AMERICAN-RUSSIAN RIVALRY
IN THE FAR EAST

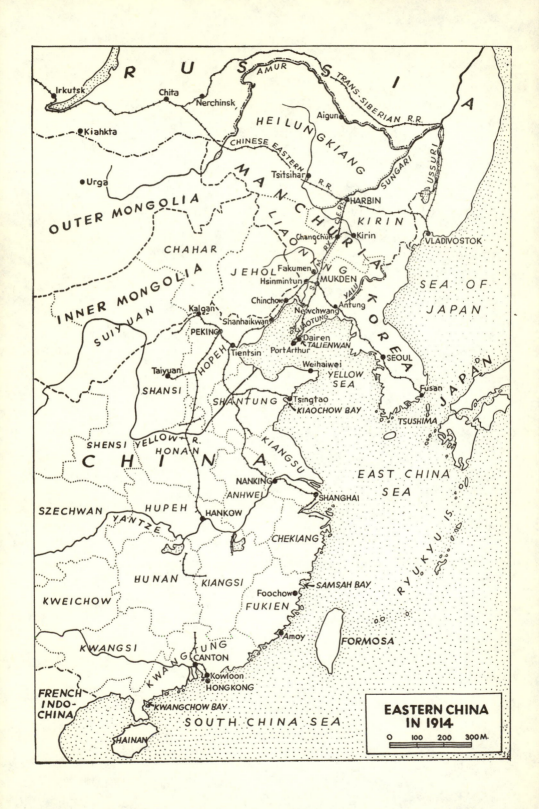

EASTERN CHINA
IN 1914

0   100   200   300 M.

AMERICAN-RUSSIAN RIVALRY IN THE FAR EAST

A STUDY IN DIPLOMACY AND POWER POLITICS

1895 - 1914

By

Edward H. Zabriskie

*Associate Professor of History
and International Relations
University of Newark*

GREENWOOD PRESS, PUBLISHERS
WESTPORT, CONNECTICUT

The Library of Congress has catalogued this publication as follows:

Library of Congress Cataloging in Publication Data

Zabriskie, Edward Henry, 1892-1951.
   American-Russian rivalry in the Far East.

   Issued in part as the author's thesis, Chicago
University.
   Bibliography: p.
   1. United States--Foreign relations--Russia.
2. Russia--Foreign relations--United States.
3. Eastern question (Far East)   I. Title.
E183.8.R9Z3 1973   327.73'047   72-11484
ISBN 0-8371-6666-7

PREFACE

WITH American expansion Eastward in the last decade of the nineteenth century, the tradition of friendship between the United States and Russia, which had existed for almost a hundred years, gave way to a period of rivalry. This rivalry in the Far East, the subject of the present study, was, in the main, a result of economic competition in Manchuria which began as early as 1895. Following the Boxer upheaval of 1900, relations between the two powers became critical, and reached a climax in the Russo-Japanese War of 1904–5. They continued in a state of tension during the Taft-Knox administration until President Wilson in 1913 withdrew governmental support from the six-power consortium.

In preparing this study the author has drawn upon diplomatic correspondence in the archives of the Department of State, and Russian Foreign Office material found in Soviet official publications, the *Krasnyi Arkhiv,* and writings of Soviet historians and economists. In addition, private papers, biographies, books, periodicals, and newspapers have been used. Certain diplomatic correspondence in the Department of State, as well as telegrams, despatches, and memoranda from the Foreign Office of Tsarist Russia, appear in these pages for the first time. It may be added that State Department correspondence and records for the period 1906–14 were first opened to accredited students in 1938.

I am indebted to many individuals for assistance in the preparation of this work. I am particularly grateful to Dr. E. Wilder Spaulding, Acting Chief, Division of Research and Publication, Department of State, for granting me access to the diplomatic correspondence pertaining to the field of my study, and for his generous assistance and courtesies on many occasions; to Mrs. Natalie Summers, Consultant in the Division of State Department Archives, for her helpful advice and suggestions; to Merrill S. Potts, in charge of the archives room of the Division of Research and Publication at the time I was consulting State Department records, for his patience and aid in facilitating access to the voluminous correspondence bearing on my subject; to Professor Quincy Wright, Professor Harley F. MacNair, and the late Professor Samuel N. Harper, of the University of Chicago, for reading the original manuscript and for their invaluable criticisms; to Professor H. H. Fisher of Stanford University for urging me at the outset to explore the field of American-Russian relations during the period of Tsar Nicholas II; to Professor Cairns K. Smith, of St. Lawrence University, for reading the manuscript and offer-

v

ing valuable suggestions; to Professor Thomas A. Bailey, of Stanford University, and to Dr. Alfred Vagts for bibliographical information; to Professor Howard Jewell, of the University of Newark, for criticism of the final draft of the study; to David Denson and Edward Mach for assistance in translation; to Miss Fanny Lipzer for typing the manuscript and for other invaluable services and suggestions too numerous to mention. I also wish to thank the following publishers for permission to quote from certain books: Harcourt, Brace and Company, for *The Far Eastern Policy of the United States,* by A. Whitney Griswold; Alfred A. Knopf, for *The Diplomacy of Imperialism,* Vols. I and II, by William L. Langer; The Johns Hopkins Press, for *Russo-American Relations, 1815–1867,* by Benjamin P. Thomas; The Macmillan Company, for *Deutschland und die Vereinigten Staaten in der Weltpolitik,* Vol. II, by Alfred Vagts; Charles Scribner's Sons, for *Theodore Roosevelt and His Time, I,* by J. B. Bishop.

EDWARD H. ZABRISKIE

Newark, New Jersey
June 1945

CONTENTS

Chapter I

TRADITION OF FRIENDSHIP

THE United States and Russia stand at opposite poles in respect to cultural background, traditions, and political philosophy. Despite these differences, during a major part of the nineteenth century a peculiar relation of cordiality existed between these powers which gave rise to the "historic tradition" of their friendship. Upon examination, it is found that this tradition has no basis other than the existence at given times of a common enemy and an absence of competing interests. Both countries viewed Great Britain as their actual or potential rival, and friendship between them fluctuated in the degree that rivalry with Great Britain increased or diminished. With the exception of the controversy over northwestern America, which was at length amicably settled, their territorial interests did not conflict at any point. When, however, the United States of America left the frontier behind and entered upon an era of overseas expansion, the earlier friendship of convenience was replaced by reciprocal attitudes of hostility.

In August 1775, England, confident of success in putting down the revolutionary uprising, applied to the Empress of Russia for twenty thousand soldiers to be sent to America to help suppress the rebellion.[1] It was natural that such aid should have been sought in Russia, since at that time Russia was on friendlier terms with Great Britain than with any other important power on the continent.[2] It was also natural that the most autocratic monarchy in the world should sympathize with another monarchy in its attempt to suppress revolution. The subject was discussed at length by the Imperial Council, and the sympathies of Catherine and her ministers were with Great Britain. But Panin, her minister of foreign affairs, who was the pawn of Frederick the Great,[3] led the Empress to believe that for domestic and foreign reasons compliance with British

[1] Frank A. Golder, "Catherine II and the American Revolution," *American Historical Review*, XXI, 92–93.
[2] A. W. Ward and G. P. Gooch, eds., *The Cambridge History of British Foreign Policy, 1783–1919*, I, 134, 135.
[3] Frederick, himself indifferent to the struggle of the colonies, was at outs with England over her attitude in the latter part of the Seven Years' War. He found vicarious revenge in the rebellion of the colonies and impressed on Panin, whose influence with Catherine was great, the inadvisability of granting England's application. P. L. Haworth, "Frederick the Great and the American Revolution," *American Historical Review*, IX, 460–70.

requests would be inadvisable.[4] Catherine therefore informed King George that, although it was physically impossible for Russia to supply him with a mercenary army, she would aid him in any way possible against the American rebels. In 1778, when France entered into an alliance with the new republic, that promise was fulfilled by the assurance of the Empress to the British monarch that as long as he regarded the Americans as rebels, she too would withhold recognition.[5] This assurance was faithfully adhered to, since Russia was the last of the European powers to recognize American independence, long after Great Britain herself had entered into treaty relations with the United States.

The so-called Armed Neutrality which, according to Professor Johnson, was first enunciated in 1752 by Frederick the Great,[6] in championship of the liberal principles of neutral rights, deserves mention as another illustration of a too frequent misconception of Russia's attitude during America's revolutionary struggle. The commonly accepted belief is that Catherine, in order to save the colonies, assumed leadership of this continental coalition against Great Britain which, in her attempts to cut off American trade, was interfering with the commerce of all nations on the high seas. The facts belie this conception. The real author of the doctrine of Armed Neutrality, as already stated, was Frederick the Great. Assisted by French connivance, Frederick, by playing upon the vanity of Catherine, induced her to assume the leadership of a great European league and to issue her famous proclamation of March 1780.[7]

This proclamation was sent to Great Britain, Spain, and France, the three European belligerents, but not to America, the fourth belligerent. To this unfriendly attitude may be added the fact that during the entire Revolutionary War, Russia, while freely allowing the use of her ports to European powers which were at war, refused this right to American warships—this despite Russia's repeated professions of neutrality. Again, in December 1780, the Continental Congress, having voted adherence to the Armed Neutrality, sent Francis Dana as envoy to St. Petersburg,[8] with instructions to "engage her Imperial Majesty to favor and support the sovereignty and independence of the United States," to obtain the admission of the United States as a party to the conventions of the League of Armed Neutrality, and to propose a treaty of amity and commerce which should be "founded on principles of equality and reciprocity and for the mutual advantage of both nations and agreeable to the spirit of the treaties existing between the United States and France." [9] As a result of both

[4] Ward and Gooch, op. cit., I, 134–35.

[5] Willis Fletcher Johnson, America's Foreign Relations, I, 96–97.

[6] Ibid., p. 101.

[7] Ibid., pp. 101–02. See also Haworth, op. cit., p. 476.

[8] Dana, at that time secretary to John Adams in Paris, was discouraged from going by Benjamin Franklin, and urged by Adams to set out at once for St. Petersburg. Samuel Flagg Bemis, The Diplomacy of the American Revolution, p. 114 n.

[9] John C. Hildt, "Early Diplomatic Negotiations of the United States with Russia," Johns Hopkins University Studies in Historical and Political Science, XXIV, 31–32.

French and British intrigue, combined with Catherine's lack of sympathy and her desire to retain English friendship, Dana, after two years of futile efforts to obtain an audience with the Empress, was finally refused a reception and in disgust returned home.[10] With the conclusion of peace in 1783 between Great Britain and her one-time colonies, the desire of the United States for friendly relations with Russia diminished.[11]

Gradually, however, relations between the two countries improved. Before the turn of the century both had arrived at a state of tension with France, and Russia had made an unsuccessful attempt to bring the United States into a coalition, the object of which was the complete isolation of France.[12] Cordial relations between the Russian and American Governments came into existence only with the accession to the throne of Alexander I, in 1801. The Emperor had been a fervent devotee of liberalism in his earlier years and was a great admirer of his contemporary, Thomas Jefferson, with whom he frequently exchanged letters.[13] In 1807, through the alliance of Alexander and Napoleon, a shift took place, with the consequent declaration of war by Great Britain against Russia and the interdiction of the latter's trade.[14] As Russia had been completely dependent upon Great Britain for commercial transportation, she was now compelled to look to another carrier nation as a substitute, and turned toward the United States.[15] In 1809, official diplomatic relations were established between the two governments, Emperor Alexander appointing Count Pahlen as minister to the United States, and President Madison designating, with the Senate confirming, John Quincy Adams as American minister to St. Petersburg.[16]

Adams, who was graciously received at the Imperial Court, opened negotiations for a commercial treaty with Russia which, because of her delicate relations with Great Britain, she refused to consider seriously. Although no treaty was entered into, relations between Russia and the United States continued on a friendly basis.[17] This friendship on the part of Russia was, however, of little benefit to America except in relation to

10 Johnson, op. cit., I, 99–100.
11 Bemis, op. cit., p. 167.
12 Hildt, op. cit., pp. 31–35.
13 The Writings of Thomas Jefferson (issued under the auspices of the Thomas Jefferson Memorial Assn. of the U.S., 1903–4), XI, 103, 106, 291; XII, 395; Michael Pavlovitch (pseud.), R.S.F.S.R. v. Imperialististicheskom Okruzhenii: Sovetskaia Rossiia i Kapitalisticheskaia Amerika (R.S.F.S.R. in Imperialistic Encirclement: Soviet Russia and Capitalistic America), p. 6.
14 Benjamin Platt Thomas, Russo-American Relations, 1815–1867, p. 10.
15 Ibid.
16 Department of State: Papers Relating to the Foreign Relations of the United States, III, 298; subsequently referred to as Foreign Relations. United States diplomatic correspondence, with no source indicated, is to be found in the archives of the Department of State, Washington.
17 In the war with France that was pending, Great Britain and Russia would be allies; it was impolitic, therefore, to grant America any commercial rights which were not extended to Great Britain. Johnson, op. cit., I, 273–74.

commerce in the region of the Baltic Sea. It had no effect upon the policies of Great Britain and France, whose disregard of neutral rights [18] became more obnoxious as the Napoleonic struggle increased in fury.

While Russia and Great Britain were at war, and the former was dependent upon American vessels for her trade with other countries, friendly relations continued to exist between the United States and Russia. But in 1812 Napoleon invaded Russia and, as a result, Alexander made peace with Great Britain. During this fateful year, however, the United States and Great Britain entered into war ostensibly over the question of neutral rights.[19] As conflict between the two great carrier nations meant ruin for Russia's commerce, her dilemma was real. Moreover, she feared that America might form an alliance with France, with whom England and Russia were now at war.

Realizing the necessity of bringing the Anglo-American conflict to a close, Alexander, through his minister of foreign affairs, Count Romanzov offered his services as mediator.[20] The United States accepted this offer, and on April 17, 1813, President Madison appointed Albert Gallatin, John Quincy Adams and James Bayard as envoys to conclude a treaty of peace with England, and also to negotiate a treaty of commerce with Russia. But Great Britain, faced with the vital problem of neutral rights, refused mediation, and the American envoys, like Dana long before, found themselves in a state of embarrassment. Unwilling to accept Great Britain's rejection of mediation as final, Russia, holding out hope of eventual success, urged the American envoys to remain. But with the fall of Napoleon in 1814, Russia lost interest in Anglo-American peace, and took no part in the mediation that ended the War of 1812. "The Russian project of mediation had turned out to be a bitter disappointment for the American Government. Its policy of looking to Russia to protect the interests of the United States had proved a failure." [21] However, it was during the War of 1812, when the United States began to give evidence of her maritime importance, that Russia had its first glimpse of the role that America was destined to play in international affairs. Consequently Tsarist Russia, ever looking for an opportunity to tip the scales against Great Britain, sought the friendship of the United States as a counterweight to their mutual rival.

Before the French debâcle at Waterloo, the other European powers, confronted with the debris of many years of war and revolution, made plans for the overthrow of Napoleon. The first definite step in this direction was the four-power alliance between Austria, Russia, Prussia, and Great Britain, signed March 1, 1814, and reëstablished as the Treaty of Paris, commonly known as the Quadruple Alliance, on November 20,

[18] *Ibid.*, p. 274.

[19] The War of 1812, in addition to being a conflict over neutral rights, was directly connected with plans for territorial expansion on the part of the United States. See Julius W. Pratt, *Expansionists of 1812.*

[20] Frank A. Golder, "The Russian Offer of Mediation in the War of 1812," *Political Science Quarterly*, XXXI, No. 3, 380–91.

[21] Hildt, *op. cit.*, p. 90.

1815.[22] The objective of the original alliance had been union for protection against French aggression; the final treaty was expanded to include measures for insuring "the maintenance of the peace of Europe." [23] Meanwhile, Alexander had conceived his own idea of a peace-mechanism, which took form in the Holy Alliance, signed September 26, 1815, by Russia, Prussia, and Austria, England refusing to join. The Tsar's imagination soared to include a "Holy League of Allied Sovereigns," to take charge not only of the affairs of Europe but of the entire civilized world. He saw in the United States a promising young disciple, and a cardinal factor of Alexander's foreign policy for some time was an attempt to win the adherence of America to this holy dictatorship of united sovereigns. But Washington, seeing in the Tsar's friendly overtures a design to use the increasing power of the United States as a counterpoise to Britain's maritime supremacy, refused to be drawn into European entanglements.[24]

The designs of Tsar Alexander to tempt the United States into the Holy Alliance, as well as preparations for the negotiation of a reciprocity treaty between the two countries, were interrupted by the unpleasant Koslov incident.[25] In November 1815, Koslov, Russian consul general at Philadelphia, was arrested on the charge of rape, locally confined over night, and released on bail the following day. This precipitated an acrimonious controversy between the two countries over consular immunity from criminal prosecution. Russia demanded reparation. The United States Government took the stand that consular immunity did not cover offenses against local laws.[26] André Dashkov, Russian minister at Washington, denouncing the arrest as a breach of international law, on his own initiative broke off diplomatic relations on October 31, 1816, and the Tsar refused to receive Levitt Harris, the American chargé d'affaires. The dispute was finally

22 Ward and Gooch, *op. cit.*, I, 516–18. See Walter Alison Phillips, *The Confederation of Europe*.

23 Thomas, *op. cit.*, pp. 14–15.

24 Count Romanzov asserted to John Quincy Adams, at that time minister to Russia, that it was to the interest of Russia "to encourage and strengthen and multiply the commercial powers which might be rivals of England to form a balance to her overbearing power. . . . She ought then to support and favor those who had them." MS. Despatches, Russia, II, No. 53, State Department Archives. Thomas, *op. cit.*, p. 18. W. R. King, secretary of the American Legation in Russia, reported that "the Emperor cannot fail to see that England, and England only, stands in the way ready to oppose herself with effect to the great designs which he is suspected to have formed. Under this state of things the growing importance of the United States as a naval power naturally excites the attention of all, but more particularly of Russia, who thinks she sees in her a nation likely at no distant day to become the rival of England, and at the same time from their commercial persuits [*sic*] most apt to come in contact, hence if for no other reason, the favorable disposition manifested toward America by this country. . . . It is more than probable that the powers of Europe have sung the *Te Deum* for an event which at no distant day they will repent with bitterness. They have freed themselves, 'tis true, from the shackles of France, but at the same time paved the way to their subjugation by the barbarous hordes of the north." MS. Despatches, Russia, VI, Jan. 29, 1817, State Department. *Ibid.*, pp. 18–19.

25 Hildt, *op. cit.*, pp. 92–107.

26 Thomas, *op. cit.*, p. 23.

settled by an exchange of notes, the Russian Government accepting un-conditionally the position of the United States. Dashkov, as a result of his hasty and unwarranted conduct in the Koslov episode, was recalled. Harris was reinstated at court, and William Pinckney, the new American minister, was received with acclamation. His reception at the Court of St. Petersburg was unprecedented. On New Year's day he had an audience with the Tsar, and in the evening at the court ball he was invited to join the Imperial circle, which was the first time that such an honor had been conferred on an envoy of less than ambassadorial rank. In many other ways the Tsar showed his desire to propitiate the United States.[27]

Pierre de Poletica, who succeeded Dashkov as Russian minister, arrived in Washington in April 1819.[28] Acting under instructions from the Tsar, Poletica was advised to aim at two objectives: first, the entrance of the United States into the Holy Alliance, stressing the folly of isolation as shown in the War of 1812, interspersed with subtle intimations as to the possibility of Russian protection from Great Britain; second, in relation to the South American colonies, which were struggling for freedom from Spain, to do all in his power to prevent the Washington Government from pursuing a policy antagonistic to that followed by the European pow-ers.[29]

The Tsar, eager to uphold the principle of monarchical solidarity and distressed at the contagion of revolutionary sentiment in Europe, favored the return of the colonies to the allegiance of Spain. Hence his persistent overtures, within the confines of diplomatic courtesy, to induce the United States to enter the Holy Alliance.[30] In three consecutive interviews with Secretary of State Adams, Poletica tactfully brought up the subject of the Holy Alliance, confidentially assuring Adams that "the Emperor was earnestly desirous that the United States should accede to the Holy Alli-ance.[31] But these overtures, while politely received, were of no avail.[32] Despatches from abroad convinced the American Government that the con-tinental powers were contemplating forcible intervention in the Spanish-American revolution.[33] Meanwhile George Canning, foreign secretary of England, whose commercial interests in Spanish America dictated a pol-icy which was no longer compatible with that of her one-time allies, declared in an interview with the French minister in London that she

[27] Johnson, op. cit., I, 297–98.

[28] For the first time Russia agreed to require her ministers to reside in Washington rather than in Philadelphia, as Dashkov had persisted in doing. Ibid.

[29] J. Franklin Jameson, ed., "Correspondence of the Russian Ministers in Washington, 1818–1825, I," American Historical Review, XVIII, 317.

[30] Charles Francis Adams, ed., The Memoirs of John Quincy Adams, IV, 404, 446–47; "Correspondence of the Russian Ministers in Washington," A.H.R., p. 317.

[31] Thomas, op. cit., p. 30.

[32] While the majority were in favor of isolation from European entanglements, public sentiment was by no means unanimous, and a number of peace societies, which were formed in the United States during this period, accepted the proposals of Alexander with enthusiasm. Ibid., pp. 27–30.

[33] Adams, op. cit., IV, 40, 86.

would no longer tolerate intervention in America.[34] Finally, with the proclamation of President Monroe on December 2, 1823, and the supporting British declaration of January 30, 1824,[35] whatever plans Alexander I and his allies may have had in regard to the new world were effectually foiled.

In spite of the tension and suspicion which existed in American-Russian relations during the period following Waterloo, Russia rendered friendly service to the United States and to the cause of peaceful settlement of disputes by arbitrating a dispute between Great Britain and the United States over the meaning of Article I of the Treaty of Ghent, which had concluded the War of 1812. This article provided for a reciprocal return of "all territory, places, and possessions whatsoever which had been seized." Great Britain opposed American claims to compensation for slaves seized by British troops during the war. The award which was made by the Tsar in April 1822 was entirely favorable to the United States.[36]

In the meantime, the controversy over the Russian possessions on the northwest coast of America approached a crisis. For more than a century Russian subjects had carried on a lively fur trade in this region, culminating in the formation in 1799 of the Russian-American Company, which was given exclusive fishing and trading privileges on the American coast as far south as fifty-one degrees north latitude for a period of twenty years. More and more, however, the Company's monopoly was threatened by American traders who came to this area in increasing numbers. Finally, with the renewal in 1821 of the Company's charter for another twenty years, Tsar Alexander, irked by these encroachments and failing to obtain satisfaction from the United States, issued a ukase in September 1821 claiming the Pacific coast north of the fifty-first parallel and forbidding foreign vessels from approaching within one hundred Italian miles of the shore.[37] Adams protested, contending that in 1799 the Tsar had designated the fifty-fifth parallel north as the southern boundary of Russian possessions, and that the Pacific Ocean, with its shores four thousand miles apart at the fifty-first parallel, was an open sea.[38] Adams' purpose was to keep the region open in behalf of American trading interests; with this objective in view, he instructed Henry Middleton, United States minister to Russia, to insist on the right of American citizens to fish and trade north of the fifty-first parallel.[39] After a still more vigorous protest from Adams to Baron Tuyll, the Russian minister, the Tsar, realizing that he had gone too far in his claim of 1821, showed a disposition to yield.[40]

[34] *British and Foreign State Papers*, XI, 49–53.

[35] *Ibid.*

[36] Johnson, *op. cit.*, I, 302–03.

[37] *Proceedings of the Alaskan Boundary Tribunal*, II, 25–26.

[38] J. B. Moore, *Digest of International Law*, I, 891; Hildt, *op. cit.*, Chapter ix.

[39] "Correspondence of the Russian Ministers in Washington," *American Historical Review*, XVIII, 333–34; Adams, *op. cit.*, VI, 93, 159.

[40] *Proceedings of the Alaskan Boundary Tribunal*, II, 40–41.

This controversy, together with the threat of continental intervention in Spanish South America, led to President Monroe's historic message of December 2, 1823, which, in addition to proclaiming to Europe a "hands-off" policy in South America, contained the ultimatum that "the American continents . . . are henceforth not to be considered as subjects for future colonization by any European powers."[41] Finally, after several months of not unfriendly negotiations, Middleton concluded with Poletica and Nesselrode, Russian minister of foreign affairs, a "Convention as to the Pacific Ocean and Northwest Coast of North America," which was signed on April 17, 1824.[42]

This treaty, the first formal agreement between the United States and Russia, provided for reciprocal freedom of fishing and navigation in the Pacific Ocean, and of trading with the natives inhabiting the coast; it further stipulated that Russia should make no establishments on the coast south of latitude fifty-four degrees, forty minutes north, and the United States should make none north of that line.[43] Although this treaty was only a trading agreement, it brought a thorny dispute to an amicable conclusion and assured tranquillity for a decade.

It had been expected that Great Britain, a joint claimant with the United States on the northwest coast, and therefore equally interested in resisting Russian pretensions, would coöperate in the negotiations of the United States with Russia. Displeased, however, by the threat to further European colonization of America implied in Adams' reply to Baron Tuyll, Great Britain declined to coöperate.[44]

Stimulated by the ratification of the Convention of 1824, the United States in 1829, under President Jackson, resumed her efforts to enter into treaties with Russia concerning commerce and neutral rights.[45] Further encouraged by the willingness of Tsar Nicholas I, who had succeeded Alexander I, to negotiate such treaties, providing they were not displeasing to Great Britain,[46] John Randolph of Roanoke was sent as minister to

[41] J. D. Richardson, *Messages and Papers of the Presidents*, II, 209. See Dexter Perkins, *The Monroe Doctrine, 1823-1826*. Perkins is of the opinion that the possibility of European intervention in America has been greatly exaggerated. He points out that the Tsar's future policy at the time of the Monroe promulgation was unformulated. Though the Russian ministers at Paris and Madrid may have made efforts to bring about armed intervention, the Tsar himself had only concluded that the matter should be considered at a conference of the powers (pp. 104–43).

[42] Johnson, *op. cit.*, I, 318. "It [the treaty] was a great victory for the United States; and it was the more gratifying to this country . . . for the reason that it had been made after the publication in Europe of the Monroe Doctrine with its direct defiance of the schemes of American reconquest which Russia had been foremost in pushing." *Ibid.*, I, 319.

[43] W. M. Malloy, *Treaties, Conventions, International Acts, Protocols and Agreements between the United States of America and Other Powers*, II, 1512–14.

[44] Johnson, *op. cit.*, I, 319.

[45] Since both countries had always pursued similar policies in regard to the protection of neutral commerce, such a treaty was logical.

[46] Frank A. Golder, *Guide to Materials for American History in Russian Archives*. Professor Golder, while assembling the material for this volume for the Carnegie In-

Russia in 1830, to reopen the question. Nicholas, fearful of antagonizing Great Britain, and suspicious of all republics because of a fresh outbreak of revolution in France, took no decisive steps. Further delay was caused by the turmoil in Europe, and finally the revolt in Poland, which compelled Nicholas to concentrate on matters nearer home.[47] And still fearful of Britain's maritime might, he became adamant in his refusal "to recognize by treaty any principle of public law which might be disagreeable to England."[48]

Convinced of the impossibility of concluding a maritime treaty, the United States postponed until a later day all efforts toward this end and pressed once more the desirability of a commercial agreement. Finally, thanks to the sedulous efforts of James Buchanan, who had succeeded Randolph as minister to Russia, and the friendly disposition toward the United States of Nesselrode, Russia's secretary of foreign affairs, a "Treaty of Commerce and Navigation" was signed on December 18, 1832, and ratified early in the following year.[49]

This treaty was for the most part similar to other commercial treaties concluded by the United States with other powers, and under its provisions commerce increased appreciably and cordial relations were once more entered upon. Article I of the treaty, however, ultimately gave rise to a serious controversy.[50]

In 1834, cordial relations gave way to a period of acrimonious controversy. Article IV of the Treaty of 1824 had provided that for a period of ten years citizens of both countries should have the reciprocal privilege of fishing and trading with the natives inhabiting the unsettled northwest coast of America.[51] The treaty, ambiguous in its wording as a whole, and particularly in Article IV, lent itself to different interpretations. Russia, hoping to acquire exclusive jurisdiction over the region north of 54° 40′, held that the expiration of Article IV automatically abrogated Article I, which gave practically the same right, subject to certain conditions. The United States, on the other hand, asserted that Article I still held and that, with the exception of settlements already established, the treaty gave Russia no sovereignty north of the given parallel. The Russian-American Company, which from the first had opposed the Treaty of 1824, brought strong influence to bear on the Russian Government against further concessions to the United States. The latter urged Russia to renew Article IV, which expired April 17, 1834, but she hedged.[52]

After over two years of parleying and skirmishing, an incident occurred

---

stitute, was given permission by the Tsarist Government to examine the archives of the Russian Foreign Office down to 1870. This opportunity gives his many articles unusual authenticity.

[47] Thomas, op. cit., pp. 69–71.
[48] J. B. Moore, ed., The Works of James Buchanan, II, 253–63.
[49] Malloy, op. cit., II, 1514–19.
[50] Infra, p. 18, n. 102.
[51] Malloy, op. cit., II, 1516.
[52] Thomas, op. cit., pp. 93–96.

on September 19, 1836, which might have led to grave consequences. The
American vessel *Loriot,* which had anchored in the harbor of Tuckessan
in the north Pacific to ,procure supplies, was boarded by Russian officers
from an armed vessel and peremptorily ordered to leave "the dominions
of Russia." Richard Blinn, master of the *Loriot,* refused to go, but upon
the arrival of armed Russian boats, the American vessel finally set sail.
The United States protested in vain.[53] While the incident in itself was
galling, the United States was less interested in it than in the renewal of
Article IV and in protesting Russia's claims to sovereignty in the north
Pacific. Hence more notes were exchanged, but the Russian Foreign Office
not only definitely refused to renew Article IV but gave the United States
to understand that American vessels would no longer be welcome north of
54° 40'.[54] Because of the urgency of other matters and the fact that trade
with the region was comparatively small, Secretary of State Forsythe, who
had originally taken a high tone, refused to concern himself further with
Russian claims.[55] Meanwhile, having leased a large strip of coast land to a
British company, Russia's interest in the territory declined and by 1840
her dominion in America was on the wane.[56]

With the closing of this controversy, the United States and Russia entered upon a period of cordial and largely coöperative relations which
lasted approximately fifty years. As disinterested friendship is something
unknown in international affairs, a key to an understanding of this friendly
coöperation is to be found in the mutual hostility to Great Britain on the
part of both countries.

Throughout most of the nineteenth century the decaying Ottoman Empire had been the object of considerable rivalry among the European
powers. The expansionist ambitions of Russia in the Near East brought
hostilities to a head, culminating in the Crimean War of 1854, in which
Russian pressure on Turkey was met by the united resistance of England,
France, and Sardinia. While the United States Government maintained
neutrality to the end of the war, the American press and populace were
outspoken in their hostility toward Britain and France and in their sympathy for Russia. Shortly after the declaration of war by Britain and
France, Secretary of State William Marcy informed the belligerents of
his intention to uphold the principles that free ships make free goods
and that neutral goods on an enemy ship, unless contraband of war, are
not subject to capture. At this stage many Americans anticipated war
with England over neutral rights.[57] Russia, unable to compete with Great
Britain on the sea, readily declared her acceptance of both principles;
hence on July 22, 1854, the two great continental powers interested in the

53 *Ibid.,* pp. 99–102.
54 MS. Despatches, Russia, XIII, March 14/27, 1838, State Department. Thomas, *op. cit.,*
p. 105.
55 *Ibid.,* p. 106.
56 Clarence L. Andrews, "Russian Plans for American Dominion," *Washington Historical Quarterly,* XVII, 83–92.
57 Thomas, *op. cit.,* pp. 112–16.

freedom of the seas, Russia and the United States, concluded a "Convention as to the Rights of Neutrals on the Sea." [58] This was the third formal agreement between the United States and Russia.

By the close of the Crimean War, then, links of friendship between the United States and Russia had been forged. The events which took place during the next decade brought about a still closer relationship. As the United States now played a significant part in the maintenance of European equilibrium, the outbreak of the American Civil War had immediate repercussions abroad. That Russia, with her crushing defeat in the recent war still fresh in mind, should sympathize with the North in proportion as Britain and France sympathized with the South, was a natural sequel to the chain of events which had gone before.

The proclamation of President Lincoln on April 19, 1861, announcing the blockade of southern United States ports, marked the commencement of the American Civil War in respect to third states. [59] As British shipping interests were seriously affected by this proclamation, Great Britain as well as France without delay recognized the Confederate states as belligerents. [60] While the attitudes of Great Britain and France differed on several points, [61] both governments openly favored the South and were determined to support its cause in every way possible. The indignation of the North because of this cordiality toward the Confederacy was outspoken. Diplomatic relations with England and France became strained, and at times war seemed not improbable. [62]

Russia from the outset supported the Union. Ever on the alert to weaken Britain's maritime power, she extended a helping hand to the cause of the North whenever opportunity presented itself. Before the fall of Fort Sumter, Eduard Stoeckl, the capable and respected Russian minister to the United States, went so far as to remonstrate with southern leaders, whom he knew well, in an attempt to bring about reconciliation between North and South. [63] Alexander Gortchakov, the Russian minister of foreign affairs, extended to Cassius Clay, our representative at St. Petersburg, the "unequivocal assurance" of Russia's friendship, together with the information that United States naval vessels would have the privilege of bringing prizes into Russian ports. [64] In fact, during the first two years of the war, when Union forces were by no means sure of victory, Russia's friendship was an important factor in preventing British and French intervention.

The *Trent* affair—an American model of British rights—aroused great indignation in England and almost caused a rupture in relations between

[58] Malloy, *op. cit.*, II, 1519–21.
[59] Charles G. Fenwick, *International Law*, p. 455.
[60] Randolph G. Adams, *A History of the Foreign Policy of the United States*, p. 236.
[61] Samuel F. Bemis, *A Diplomatic History of the United States*, pp. 365–66.
[62] Thomas, *op. cit.*, p. 123.
[63] Frank A. Golder, "The American Civil War through the Eyes of a Russian Diplomat," *American Historical Review*, XXVI, 454–63.
[64] MS. Despatches, Russia, XVIII, April 8/21, 1861, State Department. Thomas, *op. cit.*, p. 126.

Great Britain and the United States.[65] New conditions confronted by the North's blockading fleet resulted in the introduction of new doctrines of blockade, over which there was considerable controversy. The destruction of northern commerce by Confederate cruisers like the *Alabama,* which were constructed in British ports, was considered by the United States a flagrant violation of neutral duty and brought the two countries to the brink of war.[66] Napoleon III, with colonial designs on Mexico, looked longingly on a divided United States in order to make a treaty with the South to his own liking.[67] Under these conditions so inauspicious for the Union, plans for intervention were seriously discussed in the capitals of Europe, France taking the lead in such schemes.[68] Lord Russell, British minister of foreign affairs, looked with approval upon the proposal made by France for joint mediation but, unable to obtain Russia's adhesion to the plan, decided that the time was not ripe for action.[69] When in November 1862 Napoleon III made his formal proposal to Great Britain and Russia for a joint tender of good offices to the belligerents, the latter country flatly rejected his offer. Great Britain, which by this time had lost faith in the Confederate army, after much discussion in the Cabinet finally decided to reject the plan.[70] After this, all attempts on the part of southern sympathizers in the British Parliament to reopen the project of mediation failed.[71]

While Russia's firm stand was of significance in restraining Great Britain, especially during the earlier period of the war, it must be recognized that in view of conditions in Europe Alexander II could not with consistency have taken any other course. During the Civil War, Russia and the United States were confronted with similar problems. The years 1860 and 1861 had been tempestuous ones in Russian Poland, and in the latter year a revolt got under way. The struggle of the Poles for independence called forth a wave of sympathy in England and France, where both press and people denounced in bitter terms the Tsar's oppression of the legitimate national aspirations of this subject people.[72] The British and French Governments, having guaranteed by the Treaty of Vienna of 1815 a measure of autonomy to Russian Poland, strongly protested Russia's conduct, but the Russian Government, insisting that the revolt was solely a domestic question, branded all talk of intervention as a violation of their

[65] This episode occurred as a result of the seizure of two Confederate commissioners, John Slidell and James Mason (on their way to France and England respectively to obtain recognition), on the English steamer *Trent* by Captain Wilkes of the Federal war vessel, *San Jacinto*. Not being able to fight Great Britain and the Confederate states at the same time, Lincoln surrendered the commissioners to the British.

[66] Adams, *A History of the Foreign Policy of the United States,* pp. 236–41.

[67] Bemis, *Diplomatic History,* pp. 365-66.

[68] Ephraim D. Adams, *Great Britain and the American Civil War,* II, 39.

[69] Thomas, *op. cit.,* p. 132.

[70] *Ibid.,* p. 134.

[71] Bemis, *Diplomatic History,* p. 373.

[72] W. F. Grace, "Russia and the [London] Times in 1863 and 1867," *Cambridge Historical Journal,* I, No. 1, 95–96.

sovereign rights.[73] Confronted with such difficulties, it would have been out of the question for Russia to have entered into mediatory alliance with England and France during the critical period of the American Civil War. The revolt within her own domain must therefore be considered a strong factor in Russia's motivation.

In consideration of Russia's coöperative policy toward the United States, Secretary of State Seward reciprocated in May 1863, by rejecting the invitation of France for joint action with Britain to restrain the Tsar in his repressive measures against the Poles.[74] Also connected with the Polish question was the visit of the Russian fleet to the United States in the fall of 1863. In September of that year a Russian squadron under Admiral Lessofsky unexpectedly arrived in New York harbor. The following month another squadron anchored at San Francisco.[75] Throughout the North there was thunderous applause. There was no end of speculation. The popular belief was that the fleet had come to assist the Union in case of attack by England or France.[76] The average American citizen was convinced of the existence of a secret agreement between Russia and the United States.[77] Another popular legend was that, at this critical stage of the Civil War, Russia had sent the fleet to this country with "secret orders" that in case of European intervention the fleet would be placed at the service of our government.[78] It is now known that this pleasing legend had no foundation.[79]

The facts are that the Polish controversy reached a critical stage in the summer of 1863, and for months there had been danger of French and British intervention to bring about pacification by force.[80] Determined not to yield, Alexander II put his army on a war footing, and ordered the

[73] Thomas, *op. cit.*, p. 136.

[74] *Ibid.*, pp. 135–36.

[75] Frank A. Golder, "The Russian Fleet and the American Civil War," *American Historical Review*, XX, 807–08.

[76] Thomas, *op. cit.*, p. 137.

[77] J. Bigelow, *Retrospections of an Active Life*, I, 499–500.

[78] J. M. Callahan, *Russo-American Relations During the American Civil War*, p. 12.

[79] In MS. Despatches, Russia, LXI, State Department, there is an interesting and lengthy article, "A Page of Contemporary History," translated from the *Journal de St. Petersbourg*, June 4/17 and 5/18, 1904, where in only three short sentences the author refers to the visit of the Russian fleets to the United States in September 1863. No mention whatever is made of the so-called "secret orders." Commenting on this article, Ambassador McCormick, who sent the despatch to the State Department, says: "I have the honor of enclosing herewith a translation of a contribution to the discussion which has been proceeding for some time as to the services rendered by Russia to the United States during and toward the close of the Civil War bearing the title as it was published, 'A Page of Contemporary History.' Special interest is attached to this contribution as it is based upon data taken from the archives of the Russian Foreign Office and may very properly be called an official document. If it adds no facts to the discussion it is interesting on account of its source and because it contains some official correspondence between London and St. Petersburg and Paris and St. Petersburg which probably does not exist in the State Department archives." McCormick to Hay, June 25, 1904.

[80] Thomas, *op. cit.*, pp. 138–39.

Russian fleet to the United States, away from her own ports where in the event of war it might be blocked by the British navy or by ice. To obviate such dangers, the carefully concealed scheme provided for the vessels to be either in a friendly port or on the high seas where they could damage the British merchant fleet. Other facts concerning the episode indicate that the Russian vessels were ineffective and few in number, and that they did not come to the ports of the United States at a critical time, but after the crisis was over and the danger of European intervention past.[81]

When Alexander II narrowly escaped assassination in the spring of 1866 the assistant secretary of the navy, Gustavus Fox, was sent by Congress to convey to the Tsar a Congressional resolution of congratulations on his recent escape from 'death. Everywhere throughout his travels in Russia, Fox was received with extreme cordiality, and his mission aroused both interest and gratitude.[82]

Thus the policy of Russia during the American Civil War was one of self-interest which demanded that she give no support to a movement whose object was the disruption of the Union. A United States, strong and undivided, was a check to Great Britain; divided, the parts would become her victims. The United States as a balance against British might was the keynote of Russia's relations with us and she used her weight to preserve that equilibrium whenever possible. Nevertheless it cannot be denied that Russia's support of the Union, irrespective of motivation, was an important factor at a critical time in preventing intervention by England and France. And her constant support of the Federal Government gave a moral support to the North which had a favorable effect.

The purchase of Alaska was the next important step in American-Russian relations. Before the middle of the century the United States had shown occasional interest in this territory,[83] and during the course of the Crimean War Secretary of State Marcy and Senator Gwin of California had tried to interest Stoeckl in a transaction for its sale. Stoeckl, fearing that the territory would before long become a bone of contention between Russia and the United States, looked favorably on the proposal and did his utmost to bring Prince Gortchakov, the Russian minister of foreign affairs, to his point of view.[84] In 1859, Senator Gwin, with the professed sanction of President Buchanan, approached Stoeckl with an offer of $5,000,000. Stoeckl, well pleased with this offer, urged St. Petersburg to accept. Gortchakov, not convinced of the wisdom of letting these possessions go, demurred, but agreed to appoint a commission of inquiry to Alaska and to be guided by its report.[85] The commission investigated and in 1861, finding that the Russian-American Company, a semi-governmental corporation

81 *Ibid.*, p. 139; Johnson, *op. cit.*, II, 46, 47.

82 See J. F. Loubat, *Narrative of the Mission to Russia, in 1866, of the Honorable Gustavus Vasa Fox*, ed., John B. Champlin, Jr.

83 John W. Foster, *A Century of American Diplomacy*, p. 404.

84 Thomas, *op. cit.*, pp. 144–46.

85 *Proceedings of the Alaskan Boundary Tribunal*, II, 331–32.

which had administered Alaska since 1799,[86] was in a state of impending bankruptcy, recommended the sale.[87]

Gortchakov was now in a more amenable frame of mind, but by this time the United States, engrossed in the Civil War, was compelled to postpone all plans for expansion. Afterwards negotiations were resumed, in which Seward offered $5,000,000, Stoeckl demanded $10,000,000, and finally $7,200,000 was agreed upon.[88] Gortchakov was informed and, eager to consummate the transaction, gave Stoeckl full powers to sign the treaty on these terms. No time was lost, and in the early hours of the morning of March 30, 1867, the convention was signed and sealed.[89] Ten days later, on April 9, 1867, before the public was really aware of what was going on, the Senate ratified the treaty.[90]

Concerning the motives on both sides for the sale there is a difference of opinion. Cassius Clay, United States minister to Russia, believed—and his opinion was shared by others—that Russia hoped by her sale of the territory to humble Great Britain and finally drive her from the northwestern coast of America.[91] Further, in the event of war between the two powers, Russia believed that Britain would seize Alaska.[92] As far as the United States was concerned, with the exception of small groups on the western coast, there was little interest in the purchase of this supposedly worthless region. It has been claimed that the purchase was a token of appreciation for Russia's friendly attitude during the Civil War. But while Russian sympathy for the North may have had an indirect bearing in facilitating the transfer, there is no reason to believe that there is any direct connection between the two events. An ardent champion of "manifest destiny," Seward was avid to acquire anything that would add to the prestige and territorial extent of his country. He was particularly interested in expansion in the Far East and viewed Alaska as a suitable naval outpost toward the Asiatic terminus.[93] Whatever the motives were that underlay the Alaskan transaction, both powers were well pleased with the bargain.

For nearly three decades following the Alaskan purchase, domestic problems continued to absorb our national energies. The economic and industrial expansion of the United States, the discovery and exploitation of rich mineral resources in the West, the development of communications

[86] Bemis, *Diplomatic History*, p. 397.

[87] Thomas, *op. cit.*, p. 147.

[88] Frank A. Golder, "The Purchase of Alaska," *American Historical Review*, XXV, 420.

[89] Frederick Bancroft, *The Life of Seward*, II, 475–77. Seward, equally as eager as Gortchakov, arose from an evening game of whist and proposed that the treaty be signed at once. Thomas, *op. cit.*, p. 152.

[90] Malloy, *op. cit.*, II, 1521–24; Bemis, *Diplomatic History*, p. 398.

[91] Thomas, *op. cit.*, p. 165. "The sale of Alaska for an insignificant sum was made in order to restrict the power of Great Britain on the American continent." *Krasnyi Arkhiv*, LII, 129.

[92] Johnson, *op. cit.*, II, 60.

[93] Bancroft, *op. cit.*, II, 471.

between the east and west coasts, put a definite check upon such imperialistic designs as this country might have cherished. During this period,
however, not only economic but psychological forces were steadily gath-
ering the momentum which, toward the end of the century, would push
the United States on beyond its American boundaries to the far islands of
the Pacific. Signs of tension and friction between Russia and the United
States slowly gathered on the international horizon in the interval between
the Alaskan purchase in 1867 and the outbreak of the Sino-Japanese War
of 1894–95. Nevertheless, with the exception of the Catacazy episode in
1871,[94] relations were for a decade at least outwardly cordial. A number of
treaties and agreements were concluded between the two countries during
this period.

In 1868, an additional article to the Treaty of Commerce of 1832 had
been signed by Seward and Stoeckl in which they agreed that "any counter-
feiting in one of the two countries of the trademarks affixed in the other
on merchandise to show its origin and quality shall be strictly prohibited."
To broaden the scope of this article the two powers signed in 1874 a
declaration concerning trademark protection whereby "the citizens of the
United States of America shall enjoy in Russia and Russian subjects shall
enjoy in the United States the same protection as native citizens." In 1884
both powers signed a "Declaration Concerning the Admeasurement of
Vessels" which provided for the payment of navigation dues. The Extradi-
tion Convention of 1887, in addition to providing for the reciprocal surrender of persons convicted of, or charged with, specific crimes, stipulated
that political offenses should be non-extraditable, with the exception of
attempts against the life of the head of the government of either Russia or
the United States.[95]

The next agreement concerned fur seal fisheries in the Behring Sea.
The question of these fisheries had since 1868 given rise to international
controversy involving the United States, Canada, Great Britain, and Russia. In an endeavor to protect American interests, Congress in 1868 and
1869 enacted laws, based upon the interpretation by the United States of
the Treaty of 1867, which gave it control over Behring Sea east of the line
described in the Alaskan treaty.[96] Washington claimed to exercise jurisdiction over fur seals beyond the three-mile limit. Great Britain protested the

[94] Constantine Catacazy, Russian minister to the United States, engaged in acts which
were both impolitic and undiplomatic. He not only spoke of President Grant in abusive
terms but attempted to influence American legislation contrary to our own interests,
and endeavored to block the execution of the Treaty of Washington between the United
States and Great Britain. Johnson, op. cit., II, 120. His recall was demanded on the ground
that his conduct was such as "materially to impair his usefulness to his own government
and to render intercourse with him, for either business or social purposes, highly disagreeable." Moore, op. cit., IV, 501, par. 639. Later, James Orr, United States minister
to Russia, in a despatch to Secretary of State Hamilton Fish stated, "From the remarks
both of the Emperor and of Prince Gortchakov, I am of the opinion that the Catacazy
affair has left no unpleasant feelings behind it." For. Rel., 1873, p. 782.

[95] Malloy, op. cit., II, 1524–31.

[96] John Holladay Latané, A History of American Foreign Policies, pp. 462–63.

seizure of Canadian vessels beyond that limit; in view of successful opposition by the United States to the Tsar's ukase of 1821 and the traditional American policy of resisting all forms of visit and search on the high seas,[97] Washington could not logically oppose Great Britain's attitude. A modus vivendi was reached in 1891 under which, pending arbitration, the contending governments agreed to prohibit seal fishing east of the demarcation line of 1867.[98] Acting in accordance with the terms of the Arbitration Treaty, which had been signed in February 1892, the arbitration tribunal, after deciding all points of law against the United States, drafted articles of regulation for the protection of seal herds outside jurisdictional limits, which were later enforced by both governments.[99]

Meanwhile a controversy of a similar nature had taken place between the United States and Russia over the latter's seizure of American vessels in the Behring Sea, west of the demarcation line. This dispute led to the signature of a modus vivendi in 1894 by which the United States agreed to a limit for hunting fur seals of ten nautical miles on the Russian coasts of the Behring Sea and the North Pacific Ocean; a radius of thirty nautical miles around the Comandorsky (Commander) Islands and Tulienev (Robber) Island was further agreed upon. Russia, at the same time, was to confine the number of seals taken on the coasts of these islands to thirty thousand.[100]

In our relations with Russia a bitter controversy arose over the Jewish question. With certain other countries, Russia denied the right of expatriation to her subjects and forbade the return of such one-time citizens under the pain of infliction of severe penalties. She also refused to waive the claim of military service from subjects who had emigrated and later returned to Russia as naturalized Americans.[101] Her strictures forbidding alien Jews to enter Russia without permission were even more rigid, and her treatment of them, if admitted, correspondingly severe. As early as 1873 her treatment of American citizens of Jewish origin who attempted to visit or take up residence in Russia caused Secretary of State Hamilton Fish to lodge a strong protest with the Tsarist Government, pointing out

[97] Bemis, *Diplomatic History*, p. 414.

[98] Malloy, *op. cit.*, I, 743.

[99] Latané, *op. cit.*, pp. 470–71.

[100] Malloy, *op. cit.*, II, 1531–32. According to the terms of the claims protocol of 1900, the United States and Russia agreed to invite Mr. T. M. C. Asser, a member of the Council of State of the Netherlands, to arbitrate the American claim for damages resulting from the Russian seizures of 1892 and 1893. The award rendered in 1902 divided approximately $100,000 among several claimants. Five other treaties or conventions were concluded between the United States and Imperial Russia: Agreement regulating the Position of Corporations and other Commercial Associations, 1904, *Ibid.*, II, 1534–35; Protection of Trademarks in China, an agreement effected by an exchange of notes, 1906, *Ibid.*, II, 1535–36; Convention for the Preservation and Protection of Fur Seals, 1911, *Ibid.*, III, 2966–71; Treaty for the Advancement of Peace, 1914, *Ibid.*, III, 2815–16; Protocol of agreement Concerning the Exportation of Embargoed goods from Russia to the United States, 1911, *Ibid.*, III, 2817–19.

[101] "The Passport Question between United States and Russia." American editorial comment (unsigned). *American Journal of International Law*, VI (1912), 186.

that such acts were a violation of the Treaty of 1832.[102] The Russian reply was that the interpretation of the treaty must be in accordance with the domestic laws of Russia.[103]

The United States took no further action at this time. Meanwhile, many Russian and Polish Jews emigrated to the United States to escape persecution; many became naturalized, but for various reasons frequently desired to return temporarily to the country of their birth. The Russian Government in many cases refused to admit them to the Empire or, in the event of admission, subjected them to oppressive conditions. The United States became more and more concerned over this state of affairs and throughout the eighties repeatedly made vigorous protests.[104] In 1895, Secretary of State Olney demanded and obtained from the Russian Government a specific statement of policy concerning these issues, in which the supremacy of domestic law was again declared.[105]

After 1900 the increasing number of Jewish immigrants and exiled revolutionists who had fled from the Tsarist regime to the United States did much to arouse public opinion against Russia. Accounts of the barbarities of the Siberian exile system and of the Kishenev pogrom of 1903 were received with horror. Russia refused, in answer to an inquiry of the United States Government, to allow financial aid and supplies from American Jews to reach the relatives of victims of the massacre, and the Russian press indignantly denounced the United States.[106] Public agitation was increased by the "passport question," Russian agents in the United States refusing to visé Jewish-American passports to Russia.

Increasing demands were made for the abrogation of the Treaty of 1832, on the grounds that Russian practices were a violation of Article I of that treaty. It was held that Article I was of a general nature and did not admit of discriminations; that the Russian doctrine of indefeasible allegiance was incompatible with the laws and institutions of the country; and that the United States could not constitutionally be party to a treaty with a government which permitted racial and religious discrimination, which our government itself had no power to make.[107] The position taken by

---

102 The legal aspects involved in the question arose from Article I of the Treaty of Commerce and Navigation, concluded in 1832 between the United States and Russia. Article I reads: "There shall be between the territories of the high contracting parties, a reciprocal liberty of commerce and navigation. The inhabitants of their respective States shall mutually have liberty to enter the ports, places, and rivers of the territories of each party, wherever foreign commerce is permitted. They shall be at liberty to sojourn and reside in all parts whatsoever of said territories, in order to attend to their affairs, and they shall enjoy, to that effect, the same security and protection as natives of the country wherein they reside, on condition of their submitting to the laws and ordinances there prevailing, and particularly to the regulations in force concerning commerce."

103 Johnson, op. cit., II, 126–27.

104 Moore, op. cit., VI, 351–59.

105 Johnson, op. cit., II, 127.

106 For. Rel., 1903, p. 712; A. C. Coolidge, The United States as a World Power, pp. 217–20.

107 "The Passport Question Between the United States and Russia," A.J.I.L., VI, 186–91.

Russia was that the treaty contained no specific references to the Jewish people; that, in accordance with international law and practice, Americans and other aliens are entitled to no other treatment than that accorded to Russian subjects; that the exclusion by the United States of Mongolians, polygamists, and anarchists was analogous to her own exclusion of Jews. But the treaty was fated to go. When Congress met in December 1911, a resolution calling upon the President to abrogate the treaty was passed by a vote of 301 to 1 in the House.[108] The Russian Government protested that the language of the resolution was offensive. The Senate prepared a slightly more courteous substitute, which was unanimously adopted by the House. President Taft took matters into his own hands and in diplomatic language informed the Russian Government that the United States, in accordance with Article XII of the Treaty of 1832, would abrogate the treaty at the end of the year. The joint resolution which was shortly passed by Congress was nothing more than a ratification of the President's action.[109]

This controversy, which culminated in 1913 with the abrogation of the Treaty of 1832 by the United States, was in itself a comparatively minor episode. Yet in it, perhaps, lay the germs of a far greater conflict which, lying fallow, after the Sino-Japanese War began to take definite form in the regions of Manchuria.

[108] United States Congress, 62nd Cong. 2nd session; House Committee on Foreign Affairs, *The Abrogation of the Russian Treaty*, Report No. 179, 1911.
[109] W. H. Taft, *Our Chief Magistrate*, pp. 116–17.

Chapter II

THE UNITED STATES AND RUSSIA
LOOK EASTWARD

THE United States had scarcely emerged from her colonial swaddling clothes before she began to look Eastward, particularly toward China, with shrewd commercial eyes. Before the framing of the Constitution, at least nine voyages had been made to the Far East. In 1789, forty-seven American vessels were trading at one time in ports beyond the Cape of Good Hope.[1] In the same year,

. . . the year of Washington's inauguration, ten ships from Salem plowed the waters of the Indian Ocean. Before he delivered his "Farewell Address," warning his countrymen against foreign entanglements, American captains were at home in the ports of China, Java, Sumatra, Siam, India, the Philippines, and the Ile de France.[2]

Until 1842, American trade with China was limited to Canton, the only port through which foreign trade was permitted to enter,[3] and was subject to regulations established by the Chinese in the mid-eighteenth century which were applied impartially to all foreigners.[4] The United States, unlike the European powers, was without naval bases in Far Eastern waters upon which to depend for naval and military aid. Thrown thus upon her own ingenuity, the young republic was obliged to work out an individual technique in dealing with the Chinese. Tact, propitiation, and conciliation, not armed force, were the only weapons at hand. Al-

[1] Emory R. Johnson, *et al., History of Domestic and Foreign Commerce of the United States of America,* II, 25. See also Samuel E. Morison, *The Maritime History of Massachusetts.*

[2] Charles A. and Mary R. Beard, *The Rise of American Civilization,* I, 661.

[3] Russian trade in the north, at Peking and Kiakhta, was an exception. Trading caravans came to Peking as early as 1658. In 1689 a treaty at Nerchinsk was signed by Russia and China, the first treaty to be made between China and a European power. Among other things it provided for transfrontier trade. See Hosea Ballou Morse and Harley Farnsworth MacNair, *Far Eastern International Relations,* pp. 48 ff., 181–82.

[4] Anatole Kantorovich, *America v Borbe za Kitai* (America in the Struggle for China), p. 6. The United States, aided by her enterprise and her neutrality, soon ranked second among commercial powers in Canton. Hosea Ballou Morse, *The International Relations of the Chinese Empire,* I, 48; Bemis, *Diplomatic History,* p. 342.

though the Chinese regarded all outsiders as "barbarians" or "foreign devils," results as a whole were satisfactory. Thus the pacific practices which were of necessity adopted by American traders in Canton set the pattern which was later elaborated into the so-called policy of the United States: respect for the territorial and administrative integrity of the Chinese Empire, and equal opportunity with the nationals of other countries for trade with China.[5]

The first treaty between the United States and China was an outgrowth of the Anglo-Chinese War of 1839–42. The Treaty of Nanking of August 29, 1842, which ended this war, ceded Hongkong to the British crown, obliged China to pay Great Britain an indemnity of $21,000,000 (silver), and opened five ports, including Canton, to British trade.[6] When news of the signing of the Treaty of Nanking reached the United States, President Tyler immediately took steps to protect American trade interests in China and to secure entrance to Amoy, Ningpo, Foochow, and Shanghai, the ports newly opened to British commerce.[7] In 1843 Caleb Cushing was appointed commissioner to China to guard American interests and to attempt negotiation of a commercial treaty with China. The Treaty of Wanghia of 1844, which Cushing negotiated, contained by virtue of the most-favored-nation clause all the advantages of the English treaties and further privileges, particularly in relation to trade.[8] Rights of extraterritoriality were guaranteed to American citizens, United States consuls were received at treaty ports, and American nationals might not only reside in such ports but engage in business and in philanthropic and missionary activities without molestation.[9] Similar treaties, after the American model, were shortly concluded between China and France and also with Belgium and Sweden-Norway, thus widening the international circle of privilege in China and, at the same time, giving China greater latitude in playing one power against another.[10]

For almost a decade and a half in the middle of the nineteenth century China was torn by a civil war, known as the Taiping Rebellion, which the Imperial Government was powerless to quell. In July 1855, Humphrey Marshall, United States commissioner to China, alarmed by rumors that the Chinese Government had called upon Russia for aid, wrote Secretary of State Marcy:

Her [Russia's] assistance would probably end in passing China under a Russian protectorate, and in the extension of Russian limits to the Hoangho, or the mouth

---

[5] Bemis, *Diplomatic History*, pp. 343–44.

[6] Morse, *op. cit.*, I, 301–04.

[7] Tyler Dennett, *Americans in Eastern Asia*, p. 138. Commodore Kearny, in command of a squadron at Canton, had already received a written assurance, "executed by an Imperial edict," that the ports in question had been thrown open to all foreigners upon an equal basis. *Ibid.*, p. 146. President Tyler in his message to Congress was apparently unaware of this agreement.

[8] Bemis, *Diplomatic History*, pp. 345–46; Dennett, *op. cit.*, pp. 160–62.

[9] *Ibid.*, Latané, *op. cit.*, p. 333.

[10] Bemis, *Diplomatic History*, p. 346.

of the Yangtste. . . . I think that almost any sacrifice should be made by the United States to keep Russia from spreading her Pacific boundary, and to avoid her coming directly to interference in Chinese domestic affairs.[11]

At the close of the Crimean War in 1856, Great Britain and France invited the United States to coöperate with them in a military expedition against China, an offer which the American Government declined. In the Anglo-French War that ensued, China was defeated, and to save Peking from capture the Imperial Government hastily made peace. Although she had been unwilling to use force herself, the United States gave the allies moral support throughout the war and were quick to profit, under the most-favored-nation clause, from the military measures used by these powers.[12] Treaties were concluded at Tientsin in 1858, not only with Great Britain and France but also with Russia and the United States.[13] Renewed military action, known as the second Anglo-French War, was however required before the Manchu Emperor of China finally ratified these treaties.[14] The essential features of these treaties were: the opening of eleven additional ports, residence of foreign ministers in Peking, permission for foreigners to travel in the interior, toleration of Christianity throughout the empire, and a slight reduction in tariff duties.[15] The rich Chinese prize, however, went to Russia. Taking advantage of China's internal confusion, Russia received, in return for "friendly services" rendered during treaty negotiations, all the vast territory north of the Amur river and east of the Ussuri river, ultimately to become the maritime province of Siberia.[16] Here, in the southeastern end, Russia established the seaport of Vladivostok which, free from ice over half the year, later became the terminus of the Trans-Siberian Railroad.[17]

The period between the signing of the Treaty of Wanghia and the outbreak of the American Civil War was marked by further American advance in the Orient. Expansive forces were at work within the United States. The California gold rush of 1849 and the conquest and settlement of the west brought the Atlantic coast closer to the Pacific. The construction of a railroad across the Isthmus of Panama, the introduction of clipper ships, and later of steamships, to trans-Pacific travel increased American contacts with the Far East.[18] The acquisition of Oregon and California whetted the appetite for conquest. Prophets of "manifest destiny" arose, among them William H. Seward, who prophesied that "The

11 Dennett, op. cit., p. 215.

12 Dennett, op. cit., p. 305; Bemis, Diplomatic History, pp. 351 and 359. Kantorovich (op. cit. p. 35) states that the United States "sent an envoy to play the part of Saul holding the coats of those who committed the assault."

13 Dennett, op. cit., pp. 314–22.

14 Bemis, Diplomatic History, pp. 350–51.

15 Morse and MacNair, op. cit., pp. 197–202.

16 G. Nye Steiger, History of the Far East, p. 545. "Russia profited far more than actual belligerents: she got territory." Bemis, Diplomatic History, p. 351 n.

17 Kenneth Scott Latourette, The Development of China, p. 153.

18 Bemis, Diplomatic History, p. 347.

Pacific Ocean, its shores, its islands and the vast region beyond will become the chief theater of events in the world's great hereafter." [19]

Japan, which was later to become co-partner with Russia in opposition to American expansion in the Far East, had until 1853 been closed for over two centuries to all Western countries except Holland, with its limited trading center at Nagasaki. And while Japan, in seabound isolation, stood aloof, Commodore Matthew Perry, with four warships and an imposing array of presents, was on his way to offer her the keys to Western civilization and territorial expansion. The methods of Commodore Perry proved so persuasive that on March 31, 1854, he concluded a treaty of "amity and peace" with the Japanese. The Treaty of Kanagawa, "hardly more than a shipwreck convention," gave American ships and citizens access to two ports for supplies, promised good treatment to shipwrecked men and property, permitted trade under Japanese regulations, and gave permission for the residence of an American consul at Shimoda.[20]

This treaty, however, was but the initial step in the opening of Japan to Western trade. In 1856 Townsend Harris was appointed as first consul general from the United States to Japan, with instructions to negotiate a much-needed commercial treaty with Japan.[21] Mr. Harris arrived at a time when Japan was in a state of alarm over Russian aggression from the north and British advance from the south. Sympathizing with the Japanese and determined to win their confidence,[22] he secured from them the first of the three conventions concluded by Japan in 1857,[23] which formally confirmed in writing, under the most-favored-nation clause, privileges covering extraterritoriality, trade, and consuls; and, finally, the Treaty of 1858 which became the basis for Japan's trade relations with foreign powers until 1894. Among the provisions of the Treaty of 1858 were the opening of additional ports for purposes of trade, the exchange of consuls and envoys, the leasing of land to American citizens in open ports, with freedom of worship, and a fixed tariff. Similar treaties soon followed between Japan and the Netherlands, Russia, Great Britain, and France, the additional privileges of which were automatically extended to all other treaty powers.[24]

Negotiation of these treaties and the coming of the foreigner caused a reaction within Japan which further divided the nation into factions some of which had been long existent. The strife that ensued brought an end to institutions that had existed for centuries and paved the way for the

[19] Foster R. Dulles, America in the Pacific: a Century of Expansion, p. 63.

[20] Payson Treat, The Far East, pp. 200–01; Morse and MacNair, op. cit., pp. 300–01.

[21] Bemis, Diplomatic History, p. 358.

[22] The policy of Townsend Harris was the preservation of Japan so that it would not fall prey to any Western power or group of powers, "a policy of peaceable and profitable equipoise." Ibid., p. 360.

[23] Holland and Russia negotiated the other two conventions of 1857.

[24] Morse and MacNair, op. cit., pp. 304–07; Bemis, Diplomatic History, p. 360.

transformation of Japan into a modern state.[25] It was not until 1865 that the powers succeeded in obtaining the Nipponese Tenno's ratification of the treaties. And, finally, between 1894 and 1911, a general refurbishing of the treaties, after the Western pattern, took place, and foreigners were freely admitted to Japan. In one generation this remarkable country had leaped from an isolated feudal kingdom to a world power.[26]

Korea, which was shortly to become a bone of contention among the powers, concluded a treaty with the United States on May 22, 1882, the first to be made with a Western nation. This treaty, bearing the name of Commodore Shufeldt, to whose activities it was largely due, recognized the independence of Korea.[27] The immediate effect of the Shufeldt Treaty was the discovery that "not only Japan and China, but every Western power interested in the Far East, was involved." This treaty, in which the United States had felt only a tepid interest and which the Senate had hesitated to ratify was, according to an American historian, "by far the most important political action undertaken by the United States in Asia until the occupation of the Philippines in 1898. To disturb Korea in any way was to disturb the equilibrium of the Far East." [28] It "set in motion," in the opinion of Robert Pollard, "the train of circumstances which led to the Sino-Japanese War, then to the Russo-Japanese War, and finally to the annexation of Korea by Japan." [29]

Both Japan and China for three hundred years had attempted to obtain a protectorate over the hermit Kingdom.[30] Russia was watching Korea jealously. With her Trans-Siberian Railroad projected but not yet begun and with Vladivostok ice-bound during the winter months, Russia was in vital need of an outlet in Korea to warmer waters and southern markets. An enemy country in power would spell her commercial ruin. France, creditor to Russia, and with interests of her own in south China, lined up with Russia against China. Great Britain, equally startled by the opening of Korea, jealous of her own interests in the Yangtze Valley and India, and fearing that Russia might swallow up Korea if severed from China, welcomed China as a huge buffer between her and Russian designs.[31]

England and Germany concluded treaties with Korea in 1883, Italy and Russia in 1884, and France in 1886.[32] In 1885, Russia entered into a secret treaty with Korea by which, in return for her protection of Korean integrity, she was to supply military instructors for the army and have the use of Port Lazareff.[33] Great Britain promptly took possession of Port

---

[25] Treat, *op. cit.*, Chs. XX–XXV.

[26] Bemis, *Diplomatic History*, p. 362.

[27] Japan by the Treaty of Kianghwa of February 26, 1876, in which she acknowledged the independence of Korea, had prepared the way for the United States.

[28] Dennett, *op. cit.*, pp. 461–64, 450.

[29] *Chinese Soc. and Pol. Science Review*, XVI, (1932–33), 425.

[30] Bemis, *Diplomatic History*, p. 481.

[31] William L. Langer, *The Diplomacy of Imperialism*, 1890–1902, I, 168–70.

[32] Morse and MacNair, *op. cit.*, p. 391.

[33] Charles Denby, *China and Her People*, II, 132.

Hamilton, off the coast of Korea. The treaty, however, was never ratified, and Great Britain, after securing a promise from Russia, through China, not to occupy any part of Korean territory, evacuated Port Hamilton.[34]

The United States, caught in this network of rivalry and intrigue, decided to uphold her policy of recognizing Korea as independent and, at the same time, to maintain neutrality toward China and Japan as well as the European powers.[35] In the meantime, the juggling by Japan and China for control over Korea continued unabated, with first one, then the other in ascendency.[36] Until, finally, the slow-time fuse which Japan and the United States had planted when they recognized the independence of Korea, exploded into the flames of the Sino-Japanese War of 1894–95.

Japan, taking the initiative, declared war against China on August 1, 1894. During the critical weeks which preceded the declaration, the powers had made unsuccessful attempts to prevent the outbreak of hostilities, attempts in which Great Britain had urged the United States to join.[37] But the attitude of the United States toward the war may be summed up in the words of Secretary of State Gresham: "The deplorable war between Japan and China endangers no policy of the United States in Asia. Our attitude toward the belligerents is that of an impartial and neutral, desiring the welfare of both." [38] And again in October 1894, after the outstanding victories of the Japanese army and navy, Great Britain invited Germany, France, Russia, and the United States to join her in intervention, and Gresham replied: "While the President earnestly desires that China and Japan shall speedily agree upon terms of peace alike honorable to both, and not humiliating to Korea, he can not join England, Germany, Russia, and France in an intervention, as requested." [39]

Meanwhile, as Japanese victories continued and the decadence of the Manchu rule over China became more apparent, the powers began to take measures for protection of their own Far Eastern interests.[40] Russia,

[34] Dennett, *op. cit.*, pp. 480–81; Langer, *op. cit.*, I, 169.

[35] Dennett, *op. cit.*, p. 482. Despite American good intentions, "Great Britain working in the interest of China and Korea was never able to accomplish for China as much as the United States had wrought for Japan," which was later to merge with Russia as opponent of American aims and plans in Manchuria.

[36] The Chinese were so active that the Korean King asked protection from Russia, whose interest in Pacific problems had greatly increased since the Crimean War. But Russia, not wishing to become involved with England, declined to act. Langer, *op. cit.*, I, 168–69.

[37] Denby to Gresham, July 6, 1894. *For. Rel.*, 1894, Appendix I, p. 29.

[38] Gresham to Dun, Nov. 6, 1894. *Ibid.*, p. 76.

[39] Gresham to Goschen, telegram, Oct. 12, 1894. *Ibid.*, p. 70. Germany rejected the proposal. Russia, who feared Japanese aggression on the Chinese mainland, favored it. B. A. Romanov, *Rossia v Manchzhurii, 1892–1906: Ocherki po Istorii Vneshnei Politiki Samoderzhaviia v Epoche Imperializma* (Russia in Manchuria, 1892–1906: Essays on the History of the Foreign Policy of Tsarist Russia in the Epoch of Imperialism), pp. 66–67.

[40] Great Britain, who in the decade preceding the outbreak of the war had been a staunch supporter of China, underwent a change of mind, feeling apparently that, "the best policy for England would be to recognize frankly the appearance of a new power

at a special meeting of her Council of Ministers on February 1, 1895, decided to: (1) increase the fleet in the Pacific Ocean to a degree where it would surpass that of Japan; (2) enter into conversations with England and France for common action against Japan, the chief aim being the independence of Korea.[41]

In the same month Clifton Breckinridge, American ambassador to Russia, gave the Department of State his views upon the policy of Russia in relation to the war. Excerpts from his despatch of February 18, 1895, follow:

The attitude of our Government has been a matter of considerable interest in Europe, and I take it that our present and prospective commerce in the East . . . make this war and the policy of the great European nations most closely interested, a subject of more than ordinary importance and solicitude to us. . . .

The war has sufficiently advanced to enable us to see that it is a war between a regenerated nation of astonishing power and the moribund Empire of China; and that it affords a tempting opportunity for the acquisition of spoils and the rectification of objectionable frontiers.

Three European nations have extensive possessions so situated upon the continent of Asia as to make them specially interested in the approaching results of the struggle. These nations are Russia, England and France. . . .

In this view of the case I think the first step is an attempt to forecast the policy of Russia. . . . I think it is historically true that Russia has developed consistently upon the principle of territorial expansion. . . . Thus, mainly to supply her present and provide for her future wants, as she construes them, Russia has been led continuously to acquire territory in the East. . . . The denial of adequate outlets in the West has concentrated and accelerated her growth in the East . . . and every resource and energy has been combined upon the Trans-Siberian Railway. . . . And, after Vladivostok is reached, it is only to find a port closed by ice from four to five months in the year, and that by a route of vast extension around the projections of Mongolia and Manchuria. . . .

Another evidence of the policy of Russia is the tone of the press. . . . I enclose translations of two characteristic articles from the "Novoe Vremia." In these the desires of Russia are clearly intimated, and in one of them the acquisition of all Mongolia, in addition to all other territory, is alluded to. In other words, it is clear from the tone of the press that Russia is ready for the partition of China.

From all the foregoing and from every part of it, I conclude that what Russia most needs and wants at this time is outlets upon the Pacific Ocean. . . . Mongolia is a desert, fit only to sustain cross ties or to act as a frontier. Manchuria is thinly populated and too far north to alone fully answer her purposes. Corea and the country about Peking, one or both, coupled with the other, more clearly meet her requirements.

The war has come too early for Russia. Her Siberian road is not completed,

---

upon the scene." Germany, fearing an Anglo-Russian rapprochement which might lead to China's dismemberment, with Germany omitted, sent friendly word to Japan on March 8 that any territorial demand on China as the price of victory would probably result in intervention by England, Russia, and France.

41 A full account of this meeting is given in A. Popov, "Pervyie Shagi Russkogo Imperializma na Dal'nem Vostoke" (First Steps of Russian Imperialism in the Far East), Krasnyi Arkhiv, LII (1932), 67–74; Romanov, op. cit., pp. 67–69.

and the great increase of her navy is not finished. Both continue to be rapidly pushed, but some years are required for their completion. She is believed in intelligent quarters to have a war chest of 640,000,000 roubles in gold, which she hoards in spite of her debt. She maintains the largest army in Europe. In a few years she could pick a quarrel with China and take what she wanted.

I take it, then, that Russia is in a state of extreme embarrassment. She may not officially reveal her full desires. . . . But if she cannot now get what I am sure she wants, she will at least leave nothing undone to prevent Japan from gaining a foothold upon the continent, and to prevent anything like a protectorate over Corea. . . . I will add that her diplomacy may, in view of the complications of the situation, abound in surprises.

In a postscript to this despatch Mr. Breckinridge added the following pertinent information:

Mr. Peirce [Herbert D. Peirce, American chargé at St. Petersburg] calls my attention to the significant fact that a route for the Eastern part of the Siberian Railway was laid off through Manchuria and carefully considered by the Russian Government before the present route was finally agreed upon. The choice of the present route is considered due solely to the political difficulties of the Manchurian route.[42]

Negotiations for peace, which had been held up for weeks by the Chinese, who still hoped for foreign intervention, finally opened at Shimonoseki on March 21, 1895, with Li Hung-chang the foremost Chinese diplomat, as China's representative.[43] On April 1, Japan submitted her peace proposals to the Chinese delegates, the chief demands of which were: recognition by China of the complete independence of Korea; the cession to Japan of Formosa, the Pescadores, and the Liaotung Peninsula, including Port Arthur; the payment of an indemnity of three hundred million taels; and the conclusion of a treaty of commerce and navigation between China and Japan, with the extension of most-favored-nation treatment to Japan.[44]

Russia at once took action. On April 6, Prince Lobanov, minister of foreign affairs, in two notes to the Tsar pointed out the menace to Russia of Japanese occupation of the Liaotung, and suggested joint intervention by the powers. "Our aim," Lobanov wrote, "is twofold: acquisition of an ice-free port on the Pacific, and the annexation of a part of Manchuria as a right of way for the Trans-Siberian Railway." [45]

On April 8, Lobanov invited France, Germany, and Great Britain to join Russia in addressing a friendly reminder to Japan that territorial annexation on the mainland would disturb the Far Eastern balance and

---

[42] Breckinridge to Gresham, Feb. 18, 1895.

[43] Philip Joseph, *Foreign Diplomacy in China*, 1894–1900, p. 101. A reasonably good biography of Li Hung-chang is: John O. P. Bland, *Li Hung-chang*.

[44] Langer, *op. cit.*, I, 178–79.

[45] On this note Nicholas commented: "Russia absolutely needs a port free and open throughout the whole year. This port must be located on the mainland (southeastern Korea) and must certainly be connected with our possessions by a strip of land." Popov, *op. cit.*, pp. 74–76; Romanov, *op. cit.*, pp. 69–70.

be a barrier to the establishment of cordial relations between China and Japan. Great Britain alone of the powers addressed refused to coöperate.

At a heated meeting held by the Council of Ministers on April 11, 1895, the Russian policy was again discussed. Minister of Finance Witte, who finally carried the day, was for immediate action. He held that if Japanese penetration of Manchuria were permitted, conflict between Russia and Japan would eventually result. Russia, in his opinion, should warn Japan not to occupy the Liaotung, and if this warning was not heeded to open hostilities upon the Japanese. In this manner, Russia might acquire the reputation of having befriended China which, in gratitude, might later agree to a "correction" of their common frontier. The Council finally decided to advise Japan in a friendly way to refrain from occupation of southern Manchuria, at the same time warning her that if she failed to comply with this friendly counsel Russia would look after her own interests. The Council also agreed to notify the European powers and China that while Russia had no designs upon territory, she felt it necessary in protection of her interests to insist that Japan should not occupy southern Manchuria.[46] In conformity with further resolutions of the Council of April 11, Lobanov on April 17 again invited the powers to join Russia in her protest to Japan.[47] And again the response was the same. Great Britain still refused to take part in the proposed four-power intervention. Germany, who feared China's partition, replied with a ready affirmative. France acted out of deference to her ally, Russia.[48]

Meanwhile, the Treaty of Shimonoseki, which brought an official end to the Sino-Japanese War and ushered in another era in the history of the Far East, was signed on April 17, 1895.[49] And a few days later Ambassador Breckinridge reported as follows from St. Petersburg:

The momentary effect of the announcement that peace had been concluded, accompanied as it was with a confident statement of the terms, was in this quarter at least, almost dramatic. All seemed to realize the gravity of Russia's position, and that the time had come when she must finally act or give up. . . . The prevailing sentiment was that Russia should take the lead in requesting a revision by the Powers. This was pitched upon the common interests of Europe. None denied, however, Russia's predominant interest, and not a few urged her independent action, to the extent of immediate war if the other Powers principally concerned refused to join in the movement. . . .

We now see as indeed was to be expected, that Russia has been making overtures to the Powers for some weeks past, and that before the last negotiations for peace began, or at least before they were fairly under way, she was joined by Germany and France in advising Japan not to seek the acquisition of any territory on the continent. The same powers having joined Russia in the subsequent protest, the anxious inquiry now is how far will they keep her company? . . .

46 Romanov, *op. cit.*, pp. 71 ff. The minutes of this meeting are given in Popov, *op. cit.*, pp. 78–83. Witte's account in his *Memoirs*, pp. 83–85 is incomplete.
47 Romanov, *op. cit.*, pp. 75–76; *Die Grosse Politik*, IX, Nos. 2243 ff.
48 Langer, *op. cit.*, I, 184–85.
49 *Ibid.*, I, 186.

In the first place the Russian demand as now generally expressed is equality of commercial privileges, that she shall guarantee the independence of Corea if any single power is to do so, but chiefly that Japan shall not acquire, in any form, a particle of territory upon the continent. . . . It is only intimated in this connection that out of gratitude China would likely let the Siberian Railway run across Manchuria, if not give her a piece of land for that purpose. . . . Russia seems to realize that she must not under present conditions make this fight alone. . . .[50]

On April 23, 1895, the ministers of the three powers—Russia, Germany, and France—under the guise of friendship for China, presented identic notes to the Japanese Foreign Office at Tokyo, advising Japan to renounce occupation of the Liaotung Peninsula.[51] Acting under advisement from their military authorities that resistance was useless, the Japanese Government on May 5th yielded to the demands of the Dreibund (Russia, Germany, and France), requesting only the ratification of the Treaty of Shimonoseki before the return of the Liaotung, and the granting of an additional indemnity to Japan for her sacrifices.[52] The Dreibund gave assent to these requests, and the Treaty of Shimonoseki was ratified at Chefoo on May 8.

Up to this point the Dreibund had, superficially, acted in unison; but after the ratification of the Treaty of Shimonoseki each power, working for its own national ends, sought to wring concessions from China, largely for services rendered in time of need. On April 26, during the period of incubation following the warning of the Dreibund to Tokyo, William II congratulated Nicholas II on the "excellent beginning" he had made in the "common action of all Europe against Japan," adding:

I shall with interest await the further development of our action and hope that, just as I will gladly help you to settle the question of eventual annexation of portions of territory for Russia, you will kindly see that Germany may also be able to acquire a Port somewhere where it does not *gêne* you.[53]

[50] Breckinridge to Gresham, April 24, 1895.

[51] Payson J. Treat, *Diplomatic Relations between the United States and Japan, 1853–1895*, II, 534.

[52] *Ibid.*, II, 540.

[53] Langer, *op. cit.*, I, 186–87. On March 6, 1895, Berlin had warned Tokyo of the intentions of the powers to intervene, and urged restraint in making demands upon China. Telegram from Berlin Foreign Office to von Gutschmid, German ambassador in Tokyo. Erich Brandenburg, *From Bismarck to the World War: A History of German Foreign Policy, 1870–1914*, p. 54. Brandenburg comments as follows on Germany's part in the Shimonoseki episode: "The German Government . . . [gave] notice in Peking, evidently with a view to winning China's good-will when the question of compensations came up, that they themselves had been the prime-movers in suggesting united action by the Powers in favor of the Celestial Empire. That was not strictly accurate, as it was an exchange of opinions, not definite measures, that had been proposed. . . . The truth of the matter is that in March, Germany only aimed at an exchange of opinions among the Powers, but early in April, by giving her consent to the course proposed by Russia she greatly facilitated matters for the Tsar's government." With the dual alliance of Russia and France in mind, the Kaiser thought that Germany's best interests would be served by supporting Russia in eastern Asia. *Ibid.* The French, who, since 1787, had increasingly

About the same time Prince Lobanov wrote to the Russian minister at Peking that, "It is no less important for our projects to bring China into a sort of dependence in relation to ourselves and not to let England extend her influence to China." [54]

And a little later, Herbert Peirce, American chargé at St. Petersburg, realizing the trend of Russian plans, reported to the State Department:

That Russia desires to take advantage of the present situation to obtain some individual advantage, seems, in spite of the protestations of Russian officials, highly probable. That a passage across Manchuria is one of the things desired is hardly to be doubted. Not only would this shorten the Siberian Railway by about 1000 versts but the engineering difficulties would be greatly simplified. These difficulties in the route as at present laid out are said to be almost insurmountable and the obstacles to keeping the road open in winter, in a mountainous country, in high latitude, must be very great. . . .

The great importance of this acquisition, as well as the control of Corea, has been warmly advocated in the Russian press. . . . But whatever may be Russia's policy regarding Corea and the Liao Tung peninsula, it requires considerable credulity to believe, that she does not desire to shorten the route of the Siberian Railway and avoid the engineering obstacles involved in the present route by carrying that road across Northern Manchuria. An official map in my possession shows this road to have been seriously considered as passing, almost in a straight line, from the Western end of Lake Baikal to Vladivostok.

That some agreement regarding this concession has been entered into between Russia and China, is commonly believed here, and already Russian troops are reported to have crossed the frontier of Manchuria. [55]

Meanwhile, as China was unable to meet her war indemnity of $161,-000,000,[56] a proposal was made for the creation of an international commission to supervise payment of the debt.[57] This plan was foiled by Russia and France, who united in taking over China's war debt, France as financial backer, Russia as guarantor of the loan. As a result of Witte's skillful manipulations, a Franco-Russian loan of 400,000,000 francs was concluded with China on July 6, 1895, in which six French banks and four Russian participated.[58] A new factor was introduced into Far Eastern policies by

---

entrenched themselves in Indo-China, were the first of the powers to obtain their reward. Two treaties, signed June 20, 1895, extended the possessions of France in Indo-China and granted additional important economic concessions. Great Britain, insisting that these treaties violated an earlier convention with England, demanded compensation and obtained a boundary treaty in February 1897, by which China surrendered certain areas on the Burmese frontier. Treat, *Far East*, pp. 127 ff., 323, 330 n.

[54] Baron A. Meyendorff, *Correspondence de M. de Staal*, II, 272–74. Langer, *op. cit.*, I, 187.

[55] Peirce to Uhl, June 1, 1895.

[56] Treat, *Far East*, p. 304.

[57] China, apparently wary of her Russian friend, had already called upon both Berlin and London bankers for aid. The discussion of this proposal among the powers led to the proposition of an international commission. Langer, *op. cit.*, I, 188.

[58] *Ibid.*

the conclusion of this loan; namely, the Franco-Russian domination of China, in which France was to supply the money and Russia the political and diplomatic influence. Russia also provided well for her own future, as may be seen by two stipulations in the contract with China: (1) in case of Chinese default, the Peking Government was to grant Russia "additional security," to be specified later; (2) China was not to grant any foreign power control over her revenues, but in case she failed to live up to these terms such power was also automatically extended to Russia.[59]

Shortly after this transaction was completed, Witte forged a fresh link in his projects for the "peaceful penetration" of China. Plans for the establishment of a Russian bank in China were carefully worked out and, with French financial assistance, came to fruition in December 1895, when the charter of the Russo-Chinese Bank was granted to the Committee of the Siberian Railway. The charter, aside from regular banking operations, gave the Russo-Chinese Bank the right to collect taxes, to coin money, to secure railway concessions, and other extensive powers and privileges throughout the Chinese Empire.[60] Witte, who planned to associate the bank with the development of the Trans-Siberian Railway, stated in a report to the Tsar on November 27, 1895, that, "It [the bank] may prove to be a very positive weapon in the hands of the Russian Government in the latter's carrying out of measures most closely connected with the completion of the construction of the Siberian Railroad.[61] Accompanying this

[59] Romanov, op. cit., pp. 86–92; Langer, op. cit., I, 188; Joseph, op. cit., p. 134.

[60] The principal Russian material used in compiling information on Russian expansionist aims in China, and especially in regard to the policy of Witte, is B. B. Glinskii, Prolog Russko-Iaponskoi Voiny: Materialy iz Arkhiva Grafa S. I. Witte (Prologue of the Russo-Japanese War: Materials from the Archives of Count Witte), pp. 25 ff., based upon the Witte papers; and Romanov, op. cit., pp. 88 ff., with its solid foundation of Russian archive material. Baron Rosen termed the bank a "hybrid political-financial institution which in reality was but a slightly disguised branch of the Russian treasury." Baron Rosen, Forty Years of Diplomacy, I, 198.

[61] Witte's plans for the Siberian Railroad were grandiose. In his opinion the new railway with its "political and strategic significance" would open "new paths and new horizons not only for the Russians but also for world trade." It would be instrumental in bringing to fruition an alliance with China, thereby undermining the colonial policy of England and giving Russia the opportunity to become mediator between Europe and Asia. At the same time, it would draw Russia and the United States closer, unveiling the "solidarity of political interests" of the two powers. Witte's report to the Emperor, Nov. 6, 1892. Romanov, op. cit., pp. 57–60. Witte also saw in the road the possibility of increasing the strength of the Russian navy in the Pacific Ocean and of controlling "the entire international commercial movement in the Pacific Ocean." Ibid., p. 60. Not only control of the Pacific, but domination of the Chinese interior through the Manchurian railway is seen as part of Witte's far-flung plans when he wrote later, in 1900, that "It did not pay because of Manchuria to fence off our garden. . . . Historically, we shall march to the South. . . . All China—all of its riches are predominantly in the South." These statements were made by Witte in the form of a notation on a report by Kuropatkin entitled "On the Tasks of the Russian Army in the 20th Century," with particular reference to Kuropatkin's opinion that "in the coming years" Russia must "avoid conflicts with European powers in China, toward which end it is necessary to refuse railroad enterprises south of the Great Wall and particularly in the Yangtse."

report were a draft of the desired railroad concession through Manchuria, and a political statement for the Russian minister to China. Also, "as gifts in such a case are usually offered to Chinese officials," Witte requested that an appropriation for this purpose be placed at the disposal of the Russian Legation at Peking.[62]

There was a delay, however, in negotiating Witte's plans with China for running a railroad through the heart of Manchuria to Vladivostok, explained in large part by the opposition of certain Russian officials to his scheme. Count Kapnist, head of the Asiatic Department of the Russian Foreign Office, took the position that the construction of a railroad so distant from Russian territory would be unprecedented, and that it would necessitate Russia's military occupation and administration of the area, which would call forth protests from other powers and eventual partition of China: all of which Witte insisted must be avoided. Kapnist therefore urged the construction of a line in the northernmost part of Manchuria. Practically the same viewpoint was advanced by General Dukhovskii, governor of the Amur province, who termed Witte's scheme a "great historical mistake." But Witte met these objections with the argument that a railroad through central Manchuria, with Vladivostok as its terminus, would give that city importance as a port of entry to the greater part of Manchuria. Hence, Russia could effectively penetrate other sections of China; since, in his own words, "the very force of circumstances will compel us before long to construct branches from this line into the depths of China." Russia, in his opinion, should make every effort "to transfer into her own hands the network of railroads in northern China." With the railroad to Vladivostok in Russia's possession, no other railways in northern China would be constructed without her consent.[63] Finally, especially as Nicholas II was an ardent exponent of Far Eastern expansion,[64] Witte carried the day and blue prints began to take shape. The Chinese, however, proving less amenable than Russia had hoped, negotiations were held in abeyance awaiting the outcome of Chinese attempts to secure a second indemnity loan from a syndicate or British and German banks. The loan was made by the Anglo-German syndicate in March 1896. And in April Count Cassini, minister to China, again took up the Russian proposals with the Chinese minister. Prior to the conclusion of the loan, early attempts had met with rebuff. The Chinese minister at St. Peters-

---

Kuropatkin Archives. A copy of the Kuropatkin report is also in the Witte Archives (No. 269) with the same notation by Witte which is, however, crossed out with the same ink used by Witte in making his comments. *Ibid.*, p. 80. Kuropatkin was Minister of War.

[62] *Ibid.*, p. 91.

[63] Memoranda of Dukhovskii and Witte of Jan. 23 and April 12, 1896. Popov, *op. cit.*, pp. 83 ff., 91 ff. Also, Romanov, *op. cit.*, pp. 97–100.

[64] Before Nicholas II became Emperor he had visited the Far East, and upon his return by way of Siberia was appointed chairman of the Committee for the Construction of the Trans-Siberian Railway. This journey marked the beginning of Nicholas' ambition to have Russia play a major role in the Far East. V. I. Gurko, *Features and Figures of the Past*, pp. 256–57.

burg flatly rejected Russia's approaches for the railroad concession. Cassini's efforts at Peking at the same time were also fruitless.[65]

In the meantime, American interests in the Far East had not lagged. Economic and financial groups in the United States, looking beyond her borders for investments overseas, saw in China a profitable field for enterprise.[66] Before the conclusion of the Treaty of Shimonoseki, Charles Denby, Jr., chargé ad interim at Peking, had written:

I have not failed on all proper occasions to urge on the Chinese authorities the preeminence of Americans in railroad construction and in the manufacture of all those products which China's railroad system will in time acquire. It would be much to be regretted should this market be allowed to pass without an effort into the hands of others.[67]

Over a year later Mr. Denby reported to the Department of State that, "the interest which American capitalists, railroad and shipbuilders are taking in China seems to be on the increase." After specifying the firms [68] and describing their operations, Denby concludes:

All these companies and agents have reported to this legation for assistance and advice which have been fully and impartially given. They have been aided by introductions to Chinese officials, by the making of translations and by unofficial assurances of the standing of the firms they represent. In the international competition at present existing in China some recognition on the part of this Legation is essential to prevent unjust discrimination against American enterprise. Great care, however, has been exercised to give no official endorsement to plans presented.[69]

A few months later Mr. Denby reported: "Much as the road [Siberian Railroad] may mean to Germany, Russia and the rest of Europe, it may mean more to us. . . . Russia has her hands full at home. The hands to help in the East are ours." [70]

One of the first American organizations to attempt operations in Manchuria on a large scale was the American China Development Company. According to the report of Count Cassini, then Russian minister to China, an American by the name of A. W. Bash arrived in Peking in the spring

[65] Langer, op. cit., I, 400–01.

[66] According to the Russian historian Kantorovich (op. cit., p. 99), "access to the Tsarist diplomatic archives throws unexpected light on this policy which in the beginning, at least, was connected with naive proposals either for close cooperation of American capital with Tsarist imperialism in Manchuria and northern China, or for preventing Russia from seizing Manchuria by beating it to the concession of the Chinese Eastern Railway."

[67] Denby to Olney, Feb. 25, 1895.

[68] American Trading Company of London, Yokohama, and Shanghai; the Cramp Shipbuilding Company; the Union Iron Works; American China Development Company; Bethlehem Iron Works; an American Railroad syndicate, and an American banking syndicate.

[69] Denby to Olney, May 25, 1896.

[70] Denby to Olney, Sept. 2, 1896.

of 1895 as representative of a large American syndicate, the aim of which was to build and equip railroads on a wholesale scale for exploitation of the mineral riches of the Chinese Empire.[71] This syndicate, incorporated as the American China Development Company, with a capital of a million dollars, was in fact, according to another Russian, proposing to take on the "building of all railroads for which China was now planning." Bash, the same writer states, proposed a secret agreement with the Russian Government by which Russia would have priority in acquiring stocks and bonds of the American Company.[72]

In confirmation of the integrity of Mr. Bash, Mr. W. N. Pethick, American secretary to Li Hung-chang, informed Count Cassini that the China Development Company was composed "of people occupying the very highest positions in banking, financial and railroad circles in the United States." [73] Its main objective, Pethick is reported to have said, was "the construction of a railway through Manchuria for the purpose of uniting the Siberian Railway with that of northern China," [74] including "the right to exploit mines and forests in Manchuria and in the adjacent sections of Mongolia." A minor objective was the taking over of the existing lines of the Tientsin-Shanghai and the Tientsin-Peking Railways,[75] "the exploitation of which is not possible under the inefficient Chinese administration." [76] Pethick then asked if the syndicate could count on Russian support, to which Cassini replied, "In regard to railroads in Manchuria, the Russian Government has no intention of turning to any foreign syndicate whatsoever." [77]

As the proposal of the American group crossed those of Russia at every point,[78] Cassini, having received instructions from St. Petersburg to obtain

[71] Cassini to Lobanov, April 10, 1896, *Arkhiv Ministerstva Inostrannikh Diel* (Ministry of Foreign Affairs hereafter referred to as *Arkhiv M.I.D.*), Chinese Table No. 114. Kantorovich, *op. cit.*, p. 99.

[72] Romanov, *op. cit.*, pp. 102–03.

[73] The syndicate included the chairmen and directors of ten of the largest railroad companies; banks (in particular, the Chase National and the Bank of America); the Pacific Mail; and a number of insurance and industrial companies, including the American Sugar Refining Company, Kantorovich, *op. cit.*, p. 100.

[74] *Ibid.* It should be kept in mind that at this time neither the Chinese Eastern Railway nor the secret Russian-Chinese treaty for its construction was in existence.

[75] At the same time that Bash and Pethick were trying to win Russia, Bash was conducting conversations with Li Hung-chang, with no mention of joining the prospective lines with the Siberian system, on a fifty-year monopoly for the construction of railroads in Manchuria. Romanov, *op. cit.*, p. 103.

[76] Kantorovich, *op. cit.*, p. 100. In a despatch from Denby to Olney (September 2, 1896) Denby said: "Russia seems determined to run a railroad through Manchuria. . . . I have never seen any reason why the United States should object to this scheme. . . . What I would like to see accomplished is the right secured to America to build and operate railroads in China to connect with the Russian lines."

[77] Cassini to Lobanov, April 10, 1896. *Arkhiv M.I.D.*, Chinese Table, No. 114. *Ibid.*, p. 99.

[78] At the same time the representative of the American China Development Company made zealous efforts to obtain a concession for the construction of a trunk line from

a concession which would exclude all foreign companies, presented the Trans-Manchurian Railway proposal to the Tsungli Yamen early in April 1896, urging compliance on the grounds that the prospective railway would afford Russia the opportunity to defend China "from the danger of new conflicts with Japan in particular and other powers in general." But the Chinese, after twelve days of deliberation, rejected the Russian demands; [79] and Cassini reported to St. Petersburg that nothing remained but "to make the Chinese Government decisively understand that a refusal will directly result in the most disastrous consequences to China." [80] The Russian threat was not put to the test, as the Chinese Government had decided in early February to send Li Hung-chang to St. Petersburg, ostensibly to represent China at the coronation of the Tsar, actually to make good terms with Russia for the prospective Manchurian railway deal.[81]

Russian negotiations with China began April 30, 1896, and were concluded on June 3, when a treaty was signed by Li Hung-chang, Lobanov, and Witte which gave the Russo-Chinese Bank [82] the concession for the construction of a railroad across Manchuria, with a time limit of eighty years, China reserving the right to repurchase the road after thirty-six years. Witte also demanded the right to build a branch road from the main line to a port on the Yellow Sea, but as he and Li could not come to terms this project was shelved.[83]

Korea, an important factor in the policies of both Russia and Japan, was also provided for in the "defensive alliance" of the treaty.[84] And

---

Canton to Peking, by way of Hankow, which was to be extended north to Shanhaikwan with railway lines to Mukden, Kirin, and Tsitsihar and thence to the Siberian railroad and to the Korean frontier. Romanov, *op. cit.*, 102–03. The Company was to be accorded the right to acquire "land, forests and mines" in any section of Manchuria and in areas in Mongolia adjacent to the railroad, and also a thirty-year monopoly for all railroad construction in Manchuria. Copy of English text of the concession of Bash in Case No. 3B. Also in the same place report of Pokotilov of April 17/30, 1896, and the despatch of Cassini of April 10/23, 1896. *Ibid.*, p. 103. The grandiose plans of the Company mentioned in these pages are confirmed by letter of June 8, 1944, to the author from J. A. Brophy, secretary of state of New Jersey.

[79] *Ibid.*, pp. 104–5. The Chinese declared to Cassini that they had "once and forever taken the firmest and most resolute decision not to grant such concessions to any one of the foreign powers or to any foreign company," and that they themselves would construct the Manchurian line. Excerpts quoted in *"Kitaiskaya Vostochnaya Jeleznaya Doroga. Istoricheskii Otcherk Sostavlenii Kantzeliariei Pravlenia Ob-a Kitaiskoy Vostochnoy j.d."* (Chinese Eastern Railway: Historical Review Compiled by the Office of the Directorate of the Chinese Eastern Railway Co.), I, (1896–1905), 4–5.

[80] Report of Cassini to Lobanov of April 19 (May 1), 1896. Case No. 3B. Romanov, *op. cit.*, p. 105.

[81] Reports of Pokotilov of Feb. 1/14, and Feb. 12/25, from Shanghai. Case No. 26. *Ibid.*, p. 105.

[82] Li, in spite of the bribes to which he frequently succumbed, flatly refused a railway concession to the Russian Government. Witte, *Vospominania*, I, 44. Romanov, *op. cit.*, pp. 110–11.

[83] Letter of Witte to Muraviev of Aug. 20, 1897. Romanov, *op. cit.*, p. 114.

[84] As a *quid pro quo* Li obtained a defensive alliance for fifteen years which provided

finally, after Russia's refusal to accept the Japanese offer of the division of Korea into halves, the northern to be dominated by Russia and the southern by Japan,[85] a protocol was signed at Moscow June 9, 1896, by which the independence of Korea was recognized and Japan and Russia agreed to combine in efforts to restore political and financial order in the disturbed country.[86]

On September 8, 1896, after the usual diplomatic delays, particularly when China was involved, a contract was made between the Russo-Chinese Bank and the Chinese Government which made secure the desired concession for the Trans-Manchurian (Chinese Eastern) Railway.[87] The next step was the organization of the Chinese Eastern Railway Company.[88] By an earlier arrangement with the Russo-Chinese Bank in May 1896, the Russian Government had promised to "guarantee the fullest influence of the railroad," or, in other words, to "transfer the concession to the disposal of the Russian Government;" and it was further agreed that the Russo-Chinese Bank would subscribe the entire capital of one thousand shares at five thousand rubles each.[89] The Russian Government, having thus fooled the public by posing as a private concern, had successfully completed the first phase of their plans for the "peaceful penetration" of Manchuria.

---

that in case of "aggression directed by Japan against Russian territory in Eastern Asia, or the territory of China or that of Korea," the two powers "should support each other reciprocally" with military and naval forces, and that neither should make peace without the consent of the other. The details of this treaty and the events which preceded it are found in Romanov, pp. 105–17 and Glinskii, *op. cit.*, pp. 33–38. The complete text of the treaty is given in Romanov, *Ibid.*, pp. 111–13. An abridged version is found in J.V.A. MacMurray, ed., *Treaties and Agreements with and Concerning China, 1894–1919*, I, 81–82.

[85] Romanov, *op. cit.*, pp. 141 ff. The grounds given by Russia for her rejection of the Japanese proposal were that she had already recognized Korean independence. One of the three motivating elements in Russia's decision given by Langer (*op. cit.*, I, 406) was fear of complications with Great Britain and the United States, both of which had sentimental, religious, and trading interests in the "Land of the Morning Calm."

[86] Russia, according to Romanov, did not live up to the terms of the agreement, secretly keeping up her separate policy and privately promising the Korean minister to send "military instructors and a financial adviser to Korea." Lobanov's letter to Witte of June 16, 1896. Romanov, *op. cit.*, p. 145.

[87] Although the Chinese Government had approved the Li-Lobanov Treaty of June 3, they balked when pinned down to actual details and concrete specifications. Langer, *op. cit.*, I, 408.

[88] *Ibid.*, I, 409.

[89] Witte's report to the Tsar, May 18, 1896. Romanov, *op. cit.*, p. 119. Of the capital of 1000 shares, 700 were to be reserved for the Russian Government and 300 assigned to the Russo-Chinese Bank. As it turned out, however, the Russian Government retained the entire thousand shares. By a prearranged plan, a public sale of 300 shares was staged. But the public held no shares. Nor did the Chinese Government. In this curious set-up the complicated financial relationship between the Russian Government, the Russo-Chinese Bank, and the Chinese Eastern Railway Company bears testimony to the astuteness of Russia's minister of finance. The financial terms are explained at length in Romanov, *Ibid.*, pp. 117–28.

Two months after the conclusion of the Russo-Chinese contract, Ambassador Breckinridge, increasingly skeptical of the traditional friendship of Russia for the United States and anticipating rivalry between the two powers, expressed his misgivings in a confidential letter to Secretary Olney.

As for us [he wrote] I fear that our country has ceased to be either warmly or seriously taken into account by Russia. Pleasant memories remain among the people; that is all. So long as we were considered a menace to England we were important. But we grow closer to that power. Also we abstain from any policy that could make our resentment seriously effective upon other continents, and thus we are practically left out of the count. Neither are the trade relations with us of a character to excite great interest. I have been slow to come to this conclusion; but except in a few small matters, dependent upon the personal amiability and courtesy of occasional officials, generally those I have entertained and shown attention to, it is consistently enforced by all our relations. The neglect of our claims, the disregard of our representations, the marked contrast with that of former years in the reception of our men of war, and many other things, all show a distinct change and disregard.

Unhappily between nations there is little consideration except from favor or fear. They (the Russians) are lavish in their considerations of China, Turkey and France, and very particular in their dealings with Great Britain and Germany. With us they are almost culpably lacking in both respects. Our people cherish the mistaken idea that in time of trouble Russia would help us. That time is past. Nothing now in sight indicates its return. If we mend matters it must be by helping ourselves. My belief is that during my brief remaining tenure of office, while being of course always polite, yet I should predicate nothing more upon traditional friendship or any other matters of that kind; and I believe it would be well, when occasion affords, if in some suitably marked way our government would show conspicuous disapprobation of the course of our relations with Russia. She does not reciprocate—she does not deserve the consideration we have always shown her.[90]

Five months later the American minister to China gave more definite information in regard to Russia's "lavish considerations" of China, and also of the importance to the United States of securing the good will of Russia.

The influence of Russia at Peking [Denby wrote] is becoming daily more marked and her dictation to the Chinese government less veiled. In all important matters touching Manchuria the Russian Legation is consulted, and no enterprise within the borders thereof is undertaken without Russian consent. . . . It is well known now that the railroads of Manchuria are to be built by a Russian company. The manager of the Russo-Chinese Bank is to be manager of the Manchurian Railroad also, and it is expected that an official of high rank is shortly to arrive at Peking to take up the position. . . . Li Hung Chang is the obedient servant of Russia. He scouts at the idea that Russia will ever absorb China, says it is newspaper talk and claims that Russia is China's best friend. . . . France seems to be working in cordial harmony with Russia. . . . The relations between Russia and

90 Breckinridge to Olney. Written from France on stationery of the United States Legation, St. Petersburg. Cleveland Papers, Vol. 344, Nov. 11, 1896.

China are of political importance to all treaty powers but to the United States the present condition will prove of commercial advantage as well. . . . To secure such contracts the good will of Russia will prove of valuable assistance, and American capitalists and manufacturers may be able to take advantage of the fact that they alone afford in their nationality no ground of objection either on the part of Russia or China.[91]

Denby's assertion regarding "the influence of Russia at Peking . . . and her dictation to the Chinese Government," may be seen in the outcome of China's plans for railway development. Lacking the funds to attempt the construction of her projected Peking-Hankow-Canton trunk line, China opened negotiations both with American and Belgian agents.[92] The American China Development Company, whose Far Eastern projects had so far proved unsuccessful, began conversations with the Chinese Government for the construction of the line from Peking to Hankow, even making preliminary surveys.[93] In the meantime, the Belgians had consolidated with the French, backed by the Russo-Chinese Bank, and their combined efforts persuaded the Chinese to give the financing of the Peking-Hankow line to a Franco-Belgian syndicate. The syndicate, including the Russo-Chinese Bank, was given the concession in May 1897.[94] The American company, however, obtained a concession for the line from Hankow to Canton, on condition that in case of violation of contract, the concession would revert to the Belgian syndicate, a convenient screen for the French-Russian-Belgian combination.[95] In this early scramble for concessions, Russia and France had scored. Commenting on this transaction, Kent says: "The Americans were ready with a more or less reasonable business proposition. The Belgians . . . were apparently willing to undertake the work on practically any terms. The Belgians accordingly carried the day."[96] Minister Denby's report on the loss of the Peking-Hankow concession is interesting:

. . . Much as it is to be regretted that the first great step in the railroad development of China should have been taken by others, it must be admitted that our fellow citizens failed solely because they were unwilling to accept the terms offered by China and which have been accepted by the Belgians. . . . This conclusion of an enterprise which has engaged the attention of American capitalists, assisted by this legation, for many months past, is exceedingly discouraging.[97]

[91] Denby to Sherman, April 2, 1897.

[92] Percy H. Kent, *Railway Enterprise in China*, pp. 96–97.

[93] The American syndicate in the fall of 1896 inspired an article which was unfriendly to Russia in the Shanghai press. Report of the Tsarist consul general at Shanghai to the adviser at Peking, Nov. 28, 1896. *Arkhiv, M.I.D.*, Chinese Table No. 354. Kantorovich, *op. cit.*, p. 100.

[94] *Ibid., op. cit.*, p. 101; Kent, *op. cit.*, 96–97; Morse, *op. cit.*, III, 86.

[95] Langer, *op. cit.*, I, 410.

[96] Kent, *op. cit.*, p. 97.

[97] The American China Development Company was repurchased by J. P. Morgan in 1905, but "nothing was done to resume construction." Mr. Morgan sold the property of the company to the Chinese for $6,750,000 gold. Herbert Croly, *Williard Straight*, pp. 287–88.

The ominous suspicion that European politics are figuring in commercial concessions in China is not promising for Americans. If the colonial ambitions of the
Great Powers of Europe lead them to support syndicates in doubtful undertakings
here Americans will be greatly handicapped, because commercial matters for
them in Asia cannot be mixed up with the schemes of political ambitions. . . . To
Russia, to England, to France every commercial enterprise is a link in a chain of
plans of natural aggrandizement and as such is pushed with all possible diplomatic pressure. . . .[98]

Meanwhile, Russia, forecasting the day when the Peking-Hankow Railway would be connected with the Chinese Eastern Railway took a step
forward in her grandiose projects. As a preliminary, Witte sent Prince
Oukhtomsky [99] to Peking with secret orders to obtain the right to build
a railroad through Manchuria further south, by way of Kirin; also a
branch line to go south to the Chinese Tientsin-Shanhaikwan line, which
was then under construction, and still another leading to a Korean port.[100]
In spite of an attempted bribe of one million rubles, Li Hung-chang remained adamant, promising only that no concession connecting the Russian and Chinese lines would be granted to any other power.[101]

Denby's comments to the State Department on the visit of the Prince
are illuminating:

The occurrences attending the arrival of Prince Oukhtomsky at Peking are
worthy of being alluded to as bearing on the position of Russia in China. This
gentleman came as bearer of very rich presents to the Emperor of China. They are
said to be worth $100,000. His exact status not being known to the members of
the Diplomatic corps here telegrams were sent by their respective ministers to
England and Germany to ascertain what it was. The answers stated that the Prince
had no diplomatic position or character, and was simply the bearer of presents.
Some of my colleagues and I discussed the treatment that should be accorded to
the Prince, and it was decided that he ought to make the first call on the foreign
ministers. The Ministers of France and Belgium took a different view and treated
him as an ambassador and made the first call. . . .

There was no communication between the Prince and Legations. . . . There
were many festivities during the Prince's stay in which no minister, except the
French and Belgian, was invited to participate. Of course the incident has tended
to create some feeling, and to accentuate the antagonism to Russia aroused on
account of her domination of China. . . .

The moral to be drawn is that Russia intends to pursue a separate and im-
perious course in China, and what the ultimate results may be can now only
dimly be foreseen. . . .

[98] Denby to Sherman, May 24, 1897.
[99] Prince Esper Oukhtomsky, poet and publicist, was appointed editor of the *Sankt-
Peterburgskiia Vedomosti* (St. Petersburg News), a government daily, in 1896, and became
head of the Russo-Chinese Bank and of the Chinese Eastern Railway Board in the late
nineties. Gurko, *op. cit.*, pp. 256–57 and p. 647.
[100] The list of questions to be negotiated by Oukhtomsky at Peking were approved by
the Tsar on March 4, 1897. Romanov, *op. cit.*, 161 ff.
[101] Auguste Gérard, *Ma Mission en Chine*, pp. 213 ff. Romanov, *op. cit.*, pp. 161–74.

In connection with this matter I will give you the report that Count Cassini, the Russian Minister here, who is now on leave, will return as Ambassador. This rank it is supposed will give him precedence over all colleagues, make him Dean of the Diplomatic Corps, and enhance his influence with China.[102]

Germany in the meantime had not been inactive. By a coincidence which fitted neatly into German expansionist ambitions, two German missionaries were killed in Shantung on November 1, 1897. Feeling that "thousands of German Christians will breathe easier when they know that the German Emperor's ships are near," the Kaiser gave orders for immediate action to the German admiral off the coast of China, and German troops were landed in Kiaochow on November 14, with more to follow. Russia protested vigorously, immediately setting up a claim to Kiaochow. On March 6, 1898, China, in spite of vigorous Russian opposition, leased Kiaochow to Germany for ninety-nine years with accompanying railroad, mining, and other rights in Shantung.[103] By obtaining this lease of about two hundred square miles bordering the bay, with its virtual control, Germany had set a new high in ingenious methods for penetration into China. Germany's acquisition of Kiaochow, with rights in the hinterland, brought considerable concern to American trading groups. The New York Chamber of Commerce sent a resolution to the President asking that "proper steps be taken . . . for the prompt and energetic defense of the existing treaty rights of American citizens in China, and for the preservation and protection of their important commercial interests in that Empire." [104]

The interval between the landing of German troops at Kiaochow in November 1897, and its lease to Germany in March 1898, had been a stormy one. Using Germany's seizure as a pretext, Foreign Minister Muraviev [105] submitted a memorandum to the Tsar on November 23, 1897, recommending the occupation of Port Arthur and Talienwan in southern Liaotung. The opposition of the Council of Ministers was so decided that, in spite of the sympathetic attitude of Nicholas II, Muraviev's plan was temporarily laid aside.[106] Meanwhile, China, needing a loan for the last installment of her war debt to Japan, approached Russia through Li Hung-chang. Witte was willing to grant the loan,[107] subject to the following conditions: (1) a monopoly on all railroads and industrial enterprises in Manchuria and Mongolia; (2) a concession for a branch railway

102 Denby to Sherman, June 10, 1897.

103 Joseph, *op. cit.*, pp. 215–16; Langer, *op. cit.*, II, 454.

104 Alfred Vagts, *Deutschland und die Vereinigten Staaten in der Weltpolitik*, II, 1017.

105 After the death of Prince Lobanov-Rostovsky in 1896, Count M. N. Muraviev became minister of foreign affairs.

106 Glinskii, *op. cit.*, pp. 43 ff.; Romanov, *op. cit.*, pp. 186 ff.; Gurko, *op. cit.*, p. 255. Muraviev's proposal was opposed by the minister of war, the minister of the navy, and by Witte who considered the plan not only premature but in violation of the Li-Lobanov Treaty of 1896.

107 By this time Witte had undergone a change of mind, and looked more favorably upon Muraviev's plans for occupation of Port Arthur. Gurko, *op. cit.*, 255–56.

from the Chinese Eastern to a harbor on the Yellow Sea; (3) the right to construct a port at this harbor for Russian ships.[108]

As a counterweight to Russia's demands, the Chinese took up the matter of the loan with the English who, increasingly suspicious of Russian advances as well as of French penetration into southern China, made comparatively modest demands. The principal British demands were: a concession for a railway from Burma to the Yangtse Valley; a guarantee not to cede the Yangtse Valley to another power; to make Talienwan a treaty port.[109] Acute tension between Great Britain and Russia followed, upon which Minister Denby reported as follows:

It seems to me that events portend a serious conflict, and perhaps armed strife between England and Russia. . . . Looking at the treaties, and international law, it is impossible to see on what grounds Russia should claim to control Manchuria and exclude other nations from equal rights with her in that country. This question may come up between the United States and Russia.

Russia represents to China that she is her friend, and ally . . . and that her interests alone must be consulted by China. . . . In the midst of these events it may not be improper to consider our own position regarding China. I am very thoroughly aware that since Washington's Farewell Address was uttered we have been, what may be called, innately conservative on the question of interfering in the affairs of foreign powers. He would be a bold man who in the United States would advocate political entanglement in the affairs of Europe, Asia or Africa. That our abnegation tends to weaken our influence and to make us a quantité négligeable is undoubtedly true, but it has its compensations in the enforcement of the Monroe Doctrine.

Still, while preserving all the sanctity of the "Farewell Address," it is worth enquiring whether there is not some middle ground on which we may stand with advantage. . . .

Partition would tend to destroy our markets. The Pacific Ocean is destined to bear on its bosom a larger commerce than the Atlantic. As the countries in the Far East and Australia develop their resources the commerce of the United States with them will assume proportions greater in their directness and scope, than our commerce with Europe.

In these countries we are destined to find our best customers. . . . Having such interests in China, is it our duty to remain mute should her autonomy be attacked? Is it exactly right to announce . . . that we take no interest in territorial questions? We have a certain moral interest in the affairs of the world, and, in my opinion, that influence should be exacted in all cases in which our interests demand its exercise. . . .[110]

Eventually, Great Britain won, and on March 1, 1898, China entered into an agreement with the Hongkong-Shanghai Bank for a private loan.[111] Great Britain's success with the loan, however, meant that Russia was only temporarily inconvenienced. Ambassador Hitchcock, from his

[108] Glinskii, *op. cit.*, pp. 47 ff.; Romanov, *op. cit.*, p. 191.
[109] Langer, *op. cit.*, II, 463.
[110] Denby to Sherman, Jan. 31, 1898.
[111] While the original British demands were not granted by the Chinese Government, several important concessions were made. Joseph, *op. cit.*, p. 226; Langer, *op. cit.*, II, 464.

station at St. Petersburg, was noting the Russian advances, and with an eye to American trade, reported that,

Russian influence in China must necessarily be paramount not only because of existing territorial and neighborly conditions, but also in view of their present and prospective trade relations which will meet with rapid and enormous development upon the completion . . . of the Siberian Railroad and its Manchurian branch to Port Arthur which, being one-third shorter in both time and distance than England's most direct route, will make Russia a formidable competitor for the trade of China's millions of buyers and sellers, while its location wholly on Russian territory, will give Russia a supreme advantage in case of war in the Far East. With my No. 24 of Jan. 19 I had the honor to send you the Finance Minister's Report on the Budget for 1898 by which you will note the enormous sums appropriated for supplies and material, a very large percentage of which must be furnished from abroad. It is also known here that within two months the Russian Government will be in the market for 24,000 tons of iron water pipe to be delivered at Odessa, while to-day it is inquiring at what price large quantities of American coal can be delivered at Port Arthur and Vladivostok.[112]

Denby, who was closer to the theater of action than Hitchcock, and was following with a degree of apprehension the movements of the Russian colossus, reported to Sherman on February 14, 1898, as follows:

It has come to this, then, that Russia dominates Manchuria and that she will allow no other nation to open ports or build railroads or operate mines therein. It will not be long before France will put forward the same claim as to the southern provinces. Germany has answered this claim by assertion on her part of like rights to Shantung. England will be urged to take like steps as to the Yangste Valley. . . . In the interests of my country I am anxious to see China preserve her autonomy and herself develop her natural resources. She will thus furnish a great field for the purchase of our manufactured articles. . . . Divided into parcels under the control of European nations freedom of trade will not exist. There will be bickering and strife. Our missionaries will disappear. The greatest markets of the world, which we are just grasping, will be lost to us.[113]

On the basis of "information from a reliable source," Denby on March 8 reported that Russia was demanding the cession of Port Arthur and Talienwan:

Information came to me from a reliable source that Russia has demanded the cession of Port Arthur and Talienwan. . . . The situation looks dangerous, and forbodes either the peaceful partition of China, or war between Russia and Japan. . . . I content myself with saying that in my opinion an energetic protest

112 Hitchcock to Sherman, Feb. 8, 1898. Vagts, reviewing Hitchcock's endeavors to build up American trade with Russia, writes: "On Hitchcock's promptings (Hitchcock to Sherman, Feb. 15, 1898), the supplies for a United States Consulate in Vladivostok were appropriated by Congress in view of the great American trade with Siberia. . . . He sought to increase the trade between the United States and Russia by promoting direct shipping routes. . . . He used his influence with the Russian Naval and Finance Ministries in order to promote the solicitation of the shipbuilding company, Cramp & Sons, for orders for cruiser and torpedo boats." Vagts, op. cit., II, 1023, n. 2.

113 Denby to Sherman, Feb. 14, 1898.

from our Government against the dismemberment of China might have a good effect in strengthening the hands of nations like Japan and Great Britain who are freer to act in this contingency than we are.[114]

After receiving confirmation of Russia's demands upon China, Denby in a despatch of March 19 writes:

> The conduct of Russia has been characterized by tortuous treachery. . . . International intercourse does not contain an episode of greater moral baseness than this. . . . With our moral support Great Britain might even now call Russia to give an account of her plans as to the occupation of Manchuria, and might save our treaty rights in that country.[115]

Meanwhile, Hitchcock in St. Petersburg had called upon Muraviev to inquire what policy Russia proposed to adopt in regard to foreign trade in the event that Russia obtained a lease on Talienwan and Port Arthur. Muraviev replied that Port Arthur was useless as a commercial port but that Russia must control it for defensive purposes in protection of her enormous interests in Siberia. The despatch continues:

> His Excellency further stated that Russia had no desire either to occupy Chinese territory, other than the ports named or to interfere in any way with the trade of other nations than China. It appears to me from Count Mouravieff's statement that the equality of opportunity at Talienwan is assured to all nations. . . .[116]

The inevitable happened. Russia, despite China's protests, succeeded in obtaining, with the aid of a bribe,[117] the lease of Port Arthur and Talienwan for twenty-five years, and other concessions, including a railroad between these points and the Chinese Eastern, the agreement being signed on March 27, 1898. Meanwhile, the other powers had not been inactive in their demands for leased ports. On the day following the signing of the Kiaochow lease, France put in her order for a lease on Kwangchowan, which was granted; and England, having decided that Port Arthur was not worth the price of war, followed by securing the lease of Weihaiwei.[118] Great Britain apparently based her acceptance of Russia's lease of Port Arthur, which was an important military stronghold, upon the Russian promise that the ports of Talienwan and Port Arthur would be "open to the commerce of all the world." [119]

Although Russia, not unlike the other powers, had driven another hard bargain with China, and in the process had come to an understanding with Germany and Great Britain, Japan remained to be reckoned with. Fearing armed opposition from Japan, with the possibility of support from England, Russia came to terms with the Japanese Government in

[114] Denby to Sherman, March 8, 1898.
[115] Denby to Sherman, March 19, 1898.
[116] Hitchcock to Sherman, March 19, 1898.
[117] For one million rubles two Chinese officials promised to obtain the Emperor's consent to the Russian demands. Gurko, *op. cit.*, p. 256.
[118] Joseph, *op. cit.*, pp. 277–78; Langer, *op. cit.*, II, 473 ff.
[119] Romanov, *op. cit.*, p. 470.

the Nishi-Rosen Agreement of April 25, 1898, by which both powers recognized the independence of Korea and promised to refrain from interference in her domestic affairs, Russia agreeing to recognize the predominant economic rights of Japan.[120]

In the meantime, the apprehensions of the United States had been temporarily quieted by Russian promises of equal commercial opportunity to all, and by Russian orders for American products. Stressing the point that Russia was not motivated by friendship for the United States, but by a desire to play America against England and Germany in East Asia, Dr. Vagts writes:

Alone of all the foreign industries, America was called on to deliver materials for the construction and operation of the Manchuria railroad. Here we may see the skillful hand of Witte who sought to remedy his careful plans which the general staff had ruined by the overhurried occupation of Port Arthur. Witte, who would have liked even to take American capital into the foreign capitalist sector of Russian industry, attempted to move certain American contractors to establish branches in Siberia, but his attempt came to naught. . . . The American companies in Vladivostok and Port Arthur which were entrusted with the railroad supplies, allied themselves closely with the Russian-Asiatic Bank, Witte's instrument of penetration. . . . In those years, Russia was ever ready to show the Americans small and large courtesies if in this way it could damage English interests.[121]

Thus ended a period of Western impact upon China. The European powers, having obtained a stranglehold on the Celestial Empire, had no intentions of relinquishing their grasp. Russia, pursuing her imperial plans in the Far East, occasionally paused to extend the hand of supposed friendship to the United States. And the United States, no longer preoccupied with her frontiers, was again, as in her post-colonial days, looking Eastward with hopeful eyes.

---

[120] Glinskii, *op. cit.*, pp. 65 ff.; Romanov, *op. cit.*, pp. 206 ff.; Rosen, *op. cit.*, I, pp. 156 ff. Earlier in the year Japan had suggested an arrangement by which Russia would have a free hand in Manchuria and Japan in Korea. Rosen, *op. cit.*, I, 155–58; *The Secret Memoirs of Count Tadasu Hayashi*, A. M. Pooley, ed.

[121] Vagts, *op. cit.*, II, 1024–25.

Chapter III

FRIENDSHIP GIVES WAY TO RIVALRY

THE year 1898 was a significant milestone in the history of the United States. The Spanish-American War, and the subsequent annexation of the Hawaiian and the Philippine Islands, following in the wake of far-reaching economic changes which had already transformed the United States from an import to an export nation,[1] widened her horizon and gave her new significance as a world power. During this crucial year traditions of a century were discarded and new obligations were assumed.

For some time the United States had viewed with apprehension the increasing restriction of the Chinese Empire as a field for competition in trade. The door of commercial opportunity which for a century had been open to Americans on terms of equality with other nations was being rapidly closed by a series of treaties between China and the European powers.[2] Under this new regime the "spheres of influence," which had been extended to include such privileges as railway and mining concessions, leased territory, and rights of priority, were an increasing threat to the principles of equal commercial opportunity which had been the traditional policy of the United States from the time of its early contacts with the Far East.[3]

Great Britain, also alarmed at the trend of developments in the Far East, and seeking to protect her own threatened lucrative stake in China, was on the lookout for practical methods by which to uphold China's rapidly disintegrating territorial integrity.[4] No longer secure in her one-time "splendid isolation," England, in an attempt to restore her lost balance of power, sought for an ally and, having failed to persuade Russia,[5] turned to the United States. In a "very confidential" inquiry of March 8, 1898, to Secretary of State Sherman, Lord Pauncefote, commenting on the methods "by which foreign powers may restrict the opening of China to the commerce of all nations," stated that,

---

[1] Kantorovich, *op. cit.*, 79 ff.; Achille Viallate, *Economic Imperialism and International Relations During the Last Fifty Years*, pp. 31 ff.

[2] Dennett, *op. cit.*, pp. 603–04.

[3] See Mingchien J. Bau, *The Open Door Doctrine in Relation to China*, p. 16.

[4] A. Witney Griswold, *The Far Eastern Policy of the United States*, p. 39. "Great Britain's trade with China was 65 per cent of China's total trade, 85 per cent being carried in British vessels." (Figures for the year 1894), Langer, *op. cit.*, II, 167.

[5] On Jan. 17, 1898, Salisbury instructed Sir Nicholas O'Connor to approach Witte in regard to an understanding. Griswold, *op. cit.*, p. 42 n.

Her Majesty's Government are anxious to know whether they could count on the cooperation of the United States in opposing such action by foreign powers and whether the United States would be prepared to join with Great Britain in opposing such measures should the contingency arise.[6]

But the United States, preoccupied at the moment with the imminent Spanish hostilities, and unprepared for such a venture, rejected the proposal. In the interval, having been unsuccessful in her advances to Russia and the United States, Great Britain had approached Japan and then Germany, with no better results.[7]

The declaration of war between Spain and the United States on April 20, 1898, offered Great Britain the desired opportunity, and she accordingly renewed her attempts to consolidate Anglo-American friendship and to draw the United States into the vortex of the Far Eastern situation. If at the outbreak of the war Great Britain's attitude was unformulated, she proved a staunch supporter of the United States during the conflict, in particular advocating American retention of the Philippines.[8] Paralleling these endeavors to strengthen the bonds of friendship between the two Anglo-Saxon countries, British members of the cabinet and others equally before the public eye were vigorously advocating the policy of an Open Door in the Far East in speeches that were given wide circulation.[9]

Careful reading of the "instructions" given by the Russian Foreign Office in January 1898, to Count Cassini, at the time of his appointment as ambassador to Washington, and of Cassini's two letters of June 22 and 23 to the Foreign Office at St. Petersburg,[10] reveals not only Russia's fear of an Anglo-American rapprochement, but will be found "of particular value in reaching an understanding of the true character of Russian-American relations toward the end of the century." [11] The instructions, in particular, make it apparent that concealed beneath the smooth surface

[6] *Ibid.*, p. 26; see also Alfred L. P. Dennis, *Adventures in American Diplomacy, 1896–1906*, pp. 170–71. It is to be noted that this British overture, which was virtually a proposal that the United States join Great Britain in upholding the principle of an Open Door in China formed the nucleus of the doctrine which was later adopted by the United States Government.

[7] Griswold, *op. cit.*, p. 47.

[8] Dennis, *op. cit.*, p. 122; Griswold, *op. cit.*, p. 18. Colonial Secretary Joseph Chamberlain practically electioneered for an alliance between the two powers. Bertha A. Reuter, *Anglo-American Relations during the Spanish-American War*, pp. 20–21, 153–57; Langer, *op. cit.*, II, 506–18; Griswold, *op. cit.*, p. 48.

[9] Langer, *op. cit.*, II, 681–82; Dennis, *op. cit.*, p. 122. Lord Charles Beresford, a British admiral and member of Parliament, in the winter of 1898–99 made a tour of China and Japan, and returned to England by way of the United States, making vigorous speeches in all three countries in behalf of an Open Door. Griswold, *op. cit.*, pp. 48–49. Later he elaborated his speeches in his *Break-up of China*, written for American as well as British consumption. Dennett, *op. cit.*, pp. 641–42.

[10] *Krasnyi Arkhiv*, "*Severo-Amerikanskie Soedinennye Stati i Tsarskaia Rossia v 90-h gg. XIX V.*" (North-American United States and Tsarist Russia in the '90s of the 19th Century), LII, 125–42. Because of their unusual interest and pertinence, both the instructions and Cassini's letters are given *in extenso* in the appendix.

[11] From the introductory comments upon these documents. *Ibid.*, p. 125.

of Russia's apparent friendship for the United States was apprehension as to American economic expansion abroad, especially in Manchuria and China.

Your Excellency [Count Muraviev instructed Cassini] must pay special attention to the significance to us of the development of American industry in the Far East. . . . Because of your knowledge of China you will doubtless be able to make a clear distinction between those enterprises which are favorable to us and those which impinge on our sphere of influence. While conducting yourself in conformity with the first, you will take energetic action against the second.[12]

After reviewing some of the bases of Russian-American "traditional friendship," Muraviev turns to the Hawaiian islands, the possible annexation of which by the United States he regards with favor since it is

undesirable to see either the formation of a second Malta or the strengthening of Japanese naval power in the Pacific Ocean by the acquisition on the part of Japan of another link. In view of their inability to remain independent, it is more desirable that these islands should become a part of the United States. In this way they will remain forever a friendly and reliable midway station and not become a hostile nest or a threat of danger from the rear.[13]

In regard to the friendship between the United States and Great Britain, still in the bud in January 1898, and the increasing friendliness between England and Japan, Muraviev admonished Cassini "to make every endeavor to create conflicts between the Federal Government and England and Japan." [14]

Nearly five months elapsed between the date of the instructions and the arrival of Count Cassini in Washington. Meanwhile, the kaleidoscope of the Spanish-American War had shifted rapidly. And the growing friendship between America and England was paralleled, as in the past, by an increasing tension in Anglo-Russian relations. Russia, who feared a coalition of the powers, headed by Great Britain, had in the five-months interval been kept well informed as to the progress of England's wooing.

Mr. de Wollant, Cassini's predecessor at Washington, had called Russia's attention to the success of British attempts at a closer relation between the two Anglo-Saxon nations.[15] Baron G. G. Stahl, Russian ambassador to London, expressed a similar opinion.[16] Vladimir Teplov, Russian consul general in New York, reported to St. Petersburg that, according to the English press, had not Great Britain objected, the other European powers would have come to the defense of Spain.[17] In this manner, Teplov writes,

[12] *Ibid.*, p. 128.
[13] *Ibid.*, p. 129.
[14] *Ibid.*, p. 131.
[15] *Ibid.*, p. 150.
[16] *Ibid.*, p. 130. In a despatch to St. Petersburg of May 26, 1898.
[17] It is true that, with the exception of England, the European press and public opinion were strongly in favor of Spain. This expression took shape in various efforts to stave off the war. As early as September 1897, Germany considered joint intervention in behalf of monarchial solidarity but nothing came of it. Dennis, *op. cit.*, p. 72. France, with heavy

the legend has been created that "there existed a hostile coalition of powers which did not achieve realization, thanks to England, which consequently is the one and only friend of America." As a result, England, according to the Russian consul general, is attempting to convince the United States that

> while there is yet time it should conclude an agreement with England and that under the influence of the English newspapers, people here are beginning to believe that Great Britain and Japan have signed a treaty covering not only various contingencies in the Far East, but also those which might arise in connection with the Spanish-American War.[18]

Vouching for a "good musical ear" and an ability "to detect every false note," [19] Cassini "took over," and in his two despatches of June 22 and 23, respectively, proceeded to analyze the trends in American foreign policy which were at the time of chief concern to Tsarist Russia. Commenting upon the marked economic changes which had taken place during the last decade of the nineteenth century within the United States, Cassini reports:

> It is quite evident to me that the United States has firmly decided to break with the traditions of the past and to enter upon a new policy with wider horizons —a policy which if they follow it with the stubbornness characteristic of their race will not be without immediate and significant influence on the fate of the entire world. . . . Having entered upon the path of conquest, and perhaps not always being selective in their policies, they cannot fail immediately to create a multitude of enemies and give occasion for serious complications.[20]

In appraising American foreign policy, Count Cassini points out that Russia should concentrate its immediate attention upon two issues:

> (1) We should follow with undivided attention each small success in the rapprochement between the Anglo-Saxon countries, not missing a single opportunity to point out to our American friends the disadvantages which confront them in the deceitful business into which they are being drawn.
>
> (2) And of more immediate importance to us is, What do the Americans intend to do about the Philippines? If you can believe them, they simply want to annex them. We could, as things appear on the surface, console ourselves with the passing of the Philippines into the hands of our friends, the Americans, whom we love and value. But the transfer of these islands to the United States, friends and possible allies in the future of Great Britain, should give us pause to think things over.[21]

---

investments in Spain, was eager to see war averted and stood ready to mediate. Porter to Sherman. No. 199, March 31, 1898. *Ibid.*, p. 72. On the eve of the outbreak of the war in April 1898, two unsuccessful attempts were made at intervention by the European powers. *Ibid.*, pp. 72–73; Griswold, *op. cit.*, p. 18.

18 *Krasnyi Arkhiv*, LII, 131.

19 Cassini to Lamsdorf, assistant minister of foreign affairs, June 23, 1898. *Ibid.*, LII, 138–39.

20 *Ibid.*, LII, 138–39.

21 Cassini to Muraviev, June 22, 1898. *Ibid.*, LII, 140.

Cassini observes that friendship between England and the United States "is beyond doubt," but, in his opinion, "this intimacy is not destined to go beyond the limits of mutual kindness and friendly assertions, and it will hardly reach the dangerous condition of an alliance." As to the Philippines, "a problem of immediate and absorbing interest to Russia," the United States "has determined to carry through the capture of this rich prize to a successful climax, by definitely annexing it herself." Cassini bitterly denounces Spanish rule of the archipelago; nevertheless, "the possessor of the Philippines after the war is of extreme importance to us politically." If the United States should then conclude that the Philippines "were suitable as a point of departure in the Far East," Russia would have to recognize the projection of a new factor of importance into the Far Eastern situation. In conclusion, Cassini states that the Philippine problem is linked with Russia's other source of apprehension, Anglo-American friendship. This friendship "which might in spite of everything lead to a closer agreement between the two great naval powers, compels us to regard the occupation of the Philippines by the United States with considerably less well-wishing." [22]

Turning from this glimpse into the Russian diplomatic mind to despatches from the American envoys at St. Petersburg, Ambassador Ethan Hitchcock and Herbert Peirce, chargé ad interim, we are told that Russia's attitude toward the Philippines was one of apprehension and watchful waiting. Mr. Hitchcock states that,

about the time of the commencement of the [Spanish-American] war, unfriendly expressions against our country, and in favor of Spain, were indulged in by a portion of the Press and the people of this city . . . but a better understanding of the facts has led to much more friendly expressions of opinion.[23]

The Foreign Office at St. Petersburg, viewing the inevitable American victory with misgivings, could not decide what course to pursue. Hitchcock, reporting to the secretary of state Muraviev's account of an interview with the Spanish ambassador who sought Muraviev's "private and unofficial opinion with respect to the situation at Manila," was of the opinion that the Spanish ambassador's enquiry was a "feeler" put out to ascertain how far Russia would go in assisting Spain. The Spanish ambassador, according to Muraviev, was disappointed that the reply was not "more emphatically on the lines of strict neutrality . . . in view of his [Muraviev's] repeated and emphatic expressions of friendship." [24]

Believing it unwise to challenge Russia's oft-repeated pledge of loyalty to the United States, Hitchcock countered instead by reading aloud two telegrams which had recently appeared in the Paris issue of the New York Herald. One stated "that a confidential interchange of opinion has taken place between several great European powers with regard to mediation

22 Cassini to Lamsdorf, June 23, 1898. Ibid., LII, 139–40.
23 Hitchcock to Day, May 25, 1898.
24 Hitchcock to Day, June 16, 1898.

between Spain and the United States is quite correct." The second read: "It is rumored here that Germany intends to propose the assembling of a European Congress to determine the future of the Philippines." [25] Mr. Hitchcock then asked the Count: "What, if any, truth was there in the statement of the telegrams?" They were without the slightest foundation, Muraviev assured the American ambassador. No communication had passed between the powers with reference either to mediation or the future of the Philippines, and without the consent of both the United States and Spain he should regard any such attempt as wholly unwarranted.[26]

To leave no doubt in the mind of the Count as to the attitude of the United States, Hitchcock informed him in positive terms that,

any attempt at mediation or interference by any of the Powers would be regarded by my Government as an unfriendly act—and that Spain would best promote her own interest by dealing solely with the United States Government when she wished to ascertain the terms upon which peace could be secured.[27]

The intentions of the United States toward the Philippines, even after the announcement of the cessation of hostilities on August 12, were nebulous and confused; although the Peace Commission, which assembled in Paris on October 12, was overwhelmingly in favor of annexation, the Cabinet was divided.[28] Subjected to pressure from many sides, President McKinley finally demanded the cession of the entire group of islands; and on October 26, 1898, John Hay, who had been appointed secretary of state in August 1898, sent his famous wire to the Peace Commission, "The cession must be the whole archipelago or none." [29] With the sending of this ultimatum the acquisition of the Philippines became a major aim of the foreign policy of the United States.

Russia viewed the march of events with ill-disguised regrets, as may be seen by Mr. Peirce's account of an interview with Count Lamsdorf, in charge of the Foreign Office during the absence of Muraviev.

I asked the Count whether, as reported in the journals, the Russian Government had any intentions of interposing any objections should the United States claim the cession of the Philippines. After a brief pause His Excellency said he had not been informed that such was the purpose of the Federal Government and asked if such was its purpose, to which I replied that I was . . . without any information on the subject from my Government . . . further than that as enunciated in the protocol . . . in which it was formally stated that the control, dis-

25 Germany, having entered the field of colonial expansion late and fearful not only of potential American commercial rivalry but also of an Anglo-American rapprochement, looked upon the Philippines with covetous eyes. *Die Grosse Politik*, XV, 5–24; Griswold, *op. cit.*, p. 20. Germany's design at first was to acquire a protectorate over the Philippines; later, she advocated the less ambitious program of neutralization or partition. Langer, *op. cit.*, II, 519.
26 Hitchcock to Day, June 16, 1898.
27 Hitchcock to Day, June 16, 1898.
28 Griswold, *op. cit.*, pp. 27–28.
29 Julius W. Pratt, *Expansionists of 1898*, p. 338.

position, and government of the Islands would be determined by the treaty of peace now under negotiation. . . . That regarding these negotiations I had no information further than as alleged in the newspapers, but that the newspapers state that the Russian Government will object should the United States acquire possession of the Islands. As His Excellency maintained silence I asked him if this was so. He replied that while he was unable to answer for His Majesty the Emperor that so far as he was aware the Imperial Government had never occupied itself with the matter . . . but that if I desired to propound the question officially he would be happy to request an expression of the Emperor's views. . . .[30]

By the treaty of peace with Spain, which was ratified February 6, 1899,[31] the Philippines were ceded to the United States. And for better or worse the American Republic became a part of the network of Far Eastern power politics.[32]

In this manner the entrance of the United States upon the arena of the western Pacific, which Russia had feared, was accomplished. Bordering the Pacific herself, and having designs of no small dimensions upon at least Manchuria and north China, Russia resented this gigantic newcomer from the Western hemisphere.

If it were not for the Philippines [wrote de Wollant] the United States because of remoteness from China, would have been compelled to have been satisfied

[30] Peirce to Hay, Nov. 10, 1898.

[31] Bemis, *Diplomatic History*, p. 473. In the Senate the treaty met with stubborn resistance from the anti-imperialists, Senator Lodge, a foremost expansionist, commenting that the battle had been "the closest, hardest fight I have ever known." Lodge to Roosevelt, Feb. 9, 1899, *Lodge Selections*, I, 391. Griswold, *op. cit.*, p. 32.

[32] From the first the Far East, as a potential market for American commerce, had its avid devotees although they did not become vocal until after Dewey's naval victory over Spain in Manila Bay, in May 1898. Griswold, *op. cit.*, pp. 15, 26. The actual trade between the United States and China in 1898 was unimposing, the combined import and export trade with China constituting only 2 per cent of the total foreign trade of the United States. Dennett, *op. cit.*, Ch. xxx. The following are typical expressions of opinion from those who envisaged the Far East as a potential treasure-house for American commerce: "It is as a base for commercial operations that the islands seem to possess the greatest importance." Frank A. Vanderlip, undersecretary of the Treasury, *Century*, August 1898. Benjamin H. Williams, *Economic Foreign Policy of the United States*, p. 322. John Barrett, former ambassador to Siam, wrote in the September 1898, issue of the *North American Review* that "We would have an unsurpassed point in the Far East from which to extend our commerce and trade and gain our share in the immense distribution of material prizes that must follow the opening of China, operating from Manila as a base as does England from Hongkong." Williams, *op. cit.*, p. 322. "The Philippine Islands are ours forever . . . and immediately behind the Philippines there is the limitless Chinese market. . . . We will not refuse one or the other." Senator Beveridge in a speech to the Senate, Jan. 9, 1900. Claude G. Bowers, *Beveridge and the Progressive Era*, pp. 19, 119. Mark Hanna exclaimed during the electoral campaign of 1900: "If it is commercialism to want the possession of a strategic point giving the American people an opportunity to maintain a foothold in the markets of the great Eastern country, for God's sake let us have commercialism." Williams, *op. cit.*, p. 323. President McKinley in a speech at Hastings, Iowa, on October 13, 1900, said: "We have pretty much everything in the country to make it happy . . . but what we want is new markets, and as trade follows the flag, it looks very much as if we were going to have new markets."

with a passive relationship to all the disorders in China. Now, the interference of America is spreading in ever wider circles.[33]

America's economic expansion beyond the frontier, her acquisition of the Philippines, were steps that led to American-Russian rivalry in the Far East. But a more important link was yet to be forged: that of Russia's reaction to Secretary Hay's still unformulated Open Door notes.

Early in 1899 American industrial interests were exerting pressure for a more dynamic Far Eastern policy. New markets for American goods, especially textiles, were being opened in Manchuria and northern China.[34] Anticipating opposition from Russia in this unexploited Far Eastern field, American business interests sought diplomatic support both from the embassy of the United States at St. Petersburg and the State Department at Washington. In response to a petition from the Pepperell Manufacturing Company of Boston, addressed to the Department of State

by prominent cotton manufacturers and merchants engaged in the exportation of textile goods to China, pointing out that they are in danger of being shut out from the markets of that portion of northern China which is already occupied or threatened by Russia . . . ,[35]

Hay in early February 1899, instructed Chargé d'affaires Peirce to request a statement from Muraviev as to Russia's intentions toward treaty rights and foreign trade in these regions.[36]

Mr. Peirce reported that while Russia's policy in regard to "foreign trade with that territory in China which she has already acquired, or may acquire in the future" is as yet indefinite, Muraviev had expressed the opinion that,

there will be no discrimination specially favoring Russian goods, so far at least as any treaty port is concerned, but that Port Arthur, for instance, never was a treaty port. As to any likelihood of there being preferential freight rates over the

---

[33] De Wollant, first secretary, Russian Embassy, Washington, to the Russian Foreign Office, June 7, 1900. *Arkhiv M.I.D.*, Chinese Table, No. 764. Kantorovich, *op. cit.*, p. 94.

[34] Vagts, *op. cit.*, II, 1038–58. Manufacturers of South Carolina in 1899 issued a resolution that "the prosperity of the cotton mill business in South Carolina depends in our opinion on the China trade." *Ibid.*, II, 1046. According to Denby American missionaries in China, approximately fifteen hundred, strongly advocated a more active American role in the Far East. Griswold, *op. cit.*, p. 61 and n.

[35] Enclosure with despatch from Hay to Peirce, Feb. 2, 1899.

[36] *Ibid.* American traders doing business in Eastern Siberia at this time were subjected to considerable inconvenience. Enoch Emery, an American citizen, "the largest importer of American goods into Siberia" reported to Ambassador Hitchcock the persistent rumors that the free entry of foreign goods into Siberian ports was about to cease. Not only was the situation of vital importance to himself, he stated, but it had a bearing "upon the general export trade of the States with the Pacific coast, the whole character of which will be inevitably changed by the imposition of duties at the hitherto free ports of Siberia." Emery to Hitchcock, Nov. 21, 1898. Peirce discussed the situation with Witte, minister of finance, who assured him that, while it was the intention of the Imperial Government to levy duties upon importations into Siberia at some future time, "the matter is one of years not of months." Peirce to Hay, Dec. 13, 1898.

Russian lines of railroad in China or from Vladivostok, or of exaction of duties at that port on goods intended for shipment into China, he is inclined to think that everything would be done to encourage traffic in foreign goods over Russian lines, but that . . . due profits on the railway lines would be exacted . . . and that all treaty rights of foreign powers with China will be fully respected.[37]

When Charlemagne Tower followed Hitchcock as ambassador to Russia [38] he was likewise instructed to confer with Muraviev in regard to Russia's attitude toward foreign trade and treaty rights. Mr. Tower was urged at each opportunity "to act energetically in the sense desired by the numerous and influential signers of the petition." [39] His efforts elicited from the Russian Foreign Office new promises to respect all treaty rights in China as well as optimistic assertions concerning American trade with Russia, especially in respect to heavy industries.[40]

Ambassador Cassini, an adept at cajolery, did his best to allay the increasing American suspicion of Russia's trade policy in China. Commenting on intimations in the English and German press that foreign encroachments in China "would have a tendency to shut out the United States from any influence in Chinese commerce," Count Cassini said that

such suggestions were destitute of common sense; that in the only port which Russia had open to commerce, Talienwan, the United States would always be most welcome . . . ; that we should be as free as Russia in all privileges of commerce in the country under her sphere of influence.

Furthermore, the Count elucidated:

It was an utterly incorrect idea that we [the United States] had any enemies in Europe; that our strength and power were universally recognized and it was to the interest of all countries to be on the most intimate and friendly relations with the United States.[41]

Ambassadors Hitchcock and Tower, accepting the reassuring generosity of the Russian diplomats as pure coin from the mint, urged Washington not to adopt policies that might prejudice American trade with Russia or Manchuria.[42] The Russian Imperial decree of August 15, 1899, opening Talienwan as a free port, received a warm welcome from Ambassador Tower as shown in his report to the State Department.

No restriction is provided . . . for the introduction of foreign commerce and trade by way of the new port into China. And I have the authority of Count Mouraviev . . . that Russia has no intention to interfere with in any manner, or to control, Chinese custom duties. Thus, the goods manufactured at the new city, as well as foreign products imported at Dalny which enter the Russian port

---

[37] Peirce to Hay, Feb. 25, 1899.

[38] Hitchcock left office in February 1899.

[39] Adee's of March 8, 1899. Vagts, *op. cit.*, II, 1047.

[40] Tower to Hay, April 26, 1899. *Ibid.*

[41] Hay memorandum of a conversation with Cassini of May 4, 1899. Dennis, *op. cit.*, p. 199.

[42] Griswold, *op. cit.*, p. 55.

free of duty, will pass on into China without restriction from Russia, and will have only Chinese regulations to deal with. This, then, in so far as Russia is concerned, is the Open Door to China. It is gratifying to me to report to you this more important decree, which not only marks a great step forward in the progress of the world but opens the way also to the future development of American trade and the certain increase of American mercantile prosperity.[43]

On the other hand Dr. Jacob Gould Schurman, chairman of a commission appointed by President McKinley in February 1899, to investigate conditions in the Philippines, was far less sanguine as to Russia's intentions. Upon his return he was quoted as saying he feared that, "Now that Russia has taken Manchuria, it will try to encroach gradually on some or all of the other eighteen provinces of China, and when it gets them it will do as that country has done hitherto—put a duty on all foreign goods." [44]

Neither did Secretary of State Hay have illusions in regard to Russia's designs,[45] and the necessity for protecting American trade in the Far East. During the early months of 1898 when British statesmen were advocating an Open Door in China, Hay had been ambassador at the Court of St. James, and reported these speeches and discussions to Washington. When Lord Charles Beresford travelled through Japan and China propounding his doctrine of an Open Door he frequently wrote to Hay, who later entertained him in Washington.[46] Secretary Hay was, therefore, conditioned for the two men who were to play an active part in his final decision. One, W. W. Rockhill, Director of the Pan-American Union and an expert on Far Eastern matters, was a close friend of Mr. Hay's; the other, Alfred Hippisley, was a British subject, formerly in the Chinese customs service. Strong advocates of an Open Door in China, both urged Hay to take the initiative and proclaim to the powers the doctrine which the United States traditionally upheld.[47] The United States, unhampered by spheres of interest or leased ports in China, was, they argued, in a more favorable position than any other power to take the initiative. On August 24, 1899, Secretary Hay requested Mr. Rockhill to draft a form for a proclamation to the powers. And on September 6, using the Rockhill memorandum as a basis, Secretary Hay issued the first Open Door notes to Russia, Great Britain, and Germany.[48] The important clauses in these practically identic notes are:

First. The recognition that no power will in any way interfere with any treaty port or any vested interest within any leased territory or within any so-called "sphere of interest" it may have in China.

Second. That the Chinese treaty tariff of the time being shall apply to all merchandise landed or shipped to all such ports as are within said "sphere of inter-

[43] Tower to Hay, Aug. 23, 1899.

[44] As quoted in the *New York Times*, Aug. 16, 1899. Griswold, *op. cit.*, p. 70.

[45] *Ibid.*, p. 55.

[46] Dennis, *op. cit.*, pp. 184–86; Griswold, *op. cit.*, pp. 48–49.

[47] Dennis, *op. cit.*, pp. 185–86; Bemis, *Diplomatic History*, p. 484.

[48] Both form and wording of the notes were substantially the same as that used by Rockhill. Dennis, *op. cit.*, p. 187; Mr. Rockhill's memorandum is found in Appendix D, Ch. viii of Dennis, pp. 208–14.

est" (unless they be "free ports"), no matter to what nationality it may belong, and that duties so leviable shall be collected by the Chinese Government.

Third. That it [each power] will levy no higher harbor dues on vessels of another nationality frequenting any port in such "sphere" than shall be levied on vessels of its own nationality, and no higher railroad charges over lines built, controlled, or operated within its "sphere" on merchandise belonging to citizens or subjects of other nationalities transported through such "sphere" than shall be levied on similar merchandise belonging to its own nationals transported over equal distances.[49]

In November 1899, similar notes were addressed to France, Italy, and Japan. Each power was also urged to coöperate with the United States in gaining assurance from the other powers addressed.[50]

In view of Russia's attitude toward foreign commerce and treaty rights, her reception of Hay's Open Door note was not surprising. As Muraviev, the Russian foreign minister, was absent during October and part of November, Ambassador Tower was unable to approach him personally for several weeks.[51] Meantime, on November 17, Cassini telegraphed St. Petersburg from Washington that the American policy in China "follows one clear and definite aim, namely, the preservation of the principle of Open Door an'd the inviolability of the Chinese territory, which alone can guarantee American interests in that country." [52] In reply, the Russian Ministry of Foreign Affairs telegraphed Cassini on November 19:

In this [American] note the editing of which is so unclear, the confusion of treaty ports, spheres of influence and leased territories is such that it is hard for us to understand the intentions of the American Government. At the first glance it would seem that we have no serious objections against the principles expounded in the note as applied to spheres of interest on the supposition that the matter relates, as far as we are concerned, to the Chinese provinces from the Great Wall to the north. We have long considered that it would be advantageous for us by means of an exchange of opinions with the Washington Government on this question to induce the latter to recognize our privileged position in this part of China. But above all we must be convinced that the claims of the United States do not spread to the Kwantung Russian leased territory; this, by the way, doesn't seem likely.[53]

On November 23, 1899, after the return of Count Muraviev, Mr. Tower called upon him and reported as follows:

I assured him [the foreign minister] that a clearer and more formal definition of the conditions which govern the commercial rights of American citizens therein is much desired by the people of the United States. . . . I brought to his atten-

[49] For. Rel., 1899, pp. 132–33.
[50] Ibid.
[51] Bemis, Diplomatic History, p. 190.
[52] This despatch and other Russian despatches which follow that bear on the policy of the Open Door are based on Russian Foreign Office correspondence for November and December 1899, in the Tsarist Foreign Archives (Arkhiv M.I.D., Nos. 20 to 105). Kantorovich, op. cit., p. 140, n. 227.
[53] Ibid.

tion especially the three paragraphs of your despatch No. 82, designated 1st, 2nd, 3rd, in which the principles which the government of the United States is particularly desirous to see formally declared by all the great Powers interested in China are specifically set forth, and I informed him that I had been instructed to urge their immediate consideration. The Minister of Foreign Affairs . . . answered that he should be able to give a definite reply within a reasonably short time; but that before doing so, the Imperial Government wished to inform itself further as to the precise meaning of certain portions of the three propositions submitted to it by the Government of the United States . . . Count Mouravief . . . appeared to express no particular objection to either of the three propositions in question, except to that portion of the 3rd paragraph which provides that it [Russia] will levy no higher railroad charges over lines built, controlled or operated within its 'sphere' on merchandise belonging to citizens or subjects of other nationalities transported through such 'sphere' than shall be levied on similar merchandise belonging to its own nationals transported over equal distances. . . .[54]

Exchanges between Muraviev and Cassini followed this interview. Meanwhile, negotiations with Cassini at Washington were ably conducted by Rockhill, emphasis being placed upon spheres of influence rather than upon leased territory.[55] Acting under instructions from Muraviev, Cassini telegraphed St. Petersburg on November 27 that he would take up the following Russian demands with the United States:

1. Differentiation between spheres of influence and leased territory within the limits of which [the latter] we shall retain freedom of action.
2. In spheres of influence the provisions of the treaties concerning navigation, import and export of foreign goods and Chinese customs collections shall remain in force. Chinese customs will also be applied without discrimination as to the origin of goods which constitute an object of import or export through the open ports of the leased territory.
3. In our spheres of influence we retain exclusive right to equip and exploit railroads, mines and other industrial enterprises. There will be no discrimination in rates on the railroads.
4. An agreement between us and the United States is subject to the condition that all other powers having spheres of influence in China shall simultaneously sign similar obligations.[56]

In reply, the Russian Ministry of Foreign Affairs on December 1, informed Cassini that the minister of finance, Witte, objected to nondiscrimination in railroad rates. Hence, the Foreign Office "proposed that it would be best at the present time to confine the answer to general terms not binding on us." [57]

On December 14, Cassini, with his characteristic lightmindedness, and apparently discounting his telegram of November 17,[58] telegraphed Muraviev attributing the American declaration to

[54] Tower to Hay, Nov. 23, 1899.
[55] Dennis, op. cit., p. 190; Griswold, op. cit., p. 76 n.
[56] Kantorovich, op. cit., p. 140.
[57] Ibid.
[58] Supra, p. 55.

the exclusive desire of the President to prepare the way for his second election by means of playing on national self-esteem and as a form of action which demonstrates his firm determination to protect the trade interests of the United States in China, the markets of which Americans would like by all means to possess in order to dispose of their products.[59]

While not binding himself with written agreements, Cassini proposed to flatter the United States by an assurance that "the commercial interests of Americans in China will be respected in our spheres of interest, as always." Muraviev acquiesced in this policy, and on December 17 requested Cassini to ascertain the attitude of the German and French ambassadors at Washington.[60]

A few days later Ambassador Tower reported to Secretary Hay as follows:

In accordance with your instructions, I called upon the Imperial Minister for Foreign Affairs. . . . I said to him . . . that in telegraphing to you to report my interview with him, I had given expression to my belief that the government of Russia intended to apply Russian customs duties within its leased territory in China and would probably reserve the right to give certain railroad privileges, upon its lines of road, to Russian shippers and merchants. He admitted that he had intimated as much to me. Thereupon I told him that you had . . . instructed me most earnestly to represent to him the desire of the government of the United States that Russia should adhere to its proposition in regard to China. He showed a slight irritation . . . that the Russian government should under any circumstances have been addressed in the form of these propositions; though these feelings disappeared when I hastened to assure him that the propositions had been made in precisely the same form to the other great powers. . . .

He then said: "The meaning of the propositions is not sufficiently clear to us. We do not understand them . . . we do not want to bind ourselves to something that we do not perfectly understand." I declared my readiness to assist him in every way. . . . But I reminded him . . . that these propositions had been made in behalf of American commerce and industry. . . . I called his attention to the fact that we are shipping from America now as much merchandise to Vladivostok as perhaps to any port in China itself or the East, that as soon as the Russian railway connection is established to the new town of Dalny, the tide of commerce will turn also toward its harbor, and that we hope soon after to see its flow in the opposite direction in a stream of international trade,—toward our own ports, where American capital is waiting at this moment to be invested in steamships that will cross the Pacific Ocean and build up this great commercial intercourse if the government of Russia will adopt such a policy as to make this possible.

The Count Mouraviev listened attentively to what I had to say . . . and he then admitted that . . . he had been in conference . . . with M. Witte . . . upon the subject of customs duties and railroad rates. He had also, he said, been in communications with other Powers, especially with the government of France. He declared that this question is such a difficult one that the Russian Cabinet itself has not been able to reach a final decision. . . . My impression is that while the Russian government would like to meet the proposition of the United States

59 Kantorovich, *op. cit.*, p. 140.
60 *Ibid.*

with a friendly spirit . . . the Imperial Ministers fear to commit themselves to a policy which may lead so far into the future. . . . He [Muraviev] went so far at least as to say that, whatever answer the Russian government should make, it would not be a refusal; and, upon my reminding him anew of the position taken in this regard by the other Powers, he said, "Say to your government that we shall do whatever France does." [61]

At length, on December 30, 1899, the Russian formal reply to Secretary Hay's note of September 6 was sent to Ambassador Tower to be relayed to Washington. On the same day Muraviev telegraphed Cassini the text of the reply, informing the Russian ambassador that he had purposely omitted all reference to the question of railroad rates.[62] The reply of the Russian Foreign Office is given in full:

I had the honor to receive your Excellency's note dated the 8th–20th of September last, relating to the principles which the Government of the United States would like to see adopted in commercial matters by the Powers which have interests in China.

In so far as the territory leased by China to Russia is concerned, the Imperial Government has already demonstrated its firm intention to follow the policy of "the open door" by creating Dalny [Talienwan] a free port; and if at some future time that port, although remaining free itself, should be separated by a customs limit from other portions of the territory in question, the customs duties would be levied in the zone subject to the tariff, upon all foreign merchandise without distinction as to nationality.

As to the ports now opened or hereafter to be opened to foreign commerce by the Chinese Government, and which lie beyond the territory leased to Russia, the settlement of the question of customs duties belongs to China herself, and the Imperial Government have no intention whatever of claiming any privileges for its own subjects to the exclusion of other foreigners. It is to be understood, however, that this assurance of the Imperial Government is given upon condition that a similar declaration shall be made by other powers having interests in China.

With the conviction that this reply is such as to satisfy the inquiry made in the afore mentioned note, the Imperial Government is happy to have complied with the wishes of the American Government, especially as it attaches the highest value to anything that may strengthen and consolidate the traditional relations of friendship existing between the two countries.[63]

[61] Tower to Hay, Dec. 28, 1899.

[62] It must be kept in mind that the Russian diplomats of this period, as well as some others, looked upon Hay as a zealous Anglophile, almost an agent of London. De Wollant from Washington, Sept. 12, 1900. *Arkhiv M.I.D.*, Chinese Table, No. 787; also, Cassini from Washington, Nov. 4, 1900, Chinese Table, No. 105. Kantorovich, *op. cit.*, p. 139, n. 192. The Russian Foreign Office was not only suspicious of but despised the term "Open Door," mainly because of its association with the English. Dennis, *op. cit.*, p. 190. Ambassador Tower may have discovered another factor that entered into the situation when he wrote: "There is probably nothing in the whole course of international relations so distasteful to the Russian Government as the necessity to bind itself by a written agreement." Tower to Hay, Feb. 12, 1900. Tyler Dennett, *John Hay*, p. 294.

[63] Muraviev to Tower, Dec. 30, 1899. On December 31 Muraviev wrote Witte that it was impossible to go "contrary to the principle generally accepted by the powers of an economic-political beginning, thereby undermining the friendly relations existing

The Russian Foreign Office had refused to make a definite commitment in regard to either its own leased territories or spheres of influence.[64] Hay, in a private letter to Tower, wrote:

If it were safe for us to quote Count Mouravief's expression to you in connection . . . that Russia will do whatever France does, that, coupled with the full and definite acceptance of our proposition by France, would be sufficient to interpret the answer of Russia in a fuller sense than its mere text would warrant. We do not want to run the risk of Russia's refusing to be bound by the oral promise given to you to do whatever France does.[65]

But Russia did refuse to be thus bound. After another conversation with Muraviev, Tower wrote that,

It would be dangerous to announce in a formal document that the action of Russia related in any manner to that of France. The government of Russia insists that it acted by itself and although the Minister for Foreign Affairs will admit his oral statement to me in regard to France, he repels the idea that Russia and France replied in concert to the note of the United States. I am sure he would deny such a statement if publicly made.[66]

Both Muraviev and Cassini apparently resented Hay's efforts to obtain concrete statements from them regarding his proposals.

I was very much interested [wrote Hay to Tower] in your despatches . . . in the temper which Count Mouravief showed, and the slight tinge of resentment which there was in his words at being forced into a corner and compelled to reply categorically to our proposals. I had the same experience here with Count Cassini. He protested rather vehemently at one time against the extent of what he called our "demands," saying "You do not yourself see the vast portée of them." . . . I am convinced that Cassini would have stood out against us here almost indefinitely if I had not by my instruction to you shifted the field of discussion from here to St. Petersburg.[67]

Muraviev, whose dislike for the term Open Door as applied to Russia was intense,[68] did not however

---

between Russia and the United States and giving the occasion for the formation of a dangerous coalition of power against our interests in the Far East." Romanov, *op. cit.*, p. 244.

[64] See also Griswold, *op. cit.*, p. 78 n.

[65] Hay to Tower, Jan. 22, 1900. Dennett, *Hay*, pp. 293–94.

[66] Tower to Hay, telegram, Feb. 9, 1900. Later Hay wrote: "He [Muraviev] did say it, he did promise, and he did enter into just that engagement. It is possible that he did so thinking France would come in, and that other Powers would not. If now they are to take a stand in opposition to the entire civilized world we shall then make up our minds what to do about it." Hay to Henry White, April 2, 1900. William R. Thayer, *Life and Letters of John Hay*, II, 243.

[67] Hay to Tower, Jan. 22, 1900. Dennett, *Hay*, p. 293.

[68] Muraviev, through Tower, requested Hay not to link the term with Russia, since "It is not a true expression, in any event, for Russia does not intend, for instance, to throw open the door at Port Arthur." Tower to Hay, Feb. 12, 1900. Dennett, *Hay*, p. 294. In deference, probably to the Russian request, the term Open Door was no longer used in public despatches relating to the general plan. Dennis, *op. cit.*, p. 190.

object to a general public statement that Russia has replied favorably to the American propositions . . . and renews the assurance that all privileges conceded to any foreign country within the sphere of influence shall be guaranteed to the United States.[69]

Nevertheless, according to Tower, the truth was

that the Russian Government did not wish to answer your proposal at all. . . . It did so because of the desire upon its part to maintain the relations subsisting between the two countries, which it would not on any account disturb. It went a great way, as Russian diplomacy goes, when it put into writing the answer which you now have.[70]

Secretary Hay, who from the first had been aware of the actual situation, decided to present a' bold front.[71]

Our object [Hay wrote to Tower] is now to give the widest significance to the Russian reply of which we are capable. Without running the risk of bringing upon ourselves a contradiction of our assumption, we want to take it for granted that Russia has acceded to our proposals without much qualification.[72]

Hence, in a circular despatch of March 20, 1900, Hay announced that satisfactory replies had been received from all the powers to which notes had been sent, and that he accepted each reply as "final and definitive." The replies to the notes were, as a rule, not only ambiguous, but each power made its acceptance contingent upon acceptance by all the others. Great Britain, whose answer was the most satisfactory, objected to the application of the Open Door principle to either Wei-hai-wei or Kowloon. A compromise was finally reached and Kowloon was exempted.[73]

Less than three months after Secretary Hay's announcement of March 20, 1900, the long latent hostility of the Chinese to the "foreign devils" came to a head in the so-called Boxer uprising,[74] and another chapter of West versus East and the West divided against itself had begun.

Since the Empress Dowager was in sympathy with the aims of the Boxers, protests of foreigners against the activities of the organization were ineffectual.[75] After attacking foreign workers on the Peking-Hankow railway and tearing up sections of the Tientsin-Peking railway, the rebels entered Peking on June 13, and two days later, by destroying telegraph lines, cut Peking from the rest of the world. The murder of the German minister and the secretary of the Japanese Embassy followed, and the siege of the

---

[69] Tower to Hay, telegram, Feb. 9, 1900.

[70] Tower to Hay, Feb. 12, 1900. Dennett, *Hay*, p. 294.

[71] Rockhill, who wrote that Muraviev's reply has "what we call in America a string attached to it," also urged its acceptance. Rockhill to Hippisley, Jan. 16, 1900. Griswold, *op. cit.*, p. 78.

[72] Hay to Tower, Jan. 22, 1900. Dennett, *Hay*, p. 293.

[73] *For. Rel.*, 1899, p. 142; Griswold, *op. cit.*, pp. 77–78; Dennis, *op. cit.*, p. 189; Treat, *Far East*, p. 334 n.

[74] Langer, *op. cit.*, II, 692.

[75] *Ibid.*

legations began. From June 20 until August 14, when an international military force relieved Peking, the foreigners who had taken refuge in the British Legation were under fire from both the rebels and Imperial troops, menaced by sickness and starvation, their fate unknown to the rest of the world.[76]

During the initial stages neither the European capitals nor Washington clearly understood the nature of the conflict that was raging in China. In fact, on the eve of the siege of the legations, Mr. Rockhill wrote that, "The day the Chinese authorities choose to put an end to it [the Boxer uprising] they can easily do so." [77] In March, Hay instructed E. H. Conger, American minister to China, to act as far as possible "singly and without the cooperation of other powers." [78] On June 8, he still advised independent action "where practicable" in protection of American interests, "and concurrently with representatives of other powers if necessity arises." [79] Two days later he telegraphed, "We have no policy in China except to protect American citizens and the legation. . . . There must be no alliances." [80]

As the gravity of the situation became clearer, Secretary Hay, realizing the futility of independent action, and determined to forestall the tightening grip which increasing disorder would give the powers upon China, addressed his second famous circular note to them on July 3, 1900. Characterizing the situation in China as one of "virtual anarchy," the circular proclaimed the purpose of the United States "to act concurrently with the other powers . . . in opening up communications with Peking . . . in aiding to prevent a spread of the disorders . . . and in protecting American nationals and all legitimate American interests." So far the purport of the circular was in line with customary American policy in the Far East. But the concluding sentence contained a new and far-reaching objective, namely:

to seek a solution which may bring about permanent safety and peace to China, preserve Chinese territorial and administrative entity, protect all rights guaranteed to friendly powers by treaty and international law, and safeguard for the world the principle of equal and impartial trade with all parts of the Chinese Empire.[81]

Unlike the Open Door notes of September 6, the July circular did not request a formal reply. A more or less perfunctory reply from Great Britain was the only response from the powers addressed.

In suggesting that the powers coöperate in preserving the territorial integrity of China, Hay had taken a long step in advance of his notes of

76 *Ibid.*, II, 693–94; Griswold, *op. cit.*, pp. 78–79.

77 Rockhill to Hay, June 1, 1900, Dennis, *op. cit.*, p. 218. Secretary Hay was ill at the time and Mr. Rockhill was the recognized unofficial expert on China at the State Department. *Ibid.*

78 Hay to Conger, March 22, 1900. *For. Rel.*, 1900, p. 111.

79 Hay to Conger, telegram, June 8, 1900. *Ibid.*, p. 143.

80 Hay to Conger, telegram, June 10, 1900. *Ibid.*

81 Hay to Peirce, telegram, July 3, 1900.

September 6, 1899, which had asked only for most-favored-nation treatment of American commerce in the spheres of influence and leased areas in China. If the American objective of a wide-open door was to be achieved, China must be sovereign in her own territory, and this sovereignty, it was hoped, would be upheld by the powers.[82] At the same time, still with the Open Door in mind, the American Government sought to localize the conflict, fearing that the powers might declare war against China and, as a result, partition the Chinese Empire, which would be disastrous to the interests of the United States.

During the earlier stages of the Boxer crisis the policy of the United States and of Russia, who came forward in the role of "defender" of China, paralleled each other closely on the surface; so much so, in fact, that Cassini could telegraph from Washington to St. Petersburg that "Secretary of State Hay shares our point of view on most questions." [83] Despite underground Tsarist plans to invade Manchuria, the Russian Foreign Office in a circular telegram sent to their ambassadors on July 12, 1900, asserted that Russia "remains and intends in the future to remain true to its program of action, which includes in the main (1) the preservation of the true governmental structure of China; and (2) the removal of everything that might lead to a partition of the Celestial Empire." [84]

When the Tsarist Government suggested that the United States should follow the Russian intention of withdrawing its legation and troops from Peking to Tientsin,[85] the United States Government, realizing the delicacy of the situation in relation to the other powers, and the opportunity that withdrawal of Russian troops would give Russia in making special terms with China, agreed, with the proviso, that "unless there is a general expression by the powers in favor of a continued occupation . . . we shall give instructions to the Commander of the American forces in China to withdraw our troops from Peking." [86]

Again, the United States and Russia opposed the bellicosity of the German Admiral Waldersee,[87] and took a common stand against Germany's

[82] "Underlying the schemes of all the other foreign offices was the principle of military intervention on a large scale." In contrast, Hay trusted more to the power of "persuasion." Dennett, *Hay*, pp. 301–02.

[83] Kantorovich, *op. cit.*, p. 127.

[84] Circular telegram to Russian ambassadors, July 12, 1900. *Arkhiv M.I.D.*, Chinese Table, No. 32. Kantorovich, *op. cit.*, p. 127. Other documents in the Tsarist archives for this period also take the stand that the partition of China was not only unprofitable but dangerous to Russia. At an earlier date, when the Shimonoseki treaty was under discussion and intervention against Japan was decided upon by the Tsarist Cabinet, Witte laid down as a principle that it was to the interest of Russia "to support with all our strength the integrity and inviolability of the Chinese Empire." Witte, *Vospominania* (Memoirs), I, 39–40. Kantorovich, *op. cit.*, p. 138, n. 176.

[85] Dennis, *op. cit.*, p. 230.

[86] Adee to the Russian Embassy, memorandum, Aug. 29, 1900. *For. Rel.*, 1901, Appendix, p. 20. Dennis, *op. cit.*, pp. 254–55. Although there was a divergence in American diplomatic opinion, both Secretary Hay and President McKinley favored the speedy withdrawal of American troops from Peking. *Ibid.*, pp. 232–33.

[87] Kantorovich, *op. cit.*, p. 127.

demand of September 18, 1900 that China surrender to the foreign powers the criminal instigators of the Boxer rebellion.[88] In regard to the indemnity to be paid by China to the powers, Russia's original proposal to submit the entire question to the Hague Tribunal was favored by the United States.[89] And the United States and Russia were in accord as to the suitability of Li Hung-chang as plenipotentiary to represent China in the forthcoming negotiations with the Western powers.[90]

Thus, did the United States and Russia, externally at least, see eye to eye in regard to important points of Chinese policy. Their apparent cooperation, however, was little more than parallel political maneuvering, each, meanwhile, aware of the play of its opponent. Russia by no means contemplated upholding the integrity of the Chinese Empire, and this Hay understood. In the summer of 1900, at the height of the crisis in China, the hand of the Russian Foreign Office may be seen in the following instructions, sent to Admiral E. I. Alexeiev [91] at Port Arthur:

Although not isolating yourself from other nations, follow carefully, nevertheless, their activities, and have in view the necessity at any moment of presenting your demands. We must, however, avoid anything which would in any way tie our hands or be proof in the eyes of the Chinese of hostile intentions on the part of Russia.[92]

Shortly after issuing these instructions, when Russia was urging the United States to follow her example and withdraw from Peking, Foreign Minister Lamsdorf informed Chargé Peirce "in the most positive terms" that, although Russia was the temporary occupant of certain points within China, she had no intentions of seeking or permanently occupying "a single inch of territory in either China or Manchuria." [93] In a report of another interview with Lamsdorf the American chargé, after setting forth the lofty motives of the Russian Foreign Office in withdrawing its legation and troops from Peking, concluded: "He [Lamsdorf] therefore deems that good faith and the dignity of Russia requires the withdrawal of the Russian forces from Peking." [94]

The confidence of Mr. Peirce in the assertions of the Russian Foreign Office [95] was not shared by the American secretary of state who a few days

[88] This demand was supported by Austria, Italy, and France. Dennis, op. cit., p. 235.

[89] Ibid., p. 246.

[90] Kantorovich, op. cit., p. 127; Dennis, op. cit., pp. 228–29; Dennett, Hay, pp. 310–11. Germany, Austria, and Italy were opposed to, while Japan, and at last Great Britain, and France, were in favor of Li Hung-chang, who was finally appointed as negotiator for China.

[91] Chief commander of the troops for the Kwantung region and of the naval forces of the Pacific, 1899–1903. Gurko, op. cit., p. 647.

[92] Lamsdorf to Alexeiev, Aug. 15, 1900. Kantorovich, op. cit., p. 140, n. 246. Muraviev, who had died suddenly on June 21, 1900, was succeeded by Lamsdorf.

[93] Peirce to Adee, Aug. 30, 1900.

[94] Peirce to Adee, Sept. 1, 1900.

[95] In a lengthy despatch to Adee (No. 314, Sept. 11, 1900) Chargé Peirce explained that with the death of Muraviev a less aggressive foreign policy was to be expected; that

later declared that Russia's "vows are as false as dicer's oaths when treachery is profitable," adding that, "In this case it is for us to take care that
treachery shall not be profitable." [96]

Meanwhile, the apparent coöperation between the powers which had
been manifest up to the lifting of the siege of Peking, gave way to acrimonious strife and suspicion, not only in Peking but in the chancellories
of Europe.[97] Russia's proposal to withdraw from Peking as a token of
"friendship" to the Chinese, aroused the suspicions of the British and especially of the Germans, who read expansionist ambitions into the Russian
behavior. It was not, however, until after the Boxer crisis that the policies
of the United States and Russia clashed, became open rivalry, and finally
reached a climax in the Russo-Japanese War.[98]

Mr. Witte was "not in sympathy with Count Muraviev's Chinese policy and would
doubtless make his powerful influence felt in Tsarist councils." Peirce concluded: "There
would seem therefore to be a fair basis for entertaining the belief that if in the past
there existed an intention to absorb Manchuria, that policy may now have been reversed under the new direction of the foreign policy of the Empire." The following day,
the more discerning Mr. Conger telegraphed the State Department from Peking: "Russia
is now withdrawing larger part of her forces. This action, withdrawing Minister and
landing forces Newchwang, indicate purpose to make their settlement in their own way."
Conger to Hay, Sept. 12, 1900. Dennis, *op. cit.*, p. 232.

[96] Dennett, *Hay*, p. 317.

[97] Dennis, *op. cit.*, pp. 226 ff.; Langer, *op. cit.*, II, 704. Commenting on the Boxer episode Professor Langer (*Ibid.*, II, 704) says the following: "European diplomats . . . had
no ground for priding themselves on the handling of the Boxer movement and its after-
math. Europe's treatment of China in the whole period from 1895 to 1900 had been
devoid of all consideration and of all understanding. The Celestial Empire to them was
simply a great market to be exploited to the full, a rich territory to be carved up like a
sirloin steak. Hardly anywhere in the diplomatic correspondence does one find any
appreciation for the feelings of the Oriental or of any sympathy for the crude efforts
made at reform. The dominant note was always that force is the father of peace and
that the only method of treating successfully with China is the method of the mailed
fist. The Boxers were considered to be simply so many ruffians, who deserved no better
treatment than that ordinarily meted out to common criminals."

[98] During and after the lifting of the siege of Peking in August 1900, communications
to St. Petersburg from the Russian Embassy in Washington are marked by ironical allu-
sions to the increasingly pro-English attitude of Hay and his cabinet. This is particularly
true of the secret telegrams of de Wollant, July 19, and Aug. 16, 1900; and of Cassini,
Dec. 20, 1900, and June 6, 1901. Kantorovich, *op. cit.*, p. 128. According to these reports
the American press, which is credited with a mounting Russophobia, ascribed the Boxer
rebellion to the machinations of the Russians. De Wollant to Russian Foreign Office, July
7, 1900, No. 764. *Ibid.*

Chapter IV

CRISIS IN AMERICAN-RUSSIAN RELATIONS

BROADLY speaking, the rivalry between the United States and Russia represented a conflict between two contrasting paths of expansion—a Russian and an American. Tsarist Russia, which until the Russo-Japanese War was looked upon as the largest military power in the Far East, sought to take advantage of China's crisis by assuming hegemony over at least Manchuria and north China. Certain expansionists even demanded outright annexation of Manchuria.[1] This desire for expansion lay at the roots of Russia's desire for a separate agreement with China, and the *leitmotif* of its policy in relation to other powers was the maintenance of absolute freedom of action.

The United States, on the other hand, in order to uphold its own trade interests in China, had developed the policy of the Open Door. Realizing the necessity of strengthening its position to meet the growing menace of Russia in Manchuria, the United States attempted: first, to create a common front of the powers as a counterweight to the separate designs of Russia and, second, to render treaty relations between China and the other powers more effective.[2]

The aggressive Russian policy with respect to Manchuria had its roots in the past. Since 1895, as we have seen, Russian diplomats had disagreed regarding Far Eastern expansion. Witte, while not advocating annexation of Manchuria, had favored an alliance with China to serve as a mask for "peaceful penetration" and control, not only of Manchuria but ultimately of a large part of China as well. Spokesmen of the Army and the Navy De-

[1] General A. N. Kuropatkin, minister of war; General Grodekov, commander of troops of the Pri-Amur region; Admiral E. I. Alexeiev, commander of the Kwantung Province and of naval forces in the Pacific; and others. See Glinskii, *op. cit.*, pp. 106 ff., 118 ff., 140 ff.; Kantorovich, *op. cit.*, p. 128; Langer, *op. cit.*, II, 695 ff.

[2] That the situation in the Far East in the post-Boxer period was not limited to conflict between Russia and the United States goes without saying. American policies during this period were by no means wholly acceptable to any other power, while the Anglo-Russian and the Russo-Japanese political and economic rivalries were considerably sharper than those between the United States and Russia. The United States was compelled to defend her policies, not only against Russia but against France, Germany and Japan as well, and later, England. The American policy, as a whole, coincided with that of Great Britain and of Japan simply because Russia was the "chief danger" in the Far East for all three countries.

partments, on the other hand, supported in part by the Foreign Office, had advocated the more opportune policy of seizing whatever possible, whenever possible. At the time of the Boxer uprising no more unanimity of opinion existed than before except that, with the death of Foreign Minister Muraviev on June 21, 1900 and the accession of Lamsdorf, Witte now had the support, such as it was, of the Foreign Office. Witte, however, had lost ground with the Tsar, who favored Minister of War Kuropatkin, while other and lesser lights were rising on the Imperial horizon.[3]

Kuropatkin, according to Witte, openly expressed his designs on Manchuria when, learning of the Boxer uprising, he exclaimed: "I am very glad. This will give us an excuse for seizing Manchuria. . . . We will turn Manchuria into a second Bokhara."[4] He was willing that Manchuria should remain a nominal part of China, but insisted that Russia should have complete commercial hegemony and in general tighten her grasp upon the country.[5] During the summer of 1900, he informed the German diplomats that Russia insisted upon freedom of action in Manchuria; that Manchuria, not the Peking Legations, was Russia's concern.[6]

The initial step which favored Kuropatkin's plans was unwittingly taken by the Chinese rebels themselves. At the height of the Boxer crisis, Witte, opposed to the taking over of Manchuria, made an unsuccessful attempt to arrange with Li Hung-chang for the protection of the Russian-owned Chinese Eastern Railway. In mid-July the attack upon the railway by Chinese hordes necessitated the rushing in of Russian troops, who instituted an extensive campaign from the north, south, and east. So successful were they that by the middle of October 1900, Russian troops, numbering 50,000, occupied Newchwang (seizing the custom house), were in complete military control of the provinces of Mukden, Kirin, and Tsitsihar, and had established control over southern Manchuria to the borders of Chili.[7] Continuing on their predatory way, the Russian forces seized the important railway line from Peking to Tientsin, and later from Tientsin to Shanhaikwan. After vigorous protests from the powers, both lines were finally surrendered: the Peking-Tientsin Railway to the powers, the Tientsin-Shanhaikwan to the British in February 1901.[8]

On November 6, 1900, it was announced that the Russian military authorities had also obtained a land concession at Tientsin from the Chinese Government, an achievement that was characterized by the American en-

[3] Langer, *op. cit.*, II, 695; Gurko, *op. cit.*, pp. 263 ff.

[4] Witte, *Memoirs*, pp. 107–08. "Bokhara was a Russian protectorate with a resident Russian political agent whose function was broadly similar to that of a British resident in a native state of India."

[5] Aleksei Kuropatkin, *The Russian Army and the Japanese War*, I, 70.

[6] *Die Grosse Politik*, XVI, Nos. 4537, 4548, 4552. Langer, *op. cit.*, II, 696. Three years later the Tsar demanded that Korea also become another Bokhara. Kuropatkin, by this time alarmed at the menace of war in the Far East in 1903, reversed his tactics and joined Witte in opposing Russia's warlike attitude. Kuropatkin, *op. cit.*, I, Ch. vi, particularly p. 164. Tyler Dennett, *Roosevelt and the Russo-Japanese War*, p. 123.

[7] Glinskii, *op. cit.*, pp. 160 ff.; Romanov, *op. cit.*, pp. 250 ff.

[8] Morse, *op. cit.*, III, 325. Langer, *op. cit.*, II, 711.

voy to China as an act of "grab." [9] This grabbing process initiated by Russia became contagious and, despite the protests of the American minister, was immediately followed by a general scramble for similar concessions on the parts of Belgium, France, Italy, Austria, and Japan.[10] Secretary Hay contradicted his own principles, under pressure from the War and Navy Departments, in November 1900, when he sought to acquire a naval base and territorial concession at Samsah Bay in Fukien Province. The Japanese, who had recently preëmpted this as a sphere of influence, objected.[11]

Having made these advances in Manchuria, Russia relaxed and endeavored to consolidate her gains. Ever since September 1900, secret exchanges had been taking place between Li Hung-chang and Prince Oukhtomsky (Witte's special agent), but without results because of Witte's determination not to pay Li a huge bribe until he had shown his willingness to grant large concessions.[12] Meanwhile, the Russian commander on the spot, Admiral Alexeiev, made his own treaty with the Tatar general at Mukden, Tseng Chi. This document, signed on November 9, 1900, and known as the Alexeiev-Tseng Agreement, provided that the civil administration of Manchuria should be restored to Chinese control, but that Russian troops should be stationed at Mukden and other points along the railway; that Chinese troops should disband and disarm; and that all military supplies should be turned over to Russian authorities, China to be content with the appointment of police guards.[13] This separate agreement was unacceptable to both Li Hung-chang and Witte. Long and heated cabinet discussions ensued in St. Petersburg, military and naval men taking sharp issue with Witte, who, upheld by the Foreign Office, adhered to his original opposition to permanent occupation of Manchuria. War Minister Kuropatkin finally carried the day and a draft agreement, which incorporated several of Witte's whittled-down ideas, was presented to China on February 8, 1901. The most important demands of the projected Russian-Chinese agreement, in addition to those of the Alexeiev-Tseng Agreement of November 9, were: in the regions adjacent to Russia, especially those of

[9] Conger to M. de Giers (Russian minister to Peking), Nov. 14, 1900. *For. Rel.*, 1900, p. 45.

[10] Morse, *op. cit.*, III, 325–27; Langer, *op. cit.*, II, 711. Dennett states that "the Open Door doctrine and the other principles which were found necessary to bolster up its [China's] essential weakness are seen to be not principles of cohesion but of division. They are in practice policies of intervention, essential neither to prosperity nor to peace." Chapter on "The Open Door" (p. 294) in Joseph Barnes, ed., *Empire in the East.*

[11] Griswold, *op. cit.*, p. 83; Morse and MacNair, *op. cit.*, p. 443; Bemis, *Diplomatic History*, p. 487. In a despatch of March 1, 1899, to Secretary Hay United States Minister Conger had suggested that in the event of the partition of China, the United States might choose as an American sphere of influence the province of Chili which together with Tientsin is "destined in the future to be commercially one of the most valuable permanent possessions in the Orient." Kantorovich, *op. cit.*, p. 103; Dennis, *op. cit.*, p. 208.

[12] Romanov, *op. cit.*, pp. 263 ff.

[13] *Ibid.*, pp. 267 ff.; Glinskii, *op. cit.*, pp. 137 ff.; Langer, *op. cit.*, II, 712.

Manchuria and Mongolia, China was to agree not to grant railway, mineral, and industrial concessions to foreigners without the consent of the Russian Government; compensation for damages done during the Boxer crisis might be paid by granting concessions to the Chinese Eastern Railway; China was to grant a concession to the Chinese Eastern Railway for a railroad from a given point on that line to the Great Wall.[14]

The Russian Government had high hopes that Li Hung-chang would get the revised agreement accepted, but in spite of the assurance of a million rubles, the wily Chinaman, resorting to subterfuge, outwardly advocated the signing of the treaty, and at the same time appealed to the powers to save China. He suggested to the British representative, Sir Ernest Satow, that "the powers demand of China communication of the negotiations now in progress between it and Russia" and added that China "would be delighted to communicate with them and place itself in the hands of the powers for protection against Russia whose demands it could not deny, and whose constant threats terrified it."[15]

With the publication of the Alexeiev-Tseng original agreement in the *Times* of London of January 3, 1901, speculation, mingled with consternation, was rife, not only in Europe but in the United States and Japan.[16] In a despatch to the State Department Conger reported from Peking:

It is credibly reported here that Russia has already completed arrangements with China whereby separate negotiations to settle all their affairs should be conducted at St. Petersburg and that the plenipotentiaries . . . have been named. If this is true, the early conference between the Russian Minister and Li Hung Chang at Tientsin and the presence of Prince Oukhtomsky are fairly explained.[17]

A week later Conger again reported:

The Russian Minister has several times said to me that . . . each power should settle all other questions . . . by separate negotiations and in its own way. Every step which Russia has taken since the capture of Peking leads along this line. The withdrawal of her troops, the temporary retirement of her Minister, the occupation of Newchwang, and the agreement made for the partial disarming of Manchuria and for a supervisory protectorate by Russian officials, . . . the arrangement for securing a permanent concession at Tientsin, and the presence here of Prince Oukhtomsky, conferring constantly with Li Hung Chang . . . confirm beyond a doubt Russia's intention to withdraw, or at least conduct separate negotiations.[18]

Rockhill, United States commissioner to China, in a telegram of later date from Peking, was more outspoken:

[14] The complete demands in fourteen articles are given in Romanov, *op. cit.*, pp. 296–99 and in Langer, *op. cit.*, II, 714–16. Romanov asserts (p. 267 n. 2), that MacMurray (*op. cit.*, I, 329) has given the text of this agreement in a "fantastic edition."

[15] Rockhill to Hay, Jan. 29, 1901. Dennis, *op. cit.*, p. 242. See Romanov, *op. cit.*, pp. 300–04.

[16] Morse, *op. cit.*, III, 345; Langer, *op. cit.*, II, 716.

[17] Conger to Hay, Jan. 5, 1901.

[18] Conger to Hay, Jan. 12, 1901. Dennis, *op. cit.*, pp. 241–42.

Japanese Minister confidentially informs me Japanese Government will insist on *status quo ante* in Manchuria. It views present position of Russia there as a grave menace. . . . I think Russian agreement as to administration Manchuria absolutely contrary to previous declaration of intentions. If tacitly accepted by Powers, it constitutes most dangerous precedent.[19]

On February 1, 1901, Secretary Hay sent telegrams to China, Russia, and the other powers protesting the Alexeiev-Tseng Agreement.[20]

Yet, despite American support of the "entity of China," the policy of the United States was still so unstable that Secretary Hay on the same day felt compelled to reply to an inquiry by Japan as to the attitude of the United States toward Russia's infringement of her public pledges that,

We were not at present prepared to attempt singly, or in concert with other powers, to enforce these views [our well-known view as to the integrity of China] in the East by any demonstration which could present a character of hostility to any other power.[21]

Four days later Conger reported that according to the understanding in Peking, "Russia is insisting upon a separate settlement of all her Manchurian affairs," and he declared that "this is such a clear violation of the general understanding between the powers . . . as to deserve vigorous protest from the other governments." After enumerating the various excuses which Russia would probably advance for her action, Conger stated that,

It has been the policy of Russia for several years to treat China as a mere child, demanding of her whatever she desired, threatening her with great military movements as severe punishment if refused . . . and China has been frightened into yielding.

Conger then added data which apparently aroused Hay from the lethargy shown in his reply of February 1, to Japan:

I have to-day received confidentially from a reliable source a statement of the demands concerning Manchuria which Russia proposes to press upon the Chinese Government and enclose a copy herewith. This, taken with the recent correspondence upon this subject between Japan and Russia, which . . . has been sent you from Tokio, fully discloses Russia's determination to secure Manchuria, as well as to recoup her military expenditures by a practical seizure of the Railway from Shanhaikwan to Newchwang. She has already stripped the line from Tientsin to Shanhaikwan of engines and other rolling stock. This is the first step, and a very long one, toward the dissolution of the Empire. Protests here are of no avail, for the Minister is simply carrying out instructions from St. Petersburg.[22]

Meanwhile, reports were circulating that St. Petersburg was the headquarters for exchanges between Russia and China in regard to a modifi-

---

19 Rockhill to Hay, Jan. 23, 1901.
20 Dennett, *Hay*, p. 322.
21 Hay to Foreign Office, Tokyo, memorandum, Feb. 1, 1901. Dennis, *op. cit.*, p. 242.
22 Conger to Hay, Feb. 5, 1901.

cation of the prospective treaty, and that Russia was exerting pressure upon China for a speedy ratification.[23] Unconvinced by another disclaimer from St. Petersburg, the Governments of the United States, Great Britain, Germany, and Japan sent protests to China [24] warning her of the danger of concluding separate treaties with any one power.[25] On February 17, Secretary Hay pointed out to the Chinese minister at Washington "the extreme danger to the interests of China of considering any private territorial or financial arrangements, at least without the full knowledge and approval of all the Powers now engaged in negotiation." Referring specifically to the circular of July 1900, he stated that this warning was based on "the preservation of the territorial integrity of China," a principle which had been recognized by all the powers.[26]

The warnings of the powers apparently made no impression upon either Peking or St. Petersburg. Russia declared that if the powers chose to disregard earlier assurances given by the Foreign Office, then "Russia would take care to safeguard her own interests;" [27] that she was simply trying to obtain adequate guarantees from China for the evacuation of her troops from Manchuria. Finally, the Chinese Government, disturbed by reports of renewed Russian demands for signature of the convention, again called upon the powers for mediation.[28] Accompanying this request was a badly modified version of the Russian-Chinese agreement.[29]

Japan, with Korea in mind, was outraged at these developments. The atmosphere was charged with talk of war.[30] In fact, had Great Britain stood by Japan in her requests that the British Government intercede to prevent France from supporting Russia, it is indeed possible, if not probable, that Japan would at this time have fought Russia.[31] Meanwhile, Japan,

[23] Sir E. Satow to Lansdowne, Jan. 6 and Feb. 5, 1901. The Russian Government, which had originally denied the existence of such an agreement, now claimed that the documents did not partake of the nature of an international convention but was simply a modus vivendi between China and Russia. Sir C. Scott to Lansdowne, Feb. 6, 1901. Morse, *op. cit.*, III, 345.

[24] Germany's "protest" to China was in keeping with her Far Eastern policy at that time. She counselled China to make no separate agreement until the amount of the indemnity to be paid by China to the powers had been decided upon; and, at the same time, informed Russia that she was unconcerned with the fate of Manchuria. *Die Grosse Politik,* XVI, Nos. 4815–16. Langer, *op. cit.,* II, 719; Dennett, *Hay,* p. 322.

[25] Morse, *op. cit.,* III, 345; Langer, *op. cit.,* II, 719.

[26] *For. Rel.* 1901, Appendix, pp. 363–64. Dennett, *Hay,* p. 322.

[27] Sir C. Scott to Lansdowne, March 7, 11, 13, 1901. Morse, *op. cit.,* III, 346.

[28] Morse, *op. cit.,* III, 345; Langer, *op. cit.,* II, 720.

[29] G. P. Gooch and H. W. V. Temperley, (eds.), *British Documents on the Origins of the World War, 1898–1914,* II, 47; subsequently referred to as *British Documents. Die Grosse Politik,* XVI, Nos. 4819–23. Langer, *op. cit.,* II, 720.

[30] *Krasny Arkhiv, "Nakanunie Russko-Iaponskoi Voini"* (On the Eve of the Russo-Japanese war), LXIII, 13 ff.

[31] Having been given repeated assurances of German neutrality, Japan was willing to tackle Russia if France, which was reported to be lukewarm to her ally, would remain neutral. Could Great Britain be induced to hold France in leash? But the British, after several important Anglo-Japanese conversations, could not decide to intervene. Premier Ito was also a restraint upon the war-bent forces. With 1895 in mind, Ito was willing to

acting upon her own initiative, protested to St. Petersburg on March 24, 1901, demanding that the Russian-Chinese draft be referred to the joint conference of diplomats which was still in Peking endeavoring to iron out the various Boxer problems. Replying promptly, Lamsdorf on March 25, insisted that the entire question concerned only Russia and China.[32]

From a report given by Cassini of a conversation held by him with Hay on March 28, 1901, it would appear that, provided American trade was protected, the secretary of state was prepared to accept Russian occupation of Manchuria. Mr. Hay, according to Cassini, stated that,

We fully recognize Russia's right to adopt such measures as she considers necessary to prevent the repetition of the grievous events of last year. We would even have understood if she had gone further along this path, in so far as it could be acknowledged necessary for her interests and projects, if we have the assurance that our trade would not suffer and that the door would remain open.[33]

Cassini professed to be nonplussed by this utterance of the American secretary of state which he could interpret only as an open admission that, "The United States in some strange way had changed its ideas regarding the inviolability of the Celestial Empire, which she so lightly would see sacrificed so long as the powers would guarantee American trade all the advantages of the open door." [34] However, a note of protest against Russian dominance in China had already been sent by Hay on February 19 to the Chinese Government and also to the interested powers.[35] This was answered by Russia in the following note of April 5, 1901, with its ironic concluding words:

---

come to an agreement with Russia, failing which, he was willing to urge war only if assured of a line-up of powers favorable to Japan. Langer, *op. cit.*, II, 720 ff.

[32] Lamsdorf informed the Japanese Ambassador that the pending agreement was the instrument through which Russia hoped to be able to leave the occupied territory as soon as possible, in conformity with her previous promises. When Russia was convinced that order had been restored, she would hasten to return this territory to China, provided the other powers had not meanwhile interfered. As to a diplomatic conference in Peking on the Manchurian question, Russia would discuss only general questions affecting all interested powers and those affecting Russia and China would be considered separately. Manchuria, in which Russia alone was interested, belonged in the latter category. "Count Lamsdorf expressed the desire to sign the above-mentioned agreement as soon as possible to demonstrate the sincerity of Russia." *Krasnyi Arkhiv, "Nakanunie Russko-Iaponskoi Voini,"* LXIII, 21.

[33] Conversation of Hay with Cassini, March 28, 1901. Romanov, *op. cit.*, p. 304.

[34] Confidential letter of Cassini to Lamsdorf, March 28, 1901, No. 75, part 3. *Ibid.*, p. 305. The Soviet economist and historian Vladimir Avarin writes that Hay definitely stated to Cassini that he [Hay] was concerned only about American trade, capital investment, and the Open Door in Manchuria, and that if necessary he would fight on the side of Japan and Great Britain against Russian domination. Telegram of Cassini from Washington, Feb. 24, 1901, No. 3118; also telegram, March 17, No. 805. Vladimir Avarin, *Imperialism v Manchzhurii: Etap Imperialisticheskoy Borbi za Manchzhuriu.* (Imperialism in Manchuria: A Phase of Imperialistic Struggle for Manchuria), I, 58.

[35] Dennis, *op. cit.*, p. 243.

In continuation of the conversation which he [Cassini] had yesterday evening with the Secretary of State, the Ambassador of Russia has the honor to confirm to him the intentions of the Government of His Majesty the Emperor, which he has orally brought to the Secretary's attention. It vies with the erroneous interpretations occasioned by the arrangements which have been projected with the purpose of the evacuation of Manchuria by the Russian troops. The Imperial Government does not insist upon its conclusion by the Chinese Government and renounces all further negotiations on the subject. Remaining immovably faithful to its original program, which has been so many times declared, the Imperial Government will quietly await the farther march of events.[36]

On April 20, Secretary Hay, with the aim of permanently safeguarding American commercial interests, replied in a note to Cassini that the President of the United States would appreciate further assurance from the Russian Government that rights of American nationals in Manchuria, or any part of China, would not be jeopardized as a result of any agreements made between Russia and China or between Russia and other powers.[37] A favorable reply to this note was received from the Russian Foreign Office on June 9, 1901.[38]

Meanwhile, the Russians, conscious of the mounting hostility of the powers, began to retreat, presenting the modified Alexeiev-Tseng Agreement of February 8, 1901, to China in an adulterated form.[39] But the Chinese, upheld by Great Britain and Japan, still refused to sign and once more called upon the powers to intervene. Supported by Great Britain, Japan sent a stiff warning to Peking, informing the Tsungli Yamen that acceptance of the Russian demands would mean the partition of China, in which Japan would demand a substantial share. This was followed on April 6 by the Japanese reply to Count Lamsdorf's statement of March 25.[40] It reads: "The Imperial Government is unable to accept the answer of Count Lamsdorf of March 25, and reserves its opinion under the present circumstances."[41]

Temporarily overwhelmed by this opposition, Russia announced on April 25 that the Russian-Chinese convention had been withdrawn, explaining that a draft of fourteen articles had never existed; that the document was only a provisional program which in no way affected China's sovereignty or integrity. This reply was greeted with skepticism by the nationals of all the powers, especially the English, one of whom observed that these Russians are "occasionally, to use their own term, colossal."[42]

---

[36] Cassini to Hay, note from the Tsarist Foreign Office, April 5, 1901. Dennis, *op. cit.*, pp. 243–44.

[37] *Ibid.*, p. 244.

[38] Lamsdorf to Cassini to Hay, note, June 9, 1901. *Ibid.*

[39] Glinskii, *op. cit.*, pp. 158 ff.

[40] *Supra*, p. 71.

[41] Ito Masanori, *Kato Takaaki* (Japanese minister to England), I, 421–27. The diplomatic correspondence may be found in *Krasnyi Arkhiv*, "Nakanunie Russko-Iaponskoi Voini," LXIII, 21 ff. Langer, *op. cit.*, II, 723.

[42] Romanov, *op. cit.*, p. 306 ff.; Glinskii, *op. cit.*, 158 ff.; Langer, *op. cit.*, II, 724.

Thus far, however, Russia had done well by herself. Kuropatkin wrote in the summer of 1901 that, "Russia in three years has moved from Vladivostok about 1000 versts southward and placed Port Arthur and Shanghai in such a position that it can easily and quickly extend strong pressure on Peking." The war minister concluded by demanding continuation for an indefinite period of the existing order of things in North Manchuria.[43] Russia wished to continue doing well by herself. Therefore, in spite of her public statement of April 25, and the opposition of the powers, especially the determined stand taken by the Japanese,[44] Russia continued to remain in Manchuria. Not until July 18, after the customary wrangling among Cabinet officials, did the latter agree upon a plan for evacuation of Manchuria, contingent upon the restoration of order in that country.

A telegram sent by the foreign minister on July 30, 1901, to the Russian diplomatic representatives at Peking and Tokyo gives insight into the technique of Tsarist diplomacy in what the latter called "evacuating" Manchuria. Lamsdorf says:

This essential reservation [that order must be restored in Manchuria] undoubtedly reserves for Russia the right to the province which she has conquered if in the near future the conduct of the powers or that of the Chinese Government shall be hostile to the outstanding settlement of Chinese affairs, or will directly violate our interests in the Far East. . . . Before taking any decision in this matter it would be desirable to know what consequences in your opinion would follow should an official announcement of Russia's intention to annex Manchuria be made.[45]

Two days later, in secret letters to the ministers of war and finance, Lamsdorf discussed the matter of problems connected with the seizure of Manchuria. They simply boiled down, he said, to the question of what constitutes interests. The letter follows:

There is no doubt that from the formal point of view, inasmuch as the question concerns the mutual relations of Russia to other powers, the annexation of Manchuria is quite possible, notwithstanding the declarations published in the official Government communications. It is true that in all of the official documents the Imperial Government has unmistakably informed foreign governments that Russia has no intentions of territorial aggrandizement at the expense of China and that it would evacuate its troops, provided the powers and China did

[43] Kuropatkin to Lamsdorf, July 30, 1901. *Arkhiv M.I.D.*, No. 722. Kantorovich, *op. cit.*, p. 146.

[44] Romanov, *op. cit.*, pp. 315–16; *Krasnyi Arkhiv*, "Nakanunie Russko-Iaponskoi Voini," LXIII, 23–31. Kuropatkin and other military men doubted Japan's war strength. Langer, *op. cit.*, II, 748. Izvolski, minister to Japan, was aware of Japan's strength but doubted Tokyo's financial ability to fight Russia. He stated that, "If we shall be compelled to assert our power in Manchuria, we shall inevitably find ourselves faced by the dilemma: either provide Japan with the corresponding advantages in Korea, or decide on an armed conflict with her." Izvolski to Tsarist Foreign Office, letter, Oct. 6, 1901. Avarin, *op. cit.*, I, 61. Witte was of the opinion that war with Japan should be avoided at all costs. Romanov, *op. cit.*, p. 312.

[45] *Krasnyi Arkhiv*, "Nakanunie Russko-Iaponskoi Voini," LXIII, 29–32.

nothing to impede this action. On the basis of the last reservation, it would not be difficult in the near future to find some objections to the conduct of the powers or to that of China, for in the behavior of China there are sufficient pretexts to furnish a basis for abrogation from our original intentions and to declare the annexation of some part of Chinese territory. Although such a decision would undoubtedly lead to unfavorable impressions in world public opinion, which would see in this only a pretext for the non-execution by the Imperial Government of its stated promises, nevertheless there are some facts to warrant the belief that none of the Western Powers would decide to defend China, and that consequently there would be no attempt on the part of Europe to resist the plans for Russian annexation.

Lamsdorf, continuing, wrote that only Japan had military intentions against Russia; therefore, the only question was whether Russia was in a position to resist Japan in case the former carried out her intentions of annexing Manchuria. Russian ambassadors and ministers, answering these letters and telegrams, were unanimous in advising the evacuation of troops from Manchuria as a deceptive measure.[46]

Meanwhile, pressure upon Washington for action against Russian maneuvers in Manchuria was being exerted by American representatives in the Far East. Mr. Henry Miller, the able American consul at Newchwang,[47] described the obnoxious nature of the Russian civil administration over Newchwang which, among other heavy burdens, had introduced an oppressive system of taxation, the native customs tax alone totaling approximately 800,000 taels for the year. The memorandum continues:

The establishment of the new system of local taxation and the arrangements for a police control of the river for several hundred miles . . . and the thoroughness with which the Russians are now in control of every part of Manchuria does not indicate any purpose on their part to withdraw from a complete and perfect mastery of this part of China.

Over one-third of the imports into Manchuria, Mr. Miller continues, far exceeding those of any other country, are from the United States, consisting in the main of cotton, oil, and flour.[48] And "it is in all of these lines that Russia is expecting to supplant us." The report goes on:

If she can accomplish this on the basis of economy of production and transportation we cannot reasonably object; but I can see no reason why we shall

---

46 *Ibid.,* pp. 33 ff.

47 United States Consul Henry B. Miller was ordered in May, 1901, to reopen the consulate in Newchwang which for years had been supervised by a merchant vice consul. Dennett, *Roosevelt,* pp. 126–27.

48 Mr. Miller, in the same despatch, stated that the total trade in Newchwang, "the true key to the commerce of Manchuria" was approximately $100,000,000 (silver) in 1899, and that this trade was still in its infancy because of the riches of the country and its potentialities for economic and trade development. In 1901, according to Tyler Dennett, Newchwang ranked third among Chinese ports in value of imports from the United States. The Russian invasion of Manchuria, and the threatened shutting off of the United States from all markets except Newchwang, was a blow to the steadily mounting American commercial prospects in that country. "Nowhere else in the world at the moment were American commercial interests so directly threatened." *Ibid.,* pp. 125–26.

submit to it by any other method. Today her trade interests here are nominal, while our imports are greater than those of any nation. By what rights does she assume to . . . establish her authority over the Customs and Civil Administration, that is so important a factor to our trade? . . . The United States has now reached a position in production and commerce where its prosperity is dependent upon its export trade along the lines consumed by the trade of Manchuria. Are we to abandon our present trade of over five million gold dollars for 1899 and an assured increase of many times that amount (if China retains Manchuria) without an effort? Must we allow the Military Power of Russia to push us out of China without any objection? . . . Once she has the full control of this country she will annihilate American trade here. . . . It is of the utmost importance to stop the domination of Russia over the Chinese Empire, and by the most active measures insist upon the full and absolute return of this port and the whole of Manchuria to the Chinese Government.[49]

On July 29, 1901, Consul Miller, in another report, comments: "We are apparently paying no respect to our interests in Manchuria. This apathy on our part is becoming the subject of serious comment on the part of other powers represented here." [50]

On August 26, Minister Conger, using a report from Mr. Miller as a basis, also complained to Secretary Hay of Russian aggression in Manchuria. He was particularly concerned over the reported application of Russian civil law in violation of international law in Newchwang.[51] In a confidential telegram Hay replied: "Russian encroachments Newchwang cause anxiety. Send facts fully by Rockhill or by mail and brief resumé by cable. Note especially any damage to American trade. Give opinions of your colleagues as far as attainable." [52]

Conger in his response summarizes the details of the Russian occupation of Manchuria since the signing of the Alexeiev-Tseng Agreement on November 9, 1900. He reports that renewed negotiations between Russia and China are expected, toward which the attitude of the powers is unpredictable. If Russia is not checked in her activities she will ultimately acquire sovereign control over Manchuria, an unpleasant prospect for the United States to contemplate. In the next paragraph Mr. Conger, perhaps taking his cue from Secretary Hay, appears in a somewhat compromising mood:

. . . When we take into consideration our treaties with China, the conditions under which Russia has taken possession of Manchuria, and the fact that she has conjointly with the other Powers successfully negotiated a settlement of her large

[49] Squiers to Hay, Peking, July 16, 1901, with enclosure from Henry B. Miller to H. Squiers, Newchwang, June 27, 1901. Many of Mr. Miller's reports to the United States Legation at Peking were published in *Foreign Relations* for the years 1902 and 1903, as enclosures in the despatches of Minister Conger. "The fact that so many of these letters were published in 'Foreign Relations' is a still further indication of the disposition of the Department of State to present an extraordinarily full record of Russian pretensions in Manchuria." Dennett, *Roosevelt*, p. 127 n.

[50] Squires to Hay (enclosure), July 29, 1901.
[51] Conger to Hay, Aug. 29, 1901.
[52] Hay to Conger, Aug. 29, 1901.

money indemnity, we might properly, if Japan and Great Britain would do like-wise, demand that in whatever agreement Russia and China may make the *status quo ante* as to trade shall be provided for and preserved, that Newchwang customs be at once turned back to the control of the Chinese, and that all Manchuria should be left free to help pay the enormous indemnity of which Russia gets the lion's share.

Mr. Conger's concluding comments, which anticipate the later Harriman around-the-world project, are of interest:

Russia will have her great Trans-Siberian railway completed in another year. Its main terminal point will be Dalny. . . . This will open up to settlement and development the only great territory, still left on the globe, so favored with soil and climate as to promise great agricultural development and its concomitant of a strong people and resultant great trade progress. Its contiguity to the United States, and the possibility of connecting its great railroad system by direct lines of steamers across the Pacific with our own transcontinental routes make friendly political and trade relations between the two peoples most desirable and impor-tant. If such relations can be established and maintained without any particular or specific alliance, it will make this trade route, which will practically encircle the globe, one of inexpressible potency and of mutual benefit. England has been losing in the past few years much of both her political and trade supremacy and especially is this the case in the Orient. These facts ought not to be lost sight of in planning for immediate or future action upon the question under discussion.[53]

In late September 1901, Minister Conger, underwriting a despatch from Consul Miller which urged the United States, in case of Russian with-drawal, to send a gunboat and a hundred marines to Newchwang for the winter, quotes Mr. Miller as saying that the Chinese have more respect for countries that are represented by navies than for those which are not. According to Mr. Miller,

The Chinese merchants cannot understand why there has not been a United States gunboat in this river for more than a year past, when our imports here are greater than that of any other country, and their conclusion is that the United States will not protect its trade interests.

Mr. Miller concludes:

The Russian officials throughout Manchuria unreservedly announce that it is the purpose of Russia to govern Manchuria and make it a part of their great empire. . . . Our effort should be to have Manchuria thrown open to the world

[53] Conger to Hay, Sept. 7, 1901, with enclosure from Consul Miller. According to Mr. Miller, Russia expected to establish regulations that would keep American kero-sene out of Manchuria and give the market exclusively to Russian oil. He further states that not only he but "all Americans and British whom I have met in Manchuria who have had business relations with the Russians are universal in their belief of the total unreliability of both the official and mercantile classes. . . . Russian methods are so varied, devious and uncertain, that I have absolutely no faith in our being able to main-tain an open door in Manchuria by any agreement with Russia. . . . If the political dom-ination of Manchuria falls into the hands of Russia, American interests will be short-lived, and Russia will build here a colony so strong that in a few years the remainder of China will be at her mercy."

for trade, commerce and development, and in that case, I have not the least doubt that we would lead all nations.[54]

Meanwhile, negotiations between Russia and China had been renewed in Peking in July 1901, at the suggestion of Li Hung-chang, who realized that the longer China delayed the more difficult it would be to oust the Russians from Manchuria. Russia, amiably acquiescing, submitted a draft to Li which provided for the return of Manchuria to China, withdrawal of Russian troops by 1902, maintenance of Chinese troops in Manchuria, and the return of the Chinese Eastern Railway.[55] This attractive agreement was about to be signed in Peking in late October when Li Hung-chang was told by D. M. Pozdneiev, Russian representative of the Chinese Eastern Railway in Peking, that before a treaty for the evacuation of troops is concluded, China must also sign a secret convention with the Russo-Chinese Bank giving assurance that she would not award railway and other concessions to any foreign power except Russia.[56] At the same time a bribe of 300,000 rubles was offered Li by Pozdneiev if he would put through the deal. In "a stormy scene" in Peking on October 10, Li Hung-chang protested, stating, "that he could never dare to accept the responsibility for such an agreement which gives over to the bank all Manchuria," and which "without question would call forth the protests of foreigners." [57] Despite Li's vigorous protests he finally gave intimation that he would sign both agreements,[58] but his sudden death in Peking on November 4 put an end to these diplomatic arrangements.[59] The collapse of the negotiations with Li Hung-chang, however, allowed the Russian Government "to quietly await the course of events." [60]

Mr. Conger, in a despatch from Peking shortly after Li's death, wrote of the stormy interview in Peking between him and Pavel Lessar, Russian minister to China, adding that,

It is also . . . reported that . . . only a few hours before the death of Li Hung Chang, while he was entirely unconscious, the Russian Minister went to his house, and tried to compel the secretaries to have affixed, in the presence of the

[54] Conger to Hay, Sept. 28, 1901, with enclosure from Miller to Conger, Newchwang, Sept. 21, 1901.

[55] Romanov, op. cit., pp. 317 ff.; Glinskii, op. cit., pp. 177 ff.

[56] Both Witte and Lamsdorf regarded the bank agreement "as secret" and considered that it must be concluded "earlier than the agreement for the return of Manchuria." Case 75, part 4, Lamsdorf to de Giers, telegram, Aug. 18, 1901; Witte to Pozdneiev, telegram, Aug. 16; Lamsdorf to de Giers, telegram, Aug. 22; and Witte to Lamsdorf, letter, Aug. 23, with a reminder that the bank agreement "must be concluded before, or simultaneously with, the agreement for the evacuation of the troops, but under no circumstances afterwards." Romanov, op. cit., p. 325; Kantorovich, op. cit., p. 148.

[57] Telegrams of Pozdneiev of Sept. 26, 1901, with complete text of agreement, and of Sept. 27, 1901. Case No. 75, part 4. Romanov, op. cit., p. 327.

[58] Pozdneiev to Witte, telegram, Oct. 17, 1901. Case No. 75, part 4. Ibid., pp. 328–29.

[59] Glinskii, op. cit., pp. 177 ff.; Langer, op. cit., II, 751.

[60] Government despatch of March 24, 1901. Case No. 25. Kantorovich, op. cit., p. 148.

dying Viceroy, official seals, but it was too late as the seals had already been placed in the custody of the Provisional Treasurer.

The work of negotiating has been carried on very secretly so that the Powers might not have evident cause for interference until the matter was a *fait accompli*. In conversation with prominent Chinese officials, they say China is helpless and can do nothing but yield to Russia's demands, unless the other powers interfere, and they ask, "Will the United States help us?" . . .

Mr. Conger continues that in his opinion since the United States, England, and Japan have a practical monopoly of foreign trade in Manchuria, they might unite in warning Russia against endangering commercial interests that have resulted from treaty provisions,

especially in regard to Newchwang, the only treaty port, and where the continued occupation of Russia is destroying our trade, and where she is collecting for her own use the native customs, which, by a protocol signed by her representatives, have been pledged for the payment of general indemnities.

The American minister feels that the United States would be amply justified in "demanding immediate evacuation and the surrender of customs collections;" but any protests made to "helpless China" or the Russian minister are in vain since the "directing power is at St. Petersburg." In conclusion Mr. Conger writes:

It will be observed that the Russians agree to surrender all of Manchuria within three years, but in the meantime they make China therein completely helpless, keep all foreign intercourse out, and will no doubt find ample reason to make, and will make, their possession and sovereignty absolute before the expiration of that period.[61]

The opening of the year 1902 found the Manchurian problem still unsettled. In late January a compromise of sorts was reached in Peking by which China, in exchange for the return of Manchuria, was to sign an agreement with the Russo-Chinese Bank granting the desired concessions to Russia.[62] Meanwhile, Secretary Hay reiterated to the Chinese minister at Washington, Wu Ting-fang, that, although the United States stood for the territorial integrity of China, China's secrecy in dealing with Russia prevented the United States from rendering her effective assistance.[63] Mr. Hay's primary interest, however, was not China but American trade, as the evidence clearly shows. Shortly after this conversation with the Chinese minister, Hay informed Cassini that on the basis of existing information the unsigned agreement between Russia and China for the evacuation of Manchuria was not, as far as the United States could judge, injurious to American interests, "and no obstacle has been put by us in the way of the signature of the treaty." He requested that "Russia should do nothing in Manchuria which would injure the commercial interests of the United

61 Conger to Hay, Nov. 9, 1901.
62 Romanov, *op. cit.*, pp. 340–48; Kantorovich, *op. cit.*, p. 148.
63 Hay Papers, undated memorandum, early 1902.

States and nothing which would diminish the capacity of China to meet her international obligations." [64]

However, when the United States had definite word from Minister Conger in Peking that the Chinese representative, Prince Ch'ing, had agreed to sign not only the agreement with Russia but also a separate convention with the Russo-Chinese Bank concerning exclusive privileges of industrial development in Manchuria [65] Washington protested to St. Petersburg. Following instructions from the State Department, Ambassador Tower in a memorandum to Foreign Minister Lamsdorf stated that, "the United States could look only with concern upon any arrangement by which China should extend to a corporate company the exclusive right within its territory to open mines, construct railroads, or to exert other industrial privileges." The United States was of the opinion "that by permitting or creating a monopoly of this character," China would contravene existing treaties, injure American rights "by restricting legitimate trade," and impair China's sovereignty. And Ambassador Tower further wrote that,

Other powers, as well, might be expected to seek similar exclusive advantages in different parts of the Chinese Empire, which would destroy the policy of equal treatment of all nations in regard to navigation and commerce throughout China. . . . The acquiring by any one Power of exclusive privileges in China for its subjects or its own commerce would be contradictory to the assurances repeatedly given by the Imperial Russian Ministry for Foreign Affairs to the United States of the intention of the Russian Government to maintain the policy of the Open Door in China as that policy has been advocated by the United States and accepted by all the Powers who have commercial interests within the Chinese Empire.

In conclusion Mr. Tower stated that he had been instructed by the United States to request that the Russian Government "will give due attention to the foregoing considerations . . . and to express to your Excellency the hope that such measures of procedure may be adopted as will allay the apprehension of the Government of the United States." [66]

On February 8, Secretary Hay, in a conversation with Ambassador Cassini, pointed out that if these exclusive privileges demanded by Russia were granted, the United States "would be left in a position so painful as to be intolerable." [67] Lamsdorf denied that any attack had been made upon the Open Door and declared that Russia did not intend "to depart from the assurances heretofore given as to the principles which invariably direct her policy." [68] Ambassador Tower reported a few days later that Lamsdorf in a personal interview had expressed surprise and regret at the recent protest of the United States, which indicated "a lack of confidence

[64] Hay to Cassini, memorandum, Jan. 16, 1902. Dennis, op. cit., p. 351.
[65] Hay to Tower, Feb. 1, 1902. For. Rel., p. 926.
[66] Tower to Lamsdorf, Feb. 3, 1902.
[67] Hay to Cassini, memorandum, Feb. 8, 1902. Ibid., pp. 926–29.
[68] Tower to Hay, telegram, Feb. 10, 1902.

in Russia's integrity . . . which ought not to have been expected from the United States Government." Unconvinced by Tower's assurance of American friendliness, and "conscious of having done no wrong," the foreign minister said that, "if the United States had sent him a verbal inquiry as to the facts of the proposed concessions he would freely have given the details and would even have shown the contract." As it was, however, he could not escape feeling that a discourtesy had been shown to Russia "by addressing a formal note to China and Russia simultaneously," and he reiterated that, under such circumstances, "no independent nation can submit its action to the approval of others." Ambassador Tower concluded by saying that Foreign Minister Lamsdorf "would be gratified by an expression on the part of the United States Government of its acceptance of Russia's statement that it intends to return Manchuria to China and that it does not intend to depart from its policy heretofore announced." [69] But the American protest had accomplished its objective. Prince Ch'ing, supported by "the categorical protests of America and Japan," [70] refused to sign the agreement with the Russo-Chinese Bank.[71]

Meanwhile, the Anglo-Japanese Alliance had been signed on January 30, 1902, and its text had been reported on February 12 to Lamsdorf by the Japanese ambassador in St. Petersburg.[72] Preliminary conversations had been initialed in London as early as August 16, 1901, by the Japanese Count Hayashi. Japan, as the pro-British Hayashi told London, was not directly interested in Manchuria, but feared that its domination by Russia would lead inevitably to Russian attempts upon Korea, in which case Japan would be compelled to fight.[73] Great Britain, uneasy about Russian expansion not only in the Far East but in Tibet, Persia, and Turkey, hesitated, and made ineffectual attempts to come to an understanding with Russia. Witte, with the possible idea of obtaining a loan in London, appears to be the only Russian who favored an agreement with England. Finally, on November 6, Lansdowne submitted a tentative draft treaty to the Japanese minister.[74] In the interval, the Japanese Cabinet, wishing to avert a possible war, and dubious as to the possibility of an Anglo-Japanese agreement, had decided to send Prince Ito, who urged a direct settlement of the Korean question with Russia, to St. Petersburg for diplomatic conversations.[75] On November 14, Ito and Hayashi met in Paris and Ito, for the

69 Tower to Hay, telegram, Feb. 13, 1902.

70 Pokotilov to St. Petersburg, telegram, Feb. 11. Romanov, *op. cit.*, p. 347. "The difficulty of immediately seizing Manchuria is conditioned by the opposition of England and Japan, exerting their entire strength for the maintenance of the *status quo* and supported also by the United States and Germany." Letter of the Governor General of the Amur to the War Ministry, April 24, 1902. Kantorovich, *op. cit.*, p. 218, n. 28.

71 Romanov, *op. cit.*, p. 347.

72 *Ibid.*

73 *Ibid.*, p. 330; Hayashi, *op. cit.*, pp. 129-31.

74 Langer, *op. cit.*, II, 756, 759 ff., 783.

75 *Ibid.*, II, pp. 759 ff. The Russian press, as well as Witte, Lamsdorf and Izvolsky favored an agreement with Japan. In late November 1901, Witte wrote that "between the two evils, an armed conflict with Japan and the complete cession of Korea, I would

first time, learned of Lansdowne's draft. Acting upon instructions from Tokyo, Ito, however, proceeded speedily to St. Petersburg for a little "harmless gossiping," as urged by Hayashi, reaching this diplomatic center on November 25. Lansdowne, suspicious of Ito's mission in St. Petersburg, strongly protested to Hayashi. Japan, seeing the error of its course in attempting parallel negotiations with the two powers, suddenly terminated the Russian conversations, and turned unreservedly to Great Britain.[76]

The important provision in the treaty between Great Britain and Japan lay in its carefully worded Article I. In this are recognized the special interests of Great Britain in China, and those of Japan in China, and also those of Japan "in a peculiar degree, politically as well as commercially and industrially in Korea." [77]

This new two-power alliance was satisfactory both to Germany [78] and the United States.[79] France, counting on a settlement with England over Morocco, was disappointed and Russia had grave apprehensions.[80] Foreign Minister Lamsdorf, greatly perturbed at this turn in the diplomatic wheel, attempted to interest Germany and France in a joint counter-declaration. Germany refused, and France, unwilling to say a flat No, continued dickering until, finally, on March 20, 1902, she joined with her ally in a vaguely worded note which did not, however, extend the Franco-Russian alliance to the Far East.[81]

In face of the united opposition, nothing remained for Russia but to agree to withdraw from Manchuria, and to drop the banking convention —not however before Witte had succeeded in incorporating into the draft agreement a reservation that the withdrawal of troops would be contingent upon order in Manchuria and non-interference by the other

---

unhesitatingly choose the second." Witte, *Memoirs*, p. 117. In his *Memoirs*, however, Witte omits a major portion of the letter just quoted in which he states that Japan would be "weakened by the tremendous expense" in Korea which would make her more amenable to Russian pressure later and which would make the conquest of Korea possible if conditions demanded it. Witte to Lamsdorf, letter, Dec. 11, 1901, Romanov, *op. cit.*, p. 338. Confirmed by Glinskii, *op. cit.*, pp. 187 ff.

[76] Langer, *op. cit.*, II, 763–64.

[77] Morse and MacNair, *op. cit.*, p. 508; Langer, *op. cit.*, II, 777; Griswold, *op. cit.*, p. 90. Great Britain did not ally with Japan for the primary purpose of using the Japanese army to force Russia out of Manchuria. In fact, Great Britain had virtually recognized the special position of Russia in Manchuria in the Anglo-Russian agreement of 1899. It was Russian advances not only in China but in the Near East that distressed Great Britain and made her willing, in order to prevent an alliance between Russia and Japan (which automatically would have included France), to take the risk that the Japanese might take advantage of the 1902 agreement to force the issue over Korea with Russia. Langer, *op. cit.*, II, 782–83.

[78] *Ibid.*, II, 780.

[79] Hay and Roosevelt, according to Griswold (*op. cit.*, p. 89), assumed that American and British Far Eastern interests were the same. Roosevelt had become President in September 1901.

[80] Langer, *op. cit.*, II, 781.

[81] Dennis, *op. cit.*, p. 352; Langer, *op. cit.*, II, 781.

powers. Although the Chinese [82] endeavored to delete this clause, a tempting bribe of 30,000 lan softened their hearts, and the evacuation agreement was finally signed on April 8, 1902. By this convention, the opening clause of which recognizes Chinese sovereignty over Manchuria, Russia agreed to evacuate Manchuria within eighteen months.[83] Three zones were marked out, from which Russian troops would be withdrawn at intervals of six months, until complete evacuation was accomplished by October 8, 1903.

On the surface it would appear that this agreement would end the Manchurian venture. Baron Stahl, at that time Russian adviser in London —and who was not in sympathy with Russian tactics in Manchuria—congratulated Lamsdorf "for returning to what we in our time called 'Grande politique.' " [84] And Hay himself, who expressed satisfaction with the agreement,[85] wrote:

We are not in any attitude of hostility towards Russia in Manchuria. On the contrary, we recognize her exceptional position in northern China. What we have been working for two years to accomplish, and what we have at last accomplished, if assurances are to count for anything, is that, no matter what happens eventually in northern China and Manchuria, the United States shall not be placed in any worse position than while the country was under the unquestioned domination of China.[86]

That neither the convention of April 8 nor the Anglo-Japanese Alliance, from which it in part stemmed, was to have any ultimate influence upon Russia's Manchurian designs was foreseen by Consul Miller in Newchwang when he wrote:

The alliance between Japan and Great Britain will not seriously alter the intentions of Russia in Manchuria; she will be more modest in appearance and more circumspect in methods, but will continue to press all of her enterprises here and nurse her desire to cultivate her determination to become the perfect master of the country.[87]

Meanwhile, suspicious that the United States might be a silent partner in the British-Japanese combination, Russia made inquiries at the State Department. Ambassador Tower, in a private interview with the Russian

[82] Liang Fang and Wang Wen-shao, representatives of Prince Ch'ing. Romanov, *op. cit.*, pp. 347–48.
[83] Lamsdorf to Witte, letter, Feb. 25, 1902. Case No. 75, part 5. Pokotilov's telegrams, March 18 and 29, 1902. Case No. 51, part 3. Altogether 40,656 rubles in Russian currency were paid as bribes. After this payment was made from the 4-million "Li Hung-chang fund," the balance of the account of the minister of finance in the Russo-Chinese Bank amounted to 2,342,228 rubles, 24 kopeks. *Ibid.*, pp. 347–48. See also Glinskii, *op. cit.*, pp. 178–83.
[84] Private letter of Baron Stahl to Lamsdorf, April 23, 1902. Kantorovich, *op. cit.*, p. 149.
[85] *Ibid., op. cit.*, p. 149.
[86] Hay to Roosevelt, May 1, 1902, Roosevelt Papers. Dennett, *Roosevelt*, pp. 135–36.
[87] Miller to Conger, Newchwang, April 30, 1902.

foreign minister, found him "very uneasy" because of reports that pressure was being exerted "to induce the United States to join in the recent agreement between Great Britain and Japan, and that the United States Government is inclined to move in that direction." While not believing the accuracy of these reports Lamsdorf nevertheless expressed "with great earnesfness the hope that the Government of the United States will not consider such a step, which could be looked upon by Russia as only an unfriendly act." [88] Secretary Hay assured the foreign minister, through both Mr. Tower and Count Cassini, "that the Government of the United States was entirely foreign to the recent agreement; that it was not even approached in regard to it; and that since its negotiation the Government of the United States has never been asked to give its adhesion to the arrangement." [89] At the same time, Cassini, speaking unofficially, expressed his opinion that sooner or later war between Russia and Japan was inevitable, and requested "some assurance as to the future conduct of the United States in case of hostilities breaking out in the Far East." Secretary Hay could only assure him that the Russian Government had nothing but friendship to anticipate from the Government of the United States, as long as America's vital interests were safeguarded.[90]

[88] Tower to Hay, telegram, March 4, 1902.

[89] Hay to Tower and to Cassini, memorandum, March 6, 1902. Dennis, *op. cit.*, p. 374.

[90] *Ibid.* A number of Soviet writers assert that the United States indirectly, at least, endorsed the Anglo-Japanese Alliance. Avarin (*op. cit.*, I, 85) quotes Pokrovsky from the collection called "1905" (chapter on Russo-Japanese War, p. 595) as saying that the Anglo-Japanese Alliance was signed with the tacit consent of the United States; that the United States, with the assistance of the bayonets of the Japanese, hoped to keep the door open in Manchuria, and saw in the continental designs of the Japanese a protection against seizure of the Philippines and Hawaii, and had not Roosevelt feared the Senate he would probably have joined the Anglo-Japanese Alliance.

The author of the introductory remarks on p. 4, Vol. LXIII of the *Krasny Arkhiv* claims that shortly after the signing of the alliance between England and Japan, American imperialism, alarmed at the penetration of Russia into China, decided to cooperate with Japan.

Another Russian authority, Baron Boris E. Nolde in *Vneshniya Politika: Istoricheskie Ocherki* (Foreign Policy: Historical Essays), speaks of "a nearly three-year diplomatic campaign against Russian occupation which Japan led jointly with the English and American Governments." He holds (p. 242) that "had Russia come to terms with Japan on the partition, they probably would have avoided the Russo-Japanese war and succeeded in evicting both England and the United States from China."

Kantorovich (*op. cit.*, p. 148) also refers to the "behind-the-scenes" coöperation of England, Japan, and the United States in their endeavor to thwart the realization of the monopolistic plans of Tsarism.

On the other hand, Secretary Hay, in addition to his memorandum of March 6, over a year after the signing of the Anglo-Japanese Alliance, wrote: "The British Government appreciates fully our attitude of independent action, does not even ask us to enter into any arrangement with them. . . . The Japanese Government is in the same position . . . but . . . are painfully anxious to know what we propose to do . . . and, if we gave them a wink would fly at the throat of Russia in a moment. But I have constantly told Takahira that the Government of the United States must pursue an independent course in these matters, and have used my utmost efforts . . . to prevent any violent action in Manchuria." Hay to Roosevelt, May 12, 1903. Dennis, *op. cit.*, pp. 376–77.

The collapse of the banking agreement impelled Witte to redouble his efforts to guarantee for Russia the complete monopoly of all concessions in Manchuria, and accordingly the Manchurian Mining Association was created in the summer of 1902, at government expense and under the control of the Minister of Finance.[91] This creation of Witte's was, however, obstructed from the beginning by a group of adventurers headed by A. M. Bezobrazov, a retired cavalry officer, and his cousin A. M. Abaza. This clique was insistent upon reckless policies in the Far East which were completely at variance with those of the Tsar's ministers, Witte, Lamsdorf and Kuropatkin. After the Boxer uprising, this group, upheld by several grand dukes and the military party, looked upon all Manchuria, the Amur Maritime Province, and Korea as their special reservation for exploitation, and battled sharply with Witte and others who opposed their plans and stood for a more orderly form of capitalistic expansion and for compromise with other powers whenever possible.[92] In fact, the entire history of events connected with Manchuria after the conclusion of the convention of April 8, 1902, centers around the conflict for mastery between these two dominating groups at the apex of the Tsarist Russian

[91] Kantorovich, op. cit., p. 149; Avarin, op. cit., I, 75. Secretary Hay was soon busy inquiring as to the reports that a special mining concession had been secured by Russia in the Kirin region. England and Japan also hotly protested this grant. The result was a flat denial by Russia that any monopoly had been established. Dennis, op. cit., p. 353. The partners of this "private" company were A. J. Rothstein, manager of the Russo-Chinese Bank, and two important officials of the Ministry of Finance, A. J. Putilov, director of Chancellery, Ministry of Finance, and L. F. Davidov, director of Credit Department, Ministry of Finance. Its capital of one million rubles was borrowed from the government. Witte's report to the Emperor of July 5, 1902. Romanov, op. cit., p. 377. During 1902 this company spent four hundred and twenty-seven thousand rubles but was not able to begin the exploitation of any of its mining concessions. Ibid.

[92] Avarin, op. cit., I, 69–70. As early as 1900, learning of a timber concession on the Yalu and Tumen rivers, on the northern border of Korea which, in their opinion, would offer a wide field for industrial exploitation and, at the same time, serve as a protection against a Japanese attack, this group induced the Tsar to purchase the concession from his own private funds. A detailed account of the adventures and schemes of Bezobrazov et al., and their conflict with Witte is given in V. M. Vonliarliarskii, "Why Russia Went to War With Japan: The Story of the Yalu Concession," Fortnightly Review, May and June 1910, pp. 816–31, 1031–44; Gurko, op. cit., Ch. 15; Romanov, op. cit., pp. 425 ff.; Avarin, op. cit., I, 62 ff.; Kantorovich, op. cit., p. 149; Treat, Far East, pp. 366–67; Dennis, op. cit., pp. 354–55. The chief members of this palace group were: V. M. Vonliarliarskii and A. M. Bezobrazov, both retired officers of the Guards; Count I. I. Vorontsov-Dashkov, former court minister; Duke Alexander Mikhailovich; Captain A. M. Abaza (later admiral); Privy Councilor Neporozhnev; Prince F. F. Yusupov, adjutant to Grand Duke Sergei Aleksandrovich; Count V. A. Gendrikov, steward of the Imperial Household. Gurko, op. cit., pp. 259 ff. Despite their disparity of methods, the basic difference between Witte's policy and that of the palace clique was one of time. The policy of Witte, with its gradual "peaceful penetration" of Manchuria, gave Russian imperialism the opportunity to achieve success and face war under more favorable circumstances. In a letter to Lamsdorf, Witte wrote: "It is necessary for us to guarantee peace in the Far East for at least ten years." Arkhiv M.I.D., Dec. 28, 1902. Avarin, op. cit., I, 78. The palace clique made little progress until late 1902 when, supported by the minister of the interior, Plehve, their schemes assumed dimensions of grandeur.

social and political pyramid.[93] Witte, as we know, declared that a war with Japan would be a disaster and was willing even to sacrifice Korea to Japan,[94] and, eager to maintain good relations with the other powers, wanted Russia to evacuate Manchuria.[95] In this duel for the control of Far Eastern policy, the palace camarilla, having won over the Tsar, not only stalled on the evacuation promises, but advanced new demands upon China.[96] "These are the facts of history," writes Dennis

> but do we find the least hint of them in the letters and despatches of Mr. Tower or of Mr. McCormick from St. Petersburg? . . . President Roosevelt used the term 'cloth dolls' of their like in the diplomatic service of the day. It is a real question whether Secretary Hay ever understood the terrific struggle for power which was going on at St. Petersburg. From Mr. Eddy and Mr. Riddle, who were diplomatic secretaries at St. Petersburg during these years, he had more information than from their superiors; but even that did not touch the real facts with regard to Manchuria and Korea.[97]

Be this as it may, the American position at this time, as reported by Cassini, was: Let Russia grant the United States full trading rights in Manchuria and the United States will not hinder Russian domination in Manchuria. "Hay made it clear to me," Cassini notified St. Petersburg, "that the Federal Government will not impede the actions of Russia in relation to Manchuria if only the freedom of American trade and enterprise will be guaranteed in this province." [98]

The first stage of the evacuation of Manchuria was carried out on October 8, 1902, in accordance with the agreement of April 8, 1902.[99] This step did not materially alter general trade conditions at Newchwang. Russia continued to exercise supervision of the customs and the civil administration, still controlled the courts, and claimed the right to collect taxes. Russia even established a customs service, independent of the Chinese Maritime Customs and supervised by a Russian commissioner, at Dalny and other Manchurian ports.[100] "The completion of the Manchurian Railway and the creation of an open commercial port at Dalny, its terminus, make additional customs facilities necessary," wrote Mr. Conger to Secre-

[93] Avarin, *op. cit.*, I, 62 ff.; Romanov, *op. cit.*, pp. 425 ff.; Dennis, *op. cit.*, pp. 354–55; Morse and MacNair, *op. cit.*, p. 511. With the resignation of Witte in the summer of 1903, the palace group suppressed the activities of the Manchurian Mining Company, not tolerating competition either from foreign capital or from its own compatriots. Avarin, *op. cit.*, I, 75, 78.

[94] Avarin, *op. cit.*, I, 79.

[95] "We must without reservation fulfill the spirit of these agreements and in the designated period remove our troops from Manchuria and return stolen property to the Chinese." Witte to Lamsdorf, letter, Dec. 28, 1900. *Ibid.*, I, 80. Witte again insists upon the removal of troops in another letter of January 14, 1901, to Lamsdorf. *Ibid.*

[96] *Ibid.*, I, 80.

[97] Dennis, *op. cit.*, p. 355.

[98] Cassini to Lamsdorf, letter, Aug. 12, 1902. Avarin, *op. cit.*, I, 71. Cf. Hay's letter to Roosevelt of May 1, 1902. *Supra*, p. 82.

[99] Conger to Hay, Oct. 30, 1902. *For. Rel.*, p. 282.

[100] Dennett, *Roosevelt*, p. 131.

tary Hay.[101] In reply Secretary Hay instructed Mr. Conger that, "The only point with which we can be concerned is that the duties levied at these places do not exceed the regular tariff duties levied at all other points in the Chinese Empire open to foreign trade." Mr. Hay considers it "natural" since there are "a number of Russians in the imperial maritime customs service" that Russian commissioners should be in charge of these customs stations. He concludes:

You will watch the arrangements that may be reached between China and Russia on this subject, and should they in any way prove a menace to American interests and violate in any way the treaty provisions, you will take such action as the circumstances may require and your experience dictates.[102]

Russia continued to make inroads. In a letter to Minister Conger, Consul Miller, after describing the Russian railroad lines in Manchuria that were either completed or contemplated, reported that Russia had established an ostensible diplomatic representative at Mukden, equal in rank to a consul general, who would remain after the withdrawal of Russian troops. His real duties, however, were to advise the Tatar General at Mukden and give orders to Chinese officials. Writing further, Mr. Miller says that:

The only feasible method of meeting this situation is to demand of China that all Manchuria be thrown open to foreign trade. . . . If this is not done, and the policy endorsed by our own country, we will most certainly lose the trade we now have. I most earnestly recommend that this course be pressed upon the Chinese Government at this time. . . . We have little to fear from the world, in the free play of industrial forces in the markets of Manchuria, our sole danger lies in the political domination of Russia.[103]

As a brake on Russia's increasing aggression, Consul Miller felt it essential that the United States appoint a consul general "who could arrange to spend a considerable time each year at each of the capitals of the three provinces." In the same despatch he told of further Russian penetration into Manchuria:

All the land along the river [Sungari] and the railway, extending several miles back each way from the railway station, has been purchased by the Chinese East-

[101] Conger to Hay, Dec. 17, 1902. This arrangement, according to Mr. Conger, "will provide a principal Customs House at Dalny, where goods to be used in Dalny and the Russian-leased territory immediately surrounding will be free. Those to be consumed in Manchuria will pay the regular Chinese import duties; those going into Russia, the Russian tariff, all being collected at one office. Another station will be located where the railway crosses the border between Manchuria and Siberia, and others where necessary. It is proposed to establish post offices where they have not yet been established by the Maritime Customs, and I understand they are to await the Russian evacuation of the second portion of the territory which should take place April 8 next."

[102] Hay to Conger, Jan. 3, 1903.

[103] Miller to Conger, Newchwang, March 5, 1903. Within two weeks Mr. Miller reported that Russia had established certain courts in Manchuria along the Chinese Eastern Railway and higher courts at Harbin, Vladivostok, and Port Arthur. Miller to Conger, March 17, 1903.

ern Railway and held so as to preclude the leasing or ownership of land to anybody but Chinese and Russians. The high Chinese officials have assisted the Russians in this scheme. This holds true of many other places as well as Harbin.[104]

Not only Mr. Miller, but practically all the foreign representatives in Peking, insisted that only the complete opening of Manchuria could end the machinations of Russia. Nevertheless, the United States demanded the opening of only three ports—Tatung, Mukden, and Harbin,[105] a demand to which the Chinese, for reasons that were soon to appear, were unresponsive.[106]

On April 18, 1903, Minister Conger reported to the State Department that the second stage of the Russian evacuation, scheduled for April 8, 1903, had not taken place.[107] Within a week reporting again, he said that the Russian Government had made the withdrawal of their troops from Manchuria contingent upon certain concessions from China. These demands known as the "convention of seven points," were: no new treaty ports or foreign consuls to be permitted in Manchuria; with the exception of Russians, no foreigners to be employed in the public service of North China; the status of the administration of Mongolia to remain as before; Newchwang Customs receipts to be deposited as usual in the Russo-Chinese Bank; the sanitary commission at Newchwang to be under Russian control; the Port Arthur-Yingkow-Mukden telegraph line to remain under Russian domination; no territory in Manchuria to be transferred to any alien power.[108] In the opinion of Mr. Conger, the Chinese would not resist these demands unless they received tangible assistance from the other powers.[109] Upon the receipt of this news, the State Department instructed both Robert McCormick, who in 1902, had followed Tower as ambassador to Russia, and Mr. Conger to "insist on our request for treaty ports and consulates in Manchuria and make objection known to the second clause excluding all foreigners but Russians from Chinese service. Other points reserved.[110]

[104] Miller to Conger, March 21, 1903.

[105] Dennett, *Roosevelt*, p. 132.

[106] *For. Rel.*, 1903, p. 55.

[107] Conger to Hay, April 18, 1903. On March 26, 1903, Admiral Alexeiev succeeded in having a detachment moved to Kwantung on the Korean border. Bezobrazov meanwhile insisted upon a larger Far Eastern army; and, over the objections of Kuropatkin, formed *hunhutse*—militant groups wearing Chinese dress, with concealed arms—for the purpose of defending the region. Gurko, *op. cit.*, p. 275.

[108] Conger to Hay, April 23, 1903. *For. Rel.*, 1903, pp. 53-54; Morse and MacNair, *op. cit.*, pp. 510-11. In January 1903, the Russian envoys from the Far East—Rosen (Japan), Lessar (China) and Pavlov (Korea)—had been summoned to St. Petersburg for a joint meeting with the Council of Ministers to reconsider the course of Russian policy in the Far East. This conference, the members disagreeing on everything except procrastination in the evacuation of Russian troops, rejected Kuropatkin's demands to continue the occupation of North Manchuria indefinitely, but decided "not to promise" further evacuation without obtaining "guarantees." The Cabinet finally agreed to attempt to come to terms with Japan over Korea, although Lamsdorf insisted that Russia wait until Japan opened the conversations. Romanov, *op. cit.*, pp. 416 ff.

[109] Dennis, *op. cit.*, p. 356.

[110] *For. Rel.*, 1903, pp. 54 and 708-09.

Secretary Hay, somewhat perplexed at these developments, wrote to President Roosevelt:

It is a delicate and difficult subject to deal with, and I think these brief despatches, taken with what I have said to the Russian Embassy here, will answer for a little while. We admit nothing and give up nothing during the process of explanation which we are inviting from Russia. The Russian Secretary, speaking in behalf of Cassini, explained to me that the power aimed at was England and not ourselves, but the first two clauses of the convention are apparently injurious to us, and there is a certain lack of courtesy also in their opposing our demands for free ports and consulates in Manchuria without notice to us, although we had frankly announced to them our intentions more than a month ago.[111]

Meanwhile, Ambassador McCormick, having carried out Hay's instructions, notified the State Department that Lamsdorf categorically denied all knowledge of a convention between Russia and China, and especially disclaimed the first two clauses which were so objectionable to the United States. The foreign minister added that,

the United States Government could rest assured that nothing would ever be done to close the door now open in Manchuria and that American commerce and American capital were, of all countries the one Russia most desired to attract for the benefit of her Chinese Eastern Railway, which would be rendered more profitable by the opening of the tributary territory.

But there were certain details, Lamsdorf continued, not the concern of other powers, that were essential before the final evacuation could be completed.[112]

Despite the purity of Russia's motives and deeds, as enunciated by Lamsdorf, his protestations are not upheld by documentary evidence.[113] Nor was Secretary Hay deceived. A few days later he wrote President Roosevelt:

We have the positive and categorical assurance of the Russian Government that the so-called 'convention of seven points' has not been proposed by Russia to China. We have this assurance from Count Cassini here, from McCormick directly from Count Lamsdorf in St. Petersburg, and through Sir Michael Herbert from the Russian Ambassador in London. In addition to this information Russia informs us that they are not demanding from China the exclusion of our consulates in Manchuria, and are not opposing our proposition of treaty ports. Per contra, we have from Conger in Peking, from our Commissioners in Shanghai, from the Japanese Legation here and from the British Embassy, substantially identical copies of the 'convention of seven points,' which there is no shadow of doubt the Russians have been, and perhaps still are, forcing upon the Government of China. Dealing with a government with whom mendacity is a science is an extremely

---

111 Hay to Roosevelt, April 25, 1903. Hay Papers. Dennis, *op. cit.*, p. 356.

112 McCormick to Hay, April 29, 1903.

113 Romanov, *op. cit.*, pp. 420 ff.; Kantorovich, *op. cit.*, p. 150; Dennis, *op. cit.*, pp. 356–57. Conger, in Peking, received the text of the Russian conditions from the Japanese, who in turn had received them from Prince Ch'ing himself. Romanov, *op. cit.*, p. 422.

difficult and delicate matter. . . . We are not charged with the cure of the Russian soul and we may let them go to the devil at their own sweet will. If they have simply lied to gain time, a situation of a certain seriousness will soon be developed.[114]

However, after the protests, not only of the United States but of England and Japan,[115] Russia modified her demands upon China in regard to ports and consulate representatives and the depositing of customs receipts in the Russo-Chinese Bank, "but their essence remained." [116]

Faced by Russia's persistence in staking off Manchuria as her own special preserve, Hay gradually retreated to his attitude in the first Open Door notes, apparently resigning himself to the fact that Manchuria was no longer an integral part of the Chinese Empire, but virtually a Russian protectorate,[117] in which an Open Door for the United States was dependent upon the outcome of the diplomatic duel being waged between the two powers. On April 28, Hay wrote to Roosevelt:

I take it for granted that Russia knows as we do that we will not fight over Manchuria, for the simple reason that we cannot. . . . If our rights and interests in opposition to Russia in the Far East were as clear as noonday, we could never get a treaty through the Senate, the object of which was to check Russian aggression.[118]

In a second letter to the President on the same day, Hay commented:

The only hopeful symptom is that they [the Russians] are really afraid of Japan. They know perfectly well that there is nothing in the situation which we would consider as justifying us in a resort to arms, but they know that, it would require the very least encouragement on the part of the United States or England to induce Japan to seek a violent solution of the question.[119]

Meanwhile, the Russian Government was a house divided against itself. The Ministries of War and Finance, with their respective satellites, were powerful rivals. One, represented by the so-called palace clique and the military, were all for an aggressive policy and the building of strategic railroads; the other, with Witte as the dominant force, favored peaceful economic penetration of Manchuria. And the Tsar, while inclined toward the aggressive policy, occasionally acted as seemed best to His Imperial Majesty, without benefit of ministers.[120]

Confusion at home resulted in confusion abroad. Tsarist diplomacy was now marked by an uncertainty, a contradiction, an evasion, and an un-

---

[114] Hay to Roosevelt, May 12, 1903, Hay Papers. Dennis, *op. cit.*, p. 357.

[115] Romanov, *op. cit.*, pp. 421–22.

[116] Kantorovich, *op. cit.*, p. 150.

[117] "As early as March 1901, Rockhill had advised him [Hay] that the Manchurian provinces seemed 'irretrievably lost' to China." Rockhill to Hay, March 28, 1901. Vagts, *op. cit.*, II, 1112 n. Griswold, *op. cit.*, p. 84 n.

[118] Hay to Roosevelt, April 28, 1903. Dennett, *Hay*, p. 405.

[119] *Ibid.*

[120] Morse and MacNair, *op. cit.*, p. 511.

friendliness unique in the history of diplomatic relations. After Lamsdorf's vehement denial of April 29,[121] the Russian chargé at Peking forbade the Chinese minister to open new ports or appoint consuls without consulting Russia.[122] Cassini, who had advocated in 1901 full freedom of access, residence, and trade in Manchuria and North China for American citizens,[123] was in April 1903, of the opinion that Russia should reject the demand of the United States for the opening of new ports,[124] yet on June 8 of the same year he asserted that Russia should not object to the opening of the ports,[125] and explained this about face "by the accumulating conviction that the Americans will attribute great significance to this question . . . and the certainty that the rejection would undoubtedly drive the United States into the embraces of our rivals in the Far East." [126]

This sprightly game of hide-and-seek between the Foreign Offices of the United States and Russia went on apace, the United States in the role of seeker and Russia, like the traditional ostrich, endeavoring to conceal her head in the sands of a shifting and distorted diplomacy. Minister Conger reported the willingness of China to open the Manchurian ports were it not for Russia, who would consider such an act a serious affront and make it an excuse for not withdrawing her troops. China dared not, Conger said, open the ports at present but would do so of her own accord after Russian evacuation. The American minister, somewhat bewildered, continued:

The declaration of the Russian authorities to you that they have absolutely no objections to opening these Ports is certainly inexplicable, in face of the indisputable facts that their Chargé d'Affaires is, in the name of the Government, strenuously objecting, and moreover, is absolutely preventing the Chinese from opening the Ports at the suggestion of the United States.[127]

In view of these conflicting statements, Secretary Hay instructed Minister Conger to obtain a written statement from the Chinese Government, giving their reasons for refusing to comply with the American request; and a few days later he requested Conger to inform the Russian minister at Peking, that the Russian Government had stated they were not opposing American demands to open ports and consulates in Manchuria and to urge him to coöperate with the Chinese Government toward these ends.[128] The reply from Peking was so evasive [129] that Secretary Hay notified the Chinese Government that, in view of China's asserted right to open ports to foreign trade at pleasure, the American Government could not allow a

121 *Supra,* p. 88.
122 Morse and MacNair, *op. cit.,* p. 511.
123 Cassini to Lamsdorf, telegram, April 14, 1901. Kantorovich, *op. cit.,* p. 150.
124 Cassini to Lamsdorf, report, April 9, 1903. *Ibid.*
125 Cassini to Lamsdorf, June 8, 1903, *Ibid.,* p. 151.
126 Cassini to Lamsdorf, June 10, 1903, *Ibid.*
127 Conger to Hay, May 14, 1903.
128 Hay to Conger, telegram, May 18, 1903. *For. Rel.,* 1903, p. 60.
129 Conger to Hay, telegram, May 28, 1903. *Ibid.*

legitimate request, such as the one under consideration, lightly to be brushed aside [130] The next report was from Mr. Conger who, in compliance with Secretary Hay's instructions, had seen Russian Minister Lessar at Peking, and been assured by him that the Russian Government was not opposed to opening the ports. Conger then "asked him if, since he was certain there was no objection on the part of Russia, he would not so state to the Chinese Government." Mr. Lessar replied that he could give no definite statement to China "until he received instructions from St. Petersburg." [31]

Secretary Hay then instructed Ambassador McCormick at St. Petersburg to ask Lamsdorf, the Russian foreign minister, if Lessar at Peking had been directed to confirm Russian acquiescence to American demands to the Chinese Foreign Office and, if not, to insist upon prompt action.[132] Meanwhile, Lamsdorf, still stalling for time, had requested Ambassador Cassini to ask Secretary Hay, "Exactly in what sense do the Americans interpret the principle of the Open Door which they have proclaimed, and just what do they want?" [133] And at the same time he inquired of Minister Lessar in Peking who, under pressure from Minister Conger, was demanding instructions: "Is there no possibility of opening the eyes of the Chinese to the danger of granting foreigners access to Manchuria on a plane of equality with the Russians?" [134] Small wonder that Mr. Conger in a letter to Secretary Hay states that,

We must, however, acknowledge, privately, to ourselves, that China is absolutely helpless in the presence of Russian opposition, and unless she is assured of effective foreign support, which is very unlikely, she dare not and cannot take definite action in the face of Russian opposition and occupation.[135]

The Russian game of double-crossing and shifting gears at convenience, from Peking to St. Petersburg to Washington and back, continued unabated. In reply to Secretary Hay's query of June 13, Foreign Minister Lamsdorf requested Mr. Conger to lay before Lessar at Peking the demands of the United States in reference to the localities to be opened to trade, promising that Minister Lessar would be instructed to give a favorable reply to the American Minister and to the Chinese Government as to the attitude of the Russian Government.

Count Lamsdorf says that at this distance and without knowing which localities are meant, he cannot blindly commit himself, as he admits there are some ports whose opening Russia would not favor before the Russian evacuation of Manchuria. . . . He recommends a frank interchange of views between the two ministers at Peking.[136]

[130] Hay to Conger, telegram, May 29, 1903. *Ibid.*, p. 61.
[131] Conger to Hay, June 9, 1903.
[132] Hay to Riddle, June 13, 1903. *For. Rel.*, 1903, p. 710.
[133] Lamsdorf to Cassini, May 27, 1903. Kantorovich, *op. cit.*, p. 151.
[134] Lessar to Lamsdorf; Lamsdorf to Lessar, May 1903, *Ibid.*
[135] Conger to Hay, June 13, 1900.
[136] Riddle to Hay, telegram, June 15, 1903.

In a despatch of June 18, Conger stated that, in compliance with the request of Lamsdorf, he had informed Lessar in Peking that the United States requested China to open Ta-tung-kou, Mukden, and Harbin for trade in Manchuria. Mr. Conger continues:

The Russian Minister Lessar informed me that the matter had been taken entirely out of his hands, and he had been instructed to await the result of the discussion of the question at Washington,[137] therefore, he could not make any statement at all concerning the matter to the Chinese Government. . . . He, however, told me that he would at once telegraph what I had said to his Government and as soon as he received reply would inform me.[138]

This further tangling of the Russo-Chinese-American diplomatic skein resulted in a prolonged conversation between Secretary Hay and Ambassador Cassini, the salient points of which are taken from an extended memorandum made by Hay.

I called to Count Cassini's attention that I could not understand what Count Lamsdorf meant by saying he did not know what localities are meant, when the matter had been long since put clearly before his attention. . . . Several weeks ago Count Lamsdorf and Count Cassini had assured us that there was no intention on the part of Russia to stand in the way of our making an agreement with China in regard to ports in Manchuria; and that, on the contrary, they welcomed the advent and development of American trade in that country.

Later, continues Hay, "as the astonishing despatch of Mr. Riddle" showed,[139] Count Lamsdorf had apparently undergone a complete change of mind and

would object to the opening of any ports which we might designate until after the evacuation of Manchuria, the date of which was left vague. . . . I told Count Cassini that I could not exaggerate the gravity of the situation . . . which seemed to indicate a lack of good will on the part of the Government of Russia towards that of the United States. He protested vehemently against any such inference saying that the promise which Count Lamsdorf had given . . . was made in good faith and would be faithfully kept.

Mr. Hay went on to say that he had practically acted as guarantor for Russian assurances to the United States Government, but he now felt that nothing remained for him except "to lay the entire correspondence before the President, to confess my failure in coming to an amicable and honorable agreement with Russia." Count Cassini, when pressed, was unable to explain the disharmony between the former assurances of Count Lamsdorf and his present attitude.

[137] The veracity of this statement is denied by Hay, who wired that the "statement of Russian Minister to China relating to discussion of the question of Washington is not true. Russian Ambassador here is without instructions." Hay to Riddle, telegram, June 24, 1903. *For. Rel.*, 1903, p. 711.
[138] Conger to Hay, June 18, 1903.
[139] Despatch of June 15, in reply to Hay's instructions of June 13. *Supra,* p. 91.

I then said, we seem to be at a deadlock; that his Excellency had no authority; that Mr. Lessar, in spite of what Count Lamsdorf said to Mr. Riddle, disclaimed any authority to discuss the matter at Peking; that Count Lamsdorf said he was too far distant from China to discuss it at Petersburg. . . . I told him that the attitude of his Government was inconceivable to me from every point of view.

Shortly after this statement to Hay, Count Cassini left, reiterating his assurances of Russian good faith.[140]

A few days after this conversation Secretary Hay, according to Kantorovich, threatened joint action with England and Japan; [141] and, as a result, Cassini warned Lamsdorf of the possibility of "most serious decisions on the part of the United States in the sense of a direct entente with England and Japan." [142] And several days later Cassini despatched a second telegram, reiterating the seriousness of the situation and warning the Russian Foreign Office that a rejection of American trade demands in Manchuria would call forth renewed declarations, and "will raise against us not only the Government but public opinion in the United States." [143]

Finally, apprehending a united front of powers against Russia, the Tsarist Government decided to meet the American demands. A meeting was called at Port Arthur, in which Kuropatkin, Alexeiev, and Lessar participated. After a lengthy discussion it was decided that, "It is necessary to inform all powers that Russia will not prevent China . . . from opening some cities in Manchuria to foreign trade." [144] The Foreign Office at St. Petersburg accepted this decision and sent a corresponding circular despatch to all Russian Ambassadors.[145]

Hence, Cassini, acting on instructions from St. Petersburg, on July 14 handed to Secretary Hay a vague pro-memoria [146] which stated that the

[140] Secretary Hay, memorandum, June 18, 1903. Dennis, *op. cit.*, pp. 377–80.

[141] *Op. cit.*, p. 151.

[142] Cassini to Lamsdorf, June 18, also June 20, 1903. Kantorovich, *op. cit.*, p. 151, n. 42. During this period Alexeiev telegraphed St. Petersburg that "the execution of the American demands for the opening of ports and consulates . . . is for us unquestionably harmful," and that "it is necessary to explain to the American Government that at the present time the economic interests of the United States in Manchuria have not developed to such a point that they can insist on the immediate establishment there of consuls and open ports." Secret telegram of Alexeiev from Port Arthur, June 23, 1903. Kantorovich, *op. cit.*, p. 151, n. 43. This telegram, relayed to Washington, was answered by Cassini as follows: "Washington Cabinet does not acknowledge the argument of Alexeiev and does not consent to an agreement on this basis." Cassini to Lamsdorf, June 25, 1903. *Ibid.*

[143] *Ibid.* While these Russian exchanges were going on, the State Department at Washington and the American Legation at Peking discussed anew the possibility of China's taking the initiative in opening the ports. Conger, again emphasizing the fact that the Chinese were helpless, advised Hay on July 1 to delay no longer in taking action to conclude a treaty with the Chinese Government. Hay to Conger, June 24 and June 27, 1903; Conger to Hay, July 1, 1903.

[144] Secret telegrams of Kuropatkin, No. 45, from Port Arthur to Lamsdorf, July 6 and July 9, 1903. Kantorovich, *op. cit.*, p. 151.

[145] *Ibid.*

[146] A pro-memoria is a "detailed statement of facts and of arguments . . . not differ-

Government of Russia had never opposed "the opening to foreign commerce . . . of certain cities in Manchuria." Harbin, which was not entirely under Chinese control, and was "situated in the zone . . . of the Chinese Eastern Railway system," was excepted. Foreign consuls were not to be admitted to this city without Russian consent.[147] By this time Roosevelt's patience was at an end and he thus expressed himself to Secretary Hay:

> I have not the slightest objection to the Russians knowing that I feel thoroughly aroused and irritated at their conduct in Manchuria; that I don't intend to give way and that I am year by year growing more confident that this country would back me in going to an extreme in this matter.[148]

Upon the receipt of Russia's pro-memoria, Secretary Hay instructed Minister Conger to present a copy of it to Prince Ch'ing, president of the Foreign Office, Peking, at the same time insisting upon the opening to trade by treaty of Ta-tung-kou and Mukden, leaving Harbin for future action.[149] Conger, complying with these instructions, was informed by Prince Ch'ing that Russia had not notified the Chinese Government of the withdrawal of its opposition to the opening of new ports; and that he could only repeat that, as long as Russia was in possession of Manchuria it was absolutely impossible for China to take action.[150] Minister Conger, like President Roosevelt, was now completely disgusted. In a personal letter to Hay he wrote of the futility of American efforts to check Russian aggression in Manchuria:

> The Manchurian question here is most annoying. I have come to the conclusion that the statements of neither the Russians nor Chinese in regard to it can be believed. . . . I think it is quite plain to all out here that Russia does not intend to give back Manchuria. The recent conference at Port Arthur, I believe, was to consult as to the best methods of strengthening the weak places in its policy, as well as in its material defense. . . . Since the adjournment of the conference, all the Russians speak of Manchuria in the sense of absolute ownership and the minor officials continually talk of their perfect preparedness for war.

Mr. Conger felt that the protests of England, Japan, and the United States directed to China against the inroads of Russia in Manchuria had been ineffectual:

> She [Russia] has moved steadily and successfully onward, gaining and holding her every point, and except as to the important declaration as to the open door secured by you from Russia, we have scored nothing. China is not grateful to us,

---

ing essentially from a Note, except that it does not begin and end with a formula of courtesy, and need not be signed, or dated." Sir Ernest Satow, *A Guide to Diplomatic Practice*, I, 77.

[147] Imperial Russian Embassy, Washington, to the Secretary of State, July 14, 1903. *For. Rel.*, 1903, p. 711.

[148] Roosevelt Papers, July 18, 1903. Dennis, *op. cit.*, p. 359.

[149] Hay to Conger, July 14, 1903. *For. Rel.*, 1903, p. 67.

[150] Conger to Hay, July 23, 1903. *Ibid.*, p. 68.

and Russia is annoyed and sore, and will grudgingly yield even our rights in the future.[151]

Secretary Hay, however, finally achieved a degree of success. He insisted upon, and Prince Ch'ing reluctantly consented to give, a written statement "agreeing to sign on October 8, the day on which Russia has agreed to finally evacuate Manchuria, a treaty providing for the opening of Mukden and Ta-tung-kou." [152]

Meanwhile, the Japanese Government on July 28, 1903, proposed to Russia a general consideration of their mutual relations in the Far East. Russia accepted, and on August 12 received a draft of the Japanese demands, in which not only the interests of Japan but those of the other powers were upheld.[153] Article I states that both powers agree to "respect the independence and territorial integrity of the Chinese and Korean Empires," as well as the principle of the Open Door. This is followed by the crux of the draft agreement which provides for

Reciprocal recognition of Japan's preponderating interests in Korea and Russia's special interest in railway enterprises in Manchuria, and of the right of Japan to take in Korea and of Russia to take in Manchuria such measures as may be necessary for the protection of their respective interests . . . subject to the provisions of Article I.

The Japanese draft collided sharply with the feudal-imperialist plans of the Bezobrazov clique, whose power to shape Russia's Far Eastern policy was rapidly increasing.[154] In addition, on the same day that the Japanese note was presented to St. Petersburg, Admiral Alexeiev was appointed Viceroy of the Far East, by an Imperial decree which came "as a thunderbolt to disturb the East." [155] By this appointment Alexeiev was released from the jurisdiction of the Tsar's ministers. Henceforward he received his orders directly from the Tsar.[156] The organization of this Viceroyalty, comprising the Kwantung and Amur provinces (with Manchuria between) was interpreted by Japanese statesmen as signifying that Russia planned to incorporate Manchuria into the Russian Empire.[157] Japan was additionally aggrieved over the fact that the creation of this new department in the Far East meant the passing of the control of Far Eastern affairs from the Russian Foreign Office into the hands of Viceroy Alexeiev and his friends Bezobrazov and Abasa.[158]

---

151 Conger to Hay, July 24, 1903. Dennis, *op. cit.*, p. 381.

152 Hay to Conger, July 26, 1903; Conger to Hay, Aug. 14, 1903. *For. Rel.*, 1903, pp. 70–73. Antung, with Chinese consent, was later substituted for Ta-tung-kou because of the latter's poor accessibility. *Ibid.*, 74–77. China extended a similar promise to Japan. Dennett, *Roosevelt*, p. 134.

153 Romanov, *op. cit.*, pp. 426 ff.; Treat, *Far East*, pp. 369 ff.

154 Romanov, *op. cit.*, pp. 426–27.

155 H. P. Griscom to Hay, Dec. 8, 1903. Dennis, *op. cit.*, p. 383.

156 Dennett, *Roosevelt*, p. 141.

157 Gurko, *op. cit.*, p. 281.

158 *Ibid.*, p. 282.

On October 3, after a delay of nearly two months, Russia presented her reply to Tokyo. Omitting reference to China and Manchuria, she confined her discussion to Korea, where she demanded the creation of a neutral zone, north of the 39th parallel, within the limits of which neither power could station troops.[159] A few days later, on October 8, when the final evacuation of Manchuria was scheduled to take place, the Russian troops still remained.[160]

The signing of the Chinese-American Treaty of October 8 [161] was preceded by several weeks of the usual diplomatic wrangling. On September 1, Minister Conger had reported to Secretary Hay that, "Every report of Russian action in Manchuria indicates a determined permanency of occupation or at least of control." Mr. Conger had little hope for improvement even though the Russian evacuation should take place:

With Admiral Alexeiev as viceroy with almost supreme power, acting through high officers with large military forces in the vicinity of all important provincial officials, the latter will be over-awed and the will of Russia carried out almost as absolutely as when in military control.[162]

Mr. Conger also points out that since Russia has made an enormous concession "in consenting to the opening of two ports and the appointment of foreign consuls," she, in turn, will expect important concessions from China. In regard to the prospective American-Chinese treaty, Mr. Conger assures Secretary Hay that, "unless otherwise instructed I shall demand the signing of the treaty on the day named, and will consent to no delay." [163]

Two days later Secretary Hay reported to the President:

I have wired Conger that there must be no doubt nor delay about the signature of our treaty on the 8th of October. He has the pessimism about Russia which is almost universal out there. "What's the use? Russia is too big, too crafty, too cruel for us to fight. She will conquer in the end. Why not give up now and be friendly?"

I have had long conversations with Liang [Chinese minister to Washington]

---

[159] Romanov, *op. cit.*, p. 447; Treat, *Far East*, p. 371. Witte had counseled acceptance of the Japanese terms, a position in which he was supported by Baron Rosen, Russian minister to Tokyo, but their suggestions were unheeded. *Ibid.*, pp. 444–46; Gurko, *op. cit.*, p. 284. Witte was now convinced that nothing remained except war between the two powers. Treat, *Far East*, p. 379. Before Witte was the choice of going along with Bezobrazov, or refusing to make the Russian treasury responsible for the colonial schemes of this adventurer. Nicholas, however, solved the problem. His Imperial Majesty, assisted by Bezobrazov, discovered that the power of autocracy was being challenged by his minister of finance, and on September 1, 1903, Witte handed in his resignation. *Krasny Arkhiv*, II, 60, 65. Romanov, *op. cit.*, pp. 444–46. Witte became president of the Council of Ministers. Treat, *Far East*, p. 370.

[160] Treat, *Far East*, p. 371.

[161] *Infra*, p. 97, n. 169.

[162] Conger to Hay, Sept. 1, 1903. The American minister scented trouble in the activities of the Russian concession hunters in north Korea, and felt that it was here, "if anywhere, that the real *casus belli* may be looked for." *Ibid.*

[163] *Ibid.*

and Takahira [Japanese ambassador]. Liang is sure his Government will keep faith and sign the treaty as agreed, but he fears Russia will somehow punish them for it.

Ambassador Takahira, fearing the worst from Russia, stated quietly that Japan would have "something to say" if Russia continued her aggression in Korea. At this point, Secretary Hay, wishing the Japanese to be under no illusions, said plainly that the United States would not participate "in any use of force in that region unless our interests were directly involved." [164]

Early in September, as the price for evacuation, Russia made new demands upon China, several of which touched American interests in Manchuria.[165] On September 23 Conger reported that China had refused to accept these demands and, as a result, Prince Ch'ing "was certain that Russia would not withdraw on October 8." In view of the danger of forcible Russian annexation of Manchuria, Ch'ing asked if the United States would be willing to extend its good offices to St. Petersburg in effecting a settlement of the Manchurian question with a view to Russian evacuation.[166] Acting Secretary of State Adee immediately replied:

The date for signing the completed treaty, October 8, is absolute and not contingent on action of Russia. This date has been formally accepted by the Chinese Government and this Government notified. . . . When treaty is signed this Government will be in a much better and stronger position to discuss questions which may affect its treaty rights and interests in China. You will decline to receive request of Prince Ch'ing for transmission here till after signing of Treaty.[167]

However, acting upon the advice of Messrs. Adee and Rockhill not to protest the September demands until the prospective treaty with China was signed, Secretary Hay took no diplomatic action against Russia.[168] And on October 8, 1903, the day upon which Russia had agreed to evacuate Manchuria, the treaty between the United States and China, which provided for the opening of Mukden and Antung to foreign trade and for the appointment of consuls to Manchuria, was signed.[169]

[164] Hay to Roosevelt. Dennet, *Hay*, p. 406.

[165] Dennis, *op. cit.*, p. 360.

[166] Conger to Hay, telegram, Sept. 23, 1903.

[167] Adee to Conger, telegram, Sept. 23, 1903. The reasons given later by the United States government to China for not intervening were a lack of sufficient data on the subject in question, and the fact that Russia had not intimated a willingness to accept American good offices. Dennis, *op. cit.*, p. 360.

[168] This was a disappointment to Japan. Even toward the end of the year when Russia was turning a deaf ear to Japanese proposals, the United States was very circumspect, refusing to be involved. *Ibid.*, pp. 360–61.

[169] The treaty was ratified by the Senate on December 18, 1903, and by China on January 10, 1904. Ratifications were exchanged January 13, 1904. *For. Rel.*, 1903, pp. 91–118. When asked in a newspaper interview, "What would the United States do in case Russia should exert pressure upon China for the purpose of preventing the ratification of the treaty?" Hay, according to Cassini, replied: "The Federal Government will be able with all the means at its disposal to compel China to make good its promises." Secret telegram of Cassini, Dec. 19, 1903, *Arkhiv M.I.D.*, Chinese Table No. 46. Kantorovich,

After the signing of the American-Chinese Treaty, the pace of events in the Far East quickened—toward catastrophe. In reply to a Russian note which was presented to Tokyo on October 23, 1903, Japan replied a week later with a number of amendments to her earlier proposals, among them specifications for a neutral zone of fifty versts on both sides of the Manchurian-Korean border. As usual, Russian councils were divided. Lamsdorf, Kuropatkin, and Rosen, willing to forfeit Korea to Japan, favored acceptance; while the group headed by Bezobrazov was determined not to abandon the Yalu concession included in the Japanese demands.[170] At a council meeting on December 15, 1903, under the chairmanship of the Tsar, Tokyo's proposals were rejected, yet it was decided to continue negotiations with the Japanese.[171]

This confusion in Russia's foreign policy was reflected in an announcement from Port Arthur that the ratification by the United States of the American-Chinese Treaty was "unfriendly and undiplomatic," and also by the alleged claim of Russia that she no longer regarded Manchuria as a part of China.[172] That Russia regarded the treaty between the United States and China as a menace to her interests may be seen in an extract from Ambassador McCormick's despatch of January 9, 1904, in which he states that the Russians feel

that in insisting upon the open door and the establishment of consulates at Mukden and Antung before a settlement of the Russian-Japanese controversy the United States is seeking to place itself in a position from which it can give aid to Japan; that under cover of a "commercial treaty"—a trojan horse in their eyes— the United States is seeking a foothold from which it can demand a voice in the political—now become, whatever it may have been before—radical question . . . of vital importance to Russia.[173]

op. cit., p. 152. By additional provisions of the treaty, American citizens could engage in trade and manufacture, and carry on any lawful industry or avocation in any of the free ports. Certain American privileges, hitherto subject to the most-favored-nation clause, were stabilized. The social status of American envoys and consuls in China was widened. American missionary societies were permitted to hold property in any part of the empire. Both the importation and manufacture of morphine, except for medical purposes, were prohibited. Provision was made for a much-needed reform in Chinese currency, which called for uniform national coinage. Morse and MacNair, *op. cit.*, p. 496. A similar treaty was signed on the same day (October 8, 1903) with Japan, a treaty with England having been concluded in 1902. *Ibid.*, p. 495. Kantorovich, *op. cit.*, p. 152.

170 Romanov, *op. cit.*, pp. 460 ff.; Gurko, *op. cit.*, pp. 281, 284; Treat, *Far East*, p. 371.

171 At this meeting the Tsar said: "A war must not be permitted. . . . Time is Russia's most trusted ally; each year sees her strength grow." Gurko, *op. cit.*, p. 285. In the previous September the Tsar had wired Alexeiev, "Take all steps to prevent war." *Ibid.*, p. 283. On January 15, 1904, Ambassador McCormick reported that in an interview with the Tsar the latter had said: "Russia does not wish war, and it is my wish and purpose to maintain peace." McCormick to Hay, Jan. 15, 1904. But Nicholas, under the influence of the palace group, was unwilling to make the necessary compromises.

172 Dennis, *op. cit.*, p. 362. During this time Bezobrazov declared that Russia planned to remain in Manchuria and "had no idea of permitting other nations to have equal commercial privileges with Russia there." Choate to Hay, telegram, Jan. 1, 1904. *Ibid.*, pp. 361–62.

173 McCormick to Hay, Jan. 9, 1904.

That Russia was not alone in interpreting American maneuvers in the Far East as having political ends in view is seen by the following excerpts from a current article in a British periodical, written by A. Maurice Low, a well-known American journalist:

It has been somewhat a mystery to Americans who are interested in foreign politics why Russia . . . should have displayed such irritation because the United States concluded a commercial treaty with China, by which ports of Manchuria are to be opened to the commerce of the world; and why the Russian press, which is never permitted to discuss international affairs unless it shall suit the authorities to have these affairs discussed, has been so bitterly offensive in its comments on American diplomacy. . . . That treaty is as much political, if not more so, as it is commercial, but American prejudices must be respected; and while the Americans are willing to have their State Department make treaties which shall redound to the glory of American commerce, they become suspicious at the thought of a treaty which ultimately shall be for political advantages. . . . By this treaty the United States obtains precisely the same rights and privileges in Manchuria that Russia nominally does. . . . Heretofore the United States has had no established standing in Manchuria. Now, under this new treaty, her status is precisely defined. . . . She is there in fulfillment of a contract duly made and entered into, and by virtue of that contractual relation she has political rights which Russia cannot infringe or violate.

At this point Mr. Low eulogizes Secretary Hay for having "put a spoke in Russia's diplomacy:"

Without the expenditure of one dollar, without moving a single ship or a single soldier, without an alliance, without buying in one place by surrendering in another, simply by straightforward honest diplomacy, he has placed such insurmountable obstacles in the path of Russia that it will be impossible for Russia to make Manchuria Russian without fighting the United States, or without paying the United States the price she may demand.

After stating that by virtue of this treaty the United States has acquired "certain well-defined political rights in Manchuria of which it cannot be divested," the writer continues:

R·-ssia was farseeing enough to catch the drift of Mr. Hay's diplomacy. . . . That is why Russia for months prevented China from signing the commercial treaty. . . . No wonder Russia is disturbed, and that responsible statesmen in St. Petersburg . . . should regard the continued interest displayed in the United States in the integrity and independence of China as one of the most disquieting features of the Far Eastern situation; and that the "Novoe Vremya" should reflect this anxiety by terming the entrance of the United States in the arena of the politics of the Old World as "one of the most important political phenomena of the twentieth century." . . . It is not inevitable that Russia and America should clash over Manchuria, but it is not improbable. Whatever the future may bring one thing is absolutely certain: Russia can no more carry on things with a high hand in Manchuria without considering the United States than she can attempt the Russianisation of Corea without running foul of Japan. Russian diplomacy has placed a red-hot poker on top of a barrel of gunpowder.[174]

And while the diplomatic atmosphere was thus electrically charged, Russia, convinced of her superiority to Japan, especially in naval forces, played with the negotiations, granted only minor concessions, and maintained her troops in Manchuria until Japanese patience came to an end.[175] Convinced that war was the only solution, Japan struck the first blow.[176] Severing diplomatic relations with Russia on February 6, 1904, Japan attacked the Russian fleet off Port Arthur on February 8, and four days later made a formal declaration of war. The long and devious trail that had begun with the Boxer Rebellion had reached the milestone of the Russo-Japanese War.[177]

[174] From "American Affairs," by A. Maurice Low, in the *National Review* (Supplement) of Dec. 1903, London. Enclosed with despatch of McCormick to Hay, Jan. 9, 1904. In a later despatch McCormick wrote: "To the Russian mind it does not seem credible that the statement made in 'American Affairs' in the *National Review* could be made without some official instruction as a foundation." Jan. 20, 1904. *Who's who in America* (1903–1904) states that Mr. Low had been in charge of the Washington bureau of The Boston *Globe* since 1886; chief American correspondent for the London *Chronicle* for several years; and had written an article on American affairs every month since 1896 for the *National Review* of London. Kantorovich (*op. cit.*, pp. 152 ff.) is of the opinion that American interests and ambitions in Manchuria during the period under discussion cannot be limited to those of trade. Hay's note of protest to Russia of February 1, 1903, shows that the term "trade" has to be given a liberal interpretation, "with the inclusion of railroads and industrial concessions. That is as an open door for the import into Manchuria of American capital." In addition, according to Kantorovich, "The commercial interests of the United States could not in practice be separated from political interests, for on the one hand they could be guaranteed by definite political conditions (the prevention of annexations), and on the other, their very guaranteeing becomes a political factor."

[175] It was well known to Russians in the Far East that Japan was planning for a war. Alexeiev was aware of this fact as early as the middle of 1903. Colonel Samoilov, military agent in the Far East, was of the opinion that Japan might declare war at any time. And Captain Russin, naval agent in Japan, on the basis of information which he obtained, reported that Japan would make a surprise attack upon the Russian fleet in late January 1904. Gurko, *op. cit.*, p. 283.

[176] Vagts (*op. cit.*, II, 1177) states that Japan considered the Anglo-Saxon countries so friendly that she could safely take the initiative in war without bringing upon herself the stigma of war guilt.

[177] Baron Rosen, the Russian envoy to Tokyo, after receiving his passport, expressed no resentment toward the United States for her obvious Japanese slant, but the baroness, less diplomatic, exclaimed angrily to the American minister, "How did you dare to pretend to be our friends while you were knifing us all the time in the back?" Lloyd Griscom, *Diplomatically Speaking*, p. 242. On February 7, Japan requested the United States to protect her subjects and interests in enemy territory. Corresponding instructions were issued by State Department on February 9. Payson Treat, *Diplomatic Relations between the United States and Japan*, III, 198.

Chapter V

ROOSEVELT'S POLICY OF BALANCED ANTAGONISMS

THE outbreak of hostilities between Russia and Japan came as a surprise to Europe, which had been assured by the foreign offices of St. Petersburg, Berlin, and Paris that no danger of immediate war existed.[1] The Tsar had also written to the Kaiser early in December 1903, guaranteeing that there would be no war because he, the Tsar, did not wish it.[2] At the same time, the German Foreign Office gave assurance to the American ambassador, up to the actual break in Russo-Japanese negotiations, that war could be avoided.[3]

Yet the United States had played an important part in the precipitation of hostilities. The vigorous policy this country had pursued in protection of her trade interests and ambitions in Manchuria revealed her attitude toward Russia, her determination to have a place of her own in the Manchurian sun.[4] More direct, however, in its bearing upon the initiative taken by the Japanese at Port Arthur was the assurance given by the American Government to the Japanese Government on January 12, 1904, nearly a month before the outbreak of hostilities, that in case of war "the American policy would be benevolent toward Japan." [5] This assurance,

[1] Baron Eckardstein, *Die Isolierung Deutschlands*, pp. 56–69, 187–93. Dennett, *Roosevelt*, pp. 26–27 n.

[2] Witte, *Memoirs*, p. 125.

[3] Vagts, *op. cit.*, II, 1174. Cf. Tower to Hay, telegrams of Dec. 31, 1903; Jan. 10, 1904; Jan. 25, 1904. *Die Grosse Politik*, XIX, 86. Vagts, *op. cit.*, II, 1174 n. 5.

[4] Vagts (*op. cit.*, II, 1175) states that the United States, although perhaps unwittingly, by her position in the Manchurian question had more to do with bringing on the war than all the calculations of the German Foreign Minister Baron von Holstein. He compares the effect of this vitalization of American policy to a high power current on a formerly low current conductor, and quotes the observation of Baron Eckardstein that it was this invigorated American policy which led the English cabinet "not only to let the Japanese have a free hand but even to goad them directly to war." *Die Grosse Politik*, XIX, 5945.

[5] "The Japanese Minister told me this morning, that after the official declarations of Germany and the United States that they would observe strict neutrality and the latter even a very benevolent neutrality, the Japanese Government were pushing their war preparations as quickly as possible and that within two weeks very likely over 100 thousand troops would have been landed in Korea." Eckardstein to Baron Alfred Rothschild, Jan. 12, 1904. *Isolierung, op. cit.*, p. 189. Dennett, *Roosevelt*, p. 27 n.

combined with the German affirmation of neutrality [6] and the alliance between England and Japan, was the impetus that led the Japanese Government to take the reins into their own hands and declare war against Russia.[7]

On February 11, the United States proclaimed neutrality.[8] On the 12th China declared herself neutral.[9] Meanwhile, acting upon the suggestion of the German Government, Secretary of State Hay had issued circulars to Great Britain, France, and Germany, calling upon them to urge the belligerents "to respect the neutrality of China and in all practicable ways her administrative entity." [10] Although the initiative for the plea to the powers came from Germany, the Americanized version differed in one very vital point from the German model, which requested Russia and Japan "to respect the neutrality of China outside the sphere of military action." In other words, since the theater of the war was in Manchuria, that section was to be left free for Russian operations after the war.[11]

> Yes [wrote President Roosevelt] it was on the suggestion of "Bill the Kaiser" that we sent out the note on the neutrality of China. But the insertion of the word "entity" was ours. His suggestion originally was in untenable form; that is, he wanted us to guarantee the integrity of China south of the latitude of the Great Wall, which would have left Russia free to gobble up what she really wanted. . . .[12]

Russia, after consultation with Germany, refused to recognize the neutralization of Manchuria, and, turning to America, inquired, through

---

[6] Vagts (op. cit., II, 1176) states that the recently repeated assurances of German neutrality weighed so heavily in the long conferences of the Genro on February 3 and 4 that they decided to break off negotiations with Russia.

[7] No attack would have been made by the Japanese upon Port Arthur on February 8, 1904, had it not been for the "benevolent neutrality" of the United States and the Anglo-Japanese Alliance. Henry F. Pringle, Theodore Roosevelt, p. 376. "To what extent the certainty of the material and moral support of America was of decisive influence in the counsels of the Japanese Government, I personally was witness when it clearly manifested itself at the time of the conversations which I had to conduct with the Japanese Government just preceding the Russo-Japanese war." Report of Baron Rosen from Washington, Feb. 25, 1910. Arkhiv M.I.D., Kantorovich, op. cit., p. 164.

[8] For. Rel., 1904, p. 2.

[9] Ibid., pp. 121, 421.

[10] Ibid., p. 301.

[11] Dennett, Roosevelt, p. 69; Pringle, op. cit., p. 378. The Kaiser's motives were to divert Russia's attention from Germany's eastern frontier to the Far East, and eventually to consummate a treaty with Russia which would render ineffective the Franco-Russian alliance. Krasny Arkhiv, V, 9, 18–19. A less obvious motive on the part of the Kaiser was to assist Russia in acquiring control of Manchuria and to share in the partition of North China and also to receive concessions in the Near East or in Africa. Dennett, Roosevelt, pp. 68–69; Griswold, op. cit., pp. 94–95. Vagts (op. cit., II, 1181) writes: "Germany wished the war exclusively between Russia and Japan as a prospective war profiteer, with the avoidance of the suspicion that she prompted the war. . . ."

[12] Roosevelt to Root, Feb. 16, 1904. Dennis, op. cit., p. 363. Although Roosevelt takes full share of credit for detecting the Kaiser's sinister motives, the original detection was apparently made by Hay. Pringle, op. cit., p. 378; Dennett, Roosevelt, p. 69.

Cassini, why the United States in her eagerness to deprive Russia of Manchuria had made no mention of the Japanese in Korea. American intentions, according to Cassini, were not clear.[13]

Yet American intentions, in the light of documentary information, are clear. The United States, holding (together with England and Japan) a monopoly of foreign trade in Manchuria,[14] knocking persistently upon doors that might close, demanding the integrity of China, had a vital interest in Manchuria and the outcome of the war. Kantorovich states that the Russo-Japanese War was not only an English but also an American war against Tsarist Russia and its policies of territorial conquests.[15] Dennett agrees when he writes that no one can go through the records of 1898–1904 and not feel that Japan was fighting the battle of the United States in Manchuria.[16] From surface appearances it was apparently to American interests that Japan, at that time considered weaker than Russia, should disturb the Russian over-balance in Manchuria. The United States considered that Japan, even if victor, would be more pliable than Russia backed by France.[17] Hence, the bias of the American Government and also of its reflection, the American public, was unquestionably pro-Japanese at the beginning of the Russo-Japanese War.[18]

President Roosevelt,[19] influenced no doubt by the usual mixed motives of the human being, immediately threw his vigorous weight on the side of Japan. His sympathies were with this small, apparently under-dog of an island kingdom.[20] But the commercial, industrial, and possibly political

13 Dennett, *Roosevelt,* pp. 69–70. The Russian reply was received on February 19; Germany, meantime, had been the first of the powers to accept the American proposal. *For. Rel.,* 1904, p. 724. However, Chancellor von Bülow assured Russia that, regardless of the American note, Germany still considered Manchuria outside of the sphere of China's "administrative entity." Tower to Richthofen, Feb. 16, 1904. *Die Grosse Politik,* XIX, i, 102–09. Griswold, *op. cit.,* pp. 96–97.

14 "The United States, England and Japan have at present, almost a monopoly of the foreign trade in Manchuria." Conger to Hay, Nov. 9, 1901. "The United States has the most powerful interests in Manchuria. . . . Until now America has exclusively supplied her nearly everything necessary." Memorandum of Lamsdorf, approved by Nicholas, June 15, 1903. Kantorovich, *op. cit.,* p. 147.

15 *Ibid.,* p. 158.

16 *Roosevelt,* p. 332.

17 Vagts, *op. cit.,* II, 1200; Pringle, *op. cit.,* p. 379.

18 According to the German ambassador to the United States, von Sternburg, only three leading American statesmen were in sympathy with Russia. These were Hitchcock, former ambassador to St. Petersburg, and Senators Hale, and Chauncey Depew, all of whom held that a Japanese victory would be more dangerous than a Russian. Vagts, *op. cit.,* II, 1184. The American minister to Japan of that period writes that the Americans in Japan were "rampantly pro-Japanese," that the Japanese responded to their presence by cheers and playing the "Star-Spangled Banner." Griscom, *op. cit.,* p. 243.

19 Throughout the Russo-Japanese War Roosevelt, who might be termed the symbol of the Government of the United States, was not only practically his own secretary of state, but exerted an almost unprecedented and arbitrary control over foreign policy. Griswold, *op. cit.,* pp. 92–93; Dennett, *Roosevelt,* p. 338.

20 Dennett, *Roosevelt,* p. 27; Allan Nevins, *Henry White,* p. 183. As late as 1906 Roosevelt wrote to a friend: "I have from the beginning favored Japan and have done all that

interests of the United States in Manchuria were also at stake.[21] Her fate in the Far East might be sealed by the outcome of the war.

In a confidential letter to one of his sons, written two days after the Japanese attack upon the Russian fleet off Port Arthur, President Roosevelt wrote in part as follows:

It has certainly opened most disastrously for the Russians and their supine carelessness is well-nigh incredible. For several years Russia has behaved very badly in the Far East, her attitude toward all nations, including us, but especially toward Japan, being grossly overbearing. We had no sufficient cause for war with her. Yet I was apprehensive lest if she at the outset whipped Japan on the sea she might assume a position well-nigh intolerable toward us. I thought Japan would probably whip her on the sea, but I could not be certain; and between ourselves— for you must not breathe it to anybody—I was thoroughly well pleased with the Japanese victory, for Japan is playing our game.[22]

Roosevelt's own assertion that he warned France and Germany at the outbreak of hostilities against intervention exists in the form of a letter to his friend Cecil Spring-Rice, British ambassador at St. Petersburg:

As soon as this war broke out, I notified Germany and France in the most polite and discreet fashion that in the event of a combination against Japan to try to do what Russia, Germany, and France did to her in 1894 [sic] I would promptly side with Japan and proceed to whatever length was necessary on her behalf. I of course knew that your government would act in the same way, and I thought it best that I should have no consultation with your people before announcing my own purpose.[23]

Although certain historians claim that, aside from Roosevelt's letter to Spring-Rice, no records exist of any warning to France and Germany,[24] yet President Roosevelt undoubtedly anticipated, and endeavored to thwart, European intervention. In a letter to Spring-Rice at the end of the year, Roosevelt commented: "If it were not for the attitude of England

---

I could do, consistent with international law, to advance her interests. I thoroughly admire and believe in the Japanese. They have always told the truth and the Russians have not." Roosevelt to Kennan, May 6, 1906. Dennett, *Roosevelt*, p. 160.

[21] Roosevelt's friend, von Sternburg, observed in early February that a visit from delegates of the Rockefeller firm, whose East Asiatic market was threatened by Russia had put Roosevelt "in a still more war-like mood than before." Vagts, *op. cit.*, II, 1178.

[22] Roosevelt to Theodore Roosevelt, Jr., Feb. 10, 1904. Pringle, *op. cit.*, p. 375. This letter seems to carry out Kantorovich's contention (*supra*, p. 103 and n. 14) that the Russo-Japanese war was also an American war. Griscom, *op. cit.*, pp. 244–45, writes that Roosevelt throughout the war sent letters to the Embassy at Tokyo by ordinary mail, in a White House envelope (often with only a two-cent stamp instead of the required five-cent stamp), in which he vigorously expressed "his detestation of the Russians."

[23] Roosevelt to Spring-Rice, July 24, 1905. Dennett, *Roosevelt*, p. 2.

[24] According to Vagts (*op. cit.*, II, 1178–79) no trace of this warning can be found in the archives of the Department of State, of the German Foreign Office, or among the personal papers of either Roosevelt or John Hay. "That Roosevelt really did do precisely this [warn France and Germany] is doubtful." Bemis, *Diplomatic History*, p. 492 n. also Griswold, *op. cit.*, p. 92.

and the United States I think that Germany and France would probably have already interfered on Russia's side." [25]

Meanwhile, as the Americans rejoiced at the favorable Japanese outlook, and Roosevelt fulminated against the Russians, Russia, equally malevolent, reciprocated in kind. The Russian press, especially the semi-officially instigated *Novoe Vremya,* under no illusions as to the neutrality of the United States, was particularly hostile from the outbreak of hostilities until the end of the war. On February 9, 1904, the following despatch was sent from the American Embassy at St. Petersburg:

I have the honor to transmit to you herewith for your information, the translation of a leading article from the Novoe Vremya of yesterday. This article is of interest because possibly officially inspired and as voicing current opinion in Russia of the policy of the United States in the present crisis.[26]

The article reads in part:

. . . In diplomatic circles in Washington it is considered that the sympathy of the United States with Japan and the extreme rapprochement of the States with England are discounted in Russia with all their importance. . . .

Of course Russia is not going to be lulled with illusions either from America or from England. Therefore Russia is not at all surprised in the great strengthening of America's fleet now centered in the Philippines, whither the "Buffalo" accompanied by five destroyers is now on its way.

Yes, were the Panama Canal ready, were the powerful fleet of America in existence, were the Americans and English in possession of that organized army and of those armies which are being prepared in America on paper . . . peace would stand very little chance in general and the Russian in particular. . . .[27]

A later despatch from Ambassador McCormick shows his concern over the attempts of certain American newspaper correspondents to foment hostility between Russia and the United States through the medium of British newspapers.

I . . . again call the Department's attention to the statements, reiterated as opportunity offered, that the United States was hostile to Russia. These statements have taken many forms. No statement could be more explicit than that made by the Washington correspondent of the Morning Post that "The fact must not be overlooked that the action of the United States in seeking to save China from Russia and in placing itself in a position where it can be of service to Japan,

---

[25] Roosevelt to Spring-Rice, Dec. 27, 1904. Dennett, *Roosevelt,* p. 30. The United States had two urgent reasons for fearing European intervention. Japan, who was fighting to release Manchuria from the strangle-hold of Russia, was rendering an important service to the United States, and intervention, should it take place, would, as in 1895, be directed against Japan. Again, should intervention occur, the powers, following established custom, would probably demand compensations, and the long-anticipated partition of the Chinese Empire would be an established fact. With China no longer a unit, but divided among the European powers, the only available Far Eastern weapons of the United States, those of the open door and the "integrity of China" would lose their effectiveness.

[26] McCormick to Hay, Feb. 9, 1904.

[27] Leading article in the *Novoe Vremya,* Feb. 8, 1904, the date of the outbreak of hostilities.

is still another proof additional to that I have already adduced in previous letters, that the present policy of the Government of the United States is distinctly anti-Russian, and the policy of the American Government is always an expression of popular sentiment, which must always be given due weight in interpreting an official American action."

Mr. McCormick, continuing, writes:

I have already called your attention to similar even more malignant attempts on the part of American correspondents of British newspapers to sow and water the seeds of hostility between Russia and the United States. . . . Whatever the difference or grounds for actual dispute or suspicion . . . between Russia and the United States, to my mind it is deplorable that they should be turned to account by those who would reap benefit by arraying two great countries against each other, countries whose relations heretofore have been of the character of those existing between Russia and the United States for forty years.[28]

In a second despatch on the same day, Ambassador McCormick wrote:

I have the honor to enclose herewith a translation of a Reuter telegram from Washington stating that the Government of the United States has approved the laying of a new cable between Japan and the Philippines and also a translation of a leading article from the "Birjevie Viedomosti" of to-day placing an interpretation on that action of the Government which I think will be of interest to you at this time.[29]

The article enclosed in Mr. McCormick's despatch states in part:

. . . Our readers will remember that, one after the other, all the Powers made known to the world their intention to maintain strict neutrality in the Russo-Japanese war, one of the first to declare its intention being the U.S.A. And the ink upon the circular note of Mr. Hay had scarcely had time to dry before a light of bad augury is thrown upon it by the Washington telegram just received.

The Government of the United States have found it necessary to lay at once a new cable between Japan, the isle of Guam and the Philippine islands, connecting it with the Pacific Ocean cable. . . . The object of the new cable, we read, is to prevent the isolation of Japan in case Russia should cut the two cables which exist between Japan and Shanghai. . . . On the scene of war only the first shot has been fired, the forces which are to be brought together have not yet been defined and the Washington Government is already alarmed at the possible success by Russia of one of the most important problems in the time of war. . . . And don't think, reader, that the urgent American measures, as viewed by the Washington Cabinet are antagonistic to strict neutrality. They are needed in order to facilitate commercial relations and do not touch neutrality at all.[30]

28 McCormick to Hay, Feb. 27, 1904.
29 McCormick to Hay, Feb. 27, 1904.
30 "A Surprise from Washington," leading article in *Birjevie Viedomosti* (Stock Exchange News), Feb. 27, 1904. On March 1st, Henry Adams, (career diplomat), wrote, "Hay went to bed yesterday . . . and I sat half an hour by his bed-side while he gasped with astonishment at receiving a notice from Russia that she would not permit us to lay a submarine cable from Guam to Japan. . . . All this Russian business is rottener than Panama." Worthington C. Ford, ed., *Letters of Henry Adams, 1892–1918*, pp. 427–28.

In March, Ambassador McCormick, fearing the danger to American trade interests in Russia of continued statements of American correspondents that the United States was hostile to Russia, again writes:

As I have before said the statements made by these correspondents almost daily in one form or another that the United States was hostile to Russia, without any question of differences between the two countries, have come to be believed, with results which seriously threaten American commercial interests here. . . .[31]

Roosevelt, as well as the majority of American bankers, politicians, and the public at large, was, as already seen, a vigorous proponent of the Japanese during the early stages of the war. "The insincere and word-breaking policy of Russia in Manchuria" and the Jewish pogroms at Kishinev had shaken American faith.[32] In contrast to the shuffling and double-crossing of Russia, Japan had proved to Roosevelt's satisfaction, according to von Sternburg, not only that her trade policy was far more sincere than that of Russia, but that she was a country with free institutions and followed "loftier ideals" which had been "formed after the American pattern." [33]

Yet, however vigorous President Roosevelt was, especially in the early stages of hostilities, in expression of both his official and unofficial anti-Russian bias, he at no time favored Japanese predominance in Manchuria.[34] His purpose, as shown at an early stage of the war, was to give Japan a free hand in Korea,[35] to render her assistance, both morally and financially in her fight to loosen the clutch of Russia in Manchuria, with its menace to American commercial and industrial interests to prolong the war for a sufficient length of time to exhaust both Russia and Japan, and to leave a weakened Russia and a strengthened Japan facing each other at the end of the war, thereby equalizing the Manchurian balance of power.[36] A war from which both powers would emerge financially, eco-

[31] McCormick to Hay, March 19, 1904.

[32] The Jewish pogroms in Russia loosened compassion and indignation in the United States that extended in widening circles beyond the Jews themselves. *Supra*, pp. 17–18. Vagts, *op. cit.*, II, 1157. Jewish bankers played an important financial role in the war. *Infra*, p. 109, n. 41.

[33] Von Sternburg's report of a conversation with President Roosevelt on the military situation in Eastern Asia, where Roosevelt "expressed great enthusiasm for the war and for Japan's success on the sea." Von Sternburg to A.A. Feb. 23, 1904. Vagts, *op. cit.*, II, 1185.

[34] *Die Grosse Politik*, XIX, 5992. Vagts, *op. cit.*, II, 1188; Dennett, *Roosevelt*, p. 165.

[35] Dennett, *Roosevelt*, p. 110. "Korea could belong to Japan if it would recognize American private concessions there. . . ." *Die Grosse Politik*, XIX, 5994. Vagts, *op. cit.*, II, 1188. Similarly Sir Percy Sykes, *Sir Mortimer Durand*, p. 276; Vagts, *op. cit.*, II, 1188. Roosevelt "by inference" was conceding Japanese rights in Korea. Pringle, *op. cit.*, p. 377. Both Hay and Rockhill were willing to accept Japanese rule in Korea. This view was shared by Allen and Griscom, U.S. ministers to Korea and Japan respectively. Allen to Rockhill, Jan. 4, 1904, Rockhill papers; Griscom to Hay, Feb. 8, 1904. Vagts, *op. cit.*, II, 1177 n. Griswold, *op. cit.*, pp. 96–97.

[36] This policy was predicated upon the belief in Japanese victory. Vagts (*op. cit.*, II, 1188) states that a quick end to the war, for which the English hoped, was foreign to the hopes of both the Reich and the American Government; both powers, according to

nomically, and physically drained, with their appetites for territory temporarily appeased, would better serve the economic and commercial interests of the American republic.

In a conversation held with the German ambassador, von Sternburg, during the second month of the war, Roosevelt, as reported by the ambassador, stated that,

. . . It is to our interest that the war between Russia and Japan should drag on, so that both powers may exhaust themselves as much as possible and that their geographical areas of friction should not be eliminated after the conclusion of peace; and that, as regards the limits of their spheres of influence they should remain opposed to each other in the same way as they were before the war. This will keep them on a war footing and reduce their appetite for other territories. Then Japan will not menace Germany in Kiaochau and us in the Philippines. Russia's attention is then diverted from her western frontier and remains concentrated upon the East.

Von Sternburg then comments: "From this conversation it was clearly evident that the President is beginning to realize the menace of Japanese predominance in the Far East, which I had called to his attention at the time the war was declared." [37]

In another conversation with the German ambassador, Roosevelt balanced, according to von Sternburg, the desirable post-war positions of Russia and Japan more precisely. The President reasoned that according to the estimate of American financiers the war would last about a year. Korea, aside from respect to be shown to the concessions of the United States in that troubled domain, was to be turned over to Japan. "A permanent establishment of Japan in China was positively undesirable," Sternburg reports Roosevelt as saying. "Russia must remain in Manchuria, but surrender Port Arthur as a fortress." The United States was, however, willing to recognize Russia's dominance in Manchuria, contingent upon freedom of American commerce there.[38] The attitude of Roosevelt, as reported by von Sternburg, coincides with that of Secretary of State Hay at an earlier date, in which he states that the American objective is, "no matter what eventually happens in northern China and Manchuria, the United States shall not be placed in any worse position than while the country was under the unquestioned domination of China." [39]

---

the same author, endorsed a policy of draining and exhaustion. From the first it was Roosevelt's conviction that a balance of power between Russia and Japan was necessary for the protection of American interests in the Far East. Pringle, op. cit., p. 379. At the same time, Roosevelt was willing to concede Manchuria to Russia after the war, provided the Open Door could be assured. And he had also become imbued with the popular American fear of the "Yellow peril" that China and Japan would unite and drive the Caucasians from Eastern Asia. Griswold, op. cit., pp. 124–25; Dennett, Roosevelt, pp. 90, 148, 152.

[37] Conversation with von Sternburg, March 21, 1904. Die Grosse Politik, XIX, Part 1, No. 5992. Dennis, op. cit., p. 364; Romanov, op. cit., p. 475; Kantorovich, op. cit., p. 163.

[38] Die Grosse Politik, XIX, Part 1, No. 5994. Dennis, op. cit., p. 365.

[39] Hay to Roosevelt, May 1, 1902. Dennis, op. cit., p. 353; supra, pp. 82, 85.

Meanwhile, as Americans rejoiced over Japanese victories,[40] to which they had contributed generously,[41] Russia, who from the first had flouted the request of the United States to regard the neutrality of China, openly defied it when the Russian foreign minister informed the American ambassador to St. Petersburg that the "Japanese course warrants extension of hostile zone anywhere in China, and that Russia will no longer consider China neutral." [42] Secretary Hay, reporting the matter to the President, wrote:

Amazing as this declaration is, I was not unprepared for it. It has seemed to me ever since the beginning of the war that Russia was itching to declare war on China—and that in spite of all her defeats, she fully expects to crush Japan, annex Manchuria and Korea, and then take as much of North China as she may think she needs. She accepted our plan for Chinese neutrality most unwillingly, and there has hardly been a week since then that Cassini has not made some complaint of China. Now in view of China's pathetic helplessness I have felt all along that the only motive of this continued complaint was the desire of the wolf to make a case against the lamb.[43]

[40] "The American bourgeoisie welcomed the first victories of Japan with undisguised enthusiasm." Cassini to Lamsdorf, Sept. 20, 1904. Again, "Although the United States is seemingly preserving a correct neutrality, after the conclusion of peace we will have against us a coalition of Japan, England and the United States." Cassini to Lamsdorf, June 1, 1904. Kantorovich, *op. cit.*, p. 165.

[41] Russia fought the war on French loans, Japan was financed by Great Britain and America. Griswold, *op. cit.*, pp. 104–05. Jacob Schiff, president of Kuhn, Loeb, and Company, was decorated after the war by King Edward for his coöperation with the Anglo-Japanese alliance. Vagts, *op. cit.*, II, 1209. Also Vagts (*Ibid.*, II, 1190) states that American capital, more openly than the government, made itself the underwriter of a Japanese victory. Jewish bankers, according to Romanov (*op. cit.*, pp. 529–47) used war loans to Japan as retaliation for Russia's barbaric anti-Semitism. Kantorovich states (*op. cit.*, p. 165) that Cassini reported in April 1904 the issue of an Anglo-American seven per cent loan of $60,000,000, of which the United States contributed $30,000,000, which was of "great political significance to Japan." Cassini to Lamsdorf, Nov. 3, 1904. Again, the subscription of an Anglo-American Loan in March-April 1905, for $150,000,000, with half in the United States, was oversubscribed several times. Cassini to Lamsdorf, May 5, 1905. Cassini, in commenting upon this, said: "Japan has obtained the possibility of continuing this war for a whole year without resorting further to foreign loans." Kantorovich (*Ibid.*, p. 166) estimates that nearly one-fifth of the entire sum spent on Japanese military activities during the Russo-Japanese War was contributed by the United States. The *New York Times* of March 9, 1910, states that it was probably true "that without the help of the United States the financial plans of Japan would have fallen through and she would have lost the war."

[42] Conger to Hay, Aug. 25, 1904. Dennis, *op. cit.*, p. 366. For full account of the Russo-Japanese neutrality difficulties in China see Treat, *Diplomatic Relations*. III, 206–11.

[43] Hay to Roosevelt, Aug. 27, 1904. Hay papers. Dennis, *op. cit.*, p. 367. In May, 1904, Hay wrote to Henry White, "On the 29th of April Cassini came to me in great distress of mind, fearing, or pretending to fear, that China was going to join with the Japanese against Russia. A long experience in Russian diplomacy has not yet sufficiently educated me to make me sure when they are in a panic, or when they are simulating a terror for diplomatic reasons." And again he wrote to White, "It is utterly impossible for us to please the Russians especially in the present circumstances. Every time they get a kick from Japan, instead of kicking back, they begin to whimper and whine that it is our fault." Nevins, *op. cit.*, p. 184.

In the same month President Roosevelt, as reported by von Sternburg, further clarified his attitude toward the belligerents, and his desire to keep the door wide open in Manchuria after the war, free from both Russian and Japanese interference. His proposal was that,

Korea remains under a Japanese protectorate, which may be tantamount to control. The powers to guarantee the neutralization of Manchuria, which is to be placed under the control of a Chinese Viceroy to be appointed by Germany, *not* England. Should the President be reelected, he would like to go hand in hand with Germany in Eastern Asia. . . .[44]

With Theodore Roosevelt's reëlection in November 1904, and the steady decline in health and finally the death of John Hay in July 1905, the President became not only his own secretary of state for foreign affairs, but "his own Cabinet," [45] if not in fact the Government of the United States personified. Dennett states that Congress had no part in the government, that senators were seldom consulted, and that the Cabinet made few contributions.[46] Aside from Roosevelt's impetuous, assertive and self-sufficient temperament, he unquestionably lacked competent American diplomatic and consular service.[47] As a result, he turned to his two trusted friends, Baron von Sternburg who, at Roosevelt's request had been sent as German ambassador to Washington, and Cecil Spring-Rice, British ambassador at St. Petersburg.[48] The British ambassador to the United States, Sir. H. Mortimer Durand, was disliked by Roosevelt, who found him cold and unapproachable, and their relations were strained.[49] To both von Sternburg and Spring-Rice, and especially the latter, Roosevelt apparently confided his most secret plans and convictions in regard to the war. In a letter to Spring-Rice, Roosevelt, shortly after his election in November 1904, expressed freely his unflattering opinion of the Russians and his doubts of the Japanese.

[44] Telegram of von Sternburg, Aug. 11, 1904. *Die Grosse Politik*, XIX, 6264. Vagts, *op. cit.*, II, 1195; Dennis, *op. cit.*, p. 390. A definite German bias is shown if von Sternburg's report is accurate. Kantorovich (*op. cit.*, p. 163), who also cites the purported conversation, considers that, since the military strength of the United States was too weak to undertake a military adventure in the Far East, this was one of Roosevelt's diplomatic attempts to make use of the conflicts between imperialistic powers in order to further American interests in Manchuria and North China.

[45] Ford, ed., *op. cit.*, p. 454.

[46] *Roosevelt*, p. 336.

[47] Roosevelt had no diplomatic and consular organization to depend upon for reliable advice and information. "The consular service was still a stench which the President had not yet had time to abate." With the single exception of George L. von Meyer, who had been appointed ambassador to Russia and did not arrive at St. Petersburg until April 1905, the influence of the American diplomatic service "was negligible." *Ibid.*, pp. 7, 336.

[48] Dennis, *op. cit.*, p. 348.

[49] "And how am I to deal with this creature of an Ambassador Durand?" Roosevelt asked the German ambassador. Von Sternburg to Foreign Office, Sept. 27, 1904. Griswold, *op. cit.*, p. 106. As a result, messages throughout the war were not sent directly through Durand but were relayed by way of Spring-Rice at St. Petersburg to the Court of St. James.

Russia for a number of years [he wrote] has treated the United States as badly as she had treated England, and almost as badly as she has treated Japan. Her diplomatists lied to us with brazen and contemptuous effrontery, and showed with cynical indifference their intention to organize China against our interest. . . . I should have liked to be friendly with her; but she simply would not permit it. . . .

The Japanese, as a government, treated us well. . . . But I wish I were certain that the Japanese at bottom did not lump Russians, English, Americans, Germans, all of us, simply as white devils inferior to themselves . . . to be treated politely only so long as would enable the Japanese to take advantage of our various national jealousies, and beat us in turn. . . .

Roosevelt, summing up the matter at the end of the letter, decided the best course for the United States was "to trust in the Lord and keep our powder dry and our eyes open." [50]

In late 1904, William II made an unsuccessful effort to conclude a secret treaty with Nicholas II as an offset to the newly-formed Anglo-French Entente of April 8, 1904.[51] This attempted treaty paved the way for the Treaty of Björkö of July 1905.[52] About the same time the Kaiser came forward with an unsubstantiated story of a French plot to partition China. To frustrate this alleged plan, William II, seeking to save Manchuria for the Tsar and at the same time to receive a reward for his service, urged Roosevelt to circularize the powers again requesting them to uphold China's territorial integrity, with the exception of "a grant of . . . territory to both belligerents eventually in North China." [53] Hay, again detecting the loophole in the paragraph relating to north China, extracted the sting from the Kaiser's proposal and, consequently, the American note did not exclude Manchuria. The neutral powers all answered the President's circular notes in the affirmative.[54]

Germany made another effort in the Morocco crisis of 1905 to break up the Anglo-French Entente, von Bülow and Holstein taking the initiative. Presenting the argument that the principles of the Open Door and territorial integrity should be upheld in Morocco no less than in China, and that a successful Anglo-French war against Germany would spell danger to American interests in the Far East, the Kaiser appealed to the President to support Germany in her demand for a conference. Roosevelt, after four successive refusals, finally brought pressure to bear upon France, and on September 28, 1905, an agreement for a conference, later known as the Algeciras Conference, was signed by France and Germany.[55] The part

[50] Roosevelt to Spring-Rice, Dec. 27, 1904. Dennett, *Roosevelt*, pp. 47–50.

[51] Cf. Isaac Don Levine, *Letters from the Kaiser to the Tsar*, pp. 123 ff.

[52] For details of the Anglo-French Entente of 1904 see Sidney B. Fay, *Origins of the World War*, I, 152 ff. For details of the Björkö Treaty, *Ibid.*, I, 171 ff.

[53] Von Bülow to von Sternburg, Jan. 4, 1905. *Die Grosse Politik*, XIX, 2, 556–57. Griswold, *op. cit.*, p. 103.

[54] *For. Rel.*, 1905, pp. 1–4.

[55] For details of the Morocco crisis of 1905 and the Algeciras Conference see Fay, *op. cit.*, I, 168–71, 177–92.

that Roosevelt played in this affair antagonized England, and was largely responsible for her lukewarm coöperation with him at Portsmouth.[56] It may be added that throughout the Russo-Japanese War one of Germany's gravest fears was that the United States would join the Anglo-Japanese Alliance, an anticipated attempt which she made every effort to thwart.[57]

Public sentiment, as the war continued, still remained largely anti-Russian. Many felt that Japan, while fighting for her own interests, was also waging an American war against Russian control in Manchuria. Professor Paul Reinsch writing in the *North American Review* stated that:

Japan is fighting our battle. . . . The very least that the Anglo-Saxon races can do for the representatives of their policy in the Orient is to counteract the diplomatic influence that would by roundabout means again deprive the Japanese of the fruits of their unexampled self-sacrifice.[58]

And, as at the outbreak of the war, the officially instigated Russian press still fulminated against the United States, accusing her of having precipitated the war, and exposing the suppositional American designs in the Far East. On April 18, 1905, Ambassador Meyer sent the following despatch to the Department of State:

I have the honor to enclose herewith copy of an article from the "Novoe Vremya" of April 5, the semi-official organ of the Russian Government. It is headed "Russia's real enemy" and refers to America as having instigated Japan to war with Russia and also to having hounded the Japanese on, at the same time invading Eastern Siberia. These same insinuations have appeared before in this paper. Should they continue would it be advisable, in a diplomatic way, to call the attention of the Foreign Office to the tenor of these remarks?[59]

After calling attention to the imperialistic designs of the United States in the Far East, with China and "its immense untouched natural resources" as an objective, the article continues:

This is the reason of their currying favor with China by returning part of the Boxer Contribution, defending China's interests in Europe and their advocacy of the integrity of the Chinese Empire as a principle of their national politics. But Russian influence was already established in Manchuria, and was moving on toward China. America, uniting the European Powers and Japan by means of the doctrine of "The Open Door," *commenced to instigate Japan to war with Russia.*

With few exceptions, our diplomacy and our press overlooked these Japanese-American relations in the same manner as they overlooked the Japanese preparations for the war which resulted from them. Whilst we sympathized with the Boers, and learned to revile the English, *the Americans not only hounded the Japanese on to us,* but at same time *invaded Eastern Siberia.*[60]

56 Dennett, *Roosevelt,* p. 214.
57 *Die Grosse Politik,* XIX, 69. Vagts, *op. cit.,* II, 1178.
58 "Japan and Asiatic Leadership," *North American Review,* Jan. 1905.
59 Meyer to Hay, April 18, 1905.
60 Italics appear in text.

After discussing the "rapid Americanization of the East Siberian coast" and the fisheries along the Russian coast, which the Americans are supposedly trying to acquire by means of the Japanese, the writer turns to Senator Beveridge:

> But their designs go much further. Senator Beveridge, who during his travels took liberal advantage of Russian hospitality and of the privileges of a so-called friend of Russia . . . propounds the eccentric principle that since the American Pacific coast belongs to the States . . . the Asiatic coast of the same ocean ought also to belong to them, at least as a field of commercial exploitation. . . . The policy thus openly outlined in Beveridge's book is that which is being closely followed by President Roosevelt, who has repeatedly announced that the Pacific Ocean, with its islands and coasts, is a sphere for American domination. . . . General Woodford, the former American Ambassador to Spain . . . said in a public speech: "Japan is now accomplishing that which in ten years' time America would otherwise have to do for herself. This war with Japan is promoting a great future for America. . . ." [61]

The first overtures that led to the final peace settlement were made by Russia.[62] On April 5, 1905, French Premier Delcassé, cautiously informed Motono, Japanese minister to France, that he had reliable information as to the intentions of Russia which convinced him that he could bring the belligerents together for the discussion of peace, provided "that Japan would consent to eliminate from the negotiations . . . cession of Russian territory and payment of money indemnity." Japan, suspicious of overtures made through the ally of Russia, turned to Roosevelt for advice, at the same time cautiously intimating that while peace itself must be made by direct negotiations with Russia, she preferred the "friendly good offices" of the United States to those of France.[63]

President Roosevelt confirmed the advisability of direct negotiations between the belligerents, and paved the way for the security of the United States by making it clear that Japan would be expected to adhere to the maintenance of the Open Door in Manchuria and to the ultimate return of that country to China.[64] Baron Komura, Japanese foreign minister, in a

---

[61] Translation of an article from the *Novoe Vremya* of April 11, 1905.

[62] Tentative peace proposals had been made at early stages in the war. Witte, who unlike the majority of the Russians, favored an early peace, had approached Count Hayashi in the summer of 1904 with proposals. Again, in February 1905, he renewed his overtures by way of France. Dennett, *Roosevelt*, pp. 171–72; E. J. Dillon, *The Eclipse of Russia*, pp. 296 ff. Japan in the same month had approached the United States with cautious inquiries as to whether the revolutionary difficulties in Russia were not propitious for Russia to suggest peace negotiations, but had retreated when Roosevelt advised that Japan take the initiative and thereby justify herself "in the eyes of the world if Russia should reject Japan's advances." Roosevelt to K. Takahira, memorandum, Feb. 27, 1905. Dennis, *op. cit.*, p. 397.

[63] B. F. Barnes, assistant secretary of war, to Roosevelt, April 18, 1905, summary of a telegram from Baron Komura to K. Takahira. Dennett, *Roosevelt*, pp. 176–77. Roosevelt at this time was vacationing in Colorado.

[64] Roosevelt to Taft, April 20, 1905. Dennett, *Roosevelt*, p. 178.

despatch of April 25, assured the President that "Japan adheres to the position of maintaining Open-Door in Manchuria and of restoring that province to China." [65] By Japan's commitment to the fundamental principles of American policy in the Far East the way was cleared for further advances.

President Roosevelt was ready for the war to end. The Japanese had achieved the desired end of loosening the clutches of Russia on Manchuria. But Roosevelt now feared that the balance of power which he sought in the Far East was threatened by the brilliant Japanese victories. On May 22, 1905, in a telegram to Lamsdorf giving the substance of a conversation with Roosevelt, Cassini stated that the President considered the position of the Russian armies after the defeat at Tsushima as hopeless.

Je crois devoir observer [continued Cassini], que le Président est sérieusement alarmé par les récents succès Japanais et me semble dans dispositions favorable à la Russie. Il exerce une influence incontestable sur le Japon, dont il pourrait, à mon avis, modérer les exigences.[66]

Several weeks later (June 16) Roosevelt wrote: "Russia had far better make peace now, if she possibly can, and find her boundaries in East Asia left without material shrinkage . . . than submit to being driven out of East Asia. While for the rest of us, while Russia's triumph would have been a blow to civilization, her destruction as an eastern Asiatic Power would also in my opinion be unfortunate. It is best that she should be left face to face with Japan so that each may have a moderative action on the other." [67]

The belligerents themselves, as records now show, were also ready for peace. They were about equally at the end of their resources. Japan, with a war on her hands at an estimated cost of $1,000,000 a day, and faced with the improbability of further foreign loans, which so far had largely financed the war, was, despite her victories, in a serious plight, especially as her manpower was becoming exhausted by the ravages of war. The total Japanese war expenditures were estimated at approximately $1,000,000,-000, not including interest, more than half of which was furnished by foreign loans floated in London and New York, with Berlin contributing a minimum.[68] Approximately one-fifth of the entire male population of about 10,000,000 was put into some form of war service, more than half the number serving in the army.[69] Takeuchi states that the war resources

[65] Barnes to Roosevelt, April 25, 1905. Dennett, *Roosevelt*, pp. 179–80.

[66] Cassini to Lamsdorf, telegram, May 22, 1905. *Arkhiv, M.I.D., Sbornik Diplomaticheskikh Dokumentov, Kasaiushchikhsia Peregovorov mezhdu Rossiei i Iaponiei o Zakliuchenii Mirnogo Dogovora, Dopolnenii Nekotorimi Dokumentami iz Arkhiva Grafa S. U. Vitte.* 24 maia–3 oktiabria 1905 goda. (Collection of Diplomatic Documents Concerning the Negotiations between Russia and Japan about the Conclusion of the Peace Treaty, Supplemented by Several Documents from the Archives of Count S. U. Witte. May 24–Oct. 3, 1905), Doc. No. 2, pp. 4–5.

[67] Dennett, *Roosevelt*, pp. 165–66.

[68] Ushisaburo Kobayashi, *War and Armament Taxes of Japan*, p. 29. Also Gotaro Ogawa, *Expenditures of the Russo-Japanese War*, p. 68. Dennett, *Roosevelt*, 297.

[69] Ogawa, *op. cit.*, pp. 113–14.

of Japan were completely exhausted at the end of March 1905; that an additional 250,000 men and 1,500,000,000 yen, of which there were no assurance, would have been required to continue the war another year.[70] Russia likewise was in a bad way. Witte, stopping off at Paris on his way to the United States in the summer of 1905, was refused further loans by French bankers. "We had exhausted all our means and had lost our credit abroad. There was not the slightest hope of floating either a domestic or a foreign loan," Witte writes in his *Memoirs*.[71] In March of that year Russia was not only losing, but was confronted with a revolution which was steadily increasing in momentum, nourished by the war itself. France, harassed by the Moroccan crisis and not having favored the war from the beginning, was in no position or mood to assist her ally.[72]

Finally, on May 31, 1905, the Japanese Government, encouraged by their naval victory in the Sea of Japan on May 26th,[73] and the fuel it had added to the Russian revolutionary movement, formally invited President Roosevelt "directly and of his own motion and initiative to invite the two belligerents to come together for the purpose of direct negotiations." [74] Russia was yet to be heard from. The Tsar was holding back. On June 3, the German Emperor, alarmed at the Russian situation and the danger to the Tsar's authority, and possibly his life, urged Nicholas to make peace without delay,[75] calling his attention to the desirability of President Roosevelt as mediator:

I may turn your attention to the fact that undoubtedly the Japanese have the highest regard for America before all other nations. . . . If anybody in the world is able to influence the Japanese or to induce them to be reasonable in their proposals, it is President Roosevelt.[76]

And again, in two messages to Roosevelt, assuring him of German support, the Kaiser stated that he had informed the Tsar that "President Roosevelt was the person to persuade Japan to make reasonable proposals for peace." [77]

As the Tsar continued obdurate, the President requested Ambassador Meyer to see him personally, point out to him the hopelessness of continuing a struggle which, in the opinion "of all outsiders, including all of

[70] Tatsu Takeuchi, *War and Diplomacy in the Japanese Empire*, p. 149.
[71] Pp. 135 ff.; also Rosen, *op. cit.*, I, 263–64; Romanov, *op. cit.*, p. 97.
[72] Dennett, *Roosevelt*, p. 301.
[73] Takeuchi, *op. cit.*, p. 149. The Russians had also delayed, hoping for a naval victory.
[74] Komura to Takahira, May 31, 1905. Transmitted to Roosevelt by Takahira. Dennett, *Roosevelt*, p. 215; Takeuchi, *op. cit.*, p. 149.
[75] The Kaiser feared the spread of the revolutionary contagion into Germany and, finding that Russia was sufficiently weakened to be pliable in listening to his proposals for a secret treaty, made a volte face and became a champion of peace.
[76] *Die Grosse Politik*, XIX, Part 2, No. 6193. Dennett, *Roosevelt*, p. 402.
[77] The President, commenting on the Kaiser's statement in a "highly confidential" letter to Senator Lodge, wrote, "I did not desire to be asked to squeeze out of Japan terms favorable to Russia." Lodge to Roosevelt, June 5, 1905. Dennett, *Roosevelt*, p. 191.

Russia's most ardent friends," could end only in the loss of all Russian possessions in Eastern Asia, and urge him to agree to direct negotiations, assuring him of absolute secrecy until Japan should agree.[78] Fearing a menace to American interests in the supremacy of Japan on the mainland, Roosevelt was convinced if the war continued, that the Japanese would drive Russia out of Siberia to the outskirts of Lake Baikal.[79] It was only after a lengthy audience with the Tsar, during which the American ambassador presented the issues forcefully yet tactfully, that the Tsar finally yielded and gave his assent to the opening of negotiations.[80] "You have come at a psychological moment [the Tsar confessed]; as yet no foot has been placed on Russian soil; but I realize that at almost any moment they [the Japanese] can make an attack on Sakhalin. Therefore it is important that the meeting should take place before that occurs." [81]

Ambassador Meyer's telegram giving the substance of his interview with the Tsar reached Washington on June 7.[82]

I then had a perfectly characteristic experience [Roosevelt wrote], showing the utterly loose way in which the Russian Government works. On June sixth, Cassini showed me a despatch from his government in which they declined my proposition, or rather did not answer it at all, but said that they would not ask either peace or mediation, but asked me to exercise a moderating influence on the demands of Japan, and to find out what these demands were. Of course, the telegram from Meyer directly contradicted the despatch to Cassini.

Cassini was not notified of this and insisted that Meyer had misquoted the Tsar and got his words wrong. I had this statement cabled over to Meyer, who got the authority of Lamsdorf to say that he had quoted the Tsar correctly and that his (Meyer's) despatch, which was shown to Lamsdorf, was an accurate account of what had been said. Cassini's words were that Meyer "might have misinterpreted or forgotten what the Emperor has said.". . . Cassini also sent . . . messages to me . . . including a protest against my seeing so much of the Japanese Minister and of the representatives of the neutral Powers. . . . I regarded this protest as impertinent, and requested that Cassini would not repeat it. He also protested that I was trying to make Russia move too quickly, and was very indignant over my order interning the Russian ships at Manila, saying "this is not the time to establish new principles of international law." As you probably saw, I had declined to allow the Russian ships to make any repairs that were rendered necessary by the results of the battle, and then had them interned. I informed Cassini that it was precisely the right time to establish a new principle of international law, when the principle was a good one, and that the principle is now (?) established.[83]

[78] Instructions to the American ambassador at St. Petersburg, June 5, 1905. *Ibid.*, pp. 192–93. The main Russian source for the despatches between Washington and St. Petersburg for the period May 24 to October 3, 1905, is to be found in *Arkhiv M.I.D., Sbornik Diplomaticheskih Documentov* etc.

[79] Dennett, *Roosevelt*, p. 165.

[80] Meyer to secretary of state, June 7, 1905. *Ibid.*, p. 195.

[81] *Ibid.*, p. 194. The Japanese did attack Sakhalin later.

[82] *Ibid.*, p. 195.

[83] Joseph Bucklin Bishop, *Theodore Roosevelt*, I, 387–88; Dennett, *Roosevelt*, pp. 195–96. After the battle of the Sea of Japan three Russian war vessels, in need of repairs, sought asylum at Manila. The United States Government refused to allow the repairs

As both St. Petersburg and Tokyo had expressed willingness to enter upon peace negotiations, President Roosevelt on June 8, 1905, issued identic invitations to both Russia and Japan, urging them, "not only for their own sakes, but in the interest of the whole civilized world, to open direct negotiations for peace with one another." [84]

Then Cassini [wrote Roosevelt] must have been told by his government what had happened, for he called upon me and notified me that the Russian government thanked me and adopted my suggestion. I am inclined to think that up to the time he had received the message which he then communicated to me, his government had told him nothing whatever as to their attitude toward peace.[85]

There now took place, in the words of Roosevelt, "a rather exasperating incident." Both belligerents had accepted the invitation.[86] The Japanese Government promised to appoint plenipotentiaries "for the purpose of negotiating and concluding terms of peace." Cassini's oral statement had been just as direct, but Lamsdorf, in his formal reply of June 12, wrote in vague and subtle terms:

With regard to the eventual meeting of Russian and Japanese plenipotentiaries, "in order to see if it is not possible for the two Powers to agree to terms of peace," the Imperial Government has no objection in principle to this endeavor if the Japanese government expresses a like desire.[87]

Roosevelt's comments on this reply were as follows:

This note is, of course, much less satisfactory than Japan's for it showed a certain slyness and an endeavor to avoid anything like a definite committal . . . while at the same time as it used the very words of my identical note it did not offer grounds for backing out of the negotiations.

"But Japan now started to play the fool," continued Roosevelt. She insisted that unless Russia "would appoint plenipotentiaries who would have full powers to make peace . . . Japan did not care for the meeting." There was further confusion and disagreement over the place of meeting, Russia pro-

---

to be made insisting that to do so would virtually be permitting Russia to increase her naval force in a neutral port. This was not a new application of international law. The vessels were interned on June 8, five days after they reached Manila. Moore, *op. cit.*, VII, 992–94.

[84] State Department to Meyer, June 8, 1905. Dennett, *Roosevelt*, p. 196; Takeuchi, *op. cit.*, p. 150; Griscom, *op. cit.*, pp. 255–56.

[85] Roosevelt's "narrative of June 16th." Dennett, *Roosevelt*, p. 197.

[86] Text of Japanese acceptance in telegram of Griscom to secretary of state, June 10, 1905. Dennett, *Roosevelt*, p. 225. The British Government had in a "somewhat noncommital memorandum" raised no objections to peace. Telegram from Marquis Lansdowne, June 3, 1905, probably delivered through the British Embassy. Dennett, *Roosevelt*, pp. 191, 210–11. The position of England, in alliance with both France and Japan, was a delicate one. German support was already assured. France, drained by loans to Russia, and occupied with the Moroccan affair, was, as already observed, strongly in favor of peace.

[87] Meyer to secretary of state, note from the Russian Foreign Office, June 12, 1905. Dennett, *Roosevelt*, p. 226.

posing Paris, and Japan, Chefoo. As a counter proposition, Roosevelt suggested the Hague. "It was crossed," wrote Roosevelt, "by a proposition from Russia that the meeting should take place in Washington." Roosevelt's assertion here is not entirely accurate. Lamsdorf, in his message of June 13, expressed a preference for Paris mentioning Washington as his second choice. Japan refused to go to Europe, her choice now being the United States. "Russia having first suggested Washington," concluded the President, "I promptly closed and notified both Japan and Russia that I had thus accepted Washington." [88]

In spite of Lamsdorf's evasive reply, Cassini informed Roosevelt that Russia would send plenipotentiaries with full powers to the conference.[89] But following this assurance, which for the time, at least, allayed Japan's fears, Russia again made trouble. Notwithstanding Lamsdorf's expressed willingness to accept Washington as a suitable city for the conference, as well as Japan's refusal to go to Europe, the Russian foreign minister now urged the Hague for the place of meeting.[90] Instructing Ambassador Meyer to see the Tsar personally, if necessary, President Roosevelt forcefully replied that as far as he was concerned the place of meeting was a closed matter.[91] Thanks to the able and determined stand of the American ambassador, Lamsdorf once more backed down. Meyer's despatch of June 18 to the Department of State paid small tribute to Lamsdorf's handling of foreign affairs.

> Yesterday and the day before [wrote Meyer] I had two heated discussions with the Minister of Foreign Affairs. . . . The fact that you cabled me the Lamsdorf instructions to Cassini was a great assistance, because I could not get it out of him the day before, when he implied that Cassini had made a mistake and gone beyond his instructions. I said it was time that he recalled Cassini at once if the President could not rely on what he said. I could not make Lamsdorf realize that, after Washington had been decided upon, it was outrageous of him endeavoring to force you to reverse your action, your decision having been made on the instructions to Cassini, and which I compelled him to acknowledge had been approved by the Tsar. . . . As it made no impression on him that Japan had refused and you had announced it to the world, I was obliged to tell him that in America when we gave our word we abided by it, and that if he did not decide to abide by Washington, I should be compelled to carry it personally before the Emperor. This did not meet with his view at all, and he answered that it was not customary for the Emperor to give audiences weekly to an Ambassador.[92]

Finally Lamsdorf made a graceful retreat, and Cassini, in accepting Washington as the place for the conference charged the entire episode to unwarranted newspaper publicity.[93]

[88] *Ibid.*, pp. 198–99 and n. 1.

[89] *Ibid.*, p. 199.

[90] Meyer to secretary of state, telegram, June 16, 1905. *Ibid.*, p. 226.

[91] Roosevelt to Meyer, June 16, 1905. *Ibid.*, p. 228.

[92] Meyer to Roosevelt, June 18, 1905. M. A. D. Howe, *George von Lengerke Meyer*, pp. 168–70.

[93] Dennett, *Roosevelt*, p. 200. According to the Russian documents the Foreign Office

The appointment of plenipotentiaries and negotiations for an armistice now came into the foreground. Sergius Witte and Baron Rosen were chosen to represent Russia, and Foreign Minister Baron Komura and K. Takahira to act for Japan at the ensuing peace conference. It was during this period that President Roosevelt sent the following message, through the American ambassador at Berlin to the Kaiser:

Whether we can get the Japanese and Russians to make peace I do not know, but I hope you will personally tell the Kaiser how much I value what he has done and that . . . it may be imperative to get his aid in order to make the Tsar conclude peace. I hope that the Japanese will be moderate in what they ask . . . but it must be kept clearly in mind that they are the victors; that their triumph has been . . . overwhelming, and that they are entitled to . . . substantial concessions as the price of peace. The difficulty will come with Russia. . . .[94]

Conditions in Russia, as reported by Ambassador Meyer, were now alarming. Attempts at revolution were made in Odessa and Libau, and serious disorders in other parts of the country were taking place.[95]

President Roosevelt, at the request of Russia, tried unsuccessfully early in July to obtain the consent of the Japanese Government to an armistice. His failure is explained in a despatch to Meyer.

I did my best [wrote the President] to get the Japanese to consent to an armistice, but they have refused. . . . Lamsdorf's trickiness has recoiled upon the Russian government. The Japanese are entirely confident that they can win whatever they wish by force of arms, whereas they are deeply distrustful of Russia's sincerity of purpose in these peace negotiations. Russia cannot expect peace unless she makes substantial concessions, for the Japanese triumph is absolute and Russia's position is critical in the extreme. I earnestly hope the Tsar will see that he must at all hazards . . . make peace with Japan now and turn his attention to internal affairs. If he does not, I believe that the disaster to Russia will be so great that she will cease to count among the great powers for a generation to come—unless, indeed, as foreshadowed in your last letter, there is a revolution which makes her count as the French did after their revolution.[96]

In mid-July, Baron Rosen replaced Cassini, (who was transferred to Madrid) as Russian ambassador to the United States.[97] In a despatch of Rosen to the Russian Foreign Office on July 14, the newly appointed ambassador reported the substance of a lengthy conversation he had held with Roosevelt at the time of tendering his diplomatic credentials. As this despatch is not mentioned either by Rosen in his autobiography or by American authorities, salient portions are here given *verbatim*:

---

at St. Petersburg was angered because Roosevelt had informed the public that Washington had been selected as the meeting place before receiving the final consent of either Japan or Russia. *Arkhiv M.I.D., Sbornik Diplomaticheskih Dokumentov* . . . , May 24–Oct. 3, 1905, Doc. No. 19, pp. 19–20.

[94] Roosevelt to Tower, June 24, 1905. Bishop, *op. cit.,* I, 398. *Die Grosse Politik*, XIX, Part 2, No. 6318. Dennis, *op. cit.,* p. 406.

[95] Meyer to Roosevelt, telegram, July 1, 1905. Howe, *op. cit.,* pp. 173–75.

[96] Roosevelt to Meyer, July 7, 1905. Bishop, *op. cit.,* I, 399–400.

[97] Rosen, *op. cit.,* I, 257.

The President . . . began to converse with me warmly about the war and impending conversations on the conclusion of peace. With the fervor characteristic of him, Roosevelt assured me of the sincerity of his sympathy for Russia, openly admitting that in the beginning of the conflict his sympathies were on the side of Japan . . . but that with the development of the war, his feelings shifted entirely to Russia. He clearly understood the fact that not Russia, but Japan is the chief rival of the United States in the field of trade and industry, and therefore a considerable strengthening of Japan cannot coincide with American interests. From the standpoint of the necessary balance of power in the Far East, he would consider the complete exclusion of Russia from the Pacific Ocean most undesirable in general, and particularly unwelcome to the United States. However, in his opinion, our obviously hopeless war situation was dangerous in that it meant that, if the war were to continue, we may lose not only Sakhalin but also our Pacific Ocean possessions. Hence, he believes that the most satisfactory outcome for us would be a speedy conclusion of peace even on the most unfavorable conditions. On the other hand, in the interests not only of the United States but of Japan herself, he was prepared to counsel moderation in the Japanese demands, the nature of the latter, however, not being known to him.

Rosen further reports Roosevelt's categorical assurance that "Japan was most unwilling to enter into peace negotiations with Russia," an assertion which the Russian ambassador discredited. Nor did Rosen share the President's confidence in Japan's ability to continue the war. For, although Japan had won brilliant victories, she possessed, in Rosen's judgment, no means for continuing the conflict to the point where Russia would be completely crushed. "It would seem to be more correct," said the Tsarist diplomat, "to assume that the Japanese Government, with much relief, accepted President Roosevelt's proposal to enter into peace negotiations with Russia." [98]

The inevitable interval of diplomatic hitches and national jealousies still continued unabated. Roosevelt, as he kept a wary eye on Japan with her easily wounded sensibilities,[99] or detected Russia in tricks unworthy of an adult nation,[100] at times grew exasperated. On July 16, 1905, he wrote:

Russia is so corrupt, so treacherous and shifty, and so incompetent, that I am utterly unable to say whether or not it will make peace or break off the negotiations at any moment. Japan is, of course, entirely selfish, though with a veneer of courtesy and with infinitely more knowledge of what it wants and capacity to get it. I should not be surprised if the peace negotiations broke off any moment.

[98] Rosen to Lamsdorf, July 14, 1905. *Arkhiv M.I.D., Sbornik Diplomaticheskih Dokumentov* . . . , Doc. No. 69, pp. 96–97. In the course of the conversation Roosevelt insisted that England did not want the peace negotiations to be successful and was encouraging Japan to use her favorable military position to deal Russia a decisive defeat thereby eliminating Russia as an important factor in the Far East.

[99] Japan feared that Russia, looking down on Japan as a small country, would not send first-class plenipotentiaries and threatened to withdraw. Dennett, *Roosevelt*, p. 198.

[100] Lamsdorf, in his formal note of acceptance, had endeavored to twist the wording of Roosevelt's invitation into a loophole of escape for Russia if found desirable. *Ibid.*

Russia, of course, does not believe in the genuineness of my motives and words, and I sometimes doubt whether Japan does.[101]

Again, on July 27, Roosevelt expressed his unflattering opinion of the Russian Government:

Before you receive this the peace negotiations I suppose will have come to an end and I rather think they will end in failure. The Russian Government have jumped from one side to the other, but I do not think they are yet in a frame of mind to accept the consequences of their defeat. If anything could have added to the unfavorable impression I already had of them it would be their conduct during these peace negotiations. They have been unable to make war and now they cannot make peace. They strike me as corrupt, tricky, and inefficient.[102]

Meanwhile, the President, uneasy over the sweeping Japanese victories, with their menace to the Far Eastern balance of power, kept watchful eyes not only upon Manchuria but upon the Philippines. Roosevelt told von Sternburg that he thought the old "abrasion fronts" between Russia and Japan should be kept in order to divert both countries from the Philippines and Kiaochow.[103] Having decided six months earlier to let Korea shift for herself,[104] he insured the Philippines against possible Japanese designs by a secret "agreed memorandum" of July 29, 1905, known as the Taft-Katsura Agreement. Secretary of War Taft, ostensibly sent on a mission to the Philippines, stopped at Tokyo, and had a conversation with the Japanese prime minister, of which an agreed memorandum was made. By the terms of this agreement, the United States Government gave its approval to Japan's suzerainty over Korea, and Japan assured the United States of its pacific intentions toward the Philippines.[105]

The peace conference opened at Portsmouth, New Hampshire, on August 10, 1905. On account of the excessive heat of Washington in

---

[101] Roosevelt to Senator Lodge. *Ibid.*, p. 5.

[102] Roosevelt to Lloyd C. Griscom, July 27, 1905. *Ibid.*, p. 241.

[103] Von Sternburg to Foreign Office, May 9, 1904. *Die Grosse Politik*, XIX, I, 112–13. Griswold, *op. cit.*, pp. 122–23.

[104] "We cannot possibly interfere for the Koreans against Japan. They could not strike one blow in their own defense." Roosevelt to Hay, Jan. 28, 1905. Dennett, *Roosevelt*, p. 110.

[105] Treat, *Diplomatic Relations*, III, 253–54. When the news of the secret agreement leaked out in Japan, it was looked upon as a triple alliance of Great Britain, Japan, and the United States: ". . . . In fact it is a Japanese-Anglo-American alliance. . . . We firmly believe that America under the leadership of the world statesman, President Roosevelt, will deal with her Oriental problems in cooperation with Japan and Great Britain." The Japanese *Kokumin*, Oct. 4, 1905. Dennett, *Roosevelt*, pp. 114–15. Treat (*Diplomatic Relations*, III, 352–54) considers that this memorandum was in no sense a secret agreement with Japan which made the United States an unsigned member of the alliance between Japan and England. Kantorovich, with his tendency to impute sinister motives to the United States, terms the Taft-Katsura Agreement a secret alliance between Japan and the United States, together with an informal alliance of the United States with Great Britain which, if the terms had become public, would have created an unprecedented political scandal. Kantorovich, *op. cit.*, pp. 167–68.

August, Portsmouth was substituted as more satisfactory. The fears of the Japanese that their "national dignity" might be impaired by the sending of Russian plenipotentiaries of minor rank, not fully clothed with power to conduct negotiations, proved unfounded. In fact, Witte and Rosen, the Russian representatives, had more direct power than the Japanese envoys, Komura and Takahira,[106] whose power to negotiate was subject to ratification by the Japanese Government. Witte, chief Russian plenipotentiary, on the other hand, had full authority to conclude a treaty. An agreement was reached by which the powers of the Russian envoys were to be regarded as no greater than those of the Japanese.

The conference was concluded in twelve sessions. At the second session the Japanese envoys presented their peace terms, the most important of which were:

the recognition by Russia of Japan's paramount political, military and economic interests in Korea; the evacuation of Manchuria by both parties; the transfer to Japan of the Russian lease of Liaotung and the railway south of Harbin; the cession of the island of Sakhalin; and indemnity to cover the actual cost of the war; the limitation of Russian naval strength in the Far East; the surrender of all Russian vessels interned in neutral ports because of battle injuries; and fishing rights for Japanese subjects along the coasts of Russia's possessions in the East.[107]

The conference had scarcely got under way before the weather vane of American public opinion, swayed by the winds of the press, began to undergo a change. In the beginning, Japan, assisted by British and American newspapers, had presented a strong case for herself. She was a brave little nation, battling for "justice and right," fighting a greedy opponent single-handed for the independence of Korea and the return of Manchuria intact to China.[108] Russia, on the other hand, "was represented as the country of dark absolutism and reaction."[109]

The peace demands of the Japanese, however, revealed them in a different aspect. The representatives of the Mongolian race were as rapacious in their demands for land and money and as imperialistic in their designs, as their Caucasian neighbors in Russia. No hint of the independence of Korea could be found in Article I of the peace terms, with its demand for Russian recognition of Japan's "paramount political, military and economic interests" in Korea. And although President Roosevelt, as a basis for his "friendly good offices," had stipulated the return of Manchuria to China, a stipulation to which Japan had agreed, yet Article III made the restoration of Manchuria to China "subject to the guarantee of reform and improved administration."[110] This proviso, in view of the fact that the

106 The Japanese ambassador to Washington.

107 Treat, *Diplomatic Relations*, III, 247. See also Takeuchi, *op. cit.*, p. 150, for the original demands which were more excessive.

108 Dennett, *Roosevelt*, pp. 238–39; Pringle, *op. cit.*, p. 387.

109 J. J. Korostovetz, *Diary*, p. 38.

110 At approximately the same time, after having given their formal consent to peace negotiations, the Japanese invaded the island of Sakhalin "in order to obtain a diplomatic advantage at the conference." Takeuchi, *op. cit.*, pp. 151–52; Rosen, *op. cit.*, I, 260.

necessity "for reform and improved administration" in Korea had been Japan's excuse for intervention in the peninsula in 1894, and that intervention had already led to Japan's control gave grounds for apprehension.[111]

But, coming into the foreground, and contributing perhaps more to the sudden swing of popular American sentiment toward Russia than did the revelation of Japanese designs, was Witte. Although displaying in his *Memoirs* a scarcely concealed contempt for American customs and manners, Witte, according to his own account, played a part foreign to his nature to further the Russian cause.

My personal behavior may also partly account for the transformation of American public opinion. I took care to treat all the Americans with whom I came in contact with the utmost simplicity of manner. When travelling . . . I thanked everyone, talked with the engineers and shook hands with them—in a word, I treated everybody, of whatever social position, as an equal. This behaviour was a heavy strain on me as all acting is to me unaccustomed, but it surely was worth the trouble . . . here they [the Americans] discovered, not without keen pleasure, that one of the highest dignitaries of the Russian Empire, the President of the Council of Ministers and the Ambassador Extraordinary of the Emperor himself, was a simple, accessible and amiable man, treating the most humble citizen as his equal.[112]

Witte had further resolved while on shipboard, "In view of the tremendous influence of the press in America, to show it every attention and to be accessible to all its representatives," [113] a resolution ably assisted by Dr. E. J. Dillon, the St. Petersburg correspondent of a London newspaper, "who performed the duties of a highly proficient 'publicity agent.' " [114]

The two Russian envoys had received instructions from the Tsar not "to pay a kopek of indemnity or yield an inch of land." [115] In a private conversation before negotiations opened they agreed that it would be difficult, if not impossible, in view of Russia's situation, to carry out these

---

111 Dennett, *Roosevelt*, p. 246. Dennett (p. 248) expresses his personal opinion, based on a general review of Roosevelt's discussions and Hay's policy, that in 1905 the United States Government would have accepted the proposed Japanese policy in Manchuria as they had accepted the Japanese order in Korea.

112 *Memoirs*, pp. 141–42. In the Russian edition (*Vospominania*, I, 375) Witte states that he was more simple, more accessible than the very democratic President Roosevelt who made much of his simplicity. Treat, *Diplomatic Relations*, III, 271, states that "the cooling of American admiration for Japan can be dated from the successful handling of American correspondents by Count Witte at Portsmouth." Gurko (*op. cit.*, p. 64) writes: "In a few days he [Witte] succeeded in winning the sympathy of the American public, a factor of the greatest importance in establishing the conditions of the treaty."

113 *Memoirs*, p. 140.

114 Dennett, *Roosevelt*, p. 238. Dr. Dillon quotes the Japanese Count Hayashi as follows: "When the negotiations were proceeding at Portsmouth it was Dr. Dillon who controlled the American press for the benefit of Witte. At that time most of the prominent British and American correspondents who had collected at Portsmouth had gone there inclined to be in favour of Japan." Dillon, *The Eclipse of Russia*, p. 303.

115 Witte, *Memoirs*, p. 135.

Imperial demands.[116] The Japanese, on the brink of financial and material disaster, were equally apprehensive. In this manner, Russia and Japan, each fearing the other, each hoping for the best of the bargain, settled down at Portsmouth to play the diplomatic game to a finish. And Witte, cabling to Russia, said,

> It is my profound conviction that we must conduct the negotiations so as to win over to our side not only the Russian people but also the public opinion of Europe and America. . . . If Europe and America cease rendering Japan material assistance and side morally with us, we shall come out victorious.[117]

Eight items of the peace terms were discussed amicably and practically disposed of in eight sessions. Witte's revised wording of the suspected Manchurian article made it apparent that both Russia and Japan would relinquish Manchuria, with the exception of the leased Liaotung Peninsula, "entirely and completely to the exclusive administration of China." [118]

Meanwhile, President Roosevelt at Oyster Bay, still acting as his own secretary of state,[119] kept close watch over the conference through his assistants at Portsmouth. Although he was still pro-Japanese,[120] yet he was beginning to counsel moderation in their demands for "the fruits of their victories." For, more and more, he feared a prolongation of the war, with continued Japanese victories, and the ultimate disruption of the balance of power in the Far East. On August 16, he wrote: ". . . I think I can get the Japanese to abandon two of the proposed articles. But there will have to be some indemnity under some name, and it is madness for the Russians to expect the Japanese to give up Sakhalin, which they have taken." [121] Both the Russian envoys felt that Roosevelt was antagonistic to Russia. Witte writes that, "President Roosevelt at first . . . tried to scare me into making considerable concessions by pointing out to me that otherwise the treaty would not be concluded. But he met with a firm determination

116 Rosen, op. cit., I, 263. Witte was in favor of a treaty of alliance with Japan in which Russia would agree to "insure" the interests of Japan in Korea and Manchuria as well as in China. In the early days of the conference he suggested the idea to Komura but received an evasive reply. Lamsdorf also did not favor the plan. Witte, Vospominania, I, 421; II, 459. Kantorovich, op. cit., p. 168; Witte, Memoirs, p. 176; Dennett, Roosevelt, pp. 246–47.

117 Memoirs, p. 154.

118 Dennett, Roosevelt, pp. 247–48.

119 John Hay had been succeeded by Elihu Root.

120 In the Russian edition of Witte's Memoirs (Vospominania, I, 476) Witte writes that throughout the conversations Roosevelt continued to support Japan; that his sympathy was with her and had been shown before the war by the trip of Alice Roosevelt with Taft to Japan. But as a clever man, Witte continues, Roosevelt realized that it was dangerous to go against the popular trend, and he began to push Japan toward concessions. Such a change in the public sentiment was also aided by the stiff attitude of the Japanese envoys, according to Witte, in contrast with his own genial warmth.

121 Roosevelt to President Charles W. Eliot of Harvard, Aug. 16, 1905. Dennett, Roosevelt, p. 251 n.

on my part not to make any such concessions." [122] Rosen, in more diplomatic language, voices the same opinion: ". . . He [Roosevelt] endeavoured to convince me of the necessity for Russia to make the necessary sacrifices in order to secure the speedy conclusion of peace, which alone could forestall the imminent danger of the loss of Vladivostok and the province of the lattoral and maybe even of the whole of Eastern Siberia as far as Lake Baikal. . . ." (Upon Roosevelt's urgent request, Baron Rosen left Portsmouth at this time for a special conference with the President.) The argument used by Roosevelt, as reported by Rosen, again shows the President's fear that Russia would be driven out of eastern Asia.[123] Dennett says that one outstanding aspect of Roosevelt's policy was that he was convinced that his intervention would prevent Russia from being driven out of this area.[124]

By August 18 the conference had apparently reached an impasse, blocked by the "almost hopeless disagreement over the questions of indemnity and the cession of Sakhalin." [125] On the same day the President received word from Meyer that the Tsar refused to make peace unless the Japanese dropped their demands for indemnity and territory.[126] If the conference failed and war continued, not only would Roosevelt's objective, the balance of power in the Far East, be endangered, but his record as a peacemaker would be damaged internationally. Von Sternburg was meanwhile assuring Roosevelt that England and France, at any hint of failure, were ready to step in and take the peace settlement into their own hands.[127] Their success would logically result in demands for compensation, the dismemberment of China, and the downfall of the American policy of the Open Door. In the opinion of Witte, Roosevelt desired peace because it was necessary to his self-esteem as the initiator of the conference; that he worked for a peace even more favorable to the Japanese than it ultimately was until he came up against Witte's resistance and the turning tide of public opinion. In his judgment neither the President nor the American people realized the danger to the United States in the excessive increase in Japan's strength.[128]

On August 19, the President, retreating from the attitude expressed in his letter to President Eliot, proposed that Russia agree to the division of Sakhalin, paying a sum to be fixed, in lieu of indemnity, by a neutral commission for the cession of the northern half.[129] A similar compromise had been suggested on August 18 by Witte and Baron Komura, each leaving record that the initial proposal came from the other.[130] On August 21

[122] *Memoirs*, p. 153.
[123] Rosen, *op. cit.*, I, 260.
[124] Dennett, *Roosevelt*, p. 202.
[125] *Ibid.*, p. 250; Takeuchi, *op. cit.*, p. 152.
[126] Dennett, *Roosevelt*, p. 251.
[127] Von Sternburg to Roosevelt, telegram, Aug. 18, 1905. Dennett, *Roosevelt*, p. 251.
[128] *Memoirs*, p. 162.
[129] Dennett, *Roosevelt*, p. 252.
[130] Korostovetz, *Diary*, p. 86.

the President followed up this proposal by an appeal to the Tsar, through Ambassador Meyer, stressing the danger to Russia of loss of territory in eastern Siberia if the war continued. Explaining to the Tsar that the Japanese, to the President's surprise and pleasure, were willing "to restore the northern half of Sakhalin to Russia, Russia . . . to pay a substantial sum for the surrender of territory by the Japanese," Roosevelt expressed his opinion that "if peace can be obtained substantially on these terms it will be both just and honorable."

Let me repeat [continued the President] how earnestly I feel that it is for Russia's interests to conclude peace on substantially these terms. No one can foretell the result of the continuance of the war and I have no doubt that it is to Japan's advantage to conclude peace. But in my judgment it is infinitely more to the advantage of Russia. If peace is not made now and war is continued, it may well be that, though the financial strain upon Japan would be severe, yet in the end Russia would be shorn of those East-Siberian provinces, which have been won for her by the heroism of her sons during the last three centuries. The proposed peace leaves the ancient Russian boundaries absolutely intact. The only change in territory will be that Japan will get the part of Sakhalin which was hers up to thirty years ago. As Sakhalin is an island, it is, humanly speaking impossible that the Russians should reconquer it in view of the disaster to their navy; and to keep the northern half of it is a guarantee for the security of Vladivostok and Eastern Siberia for Russia. It seems to me that every consideration of national self-interest, of military exigency, and of broad humanity, makes it eminently wise and right for Russia to conclude peace substantially along these lines, and it is my hope and prayer that Your Majesty will take this view.[131]

The President next turned to the Japanese, reminding them of the dangers incident to the demands for an excessive indemnity,[132] and appealing to the Emperor of Japan to "take Sakhalin and relinquish all demands for indemnity." [133] On the 23rd, Witte made the tentative offer that Japan keep all of Sakhalin and drop the demand for indemnity. Japan, through Baron Komura, refused.[134] On the 25th of August the President, stirred by

[131] Roosevelt to Meyer, Aug. 21, 1905. Dennett, *Roosevelt*, pp. 265–67. The Tsar was at first firm in his determination neither to pay indemnity nor yield territory; but before the interview with Meyer was finished, agreed to pay a "substantial sum" for the northern part of Sakhalin, while still refusing indemnity. Meyer to Roosevelt, Aug. 23, 1905. Dennett, *Roosevelt*, pp. 253–55.

[132] Roosevelt warned the Japanese, who were demanding 1,300,000,000 yen indemnity, that continuing the war for the sake of such a large indemnity would turn public sympathy from them; and in the end the expense of the war would eat up as much indemnity as, or more indemnity than, could be exacted. Roosevelt to Baron Kaneko, Aug. 22, 1905. (Kaneko was the Japanese intermediary in New York). Dennett, *Roosevelt*, pp. 254–55.

[133] Witte interprets Roosevelt's intercession with Japan as follows: "He [Roosevelt] seeing that American public opinion was becoming favourable toward Russia and fearing that the unsuccessful end of the parley might turn the sympathies of the people away from him and from the Japanese, telegraphed the Mikado, describing the trend of public opinion in America and advising him to accept my conditions." *Memoirs*, p. 153.

[134] Korostovetz states that this offer was a clever ruse on the part of Witte to win American sympathy; that he purposely brought Komura to the point where he refused, thereby making it "clear that the Japanese carried on the war for the sake of money.

the public announcement of Lamsdorf that Russia would neither pay indemnity nor give up territory, appealed a second time to the Tsar. Reminding the latter that the Japanese, already in possession of Sakhalin, had proposed to retrocede to Russia the northern half of the island, and had agreed that the sum to be paid by Russia to redeem it could be settled by negotiations, Roosevelt warned,

That if these terms are rejected it may be possible that Japan will give up any idea of making peace or of even getting money, and that she will decide to take and to keep Vladivostok and Harbin and the whole Manchurian railway, and this of course would mean that she would take East Siberia. Such a loss to Russia would in my judgment be a disaster of portentous size. . . . If peace is made on the terms I have mentioned, Russia is left at the end of this war substantially unharmed, the national honor and interest saved. . . . But if peace is now rejected. . . . The military situation is such that there is at least . . . a strong probability that though Japan will have to make heavy sacrifices she will yet take Harbin, Vladivostok, and East Siberia, and if this is once done the probabilities are overwhelming that she could never be dislodged. . . . It is chiefly to Russia's interest and perhaps to her vital interest that it [peace] should come in this way and at this time.[135]

On the same day that the President despatched his second appeal to the Tsar, the newspapers reported the news of the second Anglo-Japanese alliance, which had been concluded on August 12, 1905.[136]

On the 27th of August, despite the fury of diplomatic messages and counter messages, with the inevitable entanglements, the Portsmouth Conference had gone from bad to worse and finally had apparently crashed on the rocks of disagreement.[137] Russia, who four days earlier had been willing to pay a "substantial sum" for northern Sakhalin, now refused to divide Sakhalin at any price. Japan was still holding out for camouflaged indemnity in the form of payment for northern Sakhalin.[138] ". . . . The Japanese envoys in Portsmouth were in despair. Witte had been ordered to break off the negotiations on Monday the 28th if the demand for money was continued. . . . Roosevelt felt that he could do nothing more."[139]

Such an acknowledgment . . . would draw public opinion still more to our side." *Diary*, p. 97. Baron Rosen, on the other hand, writes (*op. cit.*, I, 263–64) that Witte acted in good faith; that his conviction of the necessity of immediate peace was so great that in case of extremity he would not have hesitated to consent to paying a war indemnity, provided it could be put into "plausible disguise."

[135] Roosevelt to Meyer, Aug. 25, 1905. Dennett, *Roosevelt*, p. 258.

[136] This alliance renewed for ten years, and strengthening the power of both Japan and England in the Far East, is interpreted by Dennett (*Roosevelt*, pp. 256–57) as indirect aid furnished by England to the United States by making it "easier for Japan to moderate her demands," pp. 257–58. Griswold states (*op. cit.*, p. 114) that the long negotiations which led up to the renewal of the alliance was "another, subtler, reason why [Prime Minister] Balfour could not cooperate with Roosevelt in 1905."

[137] Dennett, *Roosevelt*, pp. 258–59.

[138] Takeuchi (*op. cit.*, pp. 153–54) states that on August 27 Tokyo decided to relinquish Sakhalin.

[139] Dennett, *Roosevelt*, p. 259. Roosevelt had called upon the Kaiser to appeal to the

On the 27th, at the request of Japanese Ambassador Takahira, Witte cabled the Russian foreign minister, requesting a day's postponement of the session set for the threatened breaking off of negotiations on the 28th.[140] The Tsar wrote in the margin of this despatch:

> Send Witte my order to end the parley to morrow in any event. I prefer to continue the war, rather than to wait for gracious concessions on the part of Japan.
>   (Dated, Peterhof, August 28, 1905).[141]

The twelfth and final session of the Portsmouth Conference took place on August 29. Witte delivered his ultimatum in the form of a note, the last concession, he warned, that Russia would make. Russia refused to pay indemnity in any form. She would, however, consent to the division of Sakhalin, ceding the southern half to Japan and retaining for herself the northern half, without compensation on either side. The room was silent for a few seconds. Then Baron Komura, in a "well-controlled voice" consented to Russia's proposal.[142]

American enthusiasm for the Russian success took its customary exuberant form,[143] those who rejoiced at the surface triumph of the Russians forgetting, or not comprehending, that the Japanese had

> secured control of Manchuria and Korea. They have Port Arthur and Dalny, and the south half of Sakhalin. In destroying the Russian Navy they have made themselves a formidable sea power—one which, in the Pacific, is doubtless a match for any nation save England.[144]

And although the unreliable public may have been temporarily swung off its none too stable feet, President Roosevelt had not forsaken the Japanese. On August 29 he wrote: "I was pro-Japanese before, but after my experience with the peace commissioners I am far stronger pro-Japanese than ever." [145]

And two weeks later Roosevelt, in a letter to Sir George Trevelyan, British historian and public servant, gave the following appraisal of the Japanese and the Russians with a comment on Witte:

> I am bound to say that the Japs have impressed me most favorably, not only during these three months but during the four years I have been President. They have always told me the truth. They are a very secretive people, and I speedily learned

---

Tsar. Roosevelt to the Emperor of Germany, Aug. 27, 1905. But the Tsar remained unmoved.

[140] The Japanese, according to Takeuchi (*op. cit.*, pp. 152–53), had finally decided to conclude peace on that date.

[141] Witte, *Memoirs*, p. 158.

[142] For text of Russian note, see Korostovetz, *Diary*, pp. 107–08.

[143] Dennett, *Roosevelt*, pp. 261–63, from Associated Press despatch of August 29, 1905; Witte, *Memoirs*, p. 160; Korostovetz, *Diary*, p. 112.

[144] Roosevelt to George Harvey, Sept. 6, 1905. Dennett, *Roosevelt*, p. 263. Bemis, (*Diplomatic History*, p. 493) says that, "this treaty was a striking triumph for Japan, definitely establishing her position as a world power, an epoch-making step for that nation on the continent of Asia."

[145] Roosevelt to Rockhill, Aug. 29, 1905. Rockhill papers. Griswold, *op. cit.*, p. 120.

that I must never read into anything they said one word more than was actually down in black and white; but so far, whenever they have actually committed themselves I have been able to count absolutely on their doing what they said they would. Moreover, they know their own minds and all act together; whereas the Russians all pulled against one another, rarely knew their own minds, lied so to others that they finally got into the dangerous position of lying to themselves, and showed a most unhealthy and widespread corruption and selfishness.

I suppose Witte is the best man that Russia could have at the head of her affairs at present, and probably too good a man for the grand dukes to be willing to stand him. He interested me. I cannot say that I liked him, for I thought his bragging and bluster not only foolish but shockingly vulgar when compared with the gentlemanly self-respecting self-restraint of the Japanese. Moreover, he struck me as a very selfish man, totally without high ideals.[146]

"There is no real doubt," observes the Soviet historian Kantorovich, "that if the war had ended with the triumph of Russia she would have annexed Manchuria and then would have transformed the whole of north China into her patrimony." The Tsar's Government had charged its envoy at Peking beforehand to assemble materials and arguments as a basis for this annexation.[147] "This would have led to the partition of China and would have delivered a death blow to American interests in the Far East. Roosevelt, therefore, looked upon Japan as a barrier to Russia . . . and to other continental European powers with their territorial strivings in China. In this lies the germ of Roosevelt's 'Nipponophilism' of which Tsarist diplomacy accused him and with which it tried to grapple . . . suggesting the sale of Sakhalin to America." [148]

On September 5, 1905, the Treaty of Portsmouth was signed. The terms of the treaty were regarded in Tokyo by the "Japanese people" as "a national disgrace." [149] Although the Japanese were indignant at not receiving what they considered the full "fruits of their victory," nevertheless, they had apparently done very well for themselves, as well as for the United States. In the course of the war, the Russians had been driven out of Korea, Port Arthur had been captured, the Russian fleet had been destroyed, and Manchuria, south of Tiehling, seventy miles north of Mukden, had been occupied [150]—without costing the United States a life or even a cent. The

146 Roosevelt to Sir George Trevelyan, Sept. 12, 1905. Bishop, op. cit., I, 418.

147 Telegrams in cipher, March 24, July 31, 1904; Chinese Table, case No. 49. In the same case are telegrams in reply from Lessar of April 18, 19, 20 of 1904 with arguments in favor of seizure. Kantorovich, op. cit., p. 222, n. 116.

148 Lamsdorf to Cassini, secret telegram of March 30, 1905. Cassini, in reply, pointed out "that the Senate . . . would refuse to ratify agreements of this type," and therefore "it would be better to limit ourselves to the proposition of American concessions on this island which might be more acceptable since American capitalists are making their exodus from Korea." Ibid., p. 222, n. 118. "On the other hand, Japan did not cease to emphasize that she was the knight errant to the beautiful American damsel—the 'open door' doctrine—and that . . . she was ready for any form of cooperation with American capitalism in China." Ibid., p. 166.

149 Griscom, op. cit., p. 261.

150 Treat, Far East, pp. 378–80; Steiger, op. cit., pp. 722–25.

Japanese had done this at the expense of approximately $1,000,000,000, in addition to the cost of the labor of her active male population. Russia was not only halted, but also Europe. The partition of China was also indefinitely delayed. The total result was apparently a commercial and political benefit to the United States.[151] The balance of power in the Far East had been achieved. In the words of an American historian:

. . . the compromise the president desired with reference to American interests was reached; Japan got Russia's rights in Port Arthur, Dairen, and the South Manchurian Railway, but she won no indemnity to repair her impoverished treasury. So the two belligerents faced each other weakened and divided and northern China was still without an absolute master.[152]

[151] Dennett, *Roosevelt*, p. 331.
[152] C. A. and M. R. Beard, *op. cit.*, II, 497.

Chapter VI

FORMATION OF THE ANTI-AMERICAN FRONT IN MANCHURIA

THE Treaty of Portsmouth had given Japan wide political, military, and economic rights in Korea. Russia had ceded the southern half of Sakhalin Island and the Chinese Eastern Railway, from Port Arthur to Changchun, to Japan.[1] With the exception of the Liaotung peninsula, the lease of which Russia had transferred to Japan, the two powers were now facing each other in Manchuria, each agreeing "to completely and simultaneously evacuate Manchuria," and return it to "the exclusive administration of China." [2] By the terms of the Komura Treaty, concluded between China and Japan at Peking on December 22, 1905, the Chinese Government gave formal consent to the conditions and assignments of the Portsmouth Treaty, and in addition granted Japan new privileges in the form of railroad rights and timber concessions on the Yalu. The Komura Treaty contained three articles, with an additional agreement, signed on the same day, containing twelve articles and sixteen secret protocols. By the public treaty China gave her consent to the transfer of the Russian lease and railway to Japan, the latter agreeing to conform to the terms of the original treaties between China and Russia "so far as circumstances permit." The additional articles extended concessions and privileges to Japan which would increase her power in Manchuria. By the secret protocols, among other advantages to Japan, China promised never to build a main railway, or a branch line, in the vicinity of or parallel to the South Manchurian Railway.[3] The Treaty of Portsmouth and the Komura Treaty with the

[1] J. V. A. MacMurray, *op. cit.*, I, Art. VI, 523.

[2] *Ibid.*, I, Art. III, 523.

[3] The Lytton Commission reported that "the alleged engagement of the Chinese plenipotentiaries of the Peking Conference" in regard to the so-called parallel railways "is to be found in the minutes of the Conference;" that "the Chinese and Japanese official translations of this entry . . . leave no doubt that the disputed passage . . . is a statement of intention on the part of the Chinese;" and that the Chinese government, it would seem, "admitted that there was on their part an obligation not to construct railways . . . prejudicial to the interests of the South Manchurian Railway." League of Nations. Manchuria, Commission of Enquiry into Sino-Japanese Relations, pp. 43–45. *Infra*, p. 141, n. 53.

additional agreement and secret protocols "laid the foundation of Japan's rights in Manchuria." [4]

The diplomatic game played so warily at Portsmouth was ended. Russia and Japan had ostensibly returned Manchuria to China. The balance of power which had been Roosevelt's objective seemed achieved; the antagonism between Russia and Japan had been brought into temporary equilibrium. An alliance between Russia and Japan, the necessity for which had been foreseen by Witte at Portsmouth,[5] had not yet cast its shadow across the Open Door of American diplomacy in the Far East. Nothing at this time had arisen to show that Russia and Japan, in spite of the continued rivalry between them, were shortly to be united in their battle against the expansionist plans of the United States in Manchuria.[6]

Yet the seeds which were to spring up into the Russo-Japanese Treaty of July 30, 1907, and to find fruition in the treaties of 1910 and 1912 between Russia and Japan, had been scattered before the war and finally took root at Portsmouth.[7] The ink had scarcely dried on the signatures of the Treaty of Portsmouth before steps were taken by Japanese and Russian leaders toward "working for the conclusion of a Russo-Japanese Convention which should supplement the Treaty of Portsmouth." [8] During the period between the signing of the Treaty of Portsmouth and the conclusion of the treaty of July 30, 1907, straws showed that the wind was blowing, though lightly, toward an ultimate rapprochement between Russia and Japan, based in the main on Russian fear of Japanese dominance in Manchuria. A despatch from Ambassador Meyer, reporting a conversation with the Russian foreign minister, together with an enclosed newspaper article, throws light upon the wavering search in Russia both for an entente with Japan and, as a counterweight to the latter's overweening ambition, for a rapprochement with the United States. After stating that "the whole subject" of the commercial treaty which was being negotiated between Japan and Russia "was progressing very slowly and unsatisfactorily," and referring to other points of friction, Foreign Minister Izvolsky

[4] Treat, *Far East*, p. 399. Griswold also states that the Komura Treaty formed a legal basis for Japan's rapidly increasing claims. *Op. cit.*, p. 147.

[5] *Memoirs*, p. 176.

[6] Or, according to Kantorovich, (*op. cit.*, p. 172): "As a result of the Russo-Japanese War Manchuria now had two masters instead of one—Russia and Japan—and the latter was even more unceremonious about American interests."

[7] Price states that, "leading statesmen of both Russia and Japan even before the war had become convinced that, as the two nations must needs live together in North-eastern Asia, they might as well live in peace; and that the only way in which this could be accomplished was by a friendly understanding, cemented by treaty, with respect to mutual rights and interests." True, but Price underestimates the obstacles that stood in the way of concluding an effective rapprochement between the two powers. Ernest B. Price, *The Russo-Japanese Treaties of 1907–1916 Concerning Manchuria and Mongolia*, p. 24.

[8] Count Hayashi, *Secret Memoirs*, pp. 227–28. Princes Yamagata and Ito were the Japanese protagonists of such a convention, and the Russian foreign minister, Izvolsky, was "perhaps the strongest believer in the idea of a genuine rapprochement with Japan." Price, *op. cit.*, p. 28.

said that while "they [the Russian Government] were willing to give the pound of flesh, they were unwilling to grant concessions which went beyond those of the Treaty of Portsmouth." [9] Izvolsky felt that

his position at this present moment is a much more difficult one than that of the plenipotentiaries at Portsmouth, because at that time there were large armies facing each other. His eyes were opened to the helplessness of the present situation as Russia, according to his statement, has evacuated a great many more troops than Japan, while Japan can also transport an army within 48 hours. He . . . is desirous that the world should appreciate the fact that Russia is anxious and willing to live up to the agreements of the Treaty . . . but that Japan's demands are greater than Russia should be called upon to concede.

In the same despatch Ambassador Meyer enclosed a translation from the *Bourse Gazette* of December 12, 1905, "one of the important papers of Russia," on "The Necessity of a Russo-American Rapprochement." The writer states:

Our articles on the necessity of a Russo-American rapprochement for the strengthening of universal peace have not passed unnoticed in the foreign press . . . the whole western world is alarmed at the new exhibitions of Japanese chauvinism, which it is not yet too late to render harmless. Yet in contemporary Europe there is no ground upon which two or more powers could get together for the preservation of peace in Asia. For such an object only Russia and the United States could get together. There are no old scores to settle between them; there has never been a Russian-American antagonism, the ancient friendship has only suffered in consequence of temporary causes, growing out of the old Russian regime, which has now been definitely condemned. . . . The rapprochement between the two powers on the two hemispheres, has become a historical necessity. It is necessary to restrain the Asiatic storm which is again advancing on the western world. Does this mean that we preach a war of Russia and the United States against Japan? We have nothing of the kind in mind. On the contrary, a Russo-Japanese rapprochement as soon as it takes definite form will safeguard and strengthen that peace in the Far East of which Russia and the great Trans-Atlantic republic will long stand in need.

After describing the marked inefficiency of the Russian war machine and the tragic losses suffered by Imperial Russia during the war of 1904–1905, the article continues:

All this they [the Japanese] saw, and of course they could not but become imbued with the conviction of their superiority over the great power which had been considered the most puissant and invincible in the world. . . . They saw how great was the moral weakness of the western powers, who did not raise a finger for the prevention of this bloody war; it became evident to them that the boasted

[9] Meyer to State Department, Dec. 19, 1906. Russia could not agree to Japan's claim that the Treaty of Aigun of 1858 (by which, in the main, China ceded to Russia the left bank of the Amur), was abrogated by the Treaty of Portsmouth. No reference, Izvolsky claimed, was ever made to the Treaty of Aigun during the *pourparlers* which resulted in the Treaty of Portsmouth. The fishing rights were also in excess, he believed, of what could be fairly exacted.

solidarity of the western nations . . . was but an empty sound. . . . In a word, the whole Christian West suffered a complete moral bankruptcy, and in this bankruptcy . . . lies the chief source of the present Japanese chauvinism.

The first step toward reducing it, i.e. toward the moral rehabilitation of the West, would be a Russo-Japanese rapprochement. . . . Let us not forget that in the whole Anglo-Saxon world . . . the Japanese predominance in the Far East is beginning to gall, and this predominance be it said, was created in no small measure by the gold which flowed to the Japanese islands from New York and London. This sinew must be cut by means of a Russian-American rapprochement, the only obstacle to which is the disorderly condition of our internal affairs. When this disorder once ceases, the Americans will be the first to extend the hand to Russia in the preservation and strengthening of peace, equally necessary to them and to us in the Far East.[10]

Superficially, the American outlook in Manchuria had never seemed more favorable than at the end of the Russo-Japanese War. No business corporation of importance outside of the ever-present Standard Oil Company and the British-American Tobacco Company had passed through the door that was only partially ajar in Manchuria.[11] The weakening of Russia in northern China as a result of the war offered alluring possibilities to Americans of expansionist financial vision. According to two Soviet historians, the interest of the United States in Manchuria became apparent during the war itself, when "American interests offered to loan money to China to repurchase the Chinese Eastern railroad;"[12] and again in March of 1905 when Minister Conger "advanced before Washington . . . a project for the passing over of the Manchurian railroads to China 'under international guarantees.' "[13]

One of the pioneers to attempt financial penetration of post-war Manchuria was the railroad wizard, Edward H. Harriman, who wished to acquire an interest in the Trans-Siberian Railway, and hoped that Russia, as a result of her defeat in the war, "might be willing to transfer control to an American company which could prove its ability to furnish the needed capital for the improvement of its roadbed and equipment and to operate it more efficiently."[14] The Trans-Siberian Railroad and its port on the Baltic, according to Mr. Harriman's plans, were to be links in an around-the-world system of transportation. To carry out his globe-encircling projects Mr. Harriman also required an interest in the Japanese-owned South Manchurian Railway. In August, shortly before the signing of the Treaty of Portsmouth, Mr. Harriman who, in connection with

[10] Enclosure, Meyer to Root, Dec. 19, 1906. The records in the Department of State offer no evidence that the Russian Government approached the United States at this time for a rapprochement.

[11] Herbert Croly, *Willard Straight*, p. 210.

[12] Romanov, *op. cit.*, p. 535. Avarin, (*op. cit.*, I, 114) terms this offer an attempt of American capital to get a foothold in Manchuria.

[13] Kantorovich, *op. cit.*, p. 185.

[14] Croly, *op. cit.*, p. 239. See George Kennan, *E. H. Harriman*, II, Ch. xviii, "Far Eastern Plans."

Kuhn, Loeb, and Company, had assisted Japan in floating her war loans in the United States, sailed for Japan, and began conversations with Marquis Ito and Marquis Katsura at Tokyo in September, 1905.[15]

Harriman proposed to form a syndicate and acquire a half interest in the South Manchurian, together with an equal share in mining rights, subject to political control by the Japanese.[16] A tentative agreement was signed and Mr. Harriman returned to the United States "on wings of victory." [17] But when the final test came, Baron Komura, who had negotiated the Portsmouth Treaty, and meantime had returned to Japan, opposed the agreement. He found an excuse in Article VI of the treaty which stipulated that the Russian railroad rights had been transferred to Japan subject to China's approval.[18] An unsuccessful attempt to renew the project was made in 1906 when Jacob Schiff, of Kuhn, Loeb, and Company, also travelled to Japan.[19]

The rift between the United States and Japan was widening. President Roosevelt, who in his role of peacemaker, had been condemned by Japanese public opinion,[20] had at the same time to carry the added burden of the immigration problem.[21] Finally, deciding that it was time for a showdown, on March 16, 1907, he sent the American fleet on a world cruise that included Japan in its itinerary.[22] And in July 1907, the situation became so acute that the President sent directions in code to the commander of the American troops in the Philippines "for defending the islands from a momentarily expected Japanese attack." [23] President Roosevelt for several years had felt apprehensive in regard to the Philippines and was anxious to get rid of them. In 1905, he had written that the United States

[15] Dennett, *Roosevelt*, pp. 311–12.

[16] *Ibid.*, p. 312.

[17] Kantorovich, *op. cit.*, p. 185.

[18] Dennett, *Roosevelt*, pp. 312–13.

[19] Kennan, *op. cit.*, II, 22; Dennett, *Roosevelt*, p. 313; Kantorovich, *op. cit.*, p. 185. Kantorovich adds that Schiff thought, as the head of the banking house of Kuhn, Loeb, and Company, which had played so prominent a part in floating Japanese war loans on the American market, that he would have unique influence with the Japanese Government. Romanov (*op. cit.*, p. 31) interprets these attempts of Harriman and Schiff as fear of Japanese expansion in Manchuria.

[20] The Japanese populace, particularly in Tokyo, considering Roosevelt responsible for the failure of the indemnity, reacted in violent public outbreaks of anger, in which martial law had to be declared. Griswold, *op. cit.*, p. 121; Kantorovich, *op. cit.*, p. 171; Griscom, *op. cit.*, p. 263.

[21] The immigration laws of 1904, excluding Japanese, Chinese, and Korean labor from the United States, culminated in October 1906, in the mandate of the San Francisco School Board which segregated Mongolian from Caucasian pupils, an act which met with outraged protests from Japan. Griswold, *op. cit.*, p. 126. The Chinese, although less demonstrative in their reactions than the Japanese, retaliated against the immigration laws by a boycott against American commerce that lasted from May to September 1905. *Ibid.*, p. 124; Kantorovich, *op. cit.*, p. 174.

[22] Whether or not this international gesture produced the desired effect is problematical. President Roosevelt, however, termed the cruise, "the most important service I rendered to peace." *Autobiography*, p. 548. Pringle, *op. cit.*, p. 409.

[23] Griswold, *op. cit.*, p. 126.

should either strongly fortify and defend the Philippines or give them up.[24]

The following month Mr. Rockhill, who was now American minister at Peking, in a despatch to Secretary of State Root, commenting on a recently signed convention between Japan and China [25] which provided for the sale to China of one railroad and the building of another, said:

This convention and Article VI of the additional agreement of December 22, 1905, insure to Japan possession of effective control over all the railroad lines of South Manchuria for the next fifteen years. . . . This is not a cheerful outlook. It remains to be seen what concessions Russia will secure from China in Northern Manchuria on completing its military evacuation . . . from what I hear from the Consul at Harbin I have some reason to believe that they will not be agreeable to us and to our commercial interests.[26]

The first step toward Russo-Japanese solidarity against foreign intrusion was taken on June 13, 1907, when a convention designed particularly to facilitate traffic on the conflicting railway lines of the two powers was signed. A treaty of commerce and navigation and a fisheries convention followed on July 28.[27] And on July 30, 1907, an open convention was signed by Russia and Japan in which each agreed to respect the territorial integrity of the other and to uphold the principle of the Open Door in Manchuria.[28] At the same time a secret agreement was drawn up which gave

24 Roosevelt to Taft, May 31, 1905. Roosevelt Papers. Also same to same, July 3, 1905. Roosevelt Papers. Griswold, *op. cit.*, p. 123, n. 4. According to von Sternburg, President Roosevelt "would let the islands go without delay provided that he could get rid of them in an honorable manner." Von Sternburg to Berlin, Jan. 20, 1906. Vagts, *op. cit.*, II, 1232, n. 5. In 1907, the President wrote that, "The Philippine Islands form our heel of Achilles. They are all that makes the present situation with Japan dangerous. I think that in some way . . . you should state to them that if they handle themselves wisely in their legislative assembly we shall at the earliest possible moment give them a nearly complete independence. . . . I think that to have some pretty clear avowal of our intention not to permanently keep them and to give them independence would remove a temptation from Japan's way and would render our task easier. . . ." Roosevelt to Taft, Aug. 21, 1907. Pringle, *op. cit.*, pp. 408–09.

25 Convention of April 15, 1907, providing for the sale to China of the railroad Hsin-min-Fu-Mukden and for the building of the Changchun-Kirin line. By an ingenious settlement Japan managed to keep a substantial interest in these lines. See P. H. B. Kent, *Railway Enterprise in China*, p. 75.

26 Rockhill to Root, April 22, 1907. The Portsmouth Treaty, as already pointed out, had stipulated that all Manchuria except the Kwantung leased area and the Changchun–Port Arthur Railway should be returned "entirely and completely to the exclusive administration of China" (Article III, MacMurray, *op. cit.*, I, 523), but this provision was somewhat nullified both by the Komura Treaty and by Article VIII of the Portsmouth Treaty in which Japan and Russia agreed to conclude "as soon as possible . . . a separate convention for the regulation of their connecting railway services in Manchuria." *Ibid.*, I, 524. This latter agreement indicated Japan's intentions to expand her railway and other privileges beyond those specified in the Portsmouth Treaty.

27 Price, *op. cit.*, p. 33; Avarin, *op. cit.*, I, 109.

28 Kantorovich, *op. cit.*, p. 182; Morse and MacNair, *op. cit.*, pp. 519–20; Price, *op. cit.*, p. 33. Avarin (*op. cit.*, I, 109) adds that "the necessity for a general agreement was explained by the minister of foreign affairs [Izvolsky] as necessary because of the pressure of the Japanese in northern Manchuria as well as the pressure of the Chinese and for-

Japan a free hand in Korea, and recognized the spheres of interest of
Russia in North Manchuria and Outer Mongolia, and of Japan in South
Manchuria and Inner Mongolia.[29]

A treaty, signed June 10, 1907, between Japan and France, in which the
latter in exchange for similar favors recognized Japan's "rights of propin-
quity and influence" in Fukien, Manchuria, and Mongolia, had paved the
way for the Russo-Japanese Treaty of 1907.[30] In the same year the Anglo-
Russian Entente was concluded, by the terms of which the two powers came
to an understanding over Persia, Afghanistan, and Tibet.[31] By the 1907
treaties, Japan virtually became a fourth member of the Triple Entente
which stood in opposition to the Triple Alliance.

By signing the treaty of 1907, Russia and Japan had forged the first
links in a chain which was to encircle Manchuria against encroachment
by American dollars. According to the Soviet historian Kantorovich, the
Russo-Japanese Treaty of 1907 foreshadowed very unhappy prospects for
the United States,[32] a point of view shared by the Russian ambassador to
Peking of that period, who wrote: "With full agreement of action by Russia and Japan, outside interference in Manchurian affairs can have practically no influence on the course of the latter." [33] It was therefore useless,
continues Kantorovich, to talk "about re-establishing that dominant position which America occupied in Manchurian trade before the original
occupation of Manchuria by Russia." [34] Nor does Kantorovich feel that

---

eigners on Russian and Japanese interests in general." No. 202, *Arkhiv M.I.D.*, note, Feb.
18, 1907.

[29] Kantorovich, *op. cit.*, p. 182; Price, *op. cit.*, pp. 35–37; Morse and MacNair, *op. cit.*,
p. 520. The exact terms of the secret agreement are given in Victor A. Yakhontoff's
Russia and the Soviet Union in the Far East, pp. 374–76.

[30] Griswold, *op. cit.*, p. 149.

[31] Morse and MacNair, *op. cit.*, p. 520. In an effort to thwart the increasing power of
France (which began with the formation of the Anglo-French *Accord* of 1904) and of
Japan, the Kaiser in 1906 suggested to the Chinese minister in Berlin the possibility of an
alliance or understanding between China, Germany, and the United States, to be supported by Britain or Russia. Such a combination, the Kaiser reasoned, would keep the
balance between France and Germany and prevent the partition of China. William II
to Bulow, Dec. 30, 1907. *Die Grosse Politik*, XXV, No. 8557, 87–89; No. 8556, 85–86.
Convinced of Japanese aggressive designs, and eager for the preservation of the Chinese
Empire and the Open Door to American trade in China, Roosevelt in 1906 and 1907
viewed favorably an understanding (but not a "formal alliance") with China and Germany. Von Sternburg to Schoen, Nov. 8, 1907. *Ibid.*, No. 8553, pp. 78–79; Nov. 24, 1907,
No. 8554, p. 80; Dec. 5, 1907, No. 8555, p. 80. In 1908, however, the President feared that
a guarantee of Chinese integrity on the part of Germany and the United States might
cause China to embark upon a policy hostile to Japan. Bernstorff to Berlin, Washington,
Jan. 2, 1909. *Ibid.*, No. 8565, n. 2, p. 97. This apprehension on the part of Roosevelt, together with the procrastination of Yuan Shih-k'ai (president, Foreign Office, Peking) in
following up the German proposals, as well as his fear of antagonizing Japan, explains
the failure of the Kaiser's plan. Rex to Bulow, Peking, June 1, 1908. *Ibid.*, No. 8563, pp.
94–96.

[32] *Op. cit.*, p. 182.

[33] Pokotilov to Izvolsky, Feb. 18, 1908. Kantorovich, *op. cit.*, p. 182.

[34] *Ibid.*, p. 182.

commercial interests alone lay at the roots of American activities in Manchuria, citing an American writer as his authority:

No American economic interest explains the recurring attention to Manchuria. . . . It is adequately explained on political grounds. Manchuria has been the chief international political problem in the Far East since the end of the Sino-Japanese War. The United States has shown a keen interest in Manchurian railways because the solution of the railway problem promised a solution of the political problem.[35]

The American consul general at Shanghai, Charles Denby, was also skeptical as to the success of American interests in China. He wrote to the Department of State in part as follows:

The general conclusion to which the impartial American observer is forced to come is that the policy favored by American diplomacy of an open door in China with a strong and independent Government, has at present, notwithstanding the setback of Russia in the late war, less hope of realization than at the time it was first conceived.[36]

American despatches during this period give evidence that the United States Government was uneasy, and suspected the existence of secret articles beneath the careful wording of the apparently innocuous Russo-Japanese Treaty. A statement from the United States Embassy at Tokyo shows that, although unverified, an accurate idea existed of the Russo-Japanese apportionment of northern China:

Re secret clause in Russo-Japanese political agreement, I have now been informed by an entirely reliable person that the Russian Minister here has admitted confidentially that two such clauses exist. Several think that by this Outer Mongolia and North Manchuria shall constitute Russia's exclusive sphere, and South Manchuria and Korea, Japan's.[37]

Later, Chargé Montgomery Schuyler sent the following despatch from St. Petersburg:

I have the honor to enclose herewith an 'Orange Book' issued by the Ministry for Foreign Affairs which contains the negotiations leading up to the conclusion of the recent treaty between Russia and Japan. It is interesting to note that when I made a request for copies of this 'Orange Book' . . . the official who came to the telephone asked if I was referring to the published or the Secret Treaty.[38]

And in March 1908, Secretary of State Elihu Root, referring to Mr. Schuyler's communication of December 7, wrote to the American chargé at St. Petersburg as follows:

35 Charles F. Remer, *Foreign Investments in China*, p. 335.
36 Charles Denby to the assistant secretary of state, Dec. 21, 1907.
37 Mr. Dodge, chargé d'affaires, Tokyo, to the secretary of state, Sept. 14, 1907.
38 Schuyler to Root, Dec. 7, 1907. Attached to this despatch is a note from the office of the third assistant secretary, Department of State, signed by H. W. (Huntington Wilson) which says: "The fact that there exists a secret Russian-Japanese Treaty is confirmed by this despatch."

In the [Russia-Japan] agreement it is stated that the Russian and Japanese Governments have exchanged copies of all their treaties, conventions, and contracts, with China. A knowledge of these would be very welcome to this Government, and the Government of Russia should hardly object to their communication in view of their declarations for the "Open Door" and the preservation of China's integrity, which are reiterated again in this latest published agreement. The Department has thus reason to believe in the existence of a secret understanding between Russia and Japan, possibly as regards their respective claims to spheres of influence or of mutually exclusive activity in Manchuria and North China. In view of the active interest always displayed and which continues as ever to be felt by this Government in the preservation of the territorial and political integrity of China in the "open door" policy, I naturally desire to obtain definite information as to the existence of any such secret agreements and also their nature and extent. You will therefore endeavor in any practicable manner to enlighten the Department on this subject.

It seems reasonably clear that any retrogression by Russia from the policy which she has so frequently declared in agreement with the Government of the United States would naturally have the immediate result of inspiring and instigating a similar tendency in the policy of the Government at Tokyo; and that it is improbable that in such an unfortunate event Russia would be the Power to profit most.[39]

In the meantime, as Russia and Japan withdrew further from the United States and into their own imperialist Manchurian schemes, a comparatively unknown young man in Mukden was visioning American expansion in the Far East and planning to bring American dollars to the rescue of the impaired territorial integrity of the Chinese Empire. This was Willard Straight, consul general at Mukden from 1906 to 1908, who, according to his biographer, saw

only one way in which he could effectively promote American interests in Manchuria and at the same time use the increased American influence for the benefit of Chinese independence. He must bring about the investment of a large volume of American capital in that region. The amount of trade which American merchants could obtain merely by exporting to Manchuria the few manufactured articles which the Chinese market could absorb was insignificant. If Americans wished to build up a lucrative business, their financiers must lend the money which the Chinese needed for the purpose of building railways and developing natural resources, and in this way create a demand for the products which their merchants wanted to sell to China.[40]

Willard Straight, according to another writer, "made his Mukden consulate a high-pressure sales agency for American commerce in Manchuria." [41] In Seoul, where Straight was vice consul, he had met E. H. Harriman in 1905 and discussed the "possibility of American investments

[39] In reply, Mr. Schuyler reported in part that "M. Izvolsky denied absolutely that there existed any unpublished agreement of any kind between Russia and Japan." Schuyler to Root, March 31, 1908.

[40] Croly, *op. cit.*, pp. 237–38.

[41] Griswold, *op. cit.*, p. 138.

in Manchuria." When Straight came to Mukden he was determined to keep "the door in Manchuria actually open. He saw opportunities for development of American trade in North China which Mr. Rockhill ignored. He detected and reported Japanese treaty infringements which were very disturbing in Peking and Washington. . . ." [42] While vice consul at Seoul his personal observation of, and experience with, Japanese technique in penetration had left him antagonistic to Japan. His sympathies were with the Chinese in "their fear of Japanese absorption of the country; of the post-bellum policy of Japan; of its vast schemes for commercial and industrial development of Manchuria; of the fate of Korea. . . ." [43] Yet, at the same time, he saw an excellent opportunity for the United States to pull a substantial plum from the Manchurian pie. When he arrived in Mukden on October 3, 1906, he entered upon a new activity, that of "the promotion of American national interests in Northern China," [44] and, as a concomitant to it, of driving Japan from its stronghold in Manchuria—Japan, who was ultimately to be the strong right arm of Russia in their union against American penetration of Manchuria.[45]

Mr. Straight made proposals to the American-educated Tang Shao-yi,[46] Governor of the province of Fengtien [47] for a northerly extension to be built and financed by the United States on the Imperial Railway from Hsinmintun to Fakumen, with the ultimate objective of a line through to Aigun far in the north on the Amur river.[48] Governor Tang agreed to the proposal, but wished it widened to include a Manchurian bank "with a capital of 20,000,000 gold dollars" for general financing of Manchurian industries and railroads.[49] Straight, having secured Tang's approval of a tentative draft of this scheme, mailed the document to Mr. Harriman and

[42] Croly, *op. cit.*, p. 235.

[43] Rockhill to Root, Feb. 18, 1907.

[44] Croly, *op. cit.*, p. 207.

[45] Russia, though weakened by the war, was forging steadily ahead in northern Manchuria. In a despatch from Rockhill to Root on July 13, 1906, the American minister lists "the Chinese texts of a number of the more important conventions and agreements" drawn up and signed between Russian agents and Chinese local officials in 1901 and 1902, and which the Russian Government now sought to have recognized by China as binding. The most important convention provided for "the operation of gold, iron and coal mines in Heilung-chiang and Kirin." "Tsarist Russia," writes Kantorovich, "although less active in the Far East after her defeat in the Russian-Japanese War, strengthened her hegemony in northern Manchuria, transforming the actual zones around the Chinese Eastern Railway into its own territory, took over the administration of this territory and established organs of local authority against which China and America vainly protested." Cf. Pokotilov to Izvolsky, Jan. 27, 31, Feb. 6, 12, 19, 1908; Korostovetz to Charykov, Aug. 20, 1908; Krupensky, secret telegram from Washington, Nov. 7, 1909. Kantorovich, *op. cit.*, p. 182; *For. Rel.*, 1910, pp. 203 ff.

[46] "The recent appointment of Tang Shao-yi, a graduate of Columbia University, as governor of this province should signalize the introduction of a business-like administration." Willard Straight to Henry B. Miller, April 24, 1907.

[47] Mukden was the provincial capital of Fengtien as well as the vice-regal capital of Manchuria.

[48] Croly, *op. cit.*, pp. 241–42.

[49] *Ibid.*, p. 242; Morse and MacNair, *op. cit.*, pp. 532–33.

recorded in his diary on August 7, 1907: "Tang approves draft. Letter mailed! Fraught with tremendous possibilities. If adopted it means we play principal part in the development of Manchuria. Our influence in China is tremendously enhanced." [50] This plan, however, was destined to failure. Mr. Harriman, influenced by the financial panic of 1907, was unresponsive; [51] and on November 8, 1907, the British firm of Pauling and Company secured the concession for the building of the proposed railroad from Hsinmintun to Fakumen, to be financed by the British and Chinese Corporation.[52] The Japanese, fearing rivalry to the South Manchurian, fought the British project for over a year, basing their objections upon the so-called secret clauses in the Komura Treaty. The Chinese made vehement denial of having signed such clauses. The British Government decided in favor of the Japanese against their own contractors, and the matter was finally dropped.[53]

In the same month Willard Straight, who, like Witte, was a believer in peaceful penetration through the medium of money, met Secretary of War Taft at Vladivostok and opened conversations with him on the subject of the "investment of American capital in China with the approval and support of the American Government." [54] Secretary Taft was interested but not encouraging although, as Straight recorded in his diary of November 18, Taft "felt strongly that China was turning to us as the one disinterested friend. He hoped that we might do something. I assured him that we could—that now is the time—and that the fruit is ripe and it is ours to pluck. With this he seemed to agree." [55] Straight, acting upon his own initiative, was so successful that when he returned to the United States in September 1908, he carried with him a draft agreement, approved by

[50] Croly, p. 241.
[51] Ibid., p. 242; Morse and MacNair, op. cit., p. 533.
[52] Griswold, op. cit., p. 150; Morse and MacNair, op. cit., p. 533.
[53] Price, op. cit., pp. 47, 137–38; Griswold, op. cit., p. 151. In regard to the secret protocols, concerning the existence and legality of which much has been written, excerpts from the following despatches from the Department of State are of interest. "Tang Shao-yi . . . assures me that there is no agreement or understanding upon which Japan can base legitimate opposition to the building of the new line." Straight to assistant secretary of state Jan. 4, 1908. On Feb. 21, 1908, W. J. Carr, chief clerk for the secretary of state, sent the following reply to Straight: "Your attention is called to the secret protocols of the China-Japan Treaty of 1905, Art. 3, copy of which is enclosed with despatch from the Embassy at Tokyo of Feb. 16, 1906, relating to this subject." On January 19, 1906, Huntington Wilson sent the following message from Tokyo to Secretary of State Root: "I have obtained the Japanese Government's consent to communicate to you in strict confidence the secret protocols of the Peking Treaty if you instruct me to ask them to do so." "Acting upon this instruction," commented Wilson in the despatch of Feb. 16, 1906, "I accordingly made the request. . . . The Minister for Foreign Affairs has today sent me, as strictly confidential, what purports to be a summary in English of those portions of the Peking Protocols which possess the character of executory agreements between Japan and China, and I have the honor to forward herewith a copy of the same." Copy of this despatch is given in the appendix. Cf. Lytton report, supra, p. 131, n. 3.
[54] Croly, op. cit., p. 250.
[55] Ibid.

Governor Tang Shao-yi, which was practically a replica of the one presented to Mr. Harriman the previous year.[56] ". . . It provided for a loan of twenty million dollars for the establishment of a bank which would finance railway construction and mining, timber and agricultural development." [57]

Meanwhile, Governor Tang Shao-yi was on his way to the United States, ostensibly to thank the United States Government for their remittance of the Boxer indemnity [58]—and also to confer in regard to a German-Chinese-American entente—in reality to give assistance to Straight in negotiating the loan.[59] Mr. Harriman and his bankers, Kuhn, Loeb, and Company, who had already been approached by Mr. Straight, looked with favor upon the loan.[60] But cross currents were setting in against the well-laid plans of Willard Straight and Tang Shao-yi. Russian diplomats, penetrating the subterfuge of Tang's mission, and alarmed at its possible effects on Russian interests in Manchuria, sent apprehensive despatches from Peking and Washington to St. Petersburg.[61] The Japanese, equally alarmed, especially over the possibility of an American-Chinese rapprochement, took action.

In October, K. Takahira, Japanese minister to Washington, approached the Department of State with a proposal for an exchange of notes between the Government of the United States and that of Japan on the preservation of the Open Door in China.[62] The notes, known as the Root-Takahira Agreement, were signed on the afternoon of the day (November 30, 1908) that Governor Tang Shao-yi reached Washington.[63] They reaffirmed the principle of the Open Door, and Japan and the United States pledged themselves to maintain "the existing status quo in the region above men-

[56] *Ibid.;* Morse and MacNair, *op. cit.,* p. 534.

[57] Croly, *op. cit.,* p. 272.

[58] *Ibid.* The United States, which was awarded approximately $25,000,000 as her share of the Boxer indemnity, having paid all claims and kept $2,000,000 as a fund for possible future adjustments, in 1908 remitted $10,785,286 of her indemnity. China, however, was to make periodical payments on the full amount of the indemnity, a portion of each payment being returned by the United States. These returned portions were used by the government of China for the education of Chinese students in this country. Treat, *Far East,* pp. 357–59.

[59] Croly, *op. cit.,* pp. 271–72.

[60] *Ibid.,* p. 272.

[61] Arsenyev to Charykov from Peking, Aug. 14, 1908; Korostovetz to Charykov from Peking, Nov. 4, 1908; Krupensky to Izvolsky from Washington, Dec. 9, 1908; Rosen to Izvolsky, Jan. 20, 1909. Kantorovich, *op. cit.,* p. 175.

[62] Croly, *op. cit.,* p. 274.

[63] Price, *op. cit.,* p. 48. Kantorovich states (*op. cit.,* p. 176) that "it was the perspective of an American-Chinese alliance . . . the transformation of Peking into an immediate weapon of American politics which impelled the Tokyo government after it had already concluded in 1907 the first treaty on Manchuria with Tsarist Russia and a political agreement with France, to put out its diplomatic shield in the direction of America." He states further, that Secretary of State Root's assistant, Robert Bacon, admitted to Ambassador Rosen that there was a direct connection between Japan's initiative in the steps that led up to the Root-Takahira agreement and her fear of an American-Chinese entente. Rosen to Izvolsky, Feb. 16, 1909. *Ibid.,* p. 225, n. 171.

tioned," which, according to the introductory paragraph of the agreement, was their respective "important insular possessions in the region of the Pacific Ocean." [64] The ambiguity of the phrasing of this document, with the term status quo undefined, led to at least two interpretations as to the significance of the accord,[65] and convinced both Straight and Tang that "the so-called Root-Takahira Agreement was an attempt on the part of Japan to convince the Chinese of the existence of confidential relations between the United States and Japan and of the hopelessness of securing American assistance against Japanese penetration." [66] It also left the United States in a delicate situation in regard to the projected Manchurian bank. While favoring a project so definitely in harmony with the Government's often avowed policy of the Open Door, the Department of State could not afford to antagonize Japan, who read into the Root-

[64] *For. Rel.*, 1908, p. 510; Bemis, *Diplomatic History*, pp. 495–96; Morse and MacNair, *op. cit.*, p. 536. Commenting on the agreement, Dr. Reid says: "Presumably Roosevelt's chief purpose was to prevent war with Japan, and his ignoring China was a secondary consideration with him. With Japan, nevertheless, it was a paramount consideration." Bryce to Grey, Washington, Dec. 1, 1908. *Brit. Doc.*, VIII, No. 362, 464. John Gilbert Reid, *The Manchu Abdication and the Powers, 1908–1912*, p. 20. The British foreign secretary, Sir Edward Grey, formally congratulated the Tokyo Foreign Office, stating that the agreement was "exceedingly welcome to us." Grey to Bryce, Dec. 4, 1908. *Brit. Doc.* VIII, No. 364, 465–66. The agreement of November 30, 1908, when considered in conjunction with the Taft-Katsura memorandum of July 29, 1905, assumes additional significance. Consequently, the German Government, which favored an anti-Japanese policy, was both surprised and disappointed. *Die Grosse Politik*, No. 8565, n. 2, p. 97. The German Minister at Peking explained the agreement of 1908, (or "armed truce," as he called it), on the grounds that both the United States and Japan wanted to remove the existing threat of war between the two countries. Rex to von Bülow, Peking, Dec. 15, 1908. *Ibid.*

[65] The interpretation commonly given by "American business men and Chinese officials who, at the moment, were seeking to test the validity of the principle of the open door as applied to Manchuria" (Price, *op. cit.*, p. 42), and also given by Griswold (*op. cit.*, p. 129) was that by the use of the term status quo, without definition, the United States Government practically gave Japan a free hand in Manchuria. Straight's record in his diary that the Root-Takahira Agreement "like the Korean withdrawal, was a terrible diplomatic blunder to be laid to the door of T. R." is cited by Griswold (*op. cit.*, p. 139 n.) as further evidence of "Roosevelt's intentional compromise with Japan." Kantorovich, on the other hand, with his usual anti-American bias, sees in Roosevelt's "swan song," as he terms the agreement, "an attempt to capitalize on the support given Japan during the war with Russia by wringing from Japan more concrete obligations in relation to the preservation of the Open Door in China and Manchuria." *Op. cit.*, p. 176.

[66] Croly, *op. cit.*, p. 275. Tsarist diplomats expressed varied opinions in their evaluation of this agreement. Krupensky wrote from Washington, December 9, 1908: "The agreement guarantees the preservation of the *status quo* and the maintenance of peace. . . . It is a big success for the Washington Cabinet." He made the reservation that "the Japanese Government has yet to show that it is being guided in its policies by the principles of this agreement." Rosen (Feb. 16, 1909) also thought that the new confirmation by Japan of the principle of the Open Door and the territorial integrity of China was a victory for America. But Malevski-Malevich, Russian ambassador to Tokyo, on the contrary, on November 20, 1908, reported from Tokyo: "Japanese diplomacy has gained a new triumph, having removed the possibility of an agreement of the United States with China threatening the Japanese position in Manchuria." Kantorovich, *op. cit.*, p. 225, n. 173.

Takahira notes recognition of her status in Manchuria. Any step which Harriman and his bankers might take in the Manchurian plan must therefore be on their own initiative. No active part could be taken by the State Department; it could only stand to one side and "play the part of a complacent abettor." [67] Meanwhile, the death of the Manchu Empress Dowager, and the resultant fall of the government with which Tang Shao-yi was allied, nullified his value as a negotiator.[68] And Willard Straight's second plan for a Manchurian bank, financed by American capital, with its primary objective a wide-open door welcoming American participation in mines, railroads, commerce, and industry, again fell short of fruition.

These failures deterred neither Straight nor Harriman from planning further and more extensive Manchurian penetration. And the inauguration of William Howard Taft in March 1909, with his volte face from the steadily ameliorating Far Eastern policies of Roosevelt to an insistent demand for a wide-open door, was to provide sympathetic and apparently valuable coöperation. "While our foreign policy," said President Taft, expressing the attitude of the new administration toward its foreign program,

should not be turned a hair's breadth from the straight path of justice, it may well be made to include active intervention to secure for our merchandise and our capitalists opportunity for profitable investment which shall inure to the benefit of both countries concerned.[69]

Russian observers in Washington were not long left in doubt as to the Far Eastern policy of the new regime. "The Far East attracts more attention in the United States not only in governmental spheres but also in general society than any other phase of foreign policy," wrote Krupensky from the Russian Embassy at Washington.[70]

The government which in Roosevelt's last year in office had been a "complacent abettor" of the Straight-Tang-Harriman plans for a Manchurian bank, now, with Taft and Secretary of State Knox in charge, became an active promoter in pressing their Far Eastern claims, at the same time widening their sphere to include not only Manchuria but provinces in central and southern China. A loan floated by Germany, France, and Great Britain in May 1909, to finance the construction of the proposed Hukuang Railways which were to extend from Hankow as a center south

[67] Croly, *op. cit.*, p. 271; Griswold, *op. cit.*, p. 152. Morse and MacNair (*op. cit.*, p. 536) state that the Root-Takahira notes made it clear that the Roosevelt administration had given Japan a free hand in Manchuria.

[68] *Ibid.*

[69] Viallate, *op. cit.*, p. 62.

[70] Krupensky to Izvolsky, Washington, July 12, 1909, Kantorovich, *op. cit.*, p. 183. Kantorovich (p. 182), writing of the Taft era, says that "it was characterized to a large degree by a rejection of all idealistic masks, of chatter about honor, prestige and duty which colored the diplomacy of the Rooseveltian epoch."

to Canton and west to Szechwan [71] had refreshed governmental memory as to American interests in the Chinese Empire.

In 1903 and 1904 the Chinese Government had assured Minister Conger,[72] that if foreign capital were needed in the construction of a road from Hankow to Szechwan, the preference would be equally divided between American and British capitalists.[73] The Chinese memory was apparently treacherous. The Department of State protested to the Wai-wu-pu and demanded, on the grounds of the promise to Conger, participation of American capital in the loan,[74] a protest and a demand which went unheeded by the Chinese Government, and which Russian Ambassador Rosen at Washington reported

was not called forth simply by the desire to grant a group of American banks participation in a small railroad loan. In it you see the first step of the administration of Taft on the road to an expansion of the sphere of American interests in China, and the entering of the United States into a more active and influential role in the Far East.[75]

Early in June 1909, a combination of American bankers drafted by the Department of State,[76] and under the management of J. P. Morgan and Company, was formed to "finance any concessions for railroads which American capitalists might obtain from the Chinese Government." [77] This powerful financial group included Morgan; Kuhn, Loeb, and Company; the First National Bank; the National City Bank; and Edward H. Harriman.[78] Whereupon Baron Rosen in another communication to Izvolsky stated that, ". . . Taft is definitely convinced that the United States must play the leading role in the Far Eastern regions, which present an extensive scope for American capital and American enterprise." The Russian Ambassador added that "in view of the especially friendly relations

---

[71] Croly, *op. cit.*, p. 281; Griswold, *op. cit.*, p. 142.

[72] Croly (*op. cit.*, p. 282) believes from records found in Willard Straight's diary of May 24, 1905, that it was Straight who stirred the Department of State to action.

[73] Griswold, *op. cit.*, p. 143 n.; Reid, *op. cit.*, p. 33. For details of the Hukuang Railway Loan see Frederick V. Field, *American Participation in the China Consortiums*, Ch. II; Croly, pp. 281–92; Reid, *op. cit.*, pp. 33–35; *For. Rel.*, 1909, pp. 144 ff. Kantorovich (*op. cit.*, p. 185) states that in March 1905, Conger presented to Washington, "evidently on the initiative of the Chinese Government a project to turn over the Manchurian railroads to China 'under international guarantees.'"

[74] *For. Rel.*, 1909, pp. 155–56. "The State Department's action was prompted 'from political motives and on its own initiative' and not by American financial interests unless Willard Straight may be thus classified." Reid, *op. cit.*, p. 33.

[75] Baron Rosen to Izvolsky, June 23, 1909. Kantorovich, *op. cit.*, p. 187.

[76] The Department of State designated this consortium of American bankers as the "official agent of American railway financing in China." Griswold, *op. cit.*, p. 142; *For. Rel.*, 1916, p. 134; Field, *Consortiums*, pp. 34–36. According to Croly (*op. cit.*, p. 340), "The majority of these bankers had gone into the group not because they were seeking Chinese investments but in order to oblige the administration."

[77] Croly, *op. cit.*, p. 281.

[78] *Ibid.*, pp. 280–85; Field, *op. cit.*, pp. 34–36; Griswold, *op. cit.*, p. 142.

with China, they [the United States] believe that this is the appropriate moment for the strengthening of American influence in China." [79]

Japan as well as Russia was aware of the increasing American interest in China. In a despatch of May 12, 1909, Thomas O'Brien, American ambassador to Japan, enclosed a clipping from a Japanese newspaper, and wrote in part as follows:

The TOKYO HOCHI SHIMBUN, in the accompanying editorial, expresses the fear that the influence of Great Britain and Japan in China is waning while that of the United States and Germany is greatly increasing. . . . It is said that while the mission to the United States of T'ang Shao-Yi was not successful China entertains the friendliest feelings for this country. It even stated that a Chinese-American-German alliance is a possibility. The editorial concludes by saying that Japan and England must work hand in hand to protect their interests in China.[80]

The editorial asks:

What is the real value of the Japanese-American Agreement in relation to this question? What is the present state of friendship between China and America? We do not possess sufficient data to make an exact estimate. All we know is that despite the failure of Tang Shao Yi's mission, the friendship between the two countries is highly intimate.[81]

Meanwhile, as the Chinese Government continued to ignore demands for the participation of American capital in the prospective French-English-German loan, the Department of State brought pressure to bear upon London, Berlin, and Paris for entrance into the consortium upon equal terms.[82] It also intimated to the Chinese Government that continued disregard of the American request might bring about a change in the American attitude toward the Boxer indemnity.[83] The Chinese Foreign Office finally saw the light and assured the American chargé at Peking [84] that it had "notified the representatives of the groups that the loan will not be concluded unless the bankers settle with the American Group." [85] In the meantime, Willard Straight, having left the government service,

---

[79] Rosen to Izvolsky, June 25, 1909. Kantorovich, *op. cit.*, p. 184. According to Krupensky (Russian Chargé, Washington), when Taft appointed Charles Crane United States minister to China in 1909, Mr. Crane believed that his chief duty was to help "American industrialists to establish a firm position in the country which promises to be one of the richest markets in the world." Krupensky to Izvolsky, July 20, 1909. *Ibid.*, p. 227, n. 219.

[80] O'Brien to Phillips, Division of Far Eastern Affairs, Department of State, May 12, 1909.

[81] Editorial, "China, Japan, England, America and Germany," *Hochi Shimbun*, April 19, 1909.

[82] Croly, *op. cit.*, p. 291; Griswold, *op. cit.*, p. 160.

[83] *Ibid.*

[84] In July, 1909, Henry P. Fletcher was sent to Peking by the Department of State to take charge of the political aspects of the negotiations. Croly, *op. cit.*, p. 295.

[85] *Ibid.*, p. 291.

sailed on June 27, 1909, by way of London [86] and Paris,[87] for Peking as agent of the group of American bankers headed by J. P. Morgan and Company. On July 7, he presented a formal demand to the European financiers in London for equal participation of American capital in the railway loan.[88] This demand the foreign bankers refused to consider; and the Department of State, equally inflexible, refused to compromise.[89] Negotiations had apparently come to a standstill when President Taft personally intervened and cabled the Prince Regent of China, insisting that he use his influence to secure "equal participation by American capital in the present railway loan." [90] Concerned, as were all the other representatives of the Great Powers, with the integrity of China, President Taft explained to Prince Ch'un that he had

an intense personal interest in making the use of American capital in the development of China an instrument for the promotion of China, and an increase of her national prosperity without entanglements or creating embarrassments affecting the growth of her independent political power and the preservation of her territorial integrity.[91]

Taft's intervention swung Chinese influence to the American side; and the center of negotiations was changed from Europe to Peking, under the surveillance of the American chargé, Henry Fletcher, and the representative of the American bankers, Willard Straight.[92] Not until the spring of 1910, however, was a reluctant consent for American participation in the loan obtained from Great Britain.

On May 23, 1910, a preliminary agreement was reached, this time to be blocked by the Chinese who, on the verge of revolution and fearing popular opposition, refused to sign, until forced to do so by Great Britain, France, and Germany, assisted by the United States.[93] Minister Calhoun had received instructions not to take the lead in this coercion but to cooperate with the other powers.[94] Despite this coercion of China, the four powers still remained deadlocked, and not until May 10, 1911, was a final

[86] The French, German, and British financial backers of the Hukuang Railways were having a conference in London.

[87] Mr. Straight stopped in Paris to hold conversations with E. H. Harriman in relation to the proposed purchase of the Chinese Eastern Railway.

[88] Croly, *op. cit.*, p. 293; Griswold, *op. cit.*, p. 160.

[89] *Ibid.*, pp. 293–94; *ibid.*, pp. 160–61.

[90] *Ibid.*, p. 295; *ibid.*, p. 161.

[91] Taft to Prince Ch'un, July 15, 1909. *For. Rel.,* 1909, p. 178. At the same time Secretary Knox wired the Chinese Foreign Office advancing arguments similar to those used by President Taft. *For. Rel.,* 1909, p. 178.

[92] Croly, *op. cit.*, p. 295.

[93] Griswold, *op. cit.*, p. 163.

[94] Adee to Calhoun, Oct. 7, 1910. *For. Rel.,* 1910, p. 291. Griswold (*op. cit.*, p. 163) states that this action "hastened the revolutionary *debacle* of the government, to the head of which President Taft had professed only the most disinterested concern for China's welfare."

agreement reached, and the United States became a member on equal terms of the now four-power consortium.[95]

During this time, tension between Russia and Japan, as a result of the latter's aggressiveness in Manchuria, was increasing. True, the secret political agreement with Japan of July 1907, together with the Anglo-Japanese Treaty of August 1905, and the Franco-Japanese agreement of June 1907, had apparently balanced the mutual interests and rights of Russia and Japan in Manchuria, Korea, and North Manchuria. Nevertheless, all reports of Russian diplomatic representatives in Korea, Tokyo, and Peking were unanimous in stating that Japan was systematically making speedy preparations for a new war and was using all of South Manchuria and Korea, with their railway lines, military arsenals, and camps, as a hinterland from which to attack.[96] By the spring of 1909, Japan, according to reports of Tsarist agents, would be in a position to occupy the whole maritime province.[97] The same agents reported that the Japanese were adopting the policy of inciting China against Russia in order to give Japan a pretext for completely removing Russia from the Pacific Ocean area.[98] The Ministry of Foreign Affairs, in an attempt to thwart these designs, proposed in late December 1908, that Russia, the United States, and China join in a triple agreement "on all questions concerning Manchuria and the Pacific Ocean area in general," on the basis "of complete non-interference by the administration of the Chinese Eastern Railway in the

[95] Griswold, *op. cit.*, pp. 163–64.

[96] Romanov states (*op. cit.*, p. 561) that "within the first two weeks after starting war operations," Japan could bring eleven divisions to the Amur region.

[97] *Journal Osobovo Sovestchania* (Journal of Special Conference), of April 27, 1909. Romanov, *op. cit.*, p. 561. Avarin, *op. cit.*, I, 112. With the exception of Reid, other writers, *e.g.* Price, Croly, Griswold, and Treat, in their accounts either ignore or very much underestimate the state of tension between Russia and Japan during these years. Not only Russian sources, but despatches from the United States Embassy at St. Petersburg also, give ample evidence of this tension, especially of Russia's fear of attack from Japan. *Infra,* Schuyler's and Rockhill's despatches of Sept. 27, 1909, and Oct. 2, 1909, respectively, to State Department, p. 152; Schuyler's despatch of Dec. 15, 1909, p. 155, n. 135; statement of governor of Amur as given in Izvolsky's report to Emperor, Nov. 21, 1909, p. 160; Straight's report to Morgan, June 22, 1910, p. 167, n. 26; see also Memorandum of Oct. 7, 1909, Division of Far Eastern Affairs, State Department, p. 151, n. 114. Writing as late as Nov. 23, 1912, Captain H. L. Wigmore, U. S. military attaché, Tokyo, reported to the War Department: "It would appear that last year when the disturbances in China necessitated the dispatch of troops to Pekin and Tientsin, Japan clearly foresaw an attempt by Russia to take over outer Mongolia and to obtain a warm water port for herself. Japan . . . made . . . it clear to Russia that . . . she . . . would protect her own interests in Korea and Manchuria, and that she would not . . . permit the acquirement by Russia of a warm water port. A mutual understanding was thus arrived at, but Japan has been constantly ready to back up her position. It would appear also that Japan has very definite ideas as to her future permanent control or annexation of Manchuria. . . . With China's movement of troops towards Mongolia and Russia's movement of troops into Mongolia, it looks as though Japan is preparing for eventualities and placing herself in readiness to defend her claim to Manchuria."

[98] Letter of Arseniev (secretary of the Russian Legation at Peking) of Jan. 4, 1909. Romanov, *op. cit.*, p. 562.

management of towns and settlements . . . which should be subject to regulations governing foreign settlements." [99]

Running practically parallel in time with these developments were the revived project of Messrs. Harriman and Straight for a world-wide transportation system. Harriman's immediate objective was the purchase and control of the South Manchurian Railway, but the Japanese refused to sell. He therefore attempted to bring Japan to terms by negotiating with Russia for the sale of the Chinese Eastern Railway; and in case this scheme failed, by obtaining the right from China to build a railroad, parallel with the South Manchurian, from Chinchow in Southern Manchuria to Aigun in the extreme north on the Amur river.[100]

As the Chinese Eastern Railway was in bad financial straits,[101] Russia was ready to sell, a recommendation to that effect having been made by B. Arseniev, secretary of the Russian Legation in Peking.[102] Hence, when the Chinese Government on February 1, 1909, presented to Korostovetz, Russian minister to China, an official note providing for the repurchase of the Chinese Eastern Railway, "thus solving all questions, and strengthening bonds of friendship, between the two countries," [103] the note was welcomed by the Russian Government.

Before making the proposal, however, the Chinese Government had been assured of the support of American capitalists who were prepared to subsidize the transaction.[104] The story, as found in Russian sources, is that Gregory Wilenkin, the agent in Washington of the Russian Ministry of Finance, returned to St. Petersburg in the summer of 1908. While there he discussed with Kokovtzev, the minister of finance, the advisability of drawing up an agreement with Japan for the sale of the South Manchurian and the Chinese Eastern Railways to "an international syndicate," and of inviting the American firm of Kuhn, Loeb, and Company to participate in Russian financial operations. Later Wilenkin, with the "approval"

99 Memorandum of the Ministry of Foreign Affairs (without signature) of Dec. 27, 1908. A copy is in Planson's Fund. *Ibid.*, p. 562. Nothing came of this proposal.

100 Reid, *op. cit.*, pp. 46–47; Morse and MacNair, *op. cit.*, p. 536; Croly, *op. cit.*, p. 297; Griswold, *op. cit.*, p. 152. According to Croly, Harriman's aims were not political. He wanted the Manchurian Railways purchased by an international syndicate which, in consequence, would bring about their effective neutralization. Internationalization to Harriman was the means of abolishing Japanese interference with his own plans. Croly, *op. cit.*, p. 298; Griswold, *op. cit.*, p. 153.

101 In 1909, the Chinese Eastern Railway's indebtedness to the Russian Government was approximately 550,577,386 rubles. Romanov, *op. cit.*, pp. 559 ff. John H. Snodgrass, American consul general at Moscow, in a despatch of Oct. 19, 1909 informed the State Department that the Russo-Chinese Railway was reported to be operating at a yearly loss of about $17,500,000.00.

102 Arseniev's memorandum of Jan. 4, 1909, with the Emperor's notation "excellent." Romanov, *op. cit.*, p. 560.

103 Korostovetz to the Russian Foreign Office, telegram, Feb. 2, 1909. Romanov, *op. cit.*, p. 563.

104 *Ibid.*, p. 563. According to Romanov, there are indications that the American capitalists themselves were drawn into the scheme by the Russian Government.

of both Kokovtzev and Foreign Minister Izvolsky, returned to New York
to present the outcome of these discussions to Mr. Schiff of Kuhn, Loeb, and
Company.[105] Wilenkin proposed that Schiff "take the initiative in the
realization of the project" of purchasing the Chinese Eastern and the
South Manchurian Railroads, which would constitute, as Schiff said, "the
internationalizing of both Manchurian railroads." Both Wilenkin and
Schiff considered Japan's participation in the scheme "the first and chief
condition necessary for the success of this project;" and only on the condition that "Russia and Japan will act concurrently" was Schiff willing
to take the initiative in forming "the syndicate which nominally, at least,
would be in American hands." [106]

But at the moment when it appeared that the Russian Government was
close to a successful conclusion of their enterprise, discussions came to a
halt because of the definite refusal of Japan "to entertain any proposal
whatever in regard to the Manchurian railway." [107] Schiff and his associate Harriman were, however, ready "to enter into negotiations with Russia
for the purpose of acquiring the Chinese Eastern Railway for China," irrespective of the results of the negotiations concerning the South Manchurian line.[108] But, following Japan's example, St. Petersburg decided
"to adopt a waiting attitude in order that the initiative of the deal would
not appear to have come from the Russian Government or any of its
agents." Wilenkin was therefore advised to stop "all negotiations with
American capitalists and to let the whole thing take its natural course in
the hope that foreign capitalists, or the Chinese Government themselves,
will approach us with reasonable offers." [109] Meanwhile, in the summer of
1909, Japan became so aggressive in Manchuria [110] that interested Ameri-

[105] Romanov, op. cit., p. 563. Letters of Wilenkin to Kokovtzev of Sept. 15/28 from
New York and of 21 Nov./Dec. 4, 1908 from London, and copy of letter from Schiff
to Wilenkin of Oct. 8, 1908.

[106] Letters from Wilenkin to Kokovtzev of 21 Nov./Dec. 4 and Dec. 1/14, 1908; letter
from Schiff to Wilenkin of Dec. 4, 1908, and also his telegram of Dec. 8, 1908. Romanov,
op. cit., p. 564. Schiff "was drawn into the sphere of Russia's financial operations" by
the "bait" not only of "industrial orders" but by the prospect of colossal financial, commercial and political profits connected with these undertakings." Ibid.

[107] Romanov, op. cit., p. 565. Wilenkin and Schiff counted on the support of the Japanese minister of communications, Baron Goto, with whom the matter had been discussed, and of the director of the Japanese bank, Mr. Tagakami, who already had begun
negotiations with Wilenkin in June and had promised his coöperation to Schiff. Ibid.
Meanwhile, Japan had managed to realize on the London market a South Manchurian
loan of two million pounds sterling which made it possible for her "not to hurry;" and
in China "political events," such as the death of the Empress Dowager on November 15,
1908, and the fall of Yuan Shih-k'ai on January 2, 1909, prompted the Tokyo Government "to await patiently the development of further events." Letter of Wilenkin to
Kokovtzev from Tokyo, Feb. 9/22, 1909. Ibid., p. 565.

[108] Ibid.

[109] Letter from Kokovtzev to Wilenkin, March 21, 1909. Ibid.

[110] Presentation of an ultimatum to China on Aug. 12: the Sino-Japanese agreement of
September 4, 1909, concerning the Antung–Mukden, the Changchun–Kirin Railways and
the Chientao region; and the retention by Japan of the Fushun and Yentai coal mines.
Romanov, op. cit., pp. 565–66. See C. Walter Young, The International Relations of
Manchuria, pp. 67–84.

can circles were apprehensive and considered "the necessity of concluding an understanding with Russia in view of Japan's threat to China's independence." [111] On the 23rd of August, Chargé d'affaires Henry Fletcher, sent to Peking by the Department of State in July, wrote in part to Secretary of State Knox:

. . . . As a result of the surrender to Japan on most points involved in the Manchurian questions, the Chinese are now more anxious than ever to secure concrete American and other non-Japanese interests in Manchuria, and a favorable opportunity is presented to the American group which is appreciated and will be taken advantage of by their representative, Mr. Straight.

Mr. Fletcher again wrote to Secretary Knox in regard to agreements signed on the 4th of September by Japan and China:

. . . . I stated that my government could not but feel strong objections to any agreement debarring American citizens from such a wide field of enterprise in contravention of the principle of the open door. . . . I have intimated to the Wai-wu-pu that if the agreement reached should be found to violate the principle of the open door and of equal commercial opportunity in Manchuria it would be a matter of serious concern to us.[112]

These agreements [113] led to a frequent exchange of American notes between Peking and Washington,[114] and to caustic comments in the Japanese press.

Not only Washington, but St. Petersburg as well, was aroused. Evidence of the growing distrust of Japan by Russia and of the latter's desire for a working arrangement with the United States may be seen in the despatches received by the State Department from St. Petersburg during the autumn of 1909. "Ever since the conclusion of the Treaty of Portsmouth," wrote Montgomery Schuyler, American chargé, from the United States Embassy at St. Petersburg,

the distrust of the Japanese by the Russians has been constantly increasing. Before and even during the late war the peoples of the two countries did not dislike each other. . . . During the past three years, however, the feelings of the majority of the Russian people have greatly changed with regard to the action and

---

[111] Cf. telegram of Somov from Seoul of Sept. 11, 1909, with Nicholas' annotation "At last!" *Arkhiv Revolutzii i Vneshnei Politiki,* Moscow. (Archives of Revolution and Foreign Policy), report of 1909. Romanov, *op. cit.,* p. 566.

[112] H. P. Fletcher to Knox, Sept. 6, 1909.

[113] *Supra,* p. 150, n. 110.

[114] "The object of the Japanese forcing the Manchurian agreement upon China is to secure such control of the mineral resources and transportation facilities of Manchuria and possibly Manchuria itself as will enable her to exploit that country. There are many indications that Japan has designs on Manchuria. . . . Her reasons . . . not only commercial . . . but strategic. They realize possibility of another conflict with Russia and the desirability of having two lines connecting the southern part of Korea with North Manchuria. . . . A joint protest by the United States and other powers should be made." General Memorandum regarding the Recent Chinese Japanese Agreements respecting Manchuria. [Signed by E. C. B.—Edward C. Baker] Division of Far Eastern Affairs, Department of State, Oct. 7, 1909.

policies of the Japanese Government. From a condition of almost apathy, the Russian public is rapidly working itself into a state of intense interest over the situation in the Far East and the ultimate intentions of Japan in that part of the world.[115]

In view of these conditions, the Russian Foreign Office, as reported by Mr. Schuyler, was eager to obtain an American-Russian entente, convinced that it would be useful for "subserving the interests of peace and harmony in Asia" by putting "a check upon the ambitions of Japan in Asia."

"It was not . . . until the conclusion of the Chinese-Japanese agreement of September 4," wrote Mr. Schuyler,

that apprehension of trouble in the Far East and the need of assuring a permanent peace there became acute in Russia. For more than a year the "Novoe Vremya" . . . had been advocating the need of an American-Russian entente to round out and complement in a satisfactory manner the existing agreements regarding the Far East, but the matter has not received much attention from responsible persons until lately. At present . . . it would seem as if the time were ripe for informal discussion of this question by the two Governments. The arguments of the "Novoe Vremya" may be stated briefly as suggesting the necessity of an informal instrument which while free from the obnoxious provisions of formal treaties would just as well subserve the interests of peace and harmony in Asia. The importance of the interests of the United States in Manchuria and the Far East . . . is recognized as sufficient to warrant the conclusion of such an arrangement . . . and it is believed that no nation would be willing to run counter to the wishes of those two Powers. It would serve moreover as a check upon the ambitions of Japan which are now seen to be boundless on the continent of Asia and would be productive of much good and no evil.[116]

Since the United States, as viewed by "responsible persons" in St. Petersburg, is looked upon "as the balance of power and the preserver of peace in 'Asia," an entente between Russia and the United States Government, in the opinion of Mr. Schuyler "merits the most careful attention." [117]

Reporting on the proposed, but vaguely defined, American-Russian "understanding," and requesting instructions as to his "future course of action," Ambassador Rockhill wrote:

I have not heard what form the Russian Government would like to see given to the understanding with the United States. . . . Probably the scheme is still in the embryonic stage. It may well be . . . that the Notes exchanged in November last between the United States and Japan declaring their intentions and policies in the Pacific and the Far East, may have suggested to their minds the desirability of taking a somewhat similar step.[118]

In reply, Huntington Wilson, acting secretary of state, informed Ambassador Rockhill that "pending the consideration by the Department of

[115] Schuyler to State Department, Sept. 27, 1909. Confirmed by the despatch of Rockhill to State Department, Oct. 2, 1909. Rockhill had been appointed ambassador to Russia the previous May.

[116] Schuyler to State Department, Sept. 27, 1909.

[117] *Ibid.*

[118] Rockhill to State Department, Oct. 2, 1909.

the Manchurian question as a whole," his attitude "regarding the matter should be receptive." [119] While copies of Schuyler's despatch of September 27, 1909, and Rockhill's of October 2, 1909, were sent by Mr. Wilson to Henry P. Fletcher, chargé at Peking, there is nothing in the records of the State Department to indicate that the United States was interested in following up Russia's vague proposal.[120]

Meanwhile, the death of E. H. Harriman had occurred on September 10, 1909. After Harriman's death, Straight did his utmost to present to members of the Group in New York the more important aspects of Harriman's Manchurian Railway plans. In these efforts Straight was unsuccessful. Above all, no one in the Group apparently realized the necessity of securing Russia's coöperation. Straight's suggestion to send an agent to Russia was turned down.[121] "No one in New York," wrote Straight later, "knew precisely what Mr. Harriman had in mind. No one was capable of carrying through his scheme. The directing genius had gone." [122]

That Willard Straight continued to push Harriman's plans may be seen by a despatch from Peking of September 17.

Mr. Straight, in conjunction with Lord ffrench, the representative of Pauling & Company, has submitted a proposal to the Chinese for the financing and construction of this line [the Chinchow-Aigun] and its operation by a company composed of Chinese, British and Americans after its construction. This proposal has been received with favor and negotiations are now proceeding with reference to it. If the enterprise is undertaken it will no doubt encounter the objection of the Japanese on the same ground that they opposed the Hsinmintun-Fakumen line, the contract for the construction of which, the Department will recall, had been given to the same firm of Pauling & Company.[123]

On October 2, 1909, Straight, acting on his own initiative, signed a formal preliminary agreement with the Manchurian viceroy on behalf of the American group of bankers and the British contractors, Pauling and Company, for the financing and construction, respectively, of some 750 miles of railroad between Chinchow and Aigun.[124] Six days later the American bankers notified Mr. Straight that they did not wish to enter into a contract until definite results had been reached in regard to the Hukuang Railway

[119] Wilson to Rockhill, Oct. 19, 1909.

[120] A number of despatches during this period from the American Embassy at St. Petersburg to the State Department make reference to certain official quarters in Russia which strongly favor the sale of the Chinese Eastern Railway to American capitalists. Schuyler to State Department telegram, Oct. 25, 1909; Schuyler to State Department telegram, Nov. 19, 1909. Also, Snodgrass, American Consulate, Moscow, to State Department, Oct. 19, 1909, No. 39. The State Department in a reply of October 30, 1909, instructed the Embassy to assume "a receptive attitude" and to report developments in detail. The following month Rockhill presented the text of a plan for the neutralization of the Manchurian railways.

[121] Croly, op. cit., pp. 306, 308–09, 320.

[122] The details of Harriman's plan are summarized by Straight in a letter to Schiff. Ibid., p. 309.

[123] Fletcher to Secretary of State Knox, Sept. 17, 1909.

[124] Croly, op. cit., p. 303; Price, op. cit., p. 48; Griswold, op. cit., p. 153.

loan.[125] Later in the month, Prince Ito, who had favored the sale of the South Manchurian Railway was assassinated by a Korean fanatic, following a conference with Kokovtsev and Korostovetz in Harbin on Russo-Japanese problems.[126]

Kokovtsev, upon his return to St. Petersburg, favored the selling of the Chinese Eastern Railway, but was opposed by Izvolsky who was inclined to an entente with Japan.[127] In a letter to J. P. Morgan and Company on November 10, 1909, Willard Straight gave warning of Russia's tightening opposition to the American plan:

> M. Korostovetz, the Russian Minister, returned to Peking on November 1st. Through various channels he intimated to Mr. Fletcher [chargé at Peking] and myself that unless the Group were prepared to come to some understanding he feared that M. Kokovtseff, the Minister of Finance, would make a pact with Japan.[128]

Mr. Fletcher's reply was not such as to foster a more favorable attitude on the part of Russia toward the United States. "The American government was committed to certain principles," he said, which "it would continue to uphold . . . no matter whether the opposition came from Russia and Japan acting individually or together." [129]

In view of this background of events, when members of the American Embassy in St. Petersburg talked persuasively in early November 1909, "about the necessity for Russia to go hand in hand with the United States in regard to Manchurian affairs," and Ambassador Rockhill offered Izvolsky a "combination" which would put a final and, so to speak, "international limit to further Japanese seizures," the Russian Foreign Office regarded these proposals as another version of the "commercial neutralization of the Manchurian railway lines" which the previous year had been advocated by Wilenkin.[130] Izvolsky drew the attention of the American ambassador to the fact that even if neutralization of Manchuria were ef-

---

[125] A little over a month later the American Government took up the Chinchow–Aigun Railway project, and the preliminary agreement signed by Straight was confirmed by Imperial Edict on January 21, 1910, followed by a construction contract signed April 26, 1910. Price, *op. cit.*, p. 48.

[126] Reid, *op. cit.*, p. 61; Croly, *op. cit.*, p. 310.

[127] *Ibid.*, p. 61; *ibid.*, pp. 310–11.

[128] Croly, *op. cit.*, p. 321; Reid, *op. cit.*, p. 61. Straight wanted to negotiate with St. Petersburg and cabled New York for permission, which was granted. He decided not to go ahead, however, until China had issued the ratification edict. The publication of the edict was delayed and negotiations were not begun. Croly, *op. cit.*, p. 321.

[129] Reid, *op. cit.*, p. 61; Croly, *op. cit.*, p. 321.

[130] Romanov, *op. cit.*, p. 566. In a confidential letter to the Russian ambassador in London on January 13, 1910, Izvolsky wrote in part as follows: "As soon . . . as Rockhill took up his new post at St. Petersburg he began to prepare us for a somewhat indefinite proposal of united procedure in the Far East. . . . Rockhill, at first in personal discussions, and later in the name of his Government, developed a plan which he termed the 'commercial neutralization' of Manchuria. . . . Later, we were also handed the complete text by Rockhill. . . ." G. A. De Siebert and Schreiner, *Entente Diplomacy and the World*, pp. 13–15.

fected in "a formal manner," as Rockhill suggested, it still would not save Russia from further attacks by Japan in the Amur province. On the contrary, it could be expected that Japan "having lost, under outer pressure, its predominant position in South Manchuria, would try to attempt to recompense itself at our expense" in the Maritime Provinces.[131]

On the same day that Rockhill made his offer, and immediately after he had left, Baron Motono, Japanese minister at St. Petersburg, called on Izvolsky and proposed a "formal alliance" before which "not only China but also all other powers will bow." In this manner, Motono argued, Russia, backed by Japan, would be able to "insist on the rights of the Chinese Eastern Railway Company provided for in the contract of 1896." Izvolsky saw other advantages. Such an alliance would guarantee to Russia protection in the rear in case of war, and eventually would lead to "a common Russian-Japanese guardianship" over Manchuria and even over entire China, in contrast to the aspirations of American and West-European powers."[132] Faced with the "necessity of choosing a *final decisive* attitude toward our Far Eastern policy," Tsar Nicholas II who previously, on five occasions, had been inclined to accept the American project [133] was now convinced that Russia's only hope "was a very close agreement with Japan." The die was cast. A second Russo-Japanese treaty was on the way.[134]

After making the decision to enter into a formal agreement with Japan, the Russian Government, as reported by Montgomery Schuyler, tried to quiet the apprehension that war with Japan was imminent which was "steadily increasing among all classes of Russian society at an astonishing rate," by publishing an official communiqué on December 15, 1909, which categorically declared that all such rumors were groundless.[135]

While events between St. Petersburg and Tokyo were gradually following their course, the Department of State at Washington, disregarding the hesitation of the American bankers, took action.[136] On November 6, 1909, Secretary of State Knox, using as a nucleus the Manchurian railway projects of the late E. H. Harriman, made two proposals to Sir Edward Grey, the British Foreign Minister. The first was that Great Britain join the United States in bringing about complete neutralization of all the railways

---

[131] Report of Izvolsky of Nov. 21, 1909, *Arkhiv Revolutzii i Vneshnei Politiki*. Romanov, *op. cit.*, p. 566.

[132] *Ibid.*, p. 567.

[133] Avarin, *op. cit.*, I, 118. Nicholas, dreaming of his Korean concessions and of the money he might make by selling them to the Americans, caused the St. Petersburg Government to vacillate, in the beginning, on the question of the American proposition.

[134] Romanov, *op. cit.*, p. 567.

[135] Schuyler to Secretary of State, Dec. 15, 1909. On December 24, Schuyler again reports "concerning the great apprehension in Russia as to trouble between Russia and Japan," and encloses press clippings.

[136] On November 6, the Group in New York informed Straight that the preliminary Mukden contract which he had signed on October 2 was "entirely satisfactory." Henry Davison to Straight, from New York, Nov. 6, 1909. Croly, *op. cit.*, p. 306 n.; Reid, *op cit.*, p. 61.

in Manchuria; the second, given as an alternative in case the neutralization plan was not acceptable, that Great Britain and the United States together with other "interested powers," should unite in the financing and construction of the proposed Chinchow-Aigun Railway, with China as the nominal owner.[137]

The British reply, although approving the "general principle" of the neutralization plan, urged its postponement until the pending negotiations for the Hukuang loan had been settled, and touched lightly upon the Chinchow-Aigun alternative.[138] Mr. Knox, undeterred by British negativism, presented his twofold plan to Tokyo on December 18–20, Peking on December 21, Paris and Berlin on December 17–18, 1909, assuring them of Great Britain's "approval in principle," and asking for their coöperation.[139] Both Peking and Berlin approved the Knox memorandum. On December 20 the Russian Government received the proposal for neutralization from Ambassador Rockhill, who withheld the alternative Chinchow-Aigun proposition, of which Russia learned only through her ambassadors.[140]

Two grave errors, as seen in the light of results, were made in carrying out the Knox proposals. First, the American Government, relying apparently on the "approval in principle" of Great Britain, the ally of Japan, failed to consult with Russia and Japan, the two powers having vital interests in the Manchurian railways, before extending their international

[137] Reid, *op. cit.,* p. 61. The full terms of the proposals are found in *For. Rel.,* 1910, pp. 234–35; Griswold, *op. cit.,* p. 154; Morse and MacNair, *op. cit.,* pp. 537–38.

[138] Grey to Reid, Nov. 25, 1909. *For. Rel.,* 1910, pp. 235–36. Sir Edward Grey suggested, however, that the United States and Great Britain should unite in an endeavor to persuade China to admit Japan, as the most interested party, as a participant in the Chinchow-Aigun proposition.

[139] Reid, *op. cit.,* p. 70.

[140] J. O. P. Bland, *Recent Events and Present Policies in China,* pp. 318–19. See also Reid, *op. cit.,* pp. 70, 84. Certain writers, among them Price (*op. cit.,* p. 49), Griswold (*op. cit.,* pp. 154–55), and Bemis, *Diplomatic History,* (p. 497) state that both the neutralization proposal and the Chinchow-Aigun alternative were presented to Russia at the same time. Mr. Bland, on the contrary, writes that Ambassador Rockhill took the responsibility of withholding the Chinchow-Aigun proposal and of presenting only the neutralization scheme to the Russian Government. He was aware, according to Mr. Bland, that the Chinchow-Aigun alternative ran counter to the terms of the Portsmouth Treaty in which Russia and Japan were pledged not to obstruct China's free hand in development of commerce and industry in Manchuria, and, using his own discretion, presented only the neutralization plan. The following American despatch from St. Petersburg verifies Mr. Bland's statement as to the presentation of only the neutralization scheme: . . . "Referring to your telegrams of November 6th and December 14th, . . . both concerning the complete neutralization of the railways of Manchuria, I have the honor to inform you that in compliance with the latter telegram, I handed to the Minister of Foreign Affairs, Mr. Iswolsky, a formal Note with accompanying Aide-Memoire, embodying the views of the Department of State as set forth in the telegram of November 6th, regarding the neutralization project. . . ." Montgomery Schuyler to secretary of state, Dec. 20, 1909. Cf. memorandum of Knox to Russian ambassador of February 8, 1910 (*Infra,* p. 163 and n. 8), in which Mr. Knox gives a version of Rockhill's reason for withholding the document which does not agree with that of Mr. Bland.

invitations.[141] The second error was the one made by Ambassador Rockhill in arousing the suspicions of the Russian Government by allowing them to learn at second-hand, through their ambassadors, of the Chinchow-Aigun alternative. They "naturally jumped to the conclusion that the American Government was playing a double game." [142]

The success of the neutralization of the Manchurian railways depended, as Mr. Harriman had foreseen, on separating Russia from Japan; yet "everything was done to irritate Russian sensitiveness and to lay the foundation for the predatory pact [July 4, 1910] which has since dominated the Far Eastern situation." [143]

Foreign Minister Izvolsky, who, wavering slightly at the beginning, had opposed the sale of the Chinese Eastern and had worked toward a Russo-Japanese entente, was to be left, as the result of the Knox diplomacy, holding the trump card.

The foreign politics of Russia are always largely dependent on the personal equation, on individual sympathies and the antipathies in high places, on the right word to the right man at the right time, on graceful amenities and social functions. Here was an occasion for delicate handling, not for blacksmith work. Mr. Knox's manner of presenting the neutralization scheme played directly into Mr. Iswolsky's hands; upon it he built up a formidable bogey of America's anti-Russian policy in the Far East and used it to persuade his colleagues that the best protection for Russian interests lay in a *rapprochement* with Japan.[144]

Kantorovich states that "Tsarist Russia and Japan naturally received the plan for neutralization with indignation," feeling insulted by the assurance that it "presented special privileges to Russia and Japan." [145] And Charles Beard writes that,

141 Bland, *op. cit.,* p. 317; Croly, *op. cit.,* p. 316. The policy of the Taft-Knox administration ignored the interpretation of the Root-Takahira notes that gave Japan a practically free hand in Manchuria. Bemis, *Diplomatic History,* p. 496.

142 Bland, *op. cit.,* p. 319. In view of the favorable exchanges which had taken place between the United States and Russia in respect to the Chinese Eastern Railway, it would logically seem that Russia instead of Great Britain should have been approached first with the twofold proposal. In this manner an entering wedge might conceivably have been driven between the loosely united interests of Russia and Japan. And Izvolsky might not so frequently have reiterated that, "The policy of the United States in Manchuria was driving Russia into the arms of Japan." Rockhill to Knox, Jan. 24, 1910.

143 Bland, *op. cit.,* p. 319. In a discussion of the presentation of the Knox plan, Professor Clyde states that the "closer relationship between Japan and Russia" was "the inevitable result of the diplomatic blundering which sought to internationalize Manchurian railways at a time when even the most tactful approach to the subject would probably have met with a similar failure." Paul H. Clyde, *International Rivalries in Manchuria,* p. 200. The writer shares this viewpoint. Japan's increasing power in the Far East; Russia's fear of Japan's military strength; and the secret approval by England and France of closer Russo-Japanese rapprochement in order not to disturb the delicate balance either in Europe or the Far East: these are facts which make it appear unlikely that any diplomatic handling of the situation by the United States, no matter how skillful could have been successful. The American policy only hastened, it is probable, that which was already inevitable.

144 Bland, *op. cit.,* pp. 319-20.

145 *Op. cit.,* p. 190. According to the German ambassador, Knox expected his neu-

frightened by the news, St. Petersburg and Tokyo, now convinced that the open-door policy was in reality a subterfuge to cover an American invasion of their Chinese property, started negotiations looking to advantages in their mutual concerns. . . .[146]

On December 17, 1909, Malevski-Malevich, Russian ambassador at Tokyo, reported the Japanese Baron Goto as saying:

That which Russia and Japan obtained in Manchuria by the blood of their sons and the expenditure of billions of national money, the Anglo-American bankers wish to receive by means of simple exchange abominations. In this way there is not only being created competition for the roads which are now in the possession of Russia and Japan but also a counterweight to their political influence. . . .[147]

And a Russian writer feels that while American pressure was directed against both countries it was felt more by Russia than by Japan since the former was the weaker at that time.[148]

A despatch from Peking to the State Department on January 19, 1910, shows the direction that Russo-Japanese plans were taking:

Strictly confidential. I am informed by private and confidential verbal message from Liang Tun Yen that the Japanese Secretary of Legation called upon him today and stated that Japan was displeased with the American proposal for the neutralization of the Manchurian railways and to intimate that China had insti-gated the scheme. He . . . mentioned a Russian-Japanese coalition as a possible result and said that Russia and Japan were likely to come to an agreement and would probably give their answers simultaneously to the United States.[149]

And the next day, Secretary Knox received the following despatch from Ambassador Rockhill:

. . . . He [Izvolsky] then said that, as he wanted to be "absolutely frank" with us, he would not conceal the fact that the Russian Government considered that it had been badly treated in the matter of the Chinchow-Aigun Railway; that Russia was the Power most interested in the matter from the military, economic, and political points of view, yet it was the last to be informed of it. Japan had been approached by us months before and Russia had been told of it for the first time only when the concession had been actually made and approved by the Chi-nese Government. He said that the Russian Government could not but fear that the United States had not only economic interests in view but ulterior political interests which might very seriously conflict with those of Russia; otherwise why should we have agreed to support diplomatically the construction of a line a con-siderable part of which (from Tsitsihar to Aigun) had no other than a strategic

tralization plan to "smoke Japan out." Von Bernstorff to Foreign Office, Dec. 30, 1909. *Die Grosse Politik,* XXXII, 71. Reid, *op. cit.,* p. 75.

[146] C. A. and M. R. Beard, *op. cit.,* II, 499.

[147] Kantorovich, *op. cit.,* p. 190.

[148] E. D. Grimm, *"Kitaiskii Vopros ot Simonosekskogo Mira do Mirovoi Voiny"* ("The Chinese Question from the Shimonoseki Peace to the World War"), *Novyi Vostok* (New East), VI, 60.

[149] Fletcher to Knox, Jan. 19, 1910.

value? We were aiding China in her aggressive policy against Russia. . . . The Russian reply might make suggestions which would put to the test the sincerity of American professions, and determine whether they are, as we say, of an economic nature and in the interests of peace. The Chinchow-Aigun project as it now stands is not in the interests of peace, but means aggressive designs on the part of China. . . .[150]

On January 21, another despatch arrived from St. Petersburg:

Memorandum replying yours neutralization Manchurian Railways just received. Iswolsky says it has received very serious consideration. . . . At the present moment nothing seems to threaten sovereignty of open door; consequently the Russian Government sees no necessity for immediate consideration questions raised. Declares that the proposed international control of Manchurian Railroads would gravely affect very important Russian interests, public and private. The project cannot therefore be received favorably. . . .

Concerning the alternative scheme, Russian Government considers Chinchow-Aigun Railway affect Russia vitally; opens a new line on its railway and Russian possessions. This shows its political and strategical importance. It would also modify relations of the railway with Eastern Mongolia and North Manchuria. The Russian Government can only determine its attitude towards the project and participation when informed of details. . . . The Russian Government reserves the right for all future projects for its financial participation in railways in Manchuria to examine them from political and military point of view and in relation to Chinese Eastern Railway. . . .[151]

Three factors primarily had made the rejection of Knox's neutralization plan inevitable. First, the inability of both the group of bankers and the State Department to understand the complicated nature of European *Realpolitik;* [152] second, their failure to take advantage of those Russian forces that preferred an agreement with the United States to one with Japan; third, their failure to grasp the fact that Japan, comparatively close to Russia, presented a more formidable Russian menace than did the United States with an ocean between.

The final step was taken on January 21, 1910, when Japan and Russia, who had entered into communication almost immediately after receiving the Knox proposals, rejected the plan for neutralization of the Manchurian railways in practically identic notes.[153] Their professed adherence to the

---

150 Rockhill to Knox, Jan. 20, 1910.

151 Rockhill to Knox, January 21, 1910.

152 It may be assumed that Taft and Knox did not understand the ramifying web of European power politics of which the Far East was inextricably a part. Both Britain and France sympathized with Japanese imperialism in Manchuria in order to divert it from their own political and economic areas of interest in China, Indo-China, India, and Tibet. Further, England and France required Japan's support against Germany's increasing power on the continent and were willing to pay for it by favoring her expansionist plans in Manchuria and Mongolia.

153 Avarin, *op. cit.,* I, 117; Price, *op. cit.,* p. 52; Reid, *op. cit.,* p. 93; Griswold, *op. cit.,* p. 155; De Siebert and Schreiner, *op. cit.,* p. 12. "Within the last few days I also had occasion to report to you that I had been informed by a thoroughly reliable person that in reaching the conclusions embodied in the Aide-Memoire on the subject of the

principles of the Open Door and the territorial integrity of China had been put to the acid test. They had met it by slamming the swinging door of Manchurian opportunity in the face of the diplomacy of the Taft-Knox administration.[154]

The historian Romanov states the Japanese advantage as follows:

To resist Japan [he says] America had only a plan for the "commercial neutralization of Manchurian railways," while Japan, by her eleven divisions stationed in Korea, could capture Vladivostok in two days and occupy the Maritime province in two weeks, as the Amur Governor General, Unterberger, stated. The choice was naturally made in favor of Japan.[155]

Or, as Izvolsky summed up the situation later at a cabinet meeting on Far Eastern affairs:

If we reject the American proposal, we will call forth the temporary cooling off of American friendship, but America will not declare war on us for this and its fleet will not arrive in Harbin, while in this connection Japan is considerably more dangerous.[156]

To borrow a term from Izvolsky, Russia's *politique mesquine* in the Far East was undoubtedly a policy of necessity instead of choice, perhaps intended to be abandoned when Russia was stronger. "Nevertheless, two former rivals were now united in opposing a third rival of both." [157]

---

neutralization of the Manchurian railways, the Russian Government had been in constant communication with Japan." Rockhill to Knox, Jan. 24, 1910. Neither Japan nor Russia rejected the Chinchow-Aigun proposal at this time.

[154] While public opinion in Japan was practically unanimous in supporting the reply of the Japanese Government, there was by no means unanimity of opinion in Russia in regard to the Russian reply. Comments in the St. Petersburg press on January 22 were "distinctly divided along purely political lines." The Government and conservative. papers were definitely against the Knox plan, the liberal papers were for it, and both were "disposed to favor a fuller consideration" of Russia's participation in the Chinchow-Aigun railway project. Reid, *op. cit.*, p. 97.

[155] Izvolsky's report to the Emperor of Nov. 21, 1909, concerning both proposals (America's and Japan's). *Arkhiv Revolutzii i Vneshnei Politiki, Ibid.*, p. 567.

[156] *Journal Osobovo Sovestchania* (Journal of Special Conference), of Dec. 11, 1909, No. 206. Avarin, *op. cit.*, I, 123.

[157] Reid, *op. cit.*, p. 96.

Chapter VII

FAILURE OF DOLLAR DIPLOMACY
IN MANCHURIA

THE fate of Secretary Knox's neutralization scheme had practically been settled by the Russian and Japanese replies of January 21, 1910. The Chinchow-Aigun project was still suspended. The consent of Russia and Japan to this plan, although in every way desirable, was not legally essential to the construction of the proposed line. China, to whom Manchuria in accordance with the provisions of the Portsmouth Treaty had been nominally returned, was technically free to build railways where she chose, financed by capital wherever she could find it, provided these lines did not infringe upon rights and concessions granted other countries. The Imperial Edict of January 21, 1910 [1] had already confirmed the preliminary agreement of October 2, 1909, signed by the Manchurian viceroy as representative of China and by Willard Straight on behalf of the American bankers and the British firm of Pauling and Company. Russia, weakened by the war of 1904–1905, struggling to regain a foothold in Manchuria against Japan, was not, when isolated, a formidable obstacle. United, however, Russia and Japan would constitute a dangerous menace to China's freedom of action. The possibility of a closer union than that of July 1907, was increased by the fact that France and Great Britain, interested not only in the Far East, but in the protection of their respective European frontiers, had turned away from the American-Chinese proposal, and secretly encouraged such a liaison between their allies.

Early in January 1910, Japan, through Prime Minister Katsura, had already made overtures to the Russian ambassador at Tokyo, stating that,

The steps taken by America are evidently based upon a belief that Russia mistrusts Japan. . . . It would be very desirable to give a visible manifestation of the will of both governments to put an end to this incorrect interpretation and to all hostile intrigues.[2]

A little later in the month American diplomats in the Far East saw signs on the international horizon of the approaching closer alliance be-

[1] *North China Herald,* January 1910. Price, p. 48.
[2] Malevsky-Malevich (Russian ambassador, Tokyo) to Izvolsky, Jan. 8, 1910. Kantorovich, *op. cit.,* p. 193, n. 276.

tween Russia and Japan.[3] On January 24th the American ambassador at
St. Petersburg in a despatch to the Department of State wrote:

In previous dispatches I have had occasion to refer to the remarks frequently
made to me by the Minister for Foreign Affairs [Isvolsky] that the policy of the
United States in Manchuria was driving Russia into the arms of Japan and that
we were encouraging an aggressive policy on the part of China.

I have reported to you also that in the conversation which I had . . . with
the Emperor, . . . His Majesty referred to the desire of the Japanese to reach
a closer understanding with Russia. . . . A section of the Russian press . . .
now finds that a complete identity of interests exists between the two countries in Far Eastern affairs, and that the opportunity should not be lost for per-
fecting an understanding between Russia and Japan which would, in their
opinion, insure the maintenance of their present positions, the conservancy of
their present interests, political as well as economic, in Manchuria, against any
and all other adverse interests and insure the peace of the Far East. . . . The fear
of a near renewal of hostilities with Japan which has for the last few months been
so strong in Russian government circles and in the public press is for the time
forgotten, and the conclusion of a formal "entente" with Japan is advocated as
the best, the only, safeguard of peace. . . .

This proposal for an entente between Russia and Japan was, Mr. Rockhill continued, supported by France and "to some degree" by Great Britain. He cited from the French press to show the trend of French thought,
and concluded that this tendency was "worthy of more than passing notice," since nothing could "be more dangerous for the peace of the Far
East and the normal development of our interests in that region" than an
arrangement between Russia and Japan which might result in "the practical dividing of Manchuria between the two Powers."[4]

Meanwhile, Mr. Knox, on January 20, had cabled Ambassador Rockhill
directing him to approach the Russian Government with a request for
opportunity to present fuller explanations concerning the "motive and
scope of the proposals recently submitted for the neutralization of the
railways in Manchuria."[5] Izvolsky, in reply, expressed his pleasure at the
prospect of further enlightenment "on the subject of the Chinchow-Aigun
Railway scheme, which is the only present subject of discussion."[6] Having
in this negative manner shown his lack of interest in further information
about the "motive and scope" of the neutralization project, the Russian
foreign minister again voiced his grievances against the American Government:

Concerning the Chinchow-Aigun railway scheme, [Izvolsky said] it was difficult
for Russia not to feel aggrieved at the way we had treated her in this matter, which

[3] Willard Straight as early as November 18, 1909, had notified J. P. Morgan of a warning he had received from the Russian minister at Peking that a pact was imminent
between Russia and Japan. Croly, op. cit., p. 321.

[4] Rockhill to Knox, Jan. 24, 1910.

[5] Rockhill to Knox, Jan. 29, 1910. In this despatch Rockhill gives the content of the
cablegram sent by Knox on January 20.

[6] Rockhill to Knox, Jan. 29, 1910.

affects her interests vitally; the first intimation Russia had had of this affair was the Memorandum of December last, when the contract for the construction of the line had already been awarded by the Chinese Government, and two months after we had approached Japan on the subject. . . .[7]

On February 8, Mr. Knox presented to the Russian Government a memorandum in which he explained the purpose and extent of not only the Chinchow-Aigun scheme, but of the already rejected neutralization project, gave assurance of the willingness of the British Government "to give diplomatic support to the Chinchow-Aigun project," apologized for Mr. Rockhill's failure to present the latter project to the Russian Government on December 14, and stated that Mr. Rockhill

had been given liberty to make informal use of the facts relative to the Manchurian project which were then in his possession for his information. Next to the Government of Great Britain, therefore, the Imperial Government of Russia was the first to which any communication of the plan was made.[8]

According to the Knox Memorandum all the American Ambassadors to whom the twofold plan had been sent were instructed not to refer to the then unpublished Imperial Edict ratifying the preliminary Agreement of October 2, 1909, for construction of the Chinchow-Aigun Railway. Rockhill, Mr. Knox states, "unfortunately misunderstood" and thought that he was instructed "to withhold any reference to the Chinchow-Aigun Railway as a whole." [9]

By February 14 relations with Foreign Minister Izvolsky had become so strained that Secretary Knox instructed Ambassador Rockhill to turn toward the Russian minister of finance, Kokovtsev, for more sympathetic understanding and, "so far as possible," to "confine yourself to written communications with the Minister for Foreign Affairs, in order not to subject yourself needlessly to further discourtesy." [10] In the same despatch Mr. Knox considers the advisability of instructing the American ambassador

to request a formal audience of His Majesty the Emperor, for the purpose of expressing to His Imperial Majesty the great surprise and regret of the President

[7] *Ibid.*

[8] Knox Memorandum of Feb. 8, 1910. The document is given *in extenso* in the Appendix. On November 10, 1909, Knox had instructed Rockhill to make "shrewd and discreet use, as if the ideas originated with yourself, of the fundamental ideas put before the Embassy in previous telegrams. . . . You will find yourself free to foster the idea of Russian co-operation in neutralizing the railroads of Manchuria, by joining with us, Great Britain and other interested governments supporting the open door." Rockhill papers. Griswold, *op. cit.,* p. 155.

[9] This does not agree with Bland's version of Rockhill's reason for withholding the second half of the twofold plan. *Supra,* p. 156, n. 140.

[10] Knox to Rockhill, Feb. 14, 1910. When Rockhill suggested to Izvolsky the possibility of American construction of a railroad, should the internationalization plan fall through, Izvolsky, considering this a threat, answered so sharply that Mr. Rockhill warned him that if he used such a tone in the future their relations would have to be confined to writing. Pourtalés from St. Petersburg to Bethmann-Hollweg, Jan. 17, 1910. *Die Grosse Politik,* XXXII, No. 11672. Avarin, *op. cit.,* I, 117.

that the proposal of the United States for the internationalization of railways in Manchuria should have been for some unknown reason so unsympathetically received by the Minister for Foreign Affairs. . . .[11]

The uncertainty of how far the United States would go in support of the Chinchow-Aigun scheme which Russia considered, as far as her interests were concerned, "politically dangerous, economically unprofitable and strategically threatening," and to what extent the project would be upheld by other powers, left doubt in Russian and Japanese diplomatic minds as to the advisability of open opposition.[12] Meanwhile Korostovetz, Russian minister at Peking, informed the Chinese Government that Russia "would consider the construction of the Chinchow-Aigun Railroad going to our undefended border as an unfriendly act on the part of China," and that concessions must not be accepted without the consent of the Russian Government.[13] This done, the Russian and Japanese Governments sat back to watch the international checkerboard before deciding upon their next moves.

They had not long to wait. The French Government lost little time in coming to the aid of their ally, declaring that Russia and Japan did not threaten the policy of the Open Door, and that their consent was essential to the realization of the American project.[14] Great Britain, more dilatory, but equally faithful to her Far Eastern ally, on January 25, 1910, instructed her minister at Peking to declare to the Chinese Government the impossibility of ignoring the interests of Russia and Japan.[15]

On February 24, 1910, Russia took the initiative [16] by rejecting the plan for the Chinchow-Aigun Railway which "would be exceedingly injurious both to the strategic and to the economic interests of Russia," [17] and by countering with a proposal that the American financiers join Russia in the construction of a railway from Kalgan to Kiakhta on the Russian border by way of Urga, with the proviso that Russia should have the sole power to build the section from Urga to Kiakhta.[18]

11 *Ibid.*

12 Secret telegram of Korostovetz to Izvolsky, Jan. 22, 1910. Kantorovich, *op. cit.,* p. 190, n. 249.

13 Korostovetz to Izvolsky, Jan. 27, and Feb. 3, 1910. *Ibid.,* p. 190, n. 250.

14 Telegram of A. Nekliudov from Paris, Jan. 21, 1910. *Ibid.,* pp. 191, 229, n. 257. Reid, *op. cit.,* p. 98.

15 Grey to Izvolsky, Jan. 27, 1910. Kantorovich, *op. cit.,* p. 191, n. 256. According to German Ambassador von Bernstorff, both Taft and Knox considered London's reply a rejection, Taft remarking to Bernstorff that he would like to know "what England expects to get from Japan for helping them." Bernstorff to Schoen, Jan. 21, 1910. *Die Grosse Politik,* XXXII, 83. Reid, *op. cit.,* pp. 93, 104; Griswold, *op. cit.,* p. 158.

16 "It is necessary to emphasize that in the further zigzagging of this question as well as in the question of the consortium the most active opponent which American imperialism had to face was Tsarist Russia." Kantorovich, *op. cit.,* p. 191.

17 Russian note to Knox, Feb. 24, 1910. Price, *op. cit.,* p. 53.

18 Circular from Russian Foreign Office to the Ambassadors, Feb. 10, 1910. Kantorovich, *op. cit.,* p. 191; Reid, *op. cit.,* pp. 109–110. This project which was officially supported by the French Government, drew no objections from England (secret telegram of Benck-

Japan, now feeling secure as to Russia's attitude, made no open objection to the construction of the Chinchow-Aigun Railway but "maneuvered" [19] and, after first warning the Chinese Government that they must do nothing in Manchuria without Japanese permission, gave her assent to the project, subject to the participation of Japan in both loan and construction and to the building of a branch line connecting the South Manchurian Railway with the proposed Chinchow-Aigun line.[20]

Russia, having turned down the Chinchow-Aigun project and Japan having shown her hand—both powers upheld by the approval of France and England—nothing remained for the United States but to retreat, or to proceed independently.[21] The Chinese Imperial Edict of January 21, 1910, had, as already seen, confirmed the preliminary agreement between the American bankers and Manchuria. Negotiations were completed in April 1910, for the final formal agreement.[22] Russia and Japan meanwhile had flaunted the Treaty of Portsmouth in the face of China by their protests to the latter against the carrying out of the Chinchow-Aigun scheme. As a result, the signature of Viceroy Hsi Liang, so essential to the conclusion of an American-Chinese convention, was held in abeyance.[23]

endorf, March 12, 1910. Kantorovich, *op. cit.*, p. 191), but met with a very cold reception in Japan. Malevski-Malevich to Izvolsky, Feb. 20, 1910. *Ibid.*, p. 191. The Japanese press in China carried on a campaign against the plan. Korostovetz to Sazonov, April 12, 1910. *Ibid.*, p. 191. In April 1910, the State Department expressed readiness to agree to the counter project of St. Petersburg on condition that the original American proposal also be carried through. Memorandum of Knox to Rosen, April 19, 1910. But the latter, adds Kantorovich, "was already the swan song of the State Department." *Ibid.*

19 *Ibid.*

20 Malevsky-Malevich to Izvolsky, Jan. 26, 1910. *Ibid.*, p. 191. The former considered that "the last Japanese demand has exceptional strategic importance and makes the project especially dangerous for Russia." *Ibid.*, p. 191; Price, *op. cit.*, p. 53.

21 Great Britain and France needed the coöperation not of the United States but of Russia, which was on the geographical spot, to counterbalance the Central European Empires. They paid the price "by becoming her accomplices in Persia and China." Croly, *op. cit.*, p. 335. In view of the delicate European situation, Germany, unwilling to antagonize Britain and France, pursued a "correct" policy during this period. The Emperor toyed with the idea of an Anglo-American-German entente to preserve China's integrity, but was opposed by his own foreign-office officials. Knox was "much occupied" with this scheme. Reid, *op. cit.*, pp. 107 ff.

22 Bland, *op. cit.*, p. 320.

23 Relations among the powers concerned in the Far East, and especially between the United States and Russia, were not improved by a speech made by Jacob Schiff in New York in early March 1910. "I have been much mortified," said Mr. Schiff according to the *Novoe Vremya*, "to find that Japan was going hand-in-hand with Russia, the enemy of the whole human race. Russia and Japan want to reduce China to a state of vassalage. Perfidious Albion has joined the pact which, during the next ten years, will constitute the greatest menace to the peace of the world. . . . War will be the inevitable result." *Novoe Vremya*, Feb. 25/March 10, 1910. Translation enclosed in despatch from Ambassador Rockhill of March 12, 1910. Commenting on this speech, the *Novoe Vremya* in the same issue said: "During the Russo-Japanese war . . . Schiff stirred up in America hatred against Russia and sympathy for . . . Japan . . . he arranged to express his sympathy . . . by taking part in the military loan that Japan placed in New York. Mr. Schiff's activities in behalf of the human race were not in vain . . . the great humani-

In June 1910, Willard Straight therefore received instructions from J. P. Morgan and Company to proceed to St. Petersburg to try to revive the expiring Chinchow-Aigun Railway project. The following entry was made by Post Wheeler, American chargé at St. Petersburg, in his "Embassy Diary:"

June 9/22, 1910.

Mr. Willard Straight arrived in St. Petersburg today. He called upon me and asked that interviews be arranged for him with the Premier (Mr. Stolypin), the Minister of Finance (Mr. Kokovtseff), the Minister for Foreign Affairs (Mr. Izvolsky) and the Minister of War (Gen. Sukhomlinof).

This was done at once. . . .

(signed) Post Wheeler [24]

A later entry made by Mr. Wheeler in the "Embassy Diary" states that,

. . . . Straight called on me this noon [June 24, 1910], after his call on Mr. Iswolsky, and gave me a brief account of the interview as "little short of open insult" and said the first half of his conversation had been made up of charges against the good faith of the United States, which he implied had acted in a circuitous and underhanded manner during the entire negotiations, and the latter half of covert threats against China should she join with the United States against Russia. . . . Straight believed that he [Isvolsky] had been deliberately trying to goad and anger him. As he put it, the gist of all Iswolsky said was: Russia cannot be responsible for anything that may happen if the Chinchow Railway is built. He went fully into the strategical objections, declaring his conviction that the road was but a means by which China would menace Russia's territory.

Straight is convinced that these objections are not real—that Iswolsky does not wish to come to any understanding in the matter, and that his present policy is to create ill-feeling in every way possible. If this is the case, it is not impossible, that behind this attitude is Iswolsky's anxiety to hasten the Russo-Japanese understanding as to Far Eastern affairs which he strongly desires. To this there has been from the first considerable Governmental opposition, arising, no doubt, from a feeling that by it Russia, for the sake of a compromise with her enemy, stands to lose the friendship of the United States, a valuable asset for her future. Iswolsky has had to fight his way against this opposition. Kokovtseff is persuaded to his way of thinking by the argument that the Road would cut the profits of the Manchurian Railway. Iswolsky needs other elements, however, to win other members of the Cabinet, and to this end a popular anti-American sentiment springing from constantly reiterated belief in American unfriendliness and aided by international friction, might be expected to aid his immediate object.[25]

---

tarian pocketed some millions . . . and complacently read the reports of how Japanese shells, bought with American money, were tearing to fragments not only the Russians, but his coreligionists in the ranks of our army." "Virulent and unreasoning as this editorial is," observed Ambassador Rockhill, "it nevertheless deserves some consideration; . . . it is to be feared that this confusion of the Jewish question, and all of the prejudices and animosities involved in it, with the question of the development of Manchurian railways, will complicate both problems." Despatch to Department of State, March 12, 1910.

[24] Enclosure, Post Wheeler, chargé d'affaires, St. Petersburg, to secretary of state, June 26, 1910.

[25] *Ibid.*

Other entries of Mr. Wheeler indicate that the minister of finance was both "courteous and amenable," that the minister of war was "open and responsive" and "would welcome the railway as a necessary adjunct to military operations of the future," and that Count Witte, no longer in office and, governmentally speaking, without influence, favored the railway project and advised the United States to go ahead without wasting time with Russia.

Disregarding the sympathy for the American project that came from certain Russian quarters, Izvolsky, still remained the immovable obstacle on the unbuilt tracks of the Chinchow-Aigun Railway.

. . . . Russia had made up her mind [Izvolsky said] that the Chinchow-Aigun Railway would be prejudicial to her interests and would oppose it with every means in her power. . . . Russia could not stop us but she could make it very disagreeable and could take means to punish China for her foolishness. He then said "I don't understand what you Americans are up to anyway. What do you want? You say you want business, why don't you take up our suggestion regarding the Kalgan-Kiachta line, if you are honest? I think you are playing politics." [26]

Recurring to his favorite grievance against the United States Izvolsky

launched into a tirade against the manner in which the Chinchow-Aigun proposition had been handled. He stated that we had consulted Japan, had consulted everyone in fact before approaching Russia, that our negotiations with China had been secret, that there had been a secret edict, that in every way we had shown a desire entirely to ignore Russia and Russian interests. . . . His emphasis on the secret Edict and the secret negotiations was obviously inspired by his desire to make out as bad a case against the United States as possible. . . . "You Americans," he said, "are inciting China against Russia. During the last few years we have had growing difficulties with the Chinese. . . ." [27]

On June 28, 1910, Mr. Straight, then in London, sent a second "full report" to J. P. Morgan and Company, outlining the results of his mission in St. Petersburg and the conclusions he drew therefrom. He foresees a

[26] Summarizing Russia's fear of the possibility of war with Japan, Straight declares that, "the party now in power in St. Petersburg realize their unpreparedness in the Far East and feel that unless Japan is conciliated she may attack Russia at once. And that therefore they have fallen in with M. Iswolsky's personal desire . . . [to effect] a rapprochement with Japan, in order to remove all friction between the two countries, and . . . by encouraging Japan's policy of spoilation in Manchuria, to gain her support in their own retention of the remains of what they once hoped might be the Manchurian Province of their Empire." Straight adds that, "opposed to the party in favor of a closer Russo-Japanese understanding however, is a very strong body of Russian public opinion, which advocates, on the contrary, a rapprochement with China and the United States." Willard Straight's report to J. P. Morgan of interview with Izvolsky, Department of State, June 22, 1910.

[27] Ibid. Beneath existent grievances still lurked resentment toward the United States for its attitude in the Russo-Japanese War. Prince P. A. Trubetzkoy, correspondent from the United States of a Russian magazine, when asked by someone in Washington his impressions of American-Russian relations, replied: "The impression, unfortunately, is not a favorable one. Russia cannot forget the position occupied by the majority of the press during the war." Russkaia Mysl (Russian Thought), June 1910.

closer union between Russia and Japan, based in his opinion upon Russia's fear not only of Japanese encroachment in Manchuria but of an actual attack from Japan. England, "whom Russia now regards as her great friend has . . . 'damned the Chinchow-Aigun line with faint praise' " and has, Mr. Straight believes, "encouraged M. Iswolsky's policy." While "France, the Russian banker, is urging Russia to come to an understanding with Japan in order that Russian troops may be free to act on the eastern frontier against Germany," and is concerned both politically and financially in combinations which are inimical to the interests of the Chinchow-Aigun Railway. This left Russia, according to Straight, not only free but encouraged to disregard China's suzerainty in Manchuria. In Straight's opinion three courses were left to the United States: (1) To support China and proceed with the plans for the Chinchow-Aigun Railway; (2) To drop China and join with Russia in the proposed Kalgan-Kiahta scheme; (3) To adopt a middle course, attempting

to reconcile Russian with Chinese interests . . . to pursue the traditional American policy of friendship for, and support of, China without pushing such action to such an extent as to provoke Russian retaliation against China or bitterness against the United States.

Straight advocated the third policy as the "wiser and safer" course to pursue.[28]

On June 29, 1910, Post Wheeler, after an interview with Izvolsky, wrote to the Department of State in regard to the conversations between Willard Straight and the Russian Foreign Minister:

. . . . What particularly annoyed him [Izvolsky] in the whole situation . . . was the coupling of the reiteration that the United States had no political aims in Manchuria with the constant tendency to discuss the Railway question from the political standpoint. . . . He [Straight] had repeated more than once that "Of course China wishes to be her own master in Manchuria." This indicated that the United States had, as its aim, the direction of China's political future. . . . If China, under the influence of the United States, arrayed herself against Russia, then Russia must settle that matter with China.[29]

Meanwhile, American despatches in regard to the approaching alliance between Russia and Japan became more definite. On May 9, 1910, the American chargé at St. Petersburg wrote that Russian newspapers were featuring, apparently with the approval of the Foreign Office, a report that

negotiations between Russia and Japan were going on, looking to an understanding as to spheres of influence in Manchuria and Mongolia and parallel exploitation of the Railways in the Far East. . . . There is little doubt in my mind that the Foreign Office wishes this report to be circulated and credited. . . .[30]

[28] Straight to J. P. Morgan and Company, London, June 28, 1910. Department of State.
[29] Post Wheeler to the Secretary of State, June 29, 1910.
[30] Post Wheeler to Knox, May 9, 1910. In a later despatch Post Wheeler commented

Japan was less outright in avowing her intentions, according to the following telegram from Tokyo: "Minister for Foreign Affairs tells me negotiations are pending with Russia but not such as reported by the press. He says no new agreement is needed by Japan but will be made chiefly to calm suspicions and alarm of Russian people." [31]

In spite of Tokyo's evasive statement, as reported by Ambassador O'Brien, the treaty, containing both public and secret provisions, was signed at St. Petersburg on July 4, 1910, by Izvolsky and Baron Motono, a delicate tribute, it is thought by certain writers, to Secretary Knox on the American national holiday.[32] Russia had submitted drafts of the complete treaty (public and private) to London and Paris for approval [33] which was granted. The Russian ambassador at London reported Sir Edward Grey, foreign secretary, as "very much satisfied," and later Great Britain received public thanks from both Russia and Japan "for her assistance against American intrusion." Grey observed "that the policy adopted by the United States in China hastened if it did not bring about this arrangement [Russo-Japanese Treaty of 1910]." [34]

This second Russo-Japanese Treaty drew lines sharply around the rights and concessions of Russia and Japan in their respective Manchurian spheres of influence, already roughly allocated in the convention of July 20, 1907. In the published treaty, there was no reference to "the integrity of China" or to the "principle of the Open Door," and the phrase "status quo" which had been submerged beneath its "resonant platitudes" emerged, in view of the Russo-Japanese attitude, with clarity from Article III of the published portion of the treaty:

In case any event of such a nature as to menace the above-mentioned *status quo* should be brought about, the two High Contracting Parties will in each instance enter into communication with each other, for the purpose of agreeing upon the

---

that, "when the agreement was first rumored, there was strong opposition to any rapprochement from the Liberal press, which deplored the success of Japan in luring Russia into an alliance in which she must give much and get little, and in alienating her from China, as she had already alienated America from Russia. These objections . . . were met by the governmental press, which through rumors of a near renewal of hostilities with Japan . . . succeeded in arousing a fear of attack. . . . At the same time the *Rossia*, the organ of the Foreign Office . . . with the *Novoe Vremya*, opened an editorial campaign which . . . was continually reiterating a conviction of the unfriendliness of the United States." Wheeler to Secretary of State, June 30, 1910.

[31] O'Brien to Knox, May 27, 1910.

[32] Bland, *op. cit.*, p. 320; Croly, *op. cit.*, p. 331. The public treaty was officially released in Japan on July 12 and in Russia on July 14, 1910; the secret treaty did not become public until the Soviet Government came into power. Price, *op. cit.*, p. 55.

[33] Post Wheeler to secretary of state, June 30, 1910; also confirmed by American Ambassador Reid, London, to secretary of state, telegram, July 6, 1910.

[34] Minutes by Grey on MacDonald (British ambassador, Tokyo), to Grey, July 2, 1910. *Brit. Doc.*, VIII, 485. Reid, *op. cit.*, pp. 127 ff., 142; Gérard, *op. cit.*, p. 128; Price, *op. cit.*, p. 54.

measures that they may judge it necessary to take for the maintenance of the said *status quo*.[35]

Once more the Portsmouth Treaty, with all its ornamental legal phrasing, had been flung in the face of China and the United States. A writer in the New York *Times,* looking at the treaty through American eyes and discovering the Russo-Japanese meaning of status quo, wrote:

When the recent agreement was disclosed as a consequence of Mr. Knox's proposals, we found out what the *status quo* in Manchuria means. . . . It is not at all the *status quo* established by the Portsmouth Treaty nor by the Treaty of July 30, 1907. . . . Manifestly the territorial integrity of China is not respected, it is flouted and trampled upon. . . .[36]

The Russian semi-official *Novoe Vremya* of July 7, viewing the treaty through the bifocal glasses of Russia and Japan, wrote:

The Russo-Japanese *rapprochement* is not a fortunate thing for the interests of those who built plans for their own prosperity based on the hostility of Russia and Japan. . . . The American plan of penetrating the continent of Asia is based on the desire to cherish misunderstanding between Russia, Japan and China and to create a hostile attitude. . . .

After stating that,

Russia and Japan agree to keep the *status quo* in Manchuria with the object of strengthening and further developing railway enterprise, with all the concerns of civilization and industry connected with it,

the writer acknowledges Russia's indebtedness to Secretary Knox:

The *rapprochement* between Russia and Japan . . . certainly received the last impulse from the recent proceedings of America. Therefore Mr. Philander Knox deserves our general gratitude. The situation of itself was tending toward crystallization; he, however, threw a foreign body into the mixture and the process of crystallization was fulfilled with a rapidity which could only be dreamed of beforehand. The same Knox we must probably thank for the introduction into the Russo-Japanese Convention of an article providing for the combined acts of Russia and Japan in cases when the Manchurian *status quo* shall be threatened from any side.[37]

---

[35] As in 1907, the more important provisions were in the secret treaty. In this treaty, after reaffirming the demarcation line of 1907, the two powers agreed to respect each other's "special interests" in the spheres indicated, and to recognize "the right of each, within its own sphere, freely to take all measures" to safeguard and defend "those interests." In the event of a threat to the latter, the two powers pledged themselves to "agree upon the measures to be taken with a view to common action . . . for the safeguarding and defense of those interests." Price, *op. cit.,* pp. 42–46; Morse and MacNair, *op. cit.,* p. 521.

[36] New York *Times,* Editorial, July 14, 1910. Price, *op. cit.,* p. 57.

[37] Enclosure in despatch, Wheeler to Knox, July 7, 1910. Bland (*op. cit.,* p. 339) expresses a similar opinion: "The fact that Mr. Knox rushed in where British diplomats feared to tread merely precipitated an arrangement so obviously profitable to Russia and Japan that it could not long have been delayed."

The favorite Russian grievance against America, that of the Chinchow-Aigun Railway proposal, in which Mr. Knox played favorites, is again brought forth:

In the question of the Chinchow-Aigun Railway, Mr. Knox entered previously into an agreement with Japan, and only after that did he present it to Russia, a *fait accompli*. It was disadvantageous for Russia and at the same time was undesirable for Japan, who obviously consented to accept the American proposal against her own wish. From the present time, such diplomatic misunderstandings will be impossible. The real importance of the Russo-Japanese Convention . . . is far beyond the letter of the text. It is above all the surest foundation of a long and stable peace in the Far East.[38]

The Convention of 1910 disposed of, "the new confederates," according to one writer, "lost no time in profiting by their pact." [39] Six weeks after the signature of the treaty, August 29, 1910, Japan formally annexed Korea, a step forward on the foundation for "a long and stable peace in the Far East." [40]

Secretary Knox, undeterred by the Russo-Japanese blows dealt to his neutralization and Chinchow-Aigun projects, again came to the aid of China in her attempts to free herself from the strangleholds of Russia and Japan. On September 22, 1910, at the suggestion of the Department of State, the Chinese Government approached the American Government with a request for an American loan of 50,000,000 taels, which, in a second proposal of October 2nd, was increased to $50,000,000, for the twofold purpose of currency reform in China as a whole, and industrial development in Manchuria itself.[41]

In the meantime, the Wall Street bankers, perturbed by the fiasco of the alternative projects, and dissatisfied with Secretary Knox, whose unfortunate mingling of finance and politics they feared would bring them into disrepute, or even precipitate a war for which the United States was not prepared, served notice on Mr. Knox that "they would be under no obligation to seek or accept contracts which aroused the irreconcilable opposition of other powers." [42] As a result the preliminary agreement for the loan to China, which was signed by the American financiers on October 27, 1910, stipulated that they should be allowed "associates." [43] On October

[38] Enclosure, Wheeler to Knox, July 7, 1910.

[39] Bland, *op. cit.*, p. 339.

[40] Avarin (*op. cit.*, I, 121) states that "American plans" hastened both the signing of the Treaty of 1910 and the annexation of Korea, and that the danger of direct annexation of Manchuria by Russia and Japan at that time was considerable.

[41] *For. Rel.*, 1912, pp. 89–90; *Field, op. cit.*, p. 57; Price, *op. cit.*, pp. 60–61.

[42] Croly, *op. cit.*, p. 344.

[43] *For. Rel.*, 1912, p. 91; Price, *op. cit.*, p. 61. It should be kept in mind that the United States as an import country not possessing "free export capital" required the coöperation of European bankers. Kantorovich, *op. cit.*, p. 197; Avarin, *op. cit.*, I, 96; Field, *op. cit.*, p. 60. "Without the help of Europe the loans cannot be issued," reported Rosen from Washington. Secret telegrams to St. Petersburg of Nov. 22, Dec. 1 and 3, 1910. Kantorovich, *op. cit.*, p. 197.

31st the governments of Great Britain, France, Germany, Russia, and Japan were notified of the conclusion of the agreement, with the statement that the American Government "would welcome the cordial support of the interested powers." On the same day the British, German, and French financiers with whom the American bankers were affiliated in the Hukuang Railway project, requested participation in the projected loan.[44]

Late in October 1910, Willard Straight, as representative of the American group of bankers, left New York and, after a stopover in London to consult with European financiers, returned to Peking on November 27, where he spent a hectic winter assuaging Chinese susceptibilities, persuading China to admit the three other members of the four-power consortium as co-signatories of the prospective loan, and endeavoring to have an American appointed as financial adviser to the Chinese Government in carrying out her proposed currency reform.[45]

Russia and Japan meanwhile were busy. On January 15, 1911, Straight wrote:

I am the more worried because Casenave [the representative of the French group] told me today that both the Russian and Japanese Ministers have been to the Wai-Wu-Pu and have stated that if China made any loan with political significance (i.e. the Currency Loan) their governments wanted Russian and Japanese bankers to participate, and that if any foreign adviser was appointed Russia and Japan each wanted one also.[46]

A telegram from the American minister at Peking of a later date verifies this statement, and outlines the policy to be followed by the American Government to circumvent Russo-Japanese designs. The message reads in part:

. . . It is apparent that Japanese intrigue has used the combination of banks under London agreement to arouse fear of Chinese . . . that some combination to control Chinese finances has been made, and doubtless Japanese have enlisted support of Russians hence their demand for participation in loan and representation in advisers. If Department can secure assurances for England, France and Germany that actual currency reform is the essential and only end desired and that if tripartite banks are admitted as signatories to loan agreement the Government aforesaid will acquiesce in appointment of single adviser whether he is American, Dutch or Swiss, and will oppose Russian and Japanese participation in loan or if the latter are admitted it shall be on condition that they waive claim to adviser.[47]

The governments of Russia and Japan lost little time in appealing to their respective allies. France was forthright and outspoken in assuring the Russian Government that she had no intentions of supporting an enterprise "which is directed against Russia." [48] Great Britain was more re-

44 For. Rel., 1912, pp. 91–92; Price, op. cit., p. 61.
45 Croly, op. cit., Ch. xii.
46 Willard Straight to Henry P. Davison, Jan. 15, 1911. Croly, op. cit., p. 382.
47 Calhoun to Knox, Jan. 23, 1911.
48 In a letter of November 23, 1910, to Russian Foreign Minister Sazonov, the Russian

served, yet reassuring, wishing first "to inquire at Washington whether the proposed loan was really destined to reform of China's finances." [49]

The Tsarist Izvolsky, like the Marxist Kantorovich, unwilling to credit the American Government with disinterested motives, was suspicious that behind the loan lay political designs on the part of the United States. In a confidential letter to the Russian minister of finance, Izvolsky commented as follows on Ambassador Rockhill's statement earlier in the month regarding the loan:

. . . he [Rockhill] spoke at the time neither of guarantees of any kind nor of the appointment of an American to the Chinese Ministry of Finance. Later on, however, he informed me that the American banking houses insist upon China's providing definite guarantees and on the appointment of an American. The Ambassador assured me that his government would welcome the participation of Russian capital in the loan. It may be inferred from all this that the American government desires to use foreign, not American money in order to attain a double profit: Firstly, a commission for the American banks, and, secondly, the appointment of an American who will in all probability attempt to exert not only economic but also political influence. The Japanese Ambassador here [Motono], who has arrived at the same conclusion, has openly expressed to me his dissatisfaction at the course the problem of the penetration of foreign capital into China has taken.[50]

Baron Rosen, Russian ambassador to Washington, pursuing the same line of thought, in a secret despatch to St. Petersburg wrote that Knox "is planning to have the Chinese use as much of the loan as will correspond with American policies in Manchuria." [51] And Kantorovich writing twenty years later that, "A policy intended to establish the monopolistic position of the United States, could not but call forth the savage resistance of the imperialistic powers already ruling in Manchuria—Russia and Japan." [52]

Russia, in greater need and therefore more desperate than Japan, went

---

chargé in London wrote: "The French Ambassador here [Paul Cambon] has told me that during a conversation with Knox [between Jusserand, French ambassador at Washington, and Knox], the latter, in his excitement, admitted that the sum of 50 million dollars would be in itself too small for the financial reform and other administrative measures in China, and that the Americans in reality desired to use this sum for the building of railways and the penetration of Manchuria. Knox intends to set up resistance in Manchuria, directed . . . against Russia and Japan, as well as their allies, France and England . . . [Grey] regards exclusively American negotiations with the Chinese Government as inexpedient. So far as Cambon is informed, the Americans are pursuing political ends. . . . Cambon inclines to the opinion that the American Government, in its displeasure at the failure of its plans last year, now seeks to call forth new complications in China, at the same time emphasizing its magnanimous attitude toward that country." De Siebert and Schreiner, op cit., pp. 22–23. See also Reid, op. cit., p. 166.

[49] De Siebert and Schreiner, op. cit., p. 22. Price, op. cit., p. 62. In a conversation with von Bernstorff, Taft commented that Germany was the only power upon which he could rely to uphold the open door in China. Reid, op. cit., p. 163.

[50] Izvolsky to the Russian minister of finance, Nov. 6/19, 1910. De Siebert and Schreiner, pp. 21–22.

[51] Rosen to Izvolsky, Nov. 29, 1910. Kantorovich, op. cit., p. 192, n. 271.

[52] Ibid., p. 194.

so far as to consider the advisability of risking a war with China by the immediate annexation of North Manchuria, the claim she had roughly staked out for herself, with the secret approval of Japan, in the secret portion of the treaty of July 30, 1907 and more definitely allocated in the recent convention of 1910. After much discussion among the Council of Ministers at an extraordinary meeting held in St. Petersburg on December 2, 1910,[53] it was agreed that ultimate annexation was an "imperative necessity" but, owing to the probable opposition of America and England, was at the moment inopportune. A decision was finally reached to postpone the annexation and instead bring pressure to bear upon China in protection of Russia's "stipulated privileges" in North Manchuria, with "no shrinking from forceful measures if necessity demanded." [54]

Before putting the screws upon China, Russia approached Japan and Great Britain through her envoys at Tokyo and London, asking support of her plans for "putting pressure upon China in order to place China under obligations to leave the status quo in Mongolia unaltered and to take no military measures there." [55] Compensation for British approval was to be the withdrawal of Russian objections to the sending of "scientific expeditions" to Tibet by Great Britain.[56]

Japan, while in principle warmly approving Russia's course, at the same time counseled prudence lest China be driven "into the arms of America and Germany." [57] The reply of Great Britain is unrecorded, but as Russia proceeded to carry out her plans for exerting pressure upon China, it may be inferred that the British Government was not unresponsive. Using alleged violation of the Treaty of 1881 between Russia and China as a pretext, Russia began putting her planned system into operation. American despatches and telegrams during this period show the technique employed. On February 19, 1911, a telegram from Peking states that,

> Chinese are somewhat confused over the Russian demand. . . . They said Russia had complained in vague and general terms of China's violation of existing treaties; that Chinese had asked for a bill of particulars; that Russian Minister had promised to furnish the same. . . .
>
> In conversation today with Russian Minister he told me that for six months past he has had repeated interviews with Foreign Office, seeking adjustment of numerous claims arising under the treaty of Eighteen Eighty One; that the Chinese had been guilty of great evasion and subterfuge in avoiding adjustment. . . . They [the claims] involved questions of taxation, tariff duties, rights of merchants, recognition of consuls etc., which arose under the plain terms of the treaty and which the Chinese had frequently and almost habitually ignored. . . .

[53] An account of this meeting is given in De Siebert and Schreiner, op. cit., pp. 24–27, taken from a "Protocol of an Extraordinary Meeting of the Ministerial Council." See also Reid, op. cit., pp. 168–72; Price, op. cit., p. 62.

[54] Ibid.

[55] De Siebert and Schreiner, op. cit., p. 23; Price, op. cit., p. 64.

[56] Price, op. cit., p. 64.

[57] De Siebert and Schreiner, op. cit., pp. 28–29; Reid, op. cit., p. 172; Price, op. cit., p. 65.

He said this demand was not accompanied by any threat or show of military force and that it was not true that reoccupation of Kuldja was threatened. . . .[58]

Before mid-March Russia was becoming more insistent and threatening military force if her demands were not complied with. On the 16th Rockhill telegraphed Secretary Knox:

. . . I am informed on good authority that on thirteenth instant Russian Minister at Peking was directed to deliver to the Chinese Government a reply to its communication on the subject of the Russian demands insisting upon full and absolute compliance within a limited period. . . . I am reliably informed that this Government has now decided upon immediate occupation of Kuldja if the reply from China is not satisfactory.[59]

At this point Japan also showed her hand.

Japanese Ambassador has just called and told me he considers the situation very serious. His Government has advised China to realize the determination of Russia to carry out threats and advised compliance as resistance is impossible and the tranquility of all China might be imperiled by refusal. The Ambassador hoped that the American Government had advised the Chinese in the same manner or would do so. . . .[60]

That American diplomats in the Far East did not understand the situation is shown by the concluding paragraph of the message: "This sudden reversal of the policy of the Minister for Foreign Affairs during his illness is surprising to those best informed and seems inexplicable." [61]

By the end of March China, not wishing to be drawn into conflict, had practically conceded the Russian demands. The possibility that the United States Government may have played a part in the pressure Russia was exerting upon China is conceded by the American minister to Peking in the final sentence of his telegram:

There seems to be a growing feeling here that the fate of Manchuria will be decided this summer, and adversely to China, and that it is possible the pending currency loan contract which provides for Manchurian expenditures may have stimulated Russian and Japanese action.[62]

On March 29, a telegram from American Minister Calhoun in Peking announced that Russia had definitely accepted "China's last note" and hoped "that China will hereafter strictly observe the treaty obligations in order that the friendly relations which happily exist between the two governments may be strengthened." [63]

The Chinese bamboo bent before the Russian wind. Peking yielded so completely on the points in question that St. Petersburg had slight ground

[58] Calhoun to Knox, telegram, February 19, 1911. Cf. Reid, *op. cit.*, pp. 196 ff.
[59] Rockhill to Knox, telegram, March 16, 1911.
[60] *Ibid.*
[61] *Ibid.*
[62] Calhoun to secretary of state, telegram, March 28, 1911.
[63] Calhoun to secretary of state, telegram, March 29, 1911.

left upon which to continue its campaign of pressure. And, in spite of the pressure exerted upon elastic China, in spite of the underground support of England and Japan, and the slight faux pas made by Secretary Knox in demanding an American adviser, the four-power Chinese Currency Reform and Industrial Loan Agreement was concluded on April 15, 1911, the signatories agreeing to the appointment of a neutral adviser.[64]

On the same day Willard Straight recorded in his diary, "The Currency Loan is finished. Dollar Diplomacy is justified at last. Knox and Wilson [assistant secretary of state] ought to be pleased." [65] And to Morgan he wrote, "Here is the first visible result of the new politics of Secretary Knox." [66] Yet the diplomacy of the dollar still had a rough road to travel; and the Currency Reform Loan was destined never to be floated.[67]

An editorial in the *Novoe Vremya* of April 24, 1911, voicing the apprehension felt, according to Ambassador Rockhill, "by Russians generally, inclusive of official circles," asks:

Why are the Chinese to receive at once a million pounds for the necessities of Manchuria? Will it not be spent in strengthening the army—perhaps the construction of strategical railways like the Aigun line? Why is the first payment made for the needs of Manchuria? And why is the loan guaranteed for the most part . . . by income from Manchurian monopolies? In a word, will not this money in the hands of the mandarins serve to incite them to make dangerous experiments in connection with the neighbouring possessions of Russia and Japan? [68]

After stating that telegrams at hand prove that "certain circles of Americans are ready to see in the loan not only a favorable interest, but in a manner a guarantee for China against Russian and Japanese claims in Manchuria," the writer suggests that England and France "in the interests of peace" stipulate that "loans for cultural needs of Manchuria are not loans for military purposes." [69]

Article 16 of the Agreement brought Russia and Japan into immediate action. This Article, referred to by Kantorovich as "the political edge" of the understanding [70] provides that the consortium is to be given an option upon furnishing additional funds, if any are needed, for carrying out "the operations contemplated in this agreement;" and if the consortium and the Chinese Government fail to agree as to terms the latter is at liberty to seek the additional loan elsewhere. The last section of Article 16 reads:

And should the Imperial Chinese Government decide to invite foreign capitalists to participate with Chinese interests in Manchurian business contemplated under

[64] Reid, *op. cit.*, pp. 221–25; Field, *op. cit.*, p. 61; Griswold, *op. cit.*, p. 165.

[65] Reid, *op. cit.*, p. 224; Croly, *op. cit.*, p. 402.

[66] Kantorovich, *op. cit.*, p. 193.

[67] A portion of the Industrial Development Loan was issued and recalled. Griswold, *op. cit.*, n. 2, p. 165; Reid, *op. cit.*, p. 254.

[68] Enclosure in despatch from Rockhill to secretary of state, April 24, 1911.

[69] *Ibid.*

[70] Kantorovich, *op. cit.*, p. 193.

this loan, or to be undertaken in connection therewith, the banks shall first be invited to so participate.[71]

"This clause 16," according to one writer, "revealed the secret aim of the activity of the American group which played the chief role in the conversations." [72] And this was the clause which both Russia and Japan found particularly objectionable.

Ambassador Rockhill reported on May 13, after an interview with Acting Foreign Minister Neratoff, that the latter

admitted that the two Governments [Russia and Japan], which he said were, in view of their community of interests in Manchuria, constantly exchanging views, had had occasion to consider the possible effect on their respective peculiar interests in Manchuria of the assignment by China, as security for the "Currency Loan," of Manchurian revenues, of the possible granting of large concessions to foreign interests, and of the application by China of the portion of the loan destined for the development of Manchuria to the creation of works which might either be dangerous to Russian and Japanese interests, such as the erection of arsenals, military works or like enterprises, or detrimental to their commercial interests.[73]

Japan began the assault with a request for participation in the loan. Russia soon followed. On May 18, 1911, the American minister at Peking wrote that, "The French are reported to be holding back advances for Manchuria because of Russian pressure." [74] On May 24, William Calhoun, American minister to China, in an optimistic frame of mind, paid a tribute to Secretary Knox:

If this loan is finally consummated, the Americans have a great part to play in China. We have perhaps, aroused the antagonism of Russia and Japan. But we have gained a place in China, and the basis on which that place has been established has demonstrated that we are not pursuing any selfish or exclusive prestige. The way these loan negotiations have been handled is strictly in line with your neutralization policy, which, as the years go on, will become as famous and as much honored in diplomatic history as is the 'open door' policy proclaimed by Mr. Hay. . . .[75]

On June 14, the officially approved *Novoe Vremya* again stepped into the arena, stating its belief that the loan contracted for by China from the four-power consortium was "a renewal in disguise of the plan of the American Secretary of State Knox for the neutralization of Manchuria." It credited Minister Calhoun, who "is a lawyer of the first rank, and a first class business man and financier" with deep laid plans for the agricultural exploitation of Manchuria under American control. After going into detail in regard to the American plan, the editorial continues:

[71] MacMurray, *op. cit.*, I, 848. Field, *op. cit.*, p. 63.
[72] Vaerstrat, *L'Emprunt Chinois et la Politique Russe*, p. 9. Kantorovich, *op. cit.*, p. 193, n. 274.
[73] Rockhill to Knox, May 13, 1911.
[74] *For. Rel.*, 1912, p. 97. Price, *op. cit.*, p. 68.
[75] Calhoun to Knox, May 24, 1911.

All that is left now for Mr. Straight, the American financial Napoleon who is representative of the four-power financial syndicate as he was formerly broker in the scheme for the neutralization of the Manchurian railways, is to pay down to the Chinese Government the sums stipulated in the contract, and the business is as good as done. The best lands in Manchuria will be under the control of the American agricultural machine trust . . . headed by the Envoy Extraordinary and Minister Plenipotentiary of the United States of North America in China, Mr. William J. Calhoun.[76]

At a special Russian conference of the Council of Ministers on June 7, 1911, the opinion of Kokovtsev, minister of finance, that the Reorganization Loan was political in scope, disguising a new attempt on the part of the United States, after the failure of the Knox scheme, to neutralize Manchuria, was unanimously accepted.

In this new form, this movement by the United States, which is hostile to us, is even more dangerous than when it was a matter of neutralization of only the railroads in Manchuria. . . . The present move threatens to squeeze us out of Manchuria without any kind of monetary compensation.[77]

A joint protest against Article 16 was made by Russia and Japan to Paris and London, and after obtaining favorable replies,[78] their protests were presented to Berlin [79] and Washington. "Behind the joint protest," according to an American authority, "was a mutual wish of St. Petersburg and Tokyo to stop further American influence in Manchuria," [80] a statement that is apparently verified by another writer who claims that, "The consortium immediately placed itself at the service of policies which were favorable to American interests but which were opposed by Russia and were harmful to her." [81]

The Russian note of protest which was presented to the American Government on July 11, 1911, reads in part as follows:

It seems that the syndicate pretends to a monopoly of financial and industrial enterprises in the region in which Russia possesses important special interests. . . . Now, the project in question having a tendency to hinder the development of Russian interests in Manchuria by creating in favor of the syndicate an altogether exceptional position the Imperial Government earnestly hopes that consideration will be given to the objections formulated above, and addresses itself to the Government of the United States with the request that it will not refuse to use its influence with a view to having clause 16 of the contract revoked.[82]

[76] Enclosure in despatch from Heintzleman, chargé d'affaires, Peking, to Knox, July 22, 1911. According to Avarin, *op. cit.*, I, 133, the Russian press began "a campaign against American independence in Manchuria."

[77] *Komissia po Izdaniu Dokumentov Epokhi Imperializma: Mezhdunarodnie Otnoshenia v Epokhu Imperializma* (Committee for the Publication of Documents on the Epoch of Imperialism: International Relations in the Epoch of Imperialism). Series 2, 1900–13, XVIII, Pt. 1, May 14, 1911–September 13, 1911, 94 ff.

[78] Reid, *op. cit.*, p. 235.

[79] With the view of creating discord between Russia and Japan, Germany encouraged China to disregard Russia's and Japan's veto of Article XVI. Bland, *op. cit.*, p. 391.

[80] Reid, *op. cit.*, p. 235.

[81] Kantorovich, *op. cit.*, p. 207, n. 330.

[82] *For. Rel.*, 1910, p. 261; Price, *op. cit.*, p. 69.

Meanwhile, the Anglo-Japanese-American triangle presented serious possibilities. Between the situation in Manchuria and the immigration problem, Japanese-American relations were strained almost to the snapping point. Great Britain, in the event of a Japanese-American war, would be obliged to come to the assistance of her ally. Realizing this, the United States had in the summer of 1910 proposed an arbitration treaty to Great Britain.[83] Great Britain regarded the proposal favorably.[84] On August 3, 1911, the Anglo-American arbitration treaty was signed, but, as the Senate refused to ratify it, American-British-Japanese relations practically stood as they had in the beginning.[85]

In July of 1911 the consortium held a meeting in London to consider ways and means of meeting Russo-Japanese objections to Article 16 and to arrange for the future issues of the prospective loan. As a result, Willard Straight was sent to Peking, "primarily for the purpose of removing the final obstacles to the issue of the Currency Loan." [86] But Fate, or a combination of events, intervened, as was invariably the case in any plan with which Straight was associated, and left Russia and Japan holding the winning hands.

A revolutionary movement in China which had been long smoldering, burst into flames on October 10, 1911. And indirectly the railway concession to the four-power group of the Hukuang Railways, the negotiations for which had been concluded on May 20, 1911, was one of the causes of

[83] Bryce to Grey, August 9, 1910, *Brit. Doc.*, VIII, 541. Griswold, *op. cit.*, p. 168.

[84] The problem of dovetailing an Anglo-American treaty with the terms of the Anglo-Japanese Alliance was solved by a renewal of the Alliance on July 13, 1911, in which Article IV reads, "Should either High Contracting Party conclude a treaty of general arbitration with a third power, it is agreed that nothing in the agreement shall entail upon such Contracting Party an obligation to go to war with the power with whom such treaty or arbitration is in force." *Brit. Doc.*, VIII, 532–33.

[85] In view of the question which is often raised as to whether a pre-1914 entente between the United States and Great Britain had been concluded, the following despatch of February 7, 1911, from the American Embassy at London, while likely of no especial significance, is at least of interest. "I have the honor to report," wrote Ambassador Phillips, "that on or about January 20, Major Slocum, the recently appointed Military Attaché of this Embassy was formally received at the War Office [British] by Mr. R. B. Haldane, Secretary of State for War. Major Slocum tells me in confidence that during the interview, which lasted nearly one hour, Mr. Haldane laid stress on his hopes that before he left office he would see either a formal or tacit agreement between the United States, Great Britain, and Japan for the purpose of observing the status quo in the Far East and mutually to assist one another in any misunderstanding which might occur in the Far East or elsewhere. On the intimation that possibly the American people might not approve of such an alliance at this time with any but a white race, Mr. Haldane remarked that the alliance which he had in mind need not be a formal undertaking but merely an understanding and that England stood ready to use her best efforts to smooth over any difficulties between the United States and Japan. This is in brief the substance of Mr. Haldane's remarks which, had they not been delivered in so forcible a manner, would perhaps not be worthy of report. They represent of course his personal views only. Major Slocum informs me that he is reporting the substance of the conversation to the War Department." Phillips to secretary of state, Feb. 7, 1911. The author was unable to find a reply to this despatch in the available records of the State Department.

[86] Croly, *op. cit.*, p. 411.

the outbreak.[87] The Russian Government, and particularly Izvolsky, hastened to fasten the blame for the revolution upon the American Government and the American financiers. On November 14, Straight wrote:

In connection with the present crisis, it is interesting to note that the Russian
Government, or at any rate its representative here, as well as our friend M. Iswol-
sky [Ambassador] in Paris, are endeavoring to blame the United States and the
American Group for the present upheaval in China.

There have been numerous indications of this in journals published in China
and subsidized by the Russian Government, and in recent conversations with
M. Korostovetz, the Russian Minister, he quite frankly stated that it was largely
through the educational work of the American missionaries; through the fact that
so many Chinese young men have been educated in America, and, owing to the
aggressive loan policy of the United States Government that the revolutionists
have found their strength and their opportunity.

Izvolsky, Straight continued, had been so successful in Paris in his insinuations about the United States and its constant incitement of China to "an
anti-Russian, anti-Japanese policy," that the French Government was
sending a representative to China to investigate and determine

whether it would be wiser for French interests to continue, as heretofore, to work
with an Anglo-German-American combination, or whether the Government had
best take steps to induce the Banque de l'Indo-Chine to leave the Quadruple
Group and come to an understanding with the Russians and Japanese.[88]

On December 5, 1911, Minister Calhoun reported from Peking that he
had learned by way of Paris that, "Russia and Japan had agreed to jointly
insist upon the elimination of Article sixteen in the Currency Loan agreement." They had also agreed that in the future

all Chinese loans negotiated for territory north of Great Wall in Mongolia or
Manchuria participation therein must be allowed Russia and Japan on the basis

[87] Morse and MacNair, op. cit., p. 422. The Chinese Imperial Government had granted
the people of Szechwan the privilege of building that portion of the line from Hankow
to Szechwan which was within their own province. A company had been organized and
had done a small amount of work. Meanwhile, its president had misappropriated a large
part of the company's funds, and the Imperial Government decided to withdraw the
privilege and nationalize the railway. In the summer of 1911 the people of Szechwan
province formed a league and "demanded the cancellation of the whole contract with
the Four Power Group." Croly, op. cit., p. 414. They further demanded that the Imperial
Government, which had appointed the president, should stand the loss of the stolen
funds. This the government refused to do. Indignation mounted. Bitter feelings increased daily. Agitators made the most of their opportunity to advocate overthrow of
the Manchu Dynasty. Sympathetic listeners were not lacking. And on October 10, 1911,
the day before Willard Straight reached Peking, there was a mutinous uprising at
Wuchang of troops under Li Yuan-hung. The old order was changing rapidly. The
Manchu Dynasty was drawing its last breath.

[88] Straight to J. P. Morgan & Company, Nov. 14, 1911. Acting Foreign Minister
Neratov, in a telegram of Nov. 7, 1911, to Izvolsky in Paris expressed St. Petersburg's
determined attitude with the statement: "all of China beyond the Great Wall must
be taken out of the sphere of influence of the four-power consortium." Neratov to Izvolsky, Nov. 7, 1911. Kantorovich, op. cit., p. 233, n. 336.

of sixty per cent for them and forty for the quadruple groups. In all future loans made south of Great Wall when for political purposes only Russia and Japan respectively must be allowed equal participation.

Izvolsky, according to the French report, further said that the policy of Russia and Japan was now identical, and that they would "resist together to the utmost limit any proposed departure therefrom," as well as "any neutralization policy proposed or attempted by the United States in Manchuria; that both Russia and Japan had acquired their interests there by the sacrifice of much blood and treasure while the Americans had made no such sacrifices." [89] And a few days later the United States ambassador at St. Petersburg reported that Acting Foreign Minister Neratov "expressed very frank disatisfaction with the past attitude of the United States in regard to Manchuria." [90]

Meanwhile, the plans of the consortium to issue the Currency Loan in support of the collapsing Manchu Government were blocked, not by Russia and Japan, but by the Chinese revolt against the expiring Manchus. On November 1, 1911, the Imperial Government, in an attempt to forestall the inevitable, called upon "its strongest statesman, Yuan Shih-kai," to take practically unlimited charge of the situation, form a cabinet, and bring order out of chaos. [91] The Manchu child emperor finally abdicated on February 12, 1912, and the Chinese Republic was established with Yuan Shih-kai as Provisional President. [92]

In November 1911, Yuan had applied to the consortium "for a loan with which to pay his troops, maintain order, and reorganize the Chinese Government." [93] A currency loan to pump life blood into an established but feeble government, thereby strengthening foreign interests in China, was one thing. To gamble on an unknown quantity, to recognize a government that had not yet learned to walk alone was a different matter. The financiers and their governments hesitated.

Russia, "on location," was prompt, however, in taking advantage of the revolution to gain the consent of weakened China to Russian control of Mongolia. On January 10, 1912, Mrs. Willard Straight wrote: "Today the news of Russia's coup has fallen like a bomb-shell into Peking. Last Sunday the Russian Chargé presented a note to the Chinese Foreign Office,

[89] Calhoun to Knox, telegram, Dec. 5, 1911.

[90] Guild to Knox, Dec. 15, 1911.

[91] Field, op. cit., p. 67. With the ascendency of Yuan events began to move rapidly in China. The Prince Regent was persuaded to consider resigning. Negotiations were begun early in December between the revolutionists and the government, personified in Yuan Shih-kai. These were interrupted by the revolutionists in the South who, on Jan. 1, 1912, inaugurated Sun Yat-sen as Provisional President, and proclaimed a new capital at Nanking. Tang Shao-yi, whose mission to the United States in 1908 had failed, was sent to the South to negotiate with the rebels. A compromise was reached. It was agreed that if Yuan Shih-kai could insure the abdication of the Manchus, Sun Yat-sen would resign in favor of Yuan.

[92] Ibid., p. 68.

[93] Griswold, op. cit., p. 170; Reid, op. cit., p. 254.

demanding that Mongolia be declared independent under the suzerainty of Russia. . . ." [94] And in a report to Nicholas II on January 23, 1912, Foreign Minister Sazonov, after observing that the new republic would need money for which guarantees would be necessary, and that Russian and Japanese interests in China were paramount, said:

Russia and Japan must . . . make use of the present exceptionally favorable moment for strengthening their position in China and put an end to the policy which the Chinese government has been following for the last few years and which has been directed against the primary political interests of Japan and Russia.[95]

The revolution had played into the hands of both Russia and Japan by offering them the weakness of China "as an excuse for aggrandizement at her expense." [96]

At the same time Russia was again exerting pressure, now upon France, with the aim of disrupting the consortium.[97] In December 1911, the Russian foreign minister, Sazonov, wrote Izvolsky: "We are working for the destruction of this Syndicate by inducing France to retire from it, and we regard our participation as only possible if it is so reconstructed that we have predominant influence north of Great Wall." [98] And in the same month Willard Straight wrote to Henry P. Davison of the Morgan group:

They [the Russians] bombard the French government and the banks with insinuations regarding our American policy. It looks to me as if a serious attempt was being made to break up the quadruple combination which is not looked on with favor by either Russia or Japan.[99]

Before the middle of March 1912, the members of the consortium as well as their respective governments had agreed upon the necessity of making a large loan to the Chinese Republic. This decision was not entirely disinterested, since China, if unassisted, would be in danger of defaulting in her payments abroad, in which case "the market value of existing investments in that country would . . . undergo a sharp decline." [100] Russia and

[94] Croly, *op. cit.*, p. 428.

[95] Report of Sazonov to Nicholas II, January 23, 1912. *Komissia po Izdaniu Dokumentov Epochi Imperializma*, etc., series 2, XIX, 33, Doc. 379.

[96] Croly, *op. cit.*, p. 428. On November 8, 1911, Mrs. Straight wrote: "Willard and I had an interesting talk the other day with Korostovetz, the Russian Minister. He came out quite openly with a statement of his policy, admitting that his only idea was to keep China weak and oppose always the establishment of a strong government." *Ibid.*, p. 421.

[97] Frederick Stieve, *Isvolsky and the World War*, pp. 26, 69.

[98] *Ibid.*, p. 29; Field, *op. cit.*, p. 104.

[99] Kantorovich, *op. cit.*, p. 208; Croly, *op. cit.*, pp. 429–30; Reid, *op. cit.*, pp. 261–63. Not only was pressure brought upon France but upon England also. Reid states (*op. cit.*, pp. 262, 272) that at this time the French were more in favor of Russo-Japanese admission into the consortium than of French withdrawal, and tried to persuade Sazonov but the latter was unconvinced. Paris believed that a four-power combination of England, France, Japan, and Russia within the consortium would thwart German and American ambitions. Lancken to Kiderlen-Waechter, from Paris, Dec. 11, 1911. *Die Grosse Politik*, XXXII, No. 11779, 199–200. Shortly, however, the new Poincaré government assured Russia of full support. Reid, *op. cit.*, p. 273.

[100] Croly, *op. cit.*, p. 442.

Japan, however, still remained formidable obstacles to American plans. Their interests in Manchuria and Mongolia were too wide, their relations with the governments of the British and French members of the consortium were too involved, their power to block action by refusing recognition to the new government was too great, to risk their displeasure. Both Russia and Japan had made it clear at an early stage of the revolution that a price must be paid if they joined the consortium, that of "recognition of their 'special interests' in Manchuria and Mongolia." [101] And on March 14, 1912, Sazonov notified the Russian ambassadors at Washington, Berlin, Paris, and London that he had informed the representatives of the four powers in St. Petersburg that Russian and Japanese participation in loans could be undertaken only upon the basis of recognition of Russia's special spheres of interest (Manchuria, Mongolia, and North China), and that in these spheres Russia wished to hold dominance in regard to loans and the income which guaranteed them.[102]

Reports during this period from American diplomats in the Far East give added proof of the attitude of Russia and Japan. An *aide memoire*, presented by the Russian foreign minister to the American Government through United States Ambassador Guild at St. Petersburg, reads in part:

. . . The Russian Government . . . learned with regret that the combination of English, French, German and American bankers had advanced to the provisional government of Nanking the sum of two million taels and another million to Yuan Shih-kai and was prepared to advance to it other sums in addition without any consultation with Russia. In view of the purely political character of these advances the Russian Government believes it should take part in them in order to maintain the principle of the solidarity of the Powers in regard to the Chinese Government.[103]

An additional *aide memoire* of later date from the same source states that,

The Russian Government is ready to participate in the loan of reorganization on terms of equality with the other governments which participate therein. In consenting to the said participation the Russian Government believes itself obliged clearly to indicate from now on that the conditions of the reorganization loan should contain nothing that may be injurious in its nature to the rights and special interests of Russia in north Manchuria, in Mongolia, and in West China. With this reservation the Russian Government is ready to designate the Russian-

[101] Price, *op. cit.*, p. 73.

[102] Telegrams of Sazonov from St. Petersburg, March 14, 1912, *Komissia po Izdaniu Dokumentov Epochi Imperializma, etc.*, series 2, XIX, Part 2, 270, Doc. 629. In earlier telegrams to the Russian ambassadors Sazonov, referring to Russia's "special interests" in Manchuria, Mongolia, and North China, said: "Approving of the idea of joint action of the powers in so far as they have in view the defense of their common interests in China, we must retain for ourselves, in relation to our special rights and interests in the aforementioned provinces, freedom to undertake such measures of security which we shall find necessary." And Sazonov requested the ambassadors to inform the particular powers to this effect. Telegrams of Sazonov to Ambassadors at Berlin, Paris, London, and Washington, March 6, 1912. *Ibid.*, Doc. 591, p. 236.

[103] Guild to Knox, telegram, March 15, 1912.

Asiatic Bank as being the representative of the Russian financial group in the Consortium which will take upon itself the issue of the Chinese reorganization loan.[104]

Japan having declared, as early as March 18, 1912, her willingness to participate in the loan with "reservations," [105] reported in May through her ambassador, Viscount Chinda, at Washington:

The Japanese Ambassador said that he was ordered by his Government to explain to us that, in view of Russia's reservation of rights in relation to Northern Manchuria, Mongolia and Western China, the Japanese Government had felt that silence might be misconstrued and that, therefore, Japan must make reservations as to Eastern Inner Mongolia (bordering on Southern Manchuria) in which quarter Japan naturally was interested.[106]

Two days before Ambassador Chinda called at the Department of State, Korostovetz, Russian minister at Peking, had sent an interesting and informative report to the Foreign Office at St. Petersburg stating that he had

gained the conviction from discussions with my foreign colleagues that we need at present fear no opposition on the part of the foreign Powers should we deem it necessary to take . . . military measures in Northern Manchuria, Mongolia and in West China. . . .

The Russian Minister continued:

Our Chargé d'Affaires informed you in his letter of March 3rd that the American representative categorically declared that his instructions contained nothing which would cause him to thwart our actions in Mongolia and Manchuria. The American Representative also expressed himself in the same terms to the British Minister. This caused Sir John Jordan to inform me that no other Power would attempt to oppose our measures. "You can now undoubtedly proceed without anxiety in West China and Outer Mongolia," my English colleague told me, "and will only have to take Japanese interests and desires into account in Manchuria." [107] This is also the opinion of the majority of my other colleagues.[108]

[104] Guild to Knox, telegram, April 17, 1912.

[105] *For. Rel.* 1912, pp. 114–15.

[106] *Ibid.* Memorandum of a conversation between Acting Secretary of State [Huntington Wilson] and the Japanese ambassador, Department of State, May 16, 1912. *Ibid.*, p. 79. Price (*op. cit.*, p. 72) states that the reply of the acting secretary of state on May 16, 1912, to the Japanese ambassador, inadvertently or otherwise, put the United States on record as upholding the principle that foreign governments might resort to "such protective measures" within their "spheres of interest" in China "as may be forced by necessity" provided that "the rights and interests" within the spheres are based on treaties or conventions with China.

[107] Commenting on this point, De Siebert and Schreiner say: ". . . there being no intimation as to Sir John's authority for such a sweeping statement, it must be accepted that he acted either upon his own initiative or upon instructions from London, paralleling Mr. Rockhill's orders from Washington." *Op. cit.*, p. 38 n.

[108] Report of the Russian minister at Peking to the Russian Ministry of Foreign Affairs, May 1/14, 1912. *Ibid.*, pp. 38–39. Russia had informed Great Britain of the "reservations" and had received a reply almost identical with that from the United States, namely, an acceptance, with the understanding that Russia's special interests to be pro-

A personal letter dated June 13th from Ambassador Herrick in Paris, shows that in his opinion Russia continued her efforts to break down the consortium almost upon the eve of her entrance. He writes, "I am inclined to the belief that Russia is the dominating factor in desiring the failure of the negotiations, that Japan is rather more inclined to stand with the other groups." He added that "It would seem that there is a certain rancour remaining between these two nations, as a result of the War, which makes it difficult for them to get on well together," and he was of the opinion that the only thing which united Russia and Japan was "their jealousy of the United States in their relations with China." [109]

Finally, on June 20, 1912, Russia and Japan, represented respectively by the Russo-Asiatic Bank and the Yokohama Specie Bank, became participants in the reorganization loan negotiations, and the four-power consortium became a six-power consortium. Russia, as already seen, had stipulated that her entrance should in no way "operate to the prejudice of the special rights and interests of Russia in the regions of northern Manchuria, Mongolia and western China;" and Japan, in the same manner, had made her entry contingent upon non-interference of the group with her "special rights and interests" in "South Manchuria and inner Mongolia adjacent to South Manchuria." [110] Although these conditions for entrance

were made, and accepted, with the characteristic ambiguity of diplomacy (which leaves each party free to interpret an agreement according to its own interests) American acceptance of them was a long step backward from the neutralization scheme and the Chinchow-Aigun project.[111]

---

tected were those covered by treaty and convention. This reply was unsatisfactory to the Russian Foreign Office. Referring to the limitations (as interpreted by Great Britain) to Russia's special interests "which arise out of our treaties with China," Sazonov in a communication to London, stated that "this limitation is not in accordance with our point of view. Geographical position and economical development draw these districts more and more toward Russia; as a result of this we have to deal with particular circumstances, and our political interests have not always found expression in our treaties with China. May I request you to bring this point to the knowledge of the British Government in order to avoid any misunderstanding with regard to the support we expect from the London Cabinet, should we take part in the Chinese Reorganization Syndicate?" Sazonov to Russian ambassador in London, telegram, April 7/20, 1912. *Ibid.*, p. 38. Also in Memorandum of the Russian Foreign Ministry to Ambassador Buchanan in St. Petersburg, April 25, 1912. *Komissia po Izdaniu Dokumentov Epochi Imperializma, etc.*, series 2, XIX, Doc. 807, No. 716, p. 456.

[109] Myron Herrick to Knox, letter, Paris, June 13, 1912.

[110] *For. Rel.*, 1912, pp. 137, 140-41; MacMurray, *op. cit.*, II, 1024, contains the texts of the Russian and Japanese reservations. Another condition exacted by the Russian Government was provision for the withdrawal of either Russia or Japan if "the object of any loan or advance were disapproved by them." Kantorovich, *op. cit.*, p. 208; Price, *op. cit.*, p. 75, n. 60.

[111] Griswold, *op. cit.*, pp. 171–72. In a compromise agreement drawn up on June 8, 1912, the British, German, French, and American groups declared, "that they were not

And, as Kantorovich states, Russia and Japan had entered the consortium as victors. No longer, to view the situation through Russian eyes, was the consortium "a weapon of anti-Russian and anti-Japanese politics whose chief carrier was the United States."

In this struggle [the Russian writer continues] the American group, reduced to the position of a partner of the second grade, already did not actively participate. The exclusion of railroad loans from the sphere of action of the consortium, in which American capital was primarily interested, was in essence, a new blow against American policies.[112]

Now that the Russian objective was achieved, Foreign Minister Sazonov could afford to assure the American Ambassador that,

. . . The Russian Government is now entirely convinced that the United States is acting in a most friendly manner. The course of events, in the last few months especially, has proved, in his [Sazonov's] opinion, in this entire question of the Chinese loans and railroads, that the United States . . . seeks to grant fair play to Russia.[113]

By July 19, 1912, rumors of an approaching third alliance between Russia and Japan began to appear in reports from American diplomats in Tokyo and St. Petersburg. Commenting on the forthcoming visit to St. Petersburg of Prince Katsura, former prime minister and also minister of war of Japan, Chargé d'affaires Charles Wilson, in a despatch from St. Petersburg on July 19, 1912, to Secretary Knox, wrote:

From unofficial but well-informed sources I learn that this visit is fraught with great political significance; that Mr. Katsura brings with him a proposal from his government that the interests of Russia and Japan in the Far East shall be definitely determined between them; that an agreement will be made so that in the event of the dissolution of the Chinese Empire each Power shall have a definite plan in regard to Mongolia and Manchuria; and it is stated further that even England may be consulted in this arrangement.[114]

Tokyo, on July 20, however, "emphatically denied" contemplating either a Russo-Japanese alliance or a revision of existing treaties.[115] On the 24th, the Japanese Government elaborating this denial through its minister of foreign affairs, stated that newspaper reports of such an alliance were "pure fabrication," and that the rumors of a revision of the exist-

---

in a position to express their views upon either of these declarations [those of Russia and Japan] upon the ground that they were not competent to deal with political questions." Price, *op. cit.*, p. 75, n. 60; Kantorovich, *op. cit.*, p. 209. Berating the governments that sanctioned "a politico-financial loan of the kind created by the 'participation' of Russia and Japan," Bland (*op. cit.*, p. 393) is of the opinion "that by becoming parties to such operations, the Powers concerned become morally responsible for the establishment of a Russo-Japanese Protectorate in the regions to the North and West of the Great Wall and *ipso facto* make the Treaty of Portsmouth of no effect."

112 Kantorovich, *op. cit.*, p. 209.
113 Guild to Secretary of State, June 23, 1912.
114 Charles Wilson to Knox, July 19, 1912.
115 Charles Page Bryan to Knox, telegram, July 20, 1912.

ing treaty were equally without foundation.[116] On July 27, Ambassador Guild at St. Petersburg, confirming Mr. Wilson's despatch of the preceding week, wrote:

During the week Prince Katsura of Japan and suite have been visiting St. Petersburg. It was generally announced in the press here from Japanese sources that Prince Katsura's visit was to confirm a treaty arranged with Russia with the consent of England, in accordance with which Japan and Russia were to engage in nothing less than an offensive and defensive alliance, especially as far as China is concerned. . . . It is generally believed in all diplomatic circles . . . that some sort of understanding . . . has been reached by Japan, Russia and England in regard to English interests in Thibet, Russian interests in Mongolia and Japanese interests in Manchuria.[117]

The Russian Government was quite as forthright, according to the ambassador, in promptly denying this report, as had been Japan.[118]

On July 30th Ambassador Guild again reported:

In conversation today with Mr. Kokovtsev, the Prime Minister, His Excellency emphatically denied that the visit of Prince Katsura of Japan had any political significance. He stated that no new treaty had been arranged either by the Prince or by Baron Motono, that no new entente even had been broached, but that of course relations of Russia and Japan have been the subject of prolonged conversations of an informal character.[119]

Yet on July 8, 1912, twenty-two days before the emphatic denial of the Russian prime minister, a secret treaty had been concluded between Russia and Japan, signed by Sazonov, Russian minister of foreign affairs, and Motono, the Japanese ambassador at St. Petersburg.[120] This secret treaty was a formal convention rounding out and giving precision to the terms of the secret treaties of 1907 and 1910. Article 1 of the new treaty prolonged the line of demarcation between North and South Manchuria, established by the secret treaty of 1907, until it accurately defined the boundary between Russian and Japanese spheres of influence in Mongolia. By the terms of Article II Inner Mongolia was divided by the meridian of 116° 27' east longitude into two parts. All west of the given meridian was recognized as Russia's sphere of interest; all east of it as Japan's.[121]

[116] Charles Page Bryan to Knox, July 24, 1912.
[117] Curtiss Guild to Knox, July 27, 1912.
[118] *Ibid.*
[119] Guild to Knox, July 30, 1912.
[120] Avarin, *op. cit.,* I, 137; Price, *op. cit.,* p. 75. As late as August 19, Ambassador Guild again reported: "I learn on the highest authority that M. Sazonoff on being questioned in regard to this [signing of the convention between Japan and Russia] by the German Ambassador denied absolutely that any written convention had been entered into." Guild to Knox, Aug. 19, 1912.
[121] Secret Convention of June 25/July 8, 1912. Avarin, *op. cit.,* I, 137. Russian copy of convention (translated apparently from the French text) in E. D. Grimm, *Sbornik Dogovorov i Drugikh Dokumentov po Istorii Mezhdunarodnykh Otnoshenii na Dal'nem Vostoke* (Collection of Treaties and other Documents concerning the History of International Relations in the Far East), p. 180. Also, appendix D; Price, *op. cit.,* p. 117.

In this manner Russia and Japan had given their final answer to the policy of the Taft-Knox administration, to the diplomacy of the American dollar in Manchuria and Mongolia. This third Russo-Japanese treaty widened the breach in the already ruptured territorial integrity of China and barred "the door to dollar diplomacy yet more firmly." [122]

The American policy, according to Bland was

irreproachable and just. . . . It aimed at placing Manchuria under an international economic protectorate, pending such time as China should be fit to walk alone. . . . It was a policy of righteousness, tempered by enlightened self-interest —but it required the delicate handling of a Metternich to make it effective and to dominate the equally enlightened self-interest of other Powers.[123]

Turning from this viewpoint to look through modern Russian eyes we are told by Kantorovich that the American policy, far from being one of "righteousness,"

consisted in the effort to put an end to the hegemony of Tsarist Russia in North China and Japan in South Manchuria and to create conditions for the establishment of American control in the form of internationalization. In New York and Washington it was calculated that once having won this position the United States would be able to smash the united front between Japan and Russia. Instead, the American advance directly led to the formation of a stronger united front, to a Russo-Japanese alliance directed against America, and to the confirmation of the monopolistic hegemony of each of the partners in its Manchurian sphere.[124]

And again this writer states: "Tsarist Russia and Japan together opposed the 'golden' consortium with the 'steel' of their exclusive positions in Manchuria and Mongolia, on which the American leaders of the consortium chiefly had their eyes." [125]

The reorganization loan agreement was finally concluded on April 26, 1913, but not with the United States as a signatory.[126] The fatal blow to dollar diplomacy had been dealt on March 18, 1913, when President Wilson withdrew governmental support from the American bankers on the grounds that it touched too closely "the administrative independence of China itself." [127] The initiative for withdrawal came, not from the idealism of the President, but from the demands of the American bankers who were weary of "the tedium of fruitless negotiations," and dissatisfied that

[122] Griswold, *op. cit.*, p. 172.

[123] Bland, *op. cit.*, p. 319.

[124] Kantorovich, *op. cit.*, p. 193.

[125] *Ibid.*, p. 207.

[126] Price, *op. cit.*, p. 144. This agreement, in which all reference to Manchurian enterprises was omitted, was a far step from the Currency Reform and Industrial Development Loan Agreement of April 15, 1911. *Ibid.* Willard Straight could no longer say, "Dollar diplomacy is justified at last."

[127] Field, *op. cit.*, p. 93; MacMurray, *op. cit.*, II, 1025. Griswold, *op. cit.*, p. 172; Morse and MacNair, *op. cit.*, p. 555. The American Government gave as its reasons for refusing to give further support to the American bankers that "it did not approve the conditions of the loan or the implications of responsibility on its own part which it was plainly told would be involved." MacMurray, *op. cit.*, II, 1025. Price, *op. cit.*, p. 144.

they were "not yet in a position to make any profit out of their endeavors." [128] Their representatives approached President Wilson the day after his inauguration, stating their unwillingness to retain membership in the consortium unless requested to do so by the Government of the United States.[129] No such request was forthcoming.

With the withdrawal of the American financial group from the consortium, animosity between the United States and Russia, with nothing upon which to feed, sank below the level of diplomatic and historical attention. American despatches during the period between the withdrawal of the United States from the consortium and the outbreak of the Great War are without Russian-American substance. On January 16, 1914, Chargé Charles Wilson, writing from St. Petersburg to the secretary of state reported that,

the "Novoe Vremya" in its number for January 1/14, gives a long summary of the relations of Russia with all the various countries, during and at the end of 1913. The relations of Russia with the United States are summed up in the single line at the very end with the statement that they have remained in the same state of cold indifference.

Russia, together with her Manchurian alter ego, Japan, had emerged as victor. Russia, triumphant in victory, made extensive plans for tightening her grip upon China and widening her scope of operations. One of these schemes was a demand upon the Chinese Government for the preferred right to construct "a list of railways mentioned which are staggering in their extent, covering practically all railways it would seem ever profitable to build in Northern Manchuria and Outer Mongolia." In addition, Russia was to demand "the right to exploitation of the mountain forest and other wealth attaching to the above lines." [130] But Russia reckoned without foreknowledge, August 1914 was rapidly approaching.

Turning to the United States, where had the Far Eastern trail upon which the American Government entered with the annexation of the Philippines led? What had been accomplished by Secretary Hay's appeal to the powers to guarantee the Open Door within their respective spheres in China, and by his promulgation of the principle of the territorial integrity of China? What had been the result of the American-Russian diplomatic duel waged over Manchuria between 1900 and 1904? What had been the outcome of Roosevelt's policy of balanced antagonisms during the Russo-Japanese War? And finally, how far had the Taft-Knox administration, backed by the financial power of American capitalists, carried out the policies of Hay, and succeeded in achieving their own Far Eastern plans and ambitions?

[128] MacMurray to Rockhill, March 18, 1913. Rockhill papers. Griswold, *op. cit.*, pp. 172–73.

[129] MacMurray to Rockhill, March 18, 1913. Griswold, *op. cit.*, p. 173.

[130] De Siebert and Schreiner, *op. cit.*, p. 43. Price, *op. cit.*, p. 76.

The Philippines, which had been annexed supposedly to protect American interests in China and to increase American Far Eastern trade, had become by 1907, in the opinion of Theodore Roosevelt, "our heel of Achilles," to be either strongly fortified or relinquished. The Open Door policy, weakened at the outset by the reservations and qualifications of the powers, became with the passing of time a veritable pretext for intervention. Nor was the principle of the integrity of China applied more satisfactorily. Even its formulator, Secretary Hay, in November 1900, under pressure from the War and Navy Departments, made an unsuccessful attempt to acquire a naval base and territorial concession at Samsah Bay in Fukien province, and later resigned himself to acceptance of Manchuria as a virtual Russian protectorate, provided that "freedom of American trade and enterprise . . . [was] guaranteed in this province." In the diplomatic duel waged between the United States and Russia from 1900 to 1904, Russia fought for political and economic domination of Manchuria, certain Tsarist officials even demanding annexation, while the United States, determined to keep the door open for her growing trade and economic interests in Manchuria, sought to prevent the realization of the Russian goal. Following the usual pattern of power politics, this diplomatic battle was fought with acrimony on both sides, and with a duplicity, even treachery, on the part of the Tsarist Foreign Office seldom found in the annals of diplomacy. Hay eventually won a victory of sorts in the Chinese-American Treaty of 1903 which provided for the opening of ports and the appointment of foreign consuls in Manchuria. As a result of Roosevelt's policy of balanced antagonisms during the Russo-Japanese War, to which Soviet historians refer as America's and Britain's war by proxy, Japan, far from being weakened, emerged a more formidable rival than Russia. After the war of 1904–5, Tsarist Russia, as evidenced by Russian Foreign Office and American State Department sources, lived in constant fear of Japanese attack, and this uneasy expectation lasted up to the outbreak of World War I despite the treaties of 1907, 1910, and 1912. Because of this fear, official Russia, as well as the press, was divided as to means of coping with the situation. One group, favoring a rapprochement with the United States, made mild and unsuccessful efforts in 1909 toward that end; the other group, cognizant of *Realpolitik* in Europe and the Far East and irked by the clumsy policies of our own State Department, favored closer ties with Japan, and won out. This Russo-Japanese combination, supported by Britain and France, increasingly undermined the position of the United States in the Manchurian field, especially after 1909 during the period of dollar diplomacy of the Taft-Knox administration. Dollar diplomacy proved no more successful than had previous policies of the American State Department, and left the territorial integrity of China more precarious than when Taft, Knox, and the American bankers entered the Far Eastern arena. Manchuria, which was to be saved intact, supposedly for China with American interests as an important side issue, had come under the control of Russia and Japan. Figures which are available for

American investments during this period show an appreciable decline between 1908 and 1914.[131] Thus, the long period of American-Russian rivalry in the Far East which had begun in 1895, came to a close on March 18, 1913, when President Wilson, at the request of the bankers themselves, withdrew governmental support from the consortium group.

But the United States, like Russia, was soon to be involved in the World War, the ill-omened shadow of which had long hovered over Europe. War, on a hitherto unprecedented scale, was rising on the international horizon. In such a war, in any war, greeds, hatreds, ambitions, aims, and schemes are temporarily submerged. And from such wars new lines of demarcation, new setups and new institutions emerge. Ambitions, schemes, greeds, hatreds, new in form, old in content, again arise. And the age-old cycle of history, apparently in an ever-widening circle, repeats itself.

[131] Of the total consortium loan of £27,000,000 to the Chinese Government, American bankers furnished only $7,299,000, this figure representing their share in the Hukuang railway loan of £6,000,000. American private investment in China in 1914 was $42,000,000 (2.8% of the total American investments abroad) together with mission property valued at $10,000,000. Remer, *op. cit.*, pp. 125–30, 249–65, 338. Kantorovich, *op. cit.*, p. 212. American finance in China had reached "a period of total stagnation" after the United States withdrew from the consortium. Tan, S. H. "The Diplomacy of American Investments in China," an unpublished dissertation of 1927 in the Library of the University of Chicago. According to Paul Reinsch (U.S. Minister to China, 1913–19) the only successful enterprises of American capital in China were the Standard Oil and the British-American Tobacco Company. Reinsch, *An American Diplomat in China*, pp. 66–67. "If national standing in China were to be determined by the holding of government concessions, America was at this time, indeed, poorly equipped." *Ibid.*, p. 67. Despite the growing friction between the United States and Japan, American trade with Japan exceeded that with China. Between 1910 and 1914 the annual American import and export trade with Japan was approximately $129,700,000; with China, $51,000,000. Frederick V. Field, ed., *Economic Handbook of the Pacific Area*, pp. 470–71. American exports to China in 1914 represented less than 1% of our total exports, Chinese imports to the United States only 2% of our total imports. Bemis, *Diplomatic History*, p. 501 n. In the light of the evidence, it would seem to the author that whenever the United States has pursued an aggressive Far Eastern policy, the initiative, in the main, has come not from financial and business groups but from the State Department and Administration.

Appendix I

INSTRUCTIONS OF THE TSARIST FOREIGN MINISTER, MURAVIEV, TO CASSINI, THE AMBASSADOR TO WASHINGTON, AND LETTERS OF CASSINI TO MURAVIEV AND LAMSDORF, 1898 *

INTRODUCTORY NOTE *

By F. Kelin

The "instructions" to the Russian diplomat, Count A. P. Cassini, at the time of his appointment as ambassador to Washington, and his two letters, one to Minister of Foreign Affairs M. N. Muraviev, the other to V. H. Lamsdorf, assistant minister of foreign affairs, which are here reproduced, are of particular value in reaching an understanding of the true character of Russian-American relations toward the end of the nineteenth century. The instructions are dated January 1898; in other words at the time when the Washington Government had succeeded in persuading the Madrid Government to permit the sending of the cruiser *Maine* to the port of Havana, the tragic fate of which was the immediate cause for the Spanish-American War. Consequently, in the instructions to Cassini, the winds already blow of the war that marked the turning point in the international relations of the United States, which, with the seizure of Cuba, Puerto-Rico, the Philippines and Guam, entered the path of colonial politics beyond America. On the other hand, the two letters of the ambassador to the Russian ministers present a clear picture of the sentiments prevailing in ruling Tsarist circles over the brilliant success of American imperialism. . . . In this connection the letters of Cassini are very enlightening documents, and the Tsarist authorities showed wisdom in separating them from the mass of information received from Washington in 1898 and placing them in their secret archives.

For a history of Russian-American relations in the nineteenth century

---

* "*Severo-Amerikanskie Soedinennye Stati i Tsarskaia Rossia v 90-h gg. XIX V.*" (North-American United States and Tsarist Russia in the Nineties of the Nineteenth Century), *Krasnyi Arkhiv*, LII, 125–42.

we refer readers to the existing Russian and foreign literature. But we wish to point out that the ties which have a "historical foundation," spoken of in the instructions to Cassini, were based mainly on the naval rivalry of Russia and the United States with the stronger England. So great was the rapprochement between the two countries in certain years of the nineteenth century, that St. Petersburg was even speaking of a Russo-American alliance. Such was the situation at the beginning of the seventies when Russia declared that the Paris Compact of 1856 was not binding upon itself. We give one clear illustration, which until now has not been found in special literature on the subject. This is a fragment from the diary of A. F. Tiutcheva who was close to the family of Alexander II, in relation to a conversation with Empress Marie Alexandrovna in Moscow in 1870.

"Her Majesty told me in this conversation," Tiutcheva writes on November 27, "that we (that is Russia) are guaranteed an alliance with America, which is ready to place its navy in war preparedness at the slightest sign of hostility on the part of England. 'This is the kind of thing,' she added, 'that is never published in newspapers.' " [1]

The official list of "good-will gestures" which Russia extended to the United States is found in the instructions to Cassini.

Having relinquished Alaska and regarded the seizure of the Hawaiian Islands by the United States "with sympathy," Tsarist Russia, according to these instructions, affirms its friendly attitude toward "the strengthening of the power of the United States on the continent in opposition to that of Great Britain," at the same time giving it the opportunity "to take an important step forward in the realization of the Monroe doctrine."

But it was clear that the ephemeral structure of Russo-American friendship would be shaken at the first serious conflict between Russian and American imperialism in the sphere of colonial politics. Such a conflict of interests we find at the end of the nineties in the nineteenth century when, having recovered from the consequences of a heavy and prolonged "secessionist war," which was a real catastrophe for the American merchant marine, the United States entered upon a period of economic growth. Exports at the end of the century reached such proportions that they were nearly half as large again as imports. The increase was particularly noticeable in the export of fabricated products. American goods began to compete in the Far East, and even on the banks of the Mediterranean, with the products of European factories. From a debtor country, the United States gradually transformed itself into a creditor country, and began to win new markets for the surplus products of its industry. True, at the end of the nineties the United States was still too weak in purely naval or marine power to enter into profitable competition with the great sea powers over colonies, or even in the "rape of Chinese soil." Externally, they still held to the classical line of conduct for a bourgeois government—not

---

[1] A. F. Tyutcheva, *Pri Dvore Dvoukh Imperatorov, Dnevnik, 1885–1882 gg.,* (At the Court of Two Emperors. Diary), I, 216.

to seize as their own any territory on the Asiatic continent. . . . But the United States did demand "access everywhere for its goods on the best possible terms available for the given place." [2]. . .

But the United States had their own active navy which, although comparatively not large, was capable of engaging in offensive sea battles as the naval events of 1898 proved. It is therefore not surprising that in 1897 the Washington Government decided to create the special "Chinese squadron" of Admiral Dewey, which played such an important role in seizing the strategic key to the sea routes to China—the Philippines—the magnet toward which all nations who desired economic and naval supremacy in the Far East were drawn.

The exceptional strength of the United States could not fail to alarm the commercial and industrial nations of Europe. An outstanding example of this alarm is found in the conversation of William II with the Russian minister of finance, S. U. Witte, at the time of the former's visit to St. Petersburg in August 1897—shortly before the "instructions" were sent to Cassini—when Germany succeeded in getting Russia's consent to the seizure of a stubborn piece of Chinese territory (Kiaochow). In the memoirs of Witte [3] we read that the German Emperor said that

America was becoming a dangerous competitor to Europe, especially in the field of agriculture; that America was growing rich at the expense of Europe; that she should not be treated as a most-favored-nation and treaties concluded with her; but that special measures should be taken in regard to tariffs by erecting a high tariff wall around Europe so as to make it impossible for America to flood us with her products.

When Witte pointed out the possible danger to Europe from England, William II replied, "That it was America and not England which was dumping agricultural products into European markets and lowering prices." To this Witte answered that "it would be difficult for Russia to take such a point of view for the reason that ever since the American Revolutionary War we have been on the best of terms with the United States of America and that we do not intend to quarrel with that country."

After William II had returned to Germany, Nicholas II handed Witte "a brief note given him by the German Emperor" which in substance, according to Witte, reiterated what William II had said to him and advised the erection of militant custom barriers against the United States.

I did not conceal from His Majesty that I had discussed the subject with the German Monarch, and also stated my own views on the subject. His Majesty, assuring me that he shared my point of view, asked me to write a reply to this note in the same spirit in which I had spoken with the German Emperor, which I did in the form of an unsigned memorandum and gave it to the Emperor. . . .

Although Tsarist Russia did not find it expedient to engage in any of

[2] M. Pokrovsky, *Diplomatia i Voini Tzarskoy Rossii* (Diplomacy and Wars of Tsarist Russia), 1924, p. 367.

[3] S. U. Witte, *Vospominania* (Memoirs), I, 98–101.

the hostile activities against the United States upon which the Emperor insisted, the economic expansion of North-American capital "on the whole western coast-line of the Pacific Ocean seriously worried the ruling circles of Russia. Moreover, in 1897 a change of sentiment in Anglo-American relations was noticed in a direction that was highly unwelcome to Russia. On January 6, 1898, the despatch of de Wollant, Cassini's predecessor in Washington, informed the Minister of Foreign Affairs that he had received confidential information that England's ambassador to Washington had renewed conversations with the Federal Government in regard to the conclusion of an arbitration treaty." De Wollant wrote:

"This treaty, concluded by the Anglophile Administration of Cleveland, was . . . rejected by the last session of Congress in the Senate. The conclusion of such a treaty would free England to act in regard to America according to its own interests." De Wollant added that the Americans "were aware of this fact, and understood that such a treaty with England might involve the United States in conflicts with other powers." He reported further that "notwithstanding the sympathy felt for the mother country, the majority of Americans were distrustful of English politics and had no desire to strengthen the power of Great Britain." [4] However, the very fact that the friction in Anglo-American relations caused by the Venezuelan question in 1895 had undergone a change made it necessary for the Russian Government to make haste in determining the basic points of its American policy.

Such an effort at revision is found in the instructions issued to Cassini. What are the outstanding factors in these instructions? Above all these: that notwithstanding the frequent references to friendly relations with the American Government, to the "fruits of healthy seeds sown by Russia," Cassini's instructions are permeated with a poorly concealed hostility toward the United States, in whom the St. Petersburg circles see a possible competitor in the Far East. We must not forget in this connection that Cassini's instructions preceded by two months the agreement for the leasing of the Liaotung peninsula (March 15, 1898), in which "Russian capital was guaranteed a monopoly."

The instructions begin with an admonition as to the "significance for Russian interests of the development of American industry in the Far East," and follow with the advice to make a sharp distinction "between those industries which are favorable to us and those which impinge on our sphere of influence. While conducting yourself in conformity with the first, you will have to act energetically against the latter, making use of your inherent tact and with caution winning the sympathy of the Federal Government."

No less characteristic as indicative of the writer's mood are the concluding words of the instructions:

[4] *Arkhiv Revolutzii i Vneshnei Politiki,* "Perepiska s Vashingtonom" za 1898 g. (Archive of Revolution and Foreign Policy, "Correspondence with Washington," 1898).

You will have therefore to determine how advantageous the secession of Canada from Great Britain would be for us. Would the consequent strengthening of the United States be an obstacle to us and perhaps even a threat to the existing good relations? Would the United States, already having assumed the status of a great power, preserve for us, after the dismemberment of Great Britain the same passive good-will toward our policies, or would it become a competitor with whom we would have to contend as we do now with Great Britain?

But the instructions of Cassini are valuable not only for the testimony they give of the alarm with which the Petersburg ruling cliques regarded the successes of American imperialism. They belong to those frank documents which are so abundant in the period of the Muraviev directorate of the Foreign Ministry. Muraviev did not like to write but, once writing, he named things unhesitantly without any diplomatic subterfuges. In the instructions to Cassini we find a series of such revelations, showing the true interests which dominated the Tsarist Government in different situations. From them we know that the sale of Alaska for an "insignificant sum" was made in order to restrict the power of Great Britain on the American continent. No less frank was the attitude of the Tsarist diplomats in relation to the Monroe doctrine. "Since Russia had no geographical proximity to the United States and possessed no colonies on the American continent, it was convenient to lend support to this popular theory of America in such cases as this where it was useful in blocking the interests of Russia's real antagonist—Great Britain, in its relation to Canada." Equally frank were the statements in regard to the American seizure of the Hawaiian Islands. "To see the Hawaiian Islands become another Malta or a new Japanese naval base was highly undesirable; better that they belong to the United States, and remain for Russia a half-way station, devoted and friendly, than to become a nest for the enemy and a hostile rear." "We are fully aware," intoned the instructions to Cassini, "that the United States has given attention to the gradual conquests of England in the Pacific Ocean and has decided to impede it in the given instance, as well as the expanding Japan."

Cassini, in turn, was subject to the same moods that dominated the theoretical considerations of the Tsarist Government, which spoke in limited terms of "Russian friendship." Five months passed between the date of the instructions and the letters from Washington—five months rich in political connotations. We consider it necessary to call the attention of the reader to those events on the political calendar for the first half of 1898 which are essential for the understanding of the present documents.

On February 15th, the cruiser *Maine* exploded in the Havana harbor. On March 15 the Spanish Government turned to the great powers with the request for mediation in its dispute with the United States. On March 28, the Chinese and the Russian Governments signed a treaty leasing the Liaotung Peninsula, with Port Arthur, to the Russians. From here on relations between Russia and England reached a high point of tension.

On the 10th of April the United States demanded that Spain withdraw its naval and military forces from the Cuban island. On April 21, diplomatic relations between the two countries were severed, after which open military operations took place. On May 1, the Spanish naval forces under Admiral Montojo stationed at Manila Bay were destroyed by the naval squadron of Admiral Dewey. England's Colonial Minister Chamberlain delivered a speech in Birmingham on May 13 calling for an alliance of England, Germany and the United States against the designs of Russia. On May 19, the Spanish squadron under Servere escaped to Santiago and was there destroyed by American forces. Within a brief period Santiago surrendered and the Spanish Government asked Washington through the French ambassador for a cessation of hostilities. On August 12, Manila had surrendered, the Federal Government laid down its demands, and a temporary armistice ensued.

During this period Anglo-American relations continued slowly to improve. In a despatch of April 28, 1898, de Wollant spoke of the success of "English agitation" in "drawing together the two Anglo-Saxon nations." [5] Moreover, he informed his government that the English ambassador, Julian Pauncefote, had received instructions from Great Britain to participate in the mediation efforts of the six powers only if English participation would be favorably looked upon by the Federal Government, although it was England which had proposed a six-power conference in the first place. De Wollant wrote:

Many signs show that Great Britain is adopting a very sympathetic attitude toward America, and is encouraging her to make war which is, in essence, not in the interests of England. The strengthening of America on this continent, the expulsion of the Spaniards from Cuba, as one well-informed Englishman said, must lead to settlement between England and the United States over the Canadian issue. But Englishmen are not accustomed to such long perspectives, and if it is insistently striving to win American friendship, it is only the immediate future it has in view and hopes to receive American support for its Far Eastern policy.

The same estimate was given by the Russian ambassador to London, Baron G. G. Stahl.[6] According to his despatch of May 26, 1898, the endeavors of England to bring about a rapprochement with the United States were motivated by two considerations: (1) the North-American market was of extreme importance to English trade; and (2) "now, more than ever, in view of events in the Far East, England needed friendly relations with America."

Stahl looked skeptically on the possibility of an Anglo-American alliance, which was the tenor of Chamberlain's speech in Birmingham, but noted the unquestionably closer relations that existed between the two countries. In confirmation of this trend he cited the establishment of an extraordinary committee in Quebec for the solution of all questions of dispute between Canada and the United States, including the question of

---

5 *Ibid.*
6 *Ibid.* "Perepiska s Londonom" za 1898 g. (Correspondence with London, 1898.)

seal fishing, while only a short time before the Washington Government had rejected an analogous proposal from the Canadian Ministry.

In early June the Russian consul general in New York informed his government of the following successful attempts at English agitation in the United States. "English newspapers," he wrote

constantly fabricate all kinds of news in order to worsen relations between America and France. . . . Naturally, since concrete facts were given their falsehood was easily proven. But Great Britain, having left the concrete basis, very artfully begins to insinuate that all the other European powers support Spain and are plotting the most sinister things against America. English daily newspapers have begun to say that had it not been for England other European powers would have intervened in defense of Spain. The Times directly said that England would not participate in the coalition directed against America, and under certain conditions would actively engage against such a coalition. In this manner the legend has been created that there existed a hostile coalition of powers which did not achieve realization, thanks to England, which consequently is the one and only friend of America. All of these assertions fall on willing ears. . . .

Consul General Teplov further wrote:

While fanning the hatred of Americans for the European continental powers in general, England is endeavoring to inculcate in the minds of the American public that while there is yet time it should conclude an agreement with England; under the influence of the English newspapers, people here are beginning to believe that Great Britain and Japan have signed a treaty covering not only various incidents in the Far East, but also those which might arise in connection with the Spanish-American War.

Such was the political situation at the time Cassini appeared in Washington. On the one hand, there was the growing friendship between England and America and, on the other, Russo-English strain over the Far Eastern question. Russia feared a coalition of powers headed by England. In this critical time, while the Spanish-American War was not yet settled, with the American army suffering defeat in Cuba, and Washington confused at the military situation, the Russian Government, which boasted of their friendship for the United States, had nothing better to offer than unrelaxing vigilance over any disposal of the Philippines that might prove unfavorable to Russia's "American friendship." Such was the real value of the friendship and disinterestedness of Tsarist Russia.

In the letter to Muraviev, Cassini boasts that he has a good musical ear, and it is true that he was not easily deceived. As can be seen from his letters, he did not think an Anglo-American alliance likely. Reality seems to bear out his skepticism. Even when the Anglophile Hay was appointed secretary of state, Cassini disparaged the significance of this act and insisted that there would be an exchange of "platonic declarations;" but even though a large section of the American people were in sympathy with the idea of an American-English alliance, this sympathy was far removed from a direct alliance involving agreement for the support of Far Eastern policy.

Nevertheless, English diplomatic intrigues in the United States had to be watched, said Cassini, and no opportunity should be lost to expose Great Britain's intrigues to the Americans, who had been temporarily led astray by the crude tactics of Russia's rivals.

The documents which follow should finally end any legend about the character of the friendship which Tsarist Russia had for the United States.

INSTRUCTIONS TO CASSINI

Jan. 29/Feb. 10, 1898

In entering upon your ambassadorship in our Embassy at Washington, your Excellency must pay special attention to the significance to us of the development of American industry in the Far East. In this connection your presence in Washington as a representative of the Imperial Government will be of special value owing to your knowledge of the Far East.

Because of your knowledge of China you are well aware what kind of aspirations direct the Americans in their commercial and trade enterprises on the entire Western seaboard of the Pacific Ocean. Since you are so well-informed, you will doubtless be able to make a clear distinction between those enterprises which are favorable to us and those which impinge on our sphere of influence. While conducting yourself in conformity with the first, you will take energetic action against the second, making use of your inherent tact, and with caution winning the sympathy of the Federal Government. The association between Russia and the United States exists, indubitably, and has a historical foundation. America has not forgotten the support which His Imperial Government gave through heavy years of internecine warfare in the United States, at the time of the uprising of the Southern states. This feeling of obligation for the services rendered, aside from many manifestations in the contemporary press, was clearly demonstrated in the year of our famine (1891) when from all corners of the United States came offers of bread and money. Emperor Alexander III, now sleeping in the lap of God, was gratified by this manifestation of sympathy from the citizens of a friendly government. As you know, His Highness, in due time, dispatched beautiful gifts to the chief organizations and individuals who contributed to the delivery of bread.

As a particular manifestation of his beneficence to be considered was the sending of a squadron by his Majesty to the Atlantic ports of the United States in 1893 to participate in the naval exercises on the occasion of the opening of the Columbus World Fair in Chicago. Our vessels, which remained a considerable time in American waters, received a warm welcome from the United States. Everyone still remembers the enthusiasm aroused in the New York population by the marching of our sailors in the parade the day following the naval review.

The sacrifice of Alaska in 1867 for an insignificant sum is witness to the fact that we looked favorably on the strengthening of the power of the

United States on the continent, in opposition to that of Great Britain. At the same time, by making this concession to the United States, we gave America the opportunity to take an important step forward in the realization of the Monroe doctrine.

Since we have no direct geographical contact with the United States, and possess no colonies on the American continent, it is most convenient for us to make use of the Monroe doctrine in cases like this where this most popular American theory diametrically conflicts with our natural enemy England, through its geographically greater colony, Canada.

In regard to the Hawaiian Islands, the Imperial Government has found a new language in its friendship for the United States. When four years ago, the Sandwich Islands carried through a revolt under American tutelage and established the Hawaiian Republic, the Imperial Government was among the first to recognize the young republic.

Today, when the Federal Government because of the increasing immigration of Japanese to the islands and for other reasons found it necessary to annex these islands in their entirety, the Imperial Government, looking very favorably on this annexation so advantageous to our interests, found another occasion to express its friendship for the United States. The Hawaiian Islands, in view of their geographical location in the center of the Pacific Ocean, present such an important station along the great ocean highways, that an independent existence would have proved neither durable nor long lasting. Sooner or later, these islands would have become the property of Great Britain, Japan or the United States. To us it would have been equally undesirable to see either the formation of a second Malta or the strengthening of Japanese naval power in the Pacific Ocean by the acquisition of another link. In view of their inability to remain independent, it was more desirable that these islands should become a part of the United States. In this way they will remain forever a friendly and reliable midway station and not become a hostile nest and a threat of danger from the rear. We are entirely certain that, concerned with its future, the Federal Government has paid attention to the gradual conquests of England in the Pacific Ocean and has decided to thwart her in the present case, as well as to prevent the expansion of Japan in the Pacific Ocean. . . .

One of the chief problems uniting Russian and American interests is that of the seal industry. You will see from the material entrusted to your Excellency in the Embassy the type of policy that the Imperial Government has pursued in the various phases of this question. For four years, up to the Washington conference of last year, the Imperial Government, wishing to preserve the breeding grounds of the seal, prohibited Russian citizens from hunting this animal in the open seas. The three governments of Russia, Japan and the United States agreed on the necessity of preventing seal catching in the open seas and of conducting research for the preservation of the species. However, this well-meaning intention on the part of the interested governments has no practical significance unless

Great Britain also makes the same acknowledgment concerning seal hunting. As you know, this power has not only refused to participate in the conference, but to date has given no sign that it intends to adhere to its resolutions. Such silence on the part of the St. James cabinet is explained by purely political motives of a rather complicated character. In the present case the metropolis supports the colony Canada, which in turn has accounts with the Federal Government.

Canada does not wish to make any concessions to the United States, not so much because it wants to keep certain profits (in fact, the industry for the last few years has hardly paid for itself), but because of the sharpened differences between the Canadian and Federal Governments in the recent period of new American protectionist tariffs and disputes over boundaries.

Your problem, therefore, your Excellency, in view of the unsettled condition of this question of seal-fishing, is one of conciliating hostile interests, and of achieving as quickly as possible unity of all interested parties on the question of seal-fishing.

The recent conference in Washington showed that while, with a few minor differences, the interests of Japan and Canada in seal-fishing were identical, pressure from the Federal Government induced Japan to sign the agreement for the discontinuance of seal hunting on the open seas as fatal to the life of the seals. The holding out is exclusively on the side of Canada, and we hope this is only temporary. The sooner this question is solved and the prohibition of seal hunting agreed upon, the better the chances for preserving this species of seal, which provides an industry on the Behring Straits islands, a means of subsistence for the natives, a valuable fur, and a source of government income. . . . .

Summarizing, then, what are the duties of your Excellency as a representative of our Imperial Government in Washington?

Maintaining and strengthening the ties which have been historically created, which means that you have to be careful, at the same time unwaveringly making use of the fruits of good seeds which we have sown for our interests.

While remaining in the aura of Russian-American friendship you must make every endeavor to create conflicts between the Federal Government and England and Japan.

In view of what has been said, you must evince complete sympathy with the interests of the Americans, but at the same time pay careful attention to the relations of the United States with Great Britain and Japan.

Of special interest in this connection are the increased tensions between the United States and Canada. The present protectionist tariffs are a serious obstacle to the improvement of relations with Canada. It must be added, incidentally, that the Federal Government, on guard for its own interests, will conduct itself in such a way that should a union of Canada and the United States take place, it will be as if spontaneously, and will have as its foundation reciprocal advantages for the Americans and Canadians. The secession of Canada from its metropolis has extreme importance for us.

You will therefore have to determine how advantageous the secession of Canada from Great Britain would be for us. Would the consequent strengthening of the United States be an obstacle and perhaps even a threat to the existing good relations? Would the United States, already having assumed the status of a great power, preserve the same passive good will toward our policies after the dismemberment of England, or would it become a competitor with whom we would have to deal as now with Great Britain?

CASSINI TO THE MINISTER OF FOREIGN AFFAIRS, MURAVIEV

Washington, June 22, 1898

My dear and good friend:

. . . .

I have been here only a few days and am trying to gain my bearings in the political and military chaos which this new country presents to me. Today I am sending a letter to Count Lamsdorf to share with him my first impressions, which are neither happy nor consoling. Not long ago a complete revolution in the ideas and political principles of this country took place. Not satisfied with the past which has made her rich, happy and honored, she wants to test the future which quite possibly conceals for her many occasions for disillusionment as well as serious difficulties.

I do not believe in the probability of an American-English alliance. The American mind is deep, too practical, too business-like, to carry things so far. But the rapprochement which has taken place between these two countries since the war began is unquestionable, and this alone is enough to put us on guard. We need in consequence to concentrate our attention on two main points: (1) We should follow with undivided attention each small success in the rapprochement between the Anglo-Saxon countries, not missing a single opportunity to point out to our American friends the disadvantages which confront them in the deceitful business into which they are being drawn; (2) and of more immediate importance to us is, What do the Americans intend to do about the Philippines? If you can believe them, they simply want to annex them. We could, as things appear on the surface, console ourselves with the passing of the Philippines into the hands of our friends, the Americans, whom we love and value. But the transfer of these islands to the United States, friends and possible allies in the future of Great Britain, should give us pause to think things over.

I shall do everything possible to convince the present government and the nation that their best friends have been, and will continue to be, Russia. I have, I believe, a good musical ear, and it seems to me I can assure you that I shall be able to detect every false note. . . .

CASSINI

LETTER OF CASSINI TO THE ASSISTANT MINISTER OF
FOREIGN AFFAIRS, LAMSDORF

Washington, June 23, 1898

Dear Count:

. . . .

My sojourn in this country is of too brief duration to form any opinion of the social trends worth transmitting to you. The only thing I can affirm is that there is a great lack of clarity in political ideas and tendencies among governmental circles; and in the direction of military operations, unbelievable collapse. As to the first, it is quite evident to me that the United States has firmly decided to break with the traditions of the past and to enter upon a new policy with wider horizons—a policy which if they follow with the stubbornness characteristic of their race will not be without immediate and significant influence on the fate of the entire world. The future will show in what measure this revolution in policy is capable of enhancing the might, the wealth and the degree of influence of the United States, which until now has had only friends. Having entered upon the path of conquest, and perhaps not always being selective in their policies, they cannot fail immediately to create a multitude of enemies and give occasion for serious complications.

As for the growing rapprochement between the United States and Great Britain—this rapprochement is beyond doubt. Great Britain, moved by the desire to win an ally in the form of the United States—which with complete foundation it fears—has resorted to a thousand small tricks in order to win the American Government and the sentiments of the people, especially in the present war. The friendliness is beyond doubt, but how far can it go, is the question. This is the question which interests us above all. In my opinion, and judging from everything which I have seen and heard, this intimacy is not destined to go beyond the limits of mutual kindness and friendly assertions, and it will hardly reach the dangerous condition of an alliance, where all the advantages would be on the side of England. The Americans are too practical to be drawn into an unprofitable bargain. To risk the danger of hostile relations with the majority of European powers for the honor of serving English interests is a perspective not very attractive, and I do not believe the United States will allow herself to be fooled.

Parallel with this friendship between the United States and Great Britain, the course of which I shall follow with the closest attention, there is another problem, and this problem is of immediate and absorbing interest to us. I refer to the Philippines. Judging from all the information which has reached me, the Government of the United States has determined to carry through the capture of this rich prize to a successful climax, by definitely annexing it herself. I must acknowledge that from the point of view of civilization and humanity, the eventual destruction of Spanish reign in this archipelago, important in its geographical situation and exceptionally rich, cannot engender the least regret. Thanks to the miserable administration and the fateful influence of the ruling religious orders which it encourages, Spain has done everything to kill the sympathy of the natives and to push them on to periodical uprisings. Instead of a source of wealth, which the Philippines should and could have been, Spain made them an object of financial sacrifices which became more burdensome from day to day. But, aside from humanity and civilization, the possessor of the Philippines after the war is of extreme importance to us politically, as well as to the other powers interested in the Far East. If our old friend the United States found, after the war, that the Philippines were suitable as a point of departure in the Far East, we would have to limit ourselves to the mere affirmation of a new factor in the Far-Eastern situation, which in the last period has attracted so many self-interested sentiments. But the rapprochement which has taken place between the United States and England during the war, a rapprochement which might in spite of everything lead to a closer agreement between these two great naval powers, compels us to regard the occupation of the Philippines by the United States with considerably less well-wishing. . . .

CASSINI

Appendix II

DESPATCHES FROM THE AMERICAN LEGA-TION AT TOKYO CONTAINING THE SECRET PROTOCOLS OF THE PEKING (KOMURA) TREATY OF 1905

AMERICAN LEGATION

Tokio

February 16, 1906

CONFIDENTIAL

No. 391

To the Honorable Elihu Root,
Secretary of State,
Washington

Sir:

I have the honor to confirm the Legation's cipher telegram of the 19th ultimo, reading as follows:

January 19, 5 p.m. I have obtained the Japanese Government's consent to communicate to you in strict confidence the secret protocols of the Peking treaty if you instruct me to ask them to do so.

WILSON.

In the course of an interview with the Minister for Foreign Affairs on January 18th I asked him whether there was anything in the secret protocols which he would be willing to communicate to us in addition to the information concerning the Mukden-Hsinmintun and Changchun-Kirin railway lines which I had from Mr. Yamaza, Chief of the Political Bureau,—and which was contained in this legation's dispatch No. 370 of the 12th ultimo. Mr. Kato said that there was nothing in the protocols, which they were not willing that the whole world should know, but that they were secret and were to remain so at the special request of the Chinese Government. His Excellency added that, in view of the friendship between our two countries, the importance of American interests in Manchuria, and the relations they hoped to have with us there, the Japanese Government would be willing to communicate the protocols in strict confidence to my Government if I were instructed to ask them to do so. He said that perhaps they would communicate them also to Great Britain. I was very glad of the prospect of being able to send you the protocols and assured the Minister for Foreign Affairs that their communication to you by his Government would be appreciated. As a result of this conversation I had the honor to dispatch to you the telegram confirmed above.

On the 21st ultimo I received your telegraphic instructions, which I have now the honor to acknowledge, reading as follows:

We would gladly receive in strict confidence and be thankful for secret protocols Peking Treaty. (Period) Make request.

ROOT.

Acting upon this instruction I accordingly made the request, by means of a personal note, and transmitted to the Minister for Foreign Affairs a paraphrase of your telegram. When I saw Mr. Kato some days later I was informed, to my surprise, that he was going to give us only the parts of the protocols which were in the nature of agreements, instead of the full text of the protocols as he had led me to expect. He said these parts of the documents were being translated into English. I was unable to obtain a Japanese text of the actual provisions, which would have been preferable.

The Minister for Foreign Affairs has today sent me, as strictly confidential, what purports to be a summary in English of those portions of the Peking protocols which possess the character of executory agreements between Japan and China, and I have the honor to forward herewith a copy of the same.

It will be observed that the chief importance of the protocols lies in securing to Japan a joint interest with China in the Changchun-Kirin and Mukden-Hsinmintun railway lines and reinforcing her grip upon the railways of Southern Manchuria. A mutual arrangement is also to be made for the working of the mines in the province of Feng Tien (Shing King) appertaining to the railways; and matters of common concern relating to the connecting railway services and to telegraph lines in this province and cables between Port Arthur and Yentai are to be adjusted by mutual consultation.

Section 4 of the enclosure looks to insistence by China upon Russia's faithful observance of her railway agreements regarding Northern Manchuria. Section 8 is noticeable in that it appears to give the Japanese Minister at Peking a voice as to the regulations for the opening under the Peking Agreement of the sixteen towns in Manchuria. Section 10 contains the engagement of the Chinese Government to guarantee peace, maintain order, and protect foreigners in Manchuria, upon the evacuation of that region by the Japanese and Russian troops.

The remaining paragraphs deal with various other details of the

Chinese-Japanese relations growing out of the war, but seem to add little of importance to the information already in the Department's hands.

Assuming the enclosed summary to contain all the important points in the protocols, there is a reason why the Japanese Government should themselves be anxious for the secrecy of the contents at this time in the fact that both the Diet and the people are inclined to believe the advantages gained at Peking to be still greater than they actually are.

I have The honor to be,

Sir,

Your obedient servant,

HUNTINGTON WILSON

Enclosure: Summary of
Protocols.
Encl. with Mr. Wilson's No. 391 of February 16, 1906.

STRICTLY CONFIDENTIAL

Whereas the protocols of the Conference recently held between the Plenipotentiaries of Japan and China with regard to Manchuria are to be kept strictly secret in deference to the desire of the Chinese Government only such portions of those Protocols as possess the character of executory agreements are given in the following summary:

1. The railway between Changchun and Kirin will be constructed by China with capital to be raised by herself. She, however, agrees to borrow from Japan the insufficient amount of capital, which amount being about one-half of the total sum required. The contract concerning the loan should, in due time, be concluded, following, *mutatis mutandis,* the loan contract entered into between the board of the Imperial Railways of North China and the Anglo-Chinese Syndicate. The term of the loan shall be twenty-five years, redeemable in yearly installments.

2. The military railway constructed by Japan between Mukden and Hsin-min-tun shall be sold to China at a price to be fairly determined in consultation by Commissioners appointed for the purpose by the two Governments. China engages to reconstruct the line, making it her own railway, and to borrow from a Japanese corporation or corporations one half of the capital required for the portion of the line east of Liao-ho for a term of eighteen years repayable in yearly installments, and a contract shall be concluded, for the purpose, following, *mutatis mutandis,* the loan contract entered into between the Board of the Imperial Railways of North China and the Anglo-Chinese Syndicate.

All the other military railways in different localities shall be removed with the evacuation of the regions.

3. The Chinese Government engage, for the purpose of protecting the interest of the South Manchurian Railway, not to construct, prior to the recovery by them of the said railway, any main line in the neighborhood of and parallel to that railway, or any branch line which might be prejudiced to the interest of the above-mentioned railway.

4. China declares that she will adopt sufficient measures for securing Russia's faithful observations of the Russo-Chinese treaties with regard to the railways which Russia continues to possess in the northern part of Manchuria, and that it is her intention in case Russia acts in contravention of such treaty stipulations, to approach her strongly with a view to have such action fully rectified.

5. When in the future, negotiations are to be opened between Japan and Russia for regulations of the connecting railway services (Article VIII of the Treaty of Peace between Japan and Russia), Japan shall give China previous notice. China shall communicate to Russia her desire to take part in the negotiations through commissioners to be despatched by her on the occasion, and Russia consenting shall participate in such negotiations.

6. With regard to the mines in the Province of Feng-tien, appertaining to the railway, whether already worked or not, fair and detailed arrangements shall be agreed upon for mutual observance.

7. The affairs relating to the connecting services as well as those of common concern in respect of the telegraph lines in the Province of Feng-tien and the cables between Port Arthur and Yen-tai shall be arranged from time to time as necessity may arise in consultation between the two countries.

8. The regulations respecting the places to be opened in Manchuria shall be made by China herself, but the Japanese Minister at Peking must be previously consulted regarding the matter.

9. If no objection be offered on the part of Russia in respect to the navigation of the Sungari (by Japanese vessels) China shall consent to such navigation after negotiations.

10. The Chinese Plenipotentiaries declare that immediately after the withdrawal of the Japanese and Russian troops from Manchuria, China will proceed to take, in virtue of her sovereign right, full administrative measures to guarantee peace in that region and endeavor, by the same right, to promote good and remove evil as well as steadily to restore order, so that the residents of that region, natives and foreigners, may equally enjoy the security of life and occupation under the perfect protection of the Chinese Government. As to the means of restoring order, the Chinese Government are to take by themselves all adequate measures.

11. While relations of intimate friendship subsisted as at the present time between China and Japan, Japan and Russia had unfortunately engaged in war and fought in the territory of China. But peace has now been reëstablished and hostilities in Manchuria have ceased. And while it is undeniable that Japanese troops, before their withdrawal, have the power of exercising the rights accruing from military occupation, the Chinese Government declare that certain Japanese subjects in Manchuria have recently been observed to sometimes interfere with the local Chinese administration and to inflict damage to public and private property of China. The Japanese Plenipotentiaries, considering that, should such interfer-

ence and infliction of damage have been carried beyond military necessity, they are not proper acts, declare that they will communicate the purport of the above declaration of the Chinese Government to the Government of Japan, so that proper steps may be taken for controlling Japanese subjects in the Province of Feng-tien and to promote the friendly relations between the two nations, and also for preventing them in future, from interfering with the Chinese administration or inflicting damage to public or private property without military necessity.

12. In regard to any public or private property of China which may have been purposely destroyed or used by Japanese subjects without any military necessity, the Governments of the two countries shall respectively make investigations and cause fair reparation to be made.

13. When the Chinese local authorities intend to despatch troops for the purpose of subduing native bandits in the regions not yet completely evacuated by Japanese troops, they shall not fail to previously consult with the Commander of the Japanese troops stationed in those regions so that all misunderstanding may be avoided.

14. The Japanese Plenipotentiaries declare that the Railway guards stationed between Chang-chun and the boundary line of the leased territory of Port Arthur and Talien, shall not be allowed, before their withdrawal, to unreasonably interfere with the local administration of China or to proceed without permission beyond the limits of the railway.

15. Chinese local authorities, who are to reside at Ingkou, shall be allowed, even before the withdrawal of the Japanese troops, to proceed to that place and transact their official business. The date of their departure is to be determined as soon as possible after the definitive conclusion of this Treaty, by the Japanese Minister to China in consultation with the Waiwupu. As there is still in that place a considerable number of Japanese troops, quarantine regulations as well as regulations for the prevention of contagious diseases, shall be established by the authorities of the two countries in consultation with each other so that epidemics may be avoided.

16. The revenue of the Maritime Customs at Ingkou shall be deposited with the Yokohama Specie Bank and delivered to the Chinese local authorities at the time of evacuation. As to the revenue of the native Customs at that place and the taxes and imposts at all other places, which are all to be appropriated for local expenditures a statement of receipts and expenditures shall be delivered to the Chinese local authorities at the time of evacuation.

Appendix III

KNOX MEMORANDUM OF FEBRUARY 8, 1910, TO THE RUSSIAN GOVERNMENT

In view of an apparent misunderstanding by the Imperial Russian Government of the nature of the proposal made by the United States for the neutralization of the railways in Manchuria and the relation of this to the project for the construction of a railway from Chinchow to Aigun, it seems proper to recount briefly the steps taken by this Government in preparing and presenting to various Powers the recent memorandum on those subjects.

On October 2, after some weeks of negotiation, an agreement was signed at Mukden by the Chinese Viceroy on the one part and representatives of a firm of British contractors and a group of American capitalists on the other part for the construction by British and American capital of a railway from Chinchow to Tsitsihar and Aigun. This agreement has since been ratified by a Chinese Imperial Edict.

The United States was asked to give diplomatic support to this project and was inclined to do so, provided (1) that similar support should be given by Great Britain, since the line was to be built by British contractors and in part with British capital, and (2) that other interested Powers pledged to the policy of "equal opportunity" should be invited to participate.

It is pertinent to recall at this point that during the month of October the Russian Government inquired, apropos of the then negotiations for the Hukuang loan, whether the Government of the United States would be disposed to welcome Russian cooperation in future railway loans in China. Just as this inquiry was naturally taken to indicate a favorable disposition on the part of Russia to loans like those involved in the propositions under discussion, so the reply of the United States was a very clear expression of a disposition entirely favorable to cordial cooperation in such cases between Russia and the United States.

Previous to these events, however, the Department of State had learned of the discussions in 1908 and 1909 between certain officials of the Chinese Eastern Railway Company and certain American interests with a view to the possible purchase by the latter of the railway just mentioned. More-

over, while the plan for the Chinchow-Aigun line was under consideration, several reports appeared in the press to the effect that Russia was considering the sale of this railway and had made overtures to China looking
to the purchase of the line by the latter, or by an international syndicate.
Similar reports reached the Department through the Embassy at St. Petersburg.

These reports led the American Government to believe that it might be
possible to avoid any question of a conflict of interests by suggesting a
more economical arrangement whereby, through an international loan to
China, all the existing railways in Manchuria, and such other lines as were
in future found necessary, might be combined into one system. When,
therefore, the British Government had intimated its willingness to give
diplomatic support to the Chinchow-Aigun project, the United States
Government, on November 6, prepared a memorandum setting forth the
advantages of the alternative plan and stating that the success of the plan
would require the cooperation of Russia, Japan, and China, the conces-
sionaries and the reversionary respectively of the existing Manchurian
Railways, as well as that of Great Britain and the United States, whose
special, in contradistinction to their general commercial interests rested
upon the contract already signed for the Chinchow-Aigun railway. It was
believed and so stated that such an arrangement would be advantageous
to the interests of all Powers concerned and to Russia and Japan certainly
no less than others.

Owing to the fact that a British company had contracted to build the
Chinchow-Aigun line, the alternative plan was presented first of all to
Great Britain and was approved in principle by that Government. In the
meantime, however, the Department learned that the outlines of the plans
were being publicly discussed in Europe and the Orient and in order to
avert the misunderstanding that might result from such uninformed discussion the American Government notified the British Foreign Office on
December 14 that it seemed highly important, as a matter of international
consideration, to lay the plan before the Governments of the other interested Powers without delay, and that the American representatives would
be instructed to do so. Accordingly on the same day, December 14, the
American Ambassadors at St. Petersburg and Tokyo were instructed by
cable in like terms to communicate formally to the Russian and Japanese
Governments the memorandum previously sent to them for their information, taking care to set forth fully the ideas contained therein.

Previous to this, however, the Ambassador at St. Petersburg had been
instructed to ascertain the truth of the reports that Russia was considering
the advisability of selling the Chinese Eastern Railway and had been given
liberty to make informal use of the facts relative to the Manchurian project which were then in his possession for his information. Next to the Government of Great Britain, therefore, the Imperial Government of Russia
was the first to which any communication of the plan was made, and it will

appear that the United States Government from the first realized the importance of securing the cooperation of Russia.

In the original instructions to the American Ambassadors reference was made to an unpublished edict which the Government of the United States had been informed had been issued by the Chinese Government ratifying the Chinchow-Aigun Railway agreement, and all the Ambassadors were alike instructed, as a matter of propriety, to withhold any reference to such edict. This instruction was unfortunately misunderstood by the American Ambassador at St. Petersburg, who regarded it as directing him to withhold any reference to the Chinchow-Aigun Railway agreement as a whole. This mistake on the part of the Ambassador was, however, promptly corrected by the Department of State as soon as it became known to the American Government and was explained by the Ambassador to the Russian Government.

The Government of the United States could naturally not suppose that any friendly Power would fail to interpret correctly its purposes in proposing a plan which it believed was in the best interests of all concerned and which was presented for consideration solely upon such merits as it might disclose. Nor did it occur to the American Government that in view of its consistent policy for many years past it should hesitate to bring to the attention of its associates any measures that might appear to further the policies to which all alike were solemnly committed.

On January 20 last, before the Imperial Russian Government had made its very prompt reply to the proposal of the United States for the internationalization of the Manchurian railways, the American Ambassador at St. Petersburg was telegraphically instructed to inform the Russian Minister for Foreign Affairs that the American Government would greatly regret to have the decision of the Imperial Russian Government, when ultimately reached, influenced by any misunderstanding as to the nature of the proposal or the motive in making it and would appreciate an opportunity of presenting a fuller explanation of certain matters directly bearing upon the question. The explanation to which the telegram referred is that contained in the statement made above.

BIBLIOGRAPHY

I. MANUSCRIPT SOURCES: OFFICIAL AND PRIVATE PAPERS
OFFICIAL

United States Department of State Archives, 1789–1918.

PRIVATE PAPERS

Cleveland, Grover. Manuscript Division, Library of Congress.
Hay, John J. Manuscript Division, Library of Congress.
Rockhill, W. W. Private collection.
Roosevelt, Theodore. Manuscript Division, Library of Congress.

II. PRINTED SOURCES: OFFICIAL DOCUMENTS ETC.

British Documents on the Origins of the World War, 1898–1914, London, 1926–1938, Gooch, G. P., and Temperly, H. W. V. (eds.).
British and Foreign State Papers, 137 vols., London, 1841–1939.
Die Grosse Politik der Europaischen Kabinette, 1871–1914, 40 vols., Berlin, 1921–1927.
Department of State: *Papers Relating to the Foreign Relations of the United States,* Washington, D.C., 1862–1945.
Golder, Frank A. *Guide to Materials for American History in Russian Archives.* Washington, D.C., Carnegie Institution of Washington, 1917.
Grimm, E. D. *Sbornik Dogovorov i Drugikh Dokumentov po Istorii Mezhdunarodnykh Otnoshenii na Dal'nem Vostoke.* Moscow, 1927.
House Report, 62nd Congress, 2nd Session, Report No. 179, to accompany H. J. Res. 166, *The Abrogation of the Russian Treaty,* Dec. 12, 1911. Washington: Government Printing Office, 1912.
Komissia po Izdaniu Dokumentov Epokhi Imperializma: Mezhdunarodnie Otnosheniia v Epokhu Imperializma, 1878–1917, Series 1 & 2, 2 vols., Moscow, 1931–1940.
Krasnyi Arkhiv, 104 vols., Moscow, 1922–1937.
———— "*Nakanunie Russo-Iaponskoi Voiny.*" LXIII (1934), 3–54.
———— Popov, A. "*Pervyie Shagi Russkogo Imperializma na Dal'nem Vostoke.*" LVII (1932), 34–124.
———— "*Severo-Amerikanskie Soedinennye Shtati i Tsarskaya Rossia v 90-kh gg. XIX v.*" LII (1932), 125–42.
League of Nations. *Manchuria, Commission of Enquiry into Sino-Japanese Relations.* Washington, D.C., Government Printing Office, 1932.

Malloy, W. M. *Treaties, Conventions, International Acts, Protocols and Agreements between the United States of America and Other Powers*, 2 vols., Washington: Government Printing Office, 1910.

MacMurray, J. V. A. (ed.). *Treaties and Agreements with and Concerning China, 1894–1919*, 2 vols. New York: Oxford University Press, 1921.

Ministerstvo Innostranykh Diel. *Sbornik Diplomaticheskikh Dokumentov Kasaiushchikhsia Peregovorov mezhdu Rossieie i Iaponiei o Zakluchenii Mirnogo Dogovora, Dopolnenii Nekotorimi Dokumentami iz Arkhiva Grafa S.U. Vitte.* St. Petersburg, tipographia V. E. Kirshbaum, 1906.

Proceedings of the Alaskan Boundary Tribunal, 7 vols., Washington: Government Printing Office, 1904.

Richardson, James D. *Messages and Papers of the Presidents*, 1788–1897, 10 vols., Washington: Government Printing Office, 1896–1899.

III. DIARIES, MEMOIRS, LETTERS

Adams, Charles Francis (ed.). *The Memoirs of John Quincy Adams*, 12 vols., Philadelphia: J. B. Lippincott & Co., 1874–1877.

Aksakova, Anna F. (Tyutcheva). *Pri Dvore Dvoukh Imperatorov., Dnevnik, 1882–85 gg.*, 2 vols., Moscow, 1928–29.

Ford, Worthington Chauncey (ed.). *Letters of Henry Adams 1892–1918.* Boston & New York: Houghton Mifflin Co., 1938.

Gérard, Auguste. *Ma Mission en Chine, 1893–1897.* Paris: Plon-Nourrit, 1918.

Hayashi, Count. *Secret Memoirs.* London: Eveleigh Nash, 1915.

Jefferson, Thomas. *Writings.* (Memorial edition), 20 vols., Washington, D.C., 1903.

Korostovetz, J. J. *Diary.* London: British Periodicals, Ltd., 1920.

Levine, Isaac Don. *Letters from the Kaiser to the Tsar.* New York: Frederick Stokes Co., 1920.

Lodge, Henry C. (ed.). *Selections from the Correspondence of Theodore Roosevelt and Henry Cabot Lodge, 1884–1918*, 2 vols., New York: C. Scribner's Sons, 1925.

Loubat, J. F. *Narrative of the Mission to Russia in 1866 of the Honorable Gustavus Vas Fox.* New York: Appleton & Co., 1873.

Masanori, Ito. *Kato Takaaki*, 2 vols., Tokyo, 1929.

Meyendorff, Baron A. *Correspondance diplomatique de M. de Staal.* Paris: M. Rivière, 1929.

Pooley, A. M. (ed.). *The Secret Memoirs of Count Tadasu Hayashi.* London: E. Nash, 1915.

Roosevelt, Theodore. *Autobiography.* New York: The Macmillan Co., 1913.

Thayer, William R. *Life and Letters of John Hay*, 2 vols., Boston: Houghton Mifflin Co., 1908.

Witte, Graff S.U. *Vospominania*, 2 vols., Berlin, 1922–23.

Yarmolinsky, Abraham (ed.). *The Memoirs of Count Witte.* New York: Doubleday, Page & Co., 1921.

IV. BIOGRAPHIES, HISTORIES, SPECIAL STUDIES, ARTICLES

Adams, Ephraim D. *Great Britain and the American Civil War*, 2 vols., Longmans, Green & Co., 1925.

Adams, Randolph G. *A History of the Foreign Policy of the United States.* New York: The Macmillan Co., 1924.

American Journal of International Law. "The Passport Question between the United States and Russia." VI (1912), 186–91.

Andrews, Clarence L. "Russian Plans for American Dominion." *Washington Historical Quarterly.* XVIII, 1927, 83–92.

Avarin, Vladimir. *Imperialism v Manchzhurii,* 2 vols., 2nd complete revised edition. Moscow, 1934.

Bailey, Thomas, A. *A Diplomatic History of the American People.* New York: F. S. Crofts & Co., 1941.

Bancroft, Frederick. *The Life of Seward,* 2 vols., New York: Harper & Brothers, 1900.

Barnes, Joseph (ed.). *Empire in the East.* New York: Doubleday, Doran & Co., 1934.

Bau, Mingchien J. *The Open Door Doctrine in Relation to China.* New York: The Macmillan Co., 1923.

Beard, Charles A. & Mary R. *The Rise of American Civilization,* 2 vols., New York: The Macmillan Co., 1930.

Bemis, Samuel F. *A Diplomatic History of the United States.* New York: Henry Holt & Co., 1936.

———— *The Diplomacy of the American Revolution.* New York: D. Appleton-Century Co., 1935.

Beresford, Lord Charles. *The Break-up of China: with An Account of its Present Commerce, Currency, Waterways, Armies, Railways, Politics, and Future Prospects.* New York & London: Harper & Brothers, 1900.

Bishop, Joseph Bucklin. *Theodore Roosevelt and His Time,* 2 vols., New York: C. Scribner's Sons, 1920.

Bland, J. O. P. *Recent Events and Present Policies in China.* London: William Heinemann, 1912.

———— *Li Hung Chang.* London: Constable & Co., 1917.

Bowers, Claude C. *Beveridge and the Progressive Era.* Boston: Houghton Mifflin, 1932.

Brandenburg, Erich. *From Bismarck to The World War: A History of German Foreign Policy, 1870–1914.* Translated by A. E. Adams. London: Oxford University Press, 1927.

Callahan, J. M. *Russo-American Relations During the American Civil War.* West Virginia University Studies in American History, Series I, No. I, Morgantown, W. Va., 1908.

Clyde, Paul Hibbert. *International Rivalries in Manchuria 1689–1922.* The Ohio State University Press, Columbus, Ohio, 1928.

Coolidge, A. C. *The United States as a World Power.* New York: The Macmillan Co., 1927.

"Correspondence of the Russian Ministers in Washington, 1818–1825 I." *American Historical Review.* XVIII (1913), 309–45.

Croly, Herbert. *Willard Straight.* New York: Macmillan Co., 1924.

Denby, Charles. *China and Her People.* 2 vols., Boston: L. C. Page & Co., 1906.

Dennett, Tyler. *Americans in Eastern Asia.* New York: The Macmillan Co., 1922.

———— *John Hay.* New York: Dodd, Mead & Co., 1933.

———— *Roosevelt and the Russo-Japanese War.* New York: Doubleday, Page & Co., 1925.

Dennis, Alfred L. P. *Adventures in American Diplomacy 1896–1906.* New York: E. P. Dutton, 1928.

De Siebert, B. and Schreiner, G. A. *Entente Diplomacy and the World: Matrix of the History of Europe, 1909–1914.* New York & London: G. P. Putnam's Sons, 1921.

Dillon, E. J. *The Eclipse of Russia.* London: J. M. Dent & Sons, 1919.

Dulles, Foster Rhea. *America in the Pacific: a Century of Expansion.* New York: Houghton Mifflin Co., 1932.

Eckardstein, Baron. *Die Isolierung Deutschlands.* Leipzig, 1921.

Fay, Sidney B. *Origins of the World War.* 2 vols in one. New York: The Macmillan Co., 1935.

Fenwick, Charles G. *International Law.* New York: The Century Co., 1924.

Field, Frederick V. *American Participation in the China Consortiums.* Chicago: University of Chicago Press, 1931.

———— (ed.). *Economic Handbook of the Pacific Area.* New York: Doubleday, Doran & Co., 1934.

Foster, John W. *A Century of American Diplomacy.* New York: Houghton Mifflin Co., 1900.

Glinskii, B. B. *Prolog Russko-Iaponskoi Voiny: Materialy iz Arkhiva Grafa S.U. Vitte.* Petrograd, 1916.

Golder, Frank A. "The American Civil War through the Eyes of a Russian Diplomat." *American Historical Review.* XXVI (1921), 454–63.

———— "Catherine II and the American Revolution." *American Historical Review.* XXI (1915), pp. 92–96.

———— "The Purchase of Alaska." *American Historical Review.* XXV (1920), 411–25.

———— "The Russian Fleet and the Civil War." *American Historical Review.* XX (1915), 801–812.

———— "The Russian Offer of Mediation in the War of 1812." *Political Science Quarterly.* XXXI (1916), 380–91.

Grace, W. F. "Russia and The *Times* [London] in 1863 and 1873." *Cambridge Historical Journal.* I (1923), 95–102.

Grimm, E. D. "Kitaiskii Vopros ot Simonosekskogo Mira do Mirovoy Voiny, 1895–1914." *Novyi Vostok,* VI (1924), 43–62.

Griscom, Lloyd. *Diplomatically Speaking.* New York: The Literary Guild of America, 1940.

Griswold, A. Whitney. *The Far Eastern Policy of the United States.* New York: Harcourt, Brace & Co., 1938.

Gurko, V. I. *Features and Figures of the Past.* The Hoover Library on War, Revolution and Peace. Publication No. 14. Stanford University Press, California, 1939.

Haworth, P. L. "Frederick the Great and the American Revolution." *American Historical Review.* IX (1904), 460–78.

Hildt, John C. "Early Diplomatic Negotiations of the United States with Russia." *Johns Hopkins University Studies in Historical and Political Science.* XXIV (1906), 9–194. Baltimore: The Johns Hopkins Press.

Howe, M. A. D. *George von Lengerke Meyer.* New York: Dodd, Mead and Company, 1919.

Johnson, Emory R. *et al. History of Domestic and Foreign Commerce of the United States of America,* 2 vols., Washington, D. C.: Carnegie Institution of Washington, 1915.

Johnson, Willis Fletcher. *America's Foreign Relations,* 2 vols., New York: The Century Co., 1916.

Joseph, Philip. *Foreign Diplomacy in China, 1894–1900.* London: George Allen & Unwin, Ltd., 1928.

Kantorovich, Anatole. *Amerika v Borbe za Kitai.* Moscow: Sotsekgiz, 1935.

Kennan, George. *E. H. Harriman,* 2 vols., New York: Houghton Mifflin Company, 1922.

Kent, Percy H. *Railway Enterprise in China.* London: Edward Arnold, 1907.

Kobayashi, Ushisaburo. *War and Armament Taxes of Japan.* New York: Oxford University Press, 1923.

Kuropatkin, Aleksei. *The Russian Army and the Japanese War,* 2 vols., tr. Capt. A. B. Lindsay; ed. Major E. D. Swinton. London: J. Murray, 1909.

Langer, William L. *The Diplomacy of Imperialism, 1890–1902,* 2 vols., New York: Alfred A. Knopf, 1935.

Latané, John Holladay. *A History of American Foreign Policy.* New York: Doubleday, Doran & Co., 1934.

Latourette, Kenneth Scott. *The Development of China.* New York: Houghton Mifflin Co., 1929.

Low, Maurice A. "American Affairs." *National Review* (Supplement). London. XLII (Dec. 1903), 594–606.

Moore, J. B. *Digest of International Law,* 8 vols., Washington: Government Printing Office, 1906.

——— (ed.). *The Works of James Buchanan,* 12 vols., Philadelphia: J. B. Lippincott & Co., 1908–1910.

Morse, Hosea Ballou. *The International Relations of the Chinese Empire,* 3 vols., New York: Longmans, Green & Co. 1910–1918.

Morse, Hosea Ballou, and MacNair, Harley Farnsworth. *Far Eastern International Relations.* New York: Houghton Mifflin Company, 1931.

Morison, Samuel E. *The Maritime History of Massachusetts.* New York: Houghton Mifflin Co., 1921.

Nevins, Allan. *Henry White.* New York: Harper & Brothers, 1930.

Nolde, Baron Boris E. *Vneshniya Politika: Istoricheskie Ocherki.* Petrograd, 1915.

Ogawa, Gotaro. *Expenditures of the Russo-Japanese War.* New York, 1923.

Pavlovitch, Michel (pseud.). *R.S.F.S.R. v Imperialisticheskom Okruzhenii: Sovetskaia Rossia i Kapitalisticheskaia Amerika.* Moscow, 1924.

Perkins, Dexter. *The Monroe Doctrine, 1823–1826.* Cambridge: Harvard University Press, 1927.

Phillips, Walter Alison. *The Confederation of Europe.* New York: Longmans, Green & Co., 1914.

Pokrovski, Mikhail N. *Diplomatia i Voini Tzarskoy Rossii v XIX V.* Moscow, 1924.

Pollard, Robert T. "American Relations with Korea, 1882–1895." *Chinese Social and Political Science Review.* XVI (1932–1933), 425–471.

Pratt, Julius W. *Expansionists of 1812.* New York: The Macmillan Co., 1925.

——— *Expansionists of 1898.* Baltimore: The Johns Hopkins Press, 1936.

Price, Ernest B. *The Russo-Japanese Treaties of 1907–1916 Concerning Manchuria and Mongolia.* Baltimore: The Johns Hopkins Press, 1933.

Pringle, Henry F. *Theodore Roosevelt.* New York: Harcourt, Brace & Co., 1931.

Reid, John Gilbert. *The Manchu Abdication and the Powers 1908–1912.* University of California Press, Berkeley, California, 1935.

Reinsch, Paul. *An American Diplomat in China.* New York: Doubleday Page and Company, 1922.

Reinsch, Paul. "Japan and Asiatic Leadership." *North American Review*. CLXXX (Jan. 1905), 48–57.

Remer, Charles F. *Foreign Investments in China*. New York: The Macmillan Co., 1933.

Reuter, Bertha A. *Anglo-American Relations during the Spanish-American War*. New York: The Macmillan Co., 1924.

Romanov, Boris A. *Rossia v Manchzhurii, 1892–1906*. Leningrad: Izdanie Leningradskogo Vostochnogo Instituta imeni A. S. Enukidze, 1928.

Rosen, Baron, *Forty Years of Diplomacy*, 2 vols., New York: Alfred Knopf, 1922.

Satow, Sir Ernest. *A Guide to Diplomatic Practice*, 2 vols., London: Longmans, Green & Co., 1917.

Steiger, G. Nye. *History of the Far East*. New York: Ginn & Co., 1936.

Stieve, Frederick. *Isvolsky and the World War; tr.* E. W. Dickes. London: G. Allen & Unwin, 1926.

Sykes, Sir Percy. *Sir Mortimer Durand*. London: Cassell and Co., Ltd., 1926.

Taft, W. H. *Our Chief Magistrate and his Powers*. New York: Columbia University Press, 1916.

Takeuchi, Tatsuji. *War and Diplomacy in the Japanese Empire*. New York: Doubleday, Doran & Co., 1935.

Tan, S. H. "The Diplomacy of American Investments in China." Unpublished dissertation of 1927 in the Library of the University of Chicago.

Thomas, Benjamin Platt. *Russo-American Relations 1815–1867*. Johns Hopkins University Studies in Historical and Political Science, Series XLVIII. Baltimore: The Johns Hopkins Press, 1930.

Treat, Payson, *The Far East*. New York: Harper & Brothers, 1935.

——— *Diplomatic Relations Between the United States and Japan, 1853–1905*, 3 vols., Stanford University Press, California, 1932–38.

Vagts, Alfred. *Deutschland und die Vereinigten Staaten in der Weltpolitik*, 2 vols., New York: The Macmillan Co., 1935.

Viallate, Achille. *Economic Imperialism and International Relations during the Last Fifty Years*. New York: The Macmillan Co., 1923.

Ward, A. W. and Gooch, G. P. (eds.). *The Cambridge History of British Foreign Policy, 1783–1919*, 3 vols., Cambridge: The University Press, 1922–1923.

Williams, Benjamin H. *Economic Foreign Policy of the United States*. New York: McGraw-Hill Book Company, 1929.

Yakhontoff, Victor A. *Russia and the Soviet Union in the Far East*. New York: Coward-McCann, 1931.

Young, Walter C. *The International Relations of Manchuria*. Chicago: University of Chicago Press, 1929.

V. PERIODICALS AND NEWSPAPERS

Birjevie Vedomosti. February 27, 1904.

Century. August 1896.

Fortnightly Review. May and June, 1910.

Hochi Shimbun. April 19, 1909.

New York Times. August 16, 1899. March 9, 1910. July 14, 1910.

North American Review. September 1898.

North China Herald. January 1910.

Novoe Vremya. April 11, 1905, February 8, 1904. February 25/March 10, 1910.

Russkaia Mysl. June 1910.

INDEX

Abaza, A. M., 84 and n. 92, 95
Adams, Henry, 106 n. 30
Adams, John Quincy, 2 n. 8, 3-4, 5 n. 24, 6-8
Adee, A. A., acting secretary of state, 97
Aigun, 140, 149
Alabama, 12
Alaska, 14-16
Alexander I, 3-7
Alexander II, 13-14
Alexeiev, Admiral E. I., 63, 65 n. 1, 67, 93 n. 142, 95-96, 98 n. 171, 100 n. 175
Alexeiev-Tseng Agreement, 67 ff.
American China Development Company, 33-34, 38 and n. 97
American interests in the Far East, 33, 42 and n. 112, 51 n. 32, 52 and n. 34, n. 36
Anglo-Japanese Alliance, 1902, 80-82, 83 and n. 90, 111; 1905, 127 and n. 136, 179 n. 84
Antung, 95 n. 152
Avarin, Vladimir, 71 n. 34, 171 n. 40

Bash, A. W., 33-34
Behring Sea, 16-17
Beresford, Lord Charles, 46 n. 9, 54
Bernstorff, Johann von, German ambassador, Washington, 164 n. 15
Beveridge, Senator Albert J., 113
Bezobrazov, A. M., 84 and n. 92, 95, 96 n. 159
Björkö Treaty, 111
Boxer indemnity, 142 n. 60
Boxer rebellion, 60-63
Breckinridge, Clifton, U.S. ambassador, St. Petersburg, 26-29, 37
British American Tobacco Company, 134, 191 n. 131
Buchanan, James, U.S. minister, St. Petersburg, 9
Bülow, Prince Bernhard von, German chancellor, 103 n. 13, 111

Calhoun, William J., U.S. minister, Peking, 147, 172, 175
Canada, 16

Canning, George, 6-7
Cassini, Count, Russian minister, Peking; ambassador, Washington, 32-35, 40, 46, 48-49, 53, 55-59, 72, 78-79, 90, 92-93, 97 n. 169, 109 n. 41, 114, 117-18
Catacazy, Constantine, Russian minister, Washington, 16 and n. 94
Catherine II, 1-3
Changchun-Kirin Railway, 136 n. 25
China: Boxer uprising, 60-63; refuses to sign Alexeiev-Tseng Agreement, 72; agreement with Russo-Chinese Bank, 77-79, 89; convention of seven points, 87-88; signs treaty with U.S., Oct. 8, 1903, 97 and n. 169, 98; declares neutrality in Russo-Japanese War, 102; Komura Treaty, 131 and n. 3, 141 and n. 53; concludes four-power Chinese Currency Reform Loan, April 15, 1911, 176; revolution of 1911 and establishment of republic, 1912, 179-80
Chinchow-Aigun Railway project, 153, 156 and n. 140, 157-58, 163-68, 171
Chinese Eastern Railway, 36, 39, 43, 76-77, 86, 88, 131, 149 and n. 101, 153 n. 120, 155, 157 and n. 142
Chinese Eastern Railway Company, 36
Ch'ing, Prince, 79, 88 n. 113, 95, 97
Ch'un, Prince, 147
Clay, Cassius, 11, 15
Conger, Edwin H., U.S. minister, Peking, 61, 64 n. 95, 67 n. 11, 68, 75-79, 86-87, 88 n. 113, 90, 93 n. 143, 94, 96-97, 134
Consortium, four-power, 144-48; becomes six-power group, 185; withdrawal of America, 188-89
Convention of seven points, 87-88
Crimean War, 10-11
Cushing, Caleb, U.S. commissioner to China, 21

Dalny, 53, 57, 76, 85, 86 n. 101, 128
Dana, Francis, 2-3
Dashkov, André, 5-6
Davison, Henry P., 182

221